Bridging Separate Gender Worlds

Bridging Separate Gender Worlds

Why Men and Women Clash and How Therapists Can Bring Them Together

Carol L. Philpot
Gary R. Brooks
Don-David Lusterman
Roberta L. Nutt

American Psychological Association
Washington, DC

Published by
American Psychological Association
750 First Street, NE
Washington, DC 20002

Copies may be ordered from
American Psychological Association
Order Department
P.O. Box 92984
Washington, DC 20090-2984

In the UK and Europe, copies may be ordered from
American Psychological Association
3 Henrietta Street
Covent Garden, London
WC2E 8LU England

Typeset in Minion by University Graphics, Inc., York, PA
Printer: Data Reproductions Corp., Rochester Hills, MI
Cover Designer: Deborah Hodgdon Book Design, Boston, MA
Technical/Production Editor: Sarah J. Trembath

Library of Congress Cataloging-in-Publication Data
Bridging separate gender worlds : why men and women clash and how
    therapists can bring them together / Carol L. Philpot . . . [et al.].
        p.   cm.
    Includes bibliographical references and index.
    ISBN 1-55798-381-X (alk. paper)
    1. Marital psychotherapy.   2. Sex differences (Psychology).   3. Sex
role—Psychological aspects.   4. Feminism—Psychological aspects.
5. Man-woman relationships.   6. Marital conflict.   I. Philpot,
Carol L.
    RC488.5.B6835   1997
    616.89′156—dc20   96-41554
                                                                  CIP

British Cataloguing-in-Publication Data
A CIP record is available from the British Library

Printed in the United States of America
First Edition

For Clara Frost Brooks. Some debts are never repaid.
Gary R. Brooks

For my mother and father, who were my models for a
respectful gender relationship.
Don-David Lusterman

For my parents, Toni and Hass, who provided my earliest
challenge to gender role stereotyping.
Roberta L. Nutt

For my father, Fayette M. Latham, Jr., whose respect for and belief in all
people, male or female, is largely responsible for my love of men. For
my mother, Edythe C. Latham, who modeled academic, professional,
and athletic achievement in a traditional woman. And for my husband,
Tom Jensen, whose personality encompasses all the good traits in human potential—both "feminine" and "masculine."
Carol L. Philpot

Contents

Preface

Once upon a time, about a decade ago, four individuals—two men and two women—agreed to put together a symposium on gender. It was at the annual American Psychological Association Convention for the Gender Issues Committee of APA's Division 43, the Division of Family Psychology. Due to the vision and personal philosophy of the President of that Division at the time, Florence Kaslow, the structure of the committee had changed. What had once been the Women's Issues Committee had been renamed the Gender Issues Committee and was cochaired by a woman and a man, Carol Philpot and Gary Brooks, two of the coauthors of this book. Florence Kaslow had deliberately selected as cochairs individuals who had a great deal of empathy and respect for the other gender and who were knowledgeable about both men's and women's issues, with the goal of beginning a more positive dialogue between the genders. Little did she know how successful she would be, at least in terms of the four coauthors of this book!

When we first began our presentations 10 years ago, our thinking was merely to present concurrently the problems men and women suffered as a result of the gender roles they had been rigidly assigned in a patriarchal society. For this purpose we felt it important to have an expert on women's issues, Roberta L. Nutt, an expert on men's issues, Gary R. Brooks, and someone who could present a neutral view. However, it became clear that it would be beneficial to have both genders equally represented, which then necessitated two other persons—Don-David Lusterman and Carol L. Philpot—whose empathy and respect for the other gender allowed for a more conciliatory, interactive approach to gender issues.

All four of the presenters had had previous experience with gender sensitive psychotherapy in a variety of settings. Roberta Nutt and Carol

Philpot were both in academic settings as professors and administrators, and were teaching, supervising, and doing research in the areas of gender and family sytems. Both of them also had part-time private practices. Gary Brooks had been working at a VA hospital with men's groups and families, and was teaching family therapy as an adjunct at a university. Don-David Lusterman had been doing gender-sensitive psychotherapy in a private practice setting in a large metropolitan area for many years. Ever the diplomat, Don-David had always attempted to help his clients understand the pain of the other and look for common ground.

Because gender was becoming a "hot" issue in the field, we found that our program proposals were accepted year after year, which gave us opportunities to further develop our ideas. As systemic therapists, we already used a paradigm that considered the interactions among the parts of a system within a particular context, which was an approach that led to our endorsement of such concepts as the gender ecosystem, gender socialization, androgyny, and the gender role journey. We developed guidelines for conducting gender-sensitive psychotherapy that emphasized the systemic nature of gender socialization. We also began to see clearly how men and women participated in the process of socializing one another, a process that could have either negative, rigidifying effects or produce positive, growth-enhancing coevolution. We worked with our clients and students in ways that educated them about the effects of gender socialization and their own participation in the process with the idea of creating more than just a cognitive understanding of gender socialization. Our goal was *empathic knowing:* that is, an emotional understanding of the other gender's experience gained by "walking in the shoes of the other." Once empathic knowing had been achieved, we found that our clients were able to resolve their differences in constructive ways. To that end, we independently developed a variety of techniques and approaches to therapy that appeared to be effective with the diverse populations we each served. We began to share these ideas with each other and our audiences.

As we worked together, the four of us also began to share our own personal experiences with one another. Using the same philosophy and techniques we used with our clients, we began to develop true empathy for one another's personal experience of gender. We simultaneously developed what might be termed a "passion" for helping others overcome the mutual misunderstandings and blame between the genders that we often saw, not only in our patient or student populations, but among colleagues in professional organizations as well. This passion, fed by Don-David's vision, was the genesis of this book.

In *Bridging Separate Gender Worlds* we have attempted to provide the reader with the necessary background of the effects of gender socialization on both men and women and the dangers of therapy that is not conducted in a gender-sensitive manner. The bulk of the book, however, is a discussion of the philosophy, concepts, and techniques that we developed over a period of years and case examples that illustrate our methods with individuals, couples, and families. We hope this book will inspire its readers as we were inspired by our dialogue. Our vision is the development of positive coevolution between the genders in all walks of life. Granted, this is a grandiose vision. But one has to start somewhere. This book is our attempt to further the process of bridging separate gender worlds.

Acknowledgments

There are many people whose support contributed to the production of this book. The authors would like to thank Charles Prokop, Dean of the School of Psychology, and Florida Tech for their support of Carol Philpot's sabbatical leave, which made this book possible, and for post-sabbatical time release, equipment, and staff assistance (especially Lori Sorum). We are also grateful to Ed and Frances DeFabo for the use of their beautiful home in Rafina, Greece; to "Oink," wherever he is, for his relentless criticism and suggestions; and to Michele Harway for her guidance regarding the treatment of domestic violence. Thanks also to Edythe Latham for her voluntary hours of tedious editorial work on text and references, Tom Jensen for his "real male" perspective and editorial comments, and Beth Beisel for her tireless support and organizational vision which made this book more effective. Don-David Lusterman would like to thank Jackie Kleinstern for her contributions and Judy Baumgold for the research support her dissertation provided for our philosophy. Gary Brooks would like to thank Patti Brooks, who continues to tolerate his writing illusions, and his daughters, Ashley and Allison, who teach him "stuff" he couldn't learn anywhere else. From Roberta L. Nutt, "My gratitude to Carol for providing leadership for this project and for inviting us all to Greece." And from Gary R. Brooks, "Thank you to Carol Philpot and Tom Jensen who lured us to Greece in hopes of inspiring our creative spirits."

Introduction

Gender is not a property of individuals but a socially prescribed relationship,
a process and a social construction. R. Hare-Mustin

Western society is experiencing the drama of social revolution. Men and women have participated in the process of defining one another for many centuries. In the last 30 years in the United States, women have begun to define themselves differently, and the impact of this redefinition on men, women, and couples' relationships has been revolutionary indeed. Although this endeavor is merely a moment in the evolution of human relationships, it nevertheless creates pain and turmoil for the families and couples who are caught in this transitional stage. The people psychotherapists see today are suffering from confusion, anger, and hurt as they attempt to navigate the changing rules within the context of a society that was structured with the old rules in mind. As systemic therapists, we are in a favorable position to help clients redefine one another in a manner that frees them from the restrictive dictates of gender socialization and empowers them to nurture all aspects of themselves, whether socially defined as masculine or feminine. We can do this within the context of the marital relationship, recognizing that as each member of the couple grows to view the other empathically as a whole individual with multiple possibilities, the relationship itself is greatly enhanced. Much has been written that suggests that the gender gap lies only in communication, but in fact the gap is infinitely deeper. To consider it language alone is to trivialize deep differences in history and gender socialization. This book is an effort to define a process by which the therapist can serve as a midwife for the birth of idiosyncratic resolutions to the escalating battle of the sexes presented by the couples and families who seek therapy.

IN THE WAKE OF THE FEMINIST MOVEMENT

Throughout history there have been many feminist movements that have challenged the patriarchal system that has existed around the world for most of recorded history. We have seen examples of the rise and fall of feminine consciousness, from the militance of Aristophanes's Lysistrata to the ultimate submission of Shakespeare's Kate, from the Jewish shtetl wife who managed both home and store to the corseted Victorian, from suffragette to contented suburban housewife. The most recent feminist movement, spearheaded by Betty Friedan's *The Feminine Mystique* (1963), has had a major impact on women in the United States for the last 30 years. The changes that have taken place in the family and workplace and in the attitudes of middle-class American women have shaken the foundation of what, for a short period of history, had become the "traditional" family. Access to birth control, education, and remunerative employment has given women choices they did not feel they had 50 years ago. As a result, the status quo has been toppled, and both men and women are feeling the tremors.

The feminist movement has had a mixed impact. Reactions of men and women in society at large and within the helping professions have been varied and intense. Whereas some men have been supportive, and some have welcomed the opportunity to examine the previously unrecognized dangers of "masculopathology" (Pittman, 1985), others have reacted with confusion, resistance, and bitterness. Later in this book, we explore the birth of the men's movement, which has resulted in the opening up of male consciousness and self-expression, increased participation in parenting, and greater interest in exploring feelings and improving communication skills. But there are many men for whom the change in women's roles has been an affront and who have reacted with angry withdrawal or hostility. For others, there is a sense of confusion, of feeling victimized by angry feminist confrontation. They make an effort to understand but feel the need to be on guard constantly, and they want to rediscover a more comfortable, predictable relationship with women.

The responses of women have not been uniform either. Faludi (1991) argued that the backlash in response to the women's movement set women back a decade. Changes in divorce laws, although correcting injustices previously suffered by men, went too far and did not take into consideration the economic realities in the marketplace for middle-aged women whose only skills were those of housewife and mother (Weitzman, 1985). Additionally, women increased their workload when they added full-time employment to maintenance of the home, because their husbands did not take on domestic responsibilities (Hochschild, 1989). The feminization of poverty in the United States (Morgan, 1991) is often blamed on the high divorce rate and low or nonexistent child-support payments. All of these problems are seen by many women as detrimental effects of the women's movement.

Although there are many other factors contributing to the high divorce rate in the United States, the politically conservative frequently cite the change in women's roles as a major cause. There is some evidence to support this opinion. Research has shown that marriage has a positive, protective effect on men and a negative, detrimental effect on women in terms of physical and mental health (Gove, 1972, 1979; Lewis, Beavers, Gossett, & Phillips, 1976; McGrath, Keita, Strickland, & Russo, 1990). The fact that there is a strong positive correlation between women's income and divorce (Levinger & Mole, 1976) suggests that women who have the resources to leave an institution that has proved detrimental to their health are empowered to do so. But the painful effects of the high divorce rate in our society on children and family life are also cause for concern.

Even more disturbing is the rise in reported incidents of incest, rape, wife and child abuse, and sexual harassment in the workplace (Gelles & Straus, 1989). The existence of relatively new laws that do not tolerate the abuse of women has made public the private abuse that women have endured in the past. Gelles and Straus (1989) have pointed out that the slight reduction of reported incidents of spouse abuse that occurred between their 1975 and 1985 family violence surveys is probably a result of the enforcement of those laws. Nevertheless, domestic violence and sexual harassment continue to be troubling. The research indicates that traditional gender socialization is a major contribution to each of these contemporary problems (Farrell, 1987; McGrath et al., 1990; Miedzian, 1991; O'Neil, 1982; Walker, 1984). More than ever before, a consciousness of gender roots is mandated.

THE SOCIALIZATION PROCESS

Although no one denies the obvious biological differences between men and women, it is likely that the observed gender differences in perception and behavior are the result of a complex interactive process between cultural and biological forces. The raw material an individual brings to the process of gender socialization certainly influences the outcome, but the process itself plays a significant part in the creation of separate gender ecosystems. Many families begin early in subtle and not so subtle ways to train their boys and girls to behave differently, speak differently, dress differently, even think differently. These attitudes and behaviors reflect the mores of the separate gender worlds as modeled by parents, siblings, and the surrounding society. There is even evidence to support the belief that such training so influences the expectations of children that they perceive what they expect to perceive, thus contributing to an interactive process that results in a self-fulfilling prophecy regarding gendered behavior (Geis, 1993). For therapists to deal with issues of gender that arise in the treatment of families, couples, and individuals, they must begin by considering the role that gender socialization plays in human development and subsequently in human relationships.

4

In subsequent chapters we explore in depth the gender development of both men and women. For the present, it is sufficient to note that those who deviate from traditional gender stereotypes pay a price. Hence the terms *sissy* for boys and *tomboy* for girls (O'Neil, 1982). One may think of those terms as outmoded in this era of feminism, yet one need only note the current prevalence of homophobia or the hostility aimed at women in the firehouse, on the police force, or more subtly, in the corporate boardroom to realize that gender restrictions still carry force. Even today, men who are sensitive and caring may be labeled soft or weak, whereas high-achieving women are often characterized as overly aggressive.

There is almost no area of life that is untouched by gender. From birth to death, gender affects all human relationships. During the latency period, boys and girls tend to live in separate gender ecosystems. As children enter puberty, they make their first forays into one another's social worlds. Traversing this boundary, they begin the arduous process of learning to communicate, to understand, and to work with "the other." In this process, each struggles not only to explore the other's nature, but also to overcome the misinformation, myths, and stereotypes gathered over the years. Many succeed. Others pay the price of failure in troubled marriages and dysfunctional families.

COEVOLUTION AND THE
GENDER-ROLE JOURNEY

We believe that a couple's gender patterns evolve and change during the course of their lives together, a process we call *coevolution.* When two people marry, their gender development does not stop. Rather, the behavior of each strongly affects the other, either positively or adversely. As their relationship evolves, each stage of family development is shadowed by gender. Couples face each new step in their lives from radically different gender perspectives, whether the issue is the birth of children, job problems, or any of the myriad challenges that are an inevitable part of a family's growth. Couples may become more distant and isolated or locked in angry conflict as each partner feels increasingly trapped in an assigned role.

By the same token, through their dialogue, their struggle, their journey and their search, the partners may grow in their understanding of what it is to be a woman and a man, each enhanced by the other.

It is important to place the coevolution of the couple in its larger context. Vast shifts in society's demands affect all women and men, so that there is a universal coevolution, often in a negative direction. This is evident in the persistent subjugation of women and the sacrifice of young males in time of war even as consciousness of the issues has increased. The coevolution of each individual heterosexual couple exists within this larger context, of which therapists need to be acutely conscious. It is our hope that this book will help therapists to facilitate the gender-role journey (O'Neil & Egan, 1992b; O'Neil & Roberts-Carroll, 1988) of the individuals, couples, and families in their care.

PROBLEMS WITH TRADITIONAL THERAPIES

Educated therapists often consider themselves to be immune to the pervasive influence of gender stereotypes. Feminism, an increasing male gender consciousness, and a new openness about homosexuality and lesbianism influence our views of gender. We speak of alternative lifestyles and deal in our practices with single-parent, blended, and dual-career families, each of them requiring fresh insights and approaches in treatment. However, the deeply ingrained expectations people bring to relationships are often based on traditional role models of the 1950s, which offer little help in dealing with today's family patterns. Indeed, the unrecognized messages of gender socialization interfere with the ability to cope flexibly with new patterns, leaving people confused, with no clear map to follow.

In the next chapter, we describe in detail how therapists' theories, research, and interventions are influenced by their own gender socialization in ways that are often detrimental to both men and women. We document how pioneer theorists in psychology, by using male behavior, cognitions, and feelings as the norm for healthy behavior, pathologized the other half of the human race. We also discuss the ways in which therapeutic interventions conducted without an informed gender-sensitive perspective are countertherapeutic and merely serve to reinforce a social status quo that hurts both women and men.

GENDER-SENSITIVE PSYCHOTHERAPY

When a couple seeks help, one of the most daunting tasks facing the therapist is to establish a basis of communication between two people who have grown up in separate gender worlds. The men and women who come to our offices for counseling, whether as individuals, couples, or families, are often unaware of the role that gender plays in their lives. Indeed, we therapists are not always attuned to the force of gender differences and strains. Although it is important to be knowledgeable about research findings and theoretical positions that can produce statistically significant results and characterize groups of people, we must also be able to translate these findings into clinical practice. The individuals, couples, and families we treat do not always fit our statistics, theories, and models.

As we demonstrate in subsequent chapters, gender continues to have a profound impact on both women and men in our increasingly complex society. There is great dissatisfaction with many features of traditional patterns of interaction between men and women and a strong desire to create a more egalitarian and mutually empathic society. Even those who do not consider themselves activists or agents of change, who indeed are not even conscious of these societal currents, experience a confusion and discontent that they cannot identify but that manifests itself in faulty relationships or poor communication. Therapists not only should become knowledgeable about gender issues and sensitive to their impact, but also should help those they treat to gain this recognition.

The purpose of this book is to bring together the perspectives of both female and male theoretical positions, providing the reader with the research on male and female traditional gender socialization and the literature on gender-role strain for both genders, which has occurred as a result of sociological changes since the feminist movement. We show how, despite major efforts to change the traditional gender messages, the age-old expectations still have a major impact on behavior. We point out that the feminist movement and the men's movement, although laudatory in their objectives, have given women and men gender messages that are in direct contradiction to those intransigent traditional gender dictates, thus confusing both sexes and burdening them with added requirements. Also, we provide readers with specific interventions to help their clients who are struggling to make their marriages work in the midst of this gender revolution.

WHAT TO EXPECT IN THE BOOK

The book is divided into two parts. Part I is dedicated to the process of gender socialization and its outcomes. Because a thorough knowledge of the results of gender socialization, the feminist critique of traditional methods of therapy, and the detrimental effects of rigid adherence to traditional gender roles is required before gender-sensitive psychotherapy is possible, we feel it is imperative to provide this background as a reference for the clinician who is not familiar with this literature. The reader is encouraged to remember, as this literature is reviewed, that we do not intend to endorse a radically feminist or promasculinist stance but rather to establish a baseline of theory and its clinical implications from which we develop our systemic premise. Because some of our readers are familiar with this material, we have tried to make this part more practical by including examples throughout to show what issues therapists encounter in their clinical practice.

The theoretical and research base provided in Part I describes and offers explanations for the observable gender differences in society. We admit that because we are concerned with the role of therapists as gender brokers (Pittman, 1985), we may err on the side of emphasizing differences rather than pointing out similarities. We remind the reader often that men and women are capable of possessing the whole range of characteristics, values, and behaviors and that many people do not fit the cultural stereotype. On the other hand, we recognize that the gender ecosystem has a great deal of influence on the perceptions and expectations of everyone and that even when people consciously think they disagree with the stereotype, self-fulfilling prophecies can and do occur (Geis, 1993). We describe how the expectations of each gender with regard to values, communication styles, problem-solving strategies, personality characteristics, and sexuality may lead to serious problems and misunderstandings in the relationship. We also discuss the additional strain to male–female relationships caused by the gender revolution Western society is presently experiencing.

Chapter 1 discusses the detrimental effects of traditional psychotherapy on both men and women, reviews the feminist critique of both individual and family psychological theories, and reports the research that supports the need for gender sensitive psychotherapy for *both* genders. Chapter 2 provides the reader with the literature on the process and outcomes of traditional gender socialization for women and men. Chapters 3 and 4 describe the gender-role strain placed on women and men due to changes in society as a result of the women's movement of the 1960s. Chapter 5 combines the information provided in chapters 2 through 4 and provides the reader with an understanding of how the traditional gender-socialization process and modern gender expectations have clashed, causing people to feel misunderstood and dissatisfied in heterosexual relationships.

The second half of the book focuses on gender-sensitive interventions and techniques. We discuss the conceptual foundations of gender-sensitive psychotherapy: the gender ecosystem, gender socialization, androgyny, empathic knowing, coevolution, and the gender-role journey. We emphasize the importance of the therapist's knowledge base and attitude in bringing about therapeutic change. We describe therapeutic interventions that we have found effective in working with couples who struggle with traditional gender socialization. We illustrate our discussion of our clinical methods with case examples to demonstrate the process of moving clients through the gender-role journey (O'Neil & Roberts-Carroll, 1988) from a point of egocentric entitlement to one of empathic knowing and coevolution.

Chapter 6 discusses the concepts and theoretical underpinnings of gender-sensitive psychotherapy and provides the reader with guidelines for conducting gender-sensitive therapy. Chapter 7 presents and illustrates various therapeutic interventions that may be used to resolve gender-based issues. Chapter 8 describes the unique process of gender inquiry and provides an array of developmentally based questions and case examples to illustrate the effectiveness of this technique. Chapter 9 discusses gender coevolution in heterosexual relationships, describing the process by which the couple define one another either in increasingly rigid ways, resulting in emotional isolation, or in flexible, growth-enhancing ways, which may well lead to greater intimacy.

Chapter 10 addresses the issues of power and violence in the couple relationship, cautioning therapists to assess couples carefully for the presence of violence, a condition that *contraindicates* the methods suggested in this book until the violent partner has been successfully treated. It also discusses the ways in which gender socialization contributes to the thinking and behavior of both perpetrator and victim, thus perpetuating a vicious cycle, and suggests resources for the treatment of violence. The final chapter, chapter 11, looks at the application of gender inquiry and empathic knowing to other relationships such as parent–child and work relationships. In the appendix, we provide the reader with a review of the ethical and legal issues specific to maintaining a balance between work with the couple and with the individual, particularly the limits of and strict adherence to the rules of confidentiality. Throughout the book, the emphasis is on the application of the therapist's knowledge about gender socialization and human relationships to helping heterosexual couples move beyond the battle of the sexes to empathic understanding and intimacy. The chapters are filled with case examples that illustrate the process.

WHO ARE THE CLIENTS?

Although the material in this book is intended for therapists who treat couples, it will become apparent that all of the background information and many of the techniques described can be applied to individuals and families as well. Chapters 3, 4, 8, 9, and 11 illustrate how these concepts can be used in therapeutic situations that do not involve couples.

The reader is reminded that the authors have worked most frequently with Caucasian couples ranging in socioeconomic status from lower middle class to upper middle class, with educational backgrounds ranging from below high school level to doctoral degrees and beyond. Although some of our work has been with African American couples and couples with mixed ethnic backgrounds, most of what is discussed in this book is based on the gender messages absorbed by White Americans who have lived in the United States for at least two generations. Although much of the gender socialization that occurs in this population is found to be valid cross-culturally as well, there are differences in racial and ethnic groups that might influence the results of gender socialization. When we are aware of these differences, we mention them. Readers who are expert in characteristics of a particular ethnic group are encouraged to put on their cultural lens while reading this book and make modifications accordingly. Therapists who find themselves treating a couple of a different race or ethnic background from their own without expertise in that culture are encouraged to do what all experts in treating ethnic groups advise (Boyd-Franklin, 1989; Giordano, 1995; McGoldrick, Pearce, & Giordano, 1982): Listen to the clients. Ask them. Find out what is valid for them. The beauty of the philosophy and techniques in the approach suggested by this book is that they allow one to do just that. The attitude of therapists who become gender brokers remains the same as it always has been, and so do their techniques. It is only the socialization messages that may differ.

We have been careful to indicate that we are discussing heterosexual couples in this volume. Gender socialization plays an important role in the interaction of homosexual couples as well, often exponentially increasing the detrimental effects, whether the couple is male or female. For example, lesbians often experience a great deal of difficulty with boundary setting and individuation within the relationship, because both partners have been socialized to tune into others and put their needs first (Scrivner & Eldridge, 1995). Gay male partners frequently struggle with issues of competition and hierarchy, because both partners have been socialized to view their self-worth in those terms (Scrivner & Eldridge, 1995). Although this book has not attempted to address the treatment of homosexual couples, it may sensitize the therapist who treats this population to the major role that gender socialization plays in the conflicts and struggles gay couples encounter.

THE PURPOSE OF THE BOOK

There is a tendency in the United States today, for women and men to blame one another for the dissatisfactions that arise from strict adherence to gender-role socialization. It is the strong conviction of the authors that most men and women have not conspired against one another in some malicious fashion, but that during the course of social evolution, as each gender took on more specialized roles, they each were forced to give up aspects of themselves that prevented them from realizing their full potential. Furthermore, it is our belief that the adaptations women and men have made for the good of society as a whole have had detrimental effects on both genders. We also believe that, given the technological and political advances in the United States, the potential for men and women to work cooperatively toward a more egalitarian, mutually respectful relationship is great. As therapists, we can work with individuals and groups to facilitate this process, if we can help them get beyond outrage and blame to a point of deep change that grows out of increased empathy. The aim of this book, therefore, is not merely to discuss what we know of the effects of gender socialization on heterosexual relationships, but to provide readers with a therapeutic process that allows them to help couples understand their gender roots and move away from rigid gender expectations toward mutual empathy and intimacy.

1

Warning: Sexist Therapy May Be Hazardous to Your Health

In the 1970s, feminist scholars began to question the theories and techniques of psychological practice. They pointed out that the basic concepts that psychologists viewed as "truth" were often based on a male perspective of life, which did not hold true for females. Today there exists a whole body of literature that documents and illustrates this point of view. Inadvertently, early therapists worked in ways that were often detrimental to their women clients (Abramowitz, Abramowitz, Jackson, & Gomes, 1973; Broverman, Broverman, Clarkson, Rosenkrantz, & Vogel, 1970; Fabrikant, Landau, & Rollenhagen, 1973; Maracek & Johnson, 1980; Orlinsky & Howard, 1980).

It is not just women who are hurt by therapists who are unaware of the impact of gender socialization on their clients. What has been brought to light more recently is the fact that therapists, both male and female, have acted in ways that are often detrimental to male clients as well by assuming that the value systems and roles presently endorsed by the larger society are beneficial or perhaps by not even addressing the issue of their goodness (Robertson & Fitzgerald, 1990). The recent men's movement has pointed out the damage to men of strict adherence to their gender messages (David & Brannon, 1976; Fasteau, 1974; Goldberg, 1976; Harrison, 1978; Nathanson, 1977). Therapists who merely reinforce the status quo of male socialization are contributing to the negative toll imposed on men by traditional values of manhood. Furthermore, therapy as it is presently structured requires verbal skills and attitudes that are usually associated with women's communication, a fact that makes traditional therapy an uncomfortable and potentially nonproductive undertaking for many men (Andronico, 1996).

It is vitally important for therapists to be aware of the effects of gender socialization when working with either men or women. This chapter reviews briefly some of the ways gender-blind therapy can harm clients, regardless of their gender. Sensitivity to the issues of gender in couples therapy is essential if the therapist is to avoid reinforcing the cultural status quo and aid clients in the open negotiation of their relationships.

DANGERS OF THERAPY AND THERAPIST EXPECTATIONS FOR MALE AND FEMALE CLIENTS

Women

A vast body of research, primarily published in the 1970s, demonstrated sex-role stereotyping on the part of therapists. Phyllis Chesler (1972) wrote an exposé of sexist treatment in the mental health system that stimulated many later studies. In 1984, the Women's Task Force of the Department of Mental Health in Minnesota published *Women and Mental Health: New Directions for Change* (Mowbray, Lanir, & Hulce, 1984), which was based on a thorough review of the literature up to that time. Findings reported indicated that clinicians had a double standard of mental health with different expectations for female and male clients (Brodsky & Hare-Mustin, 1980; Fabrikant, 1974; Fabrikant et al., 1973). According to these studies, women were expected to be more submissive, less independent, more neurotic, more emotional, less adventurous, more nurturing, less achieving, and more excitable than men. Therapists rated women with nontraditional and nonstereotypical interests as psychologically maladjusted. Marriage and children were more frequently prescribed as necessary for the mental well-being of women than for men. Women were kept in therapy longer than men and often received more directive therapy.

Most individual clients of psychotherapy are women (Anderson & Holder, 1989; Gove, 1980; Gove & Tudor, 1973; Mowbray et al., 1984). Suggested reasons for this include the fact that the client role is more compatible with the female gender role of being weak, irrational, childish, and submissive. Recently, information derived from psycholinguistic observation (Tannen, 1990) has indicated that women often use talk as a way to connect with others and solve their problems, whereas men tend to minimize problems as a way to comfort one another, which would certainly help to explain the preponderance of women in a talking-based therapeutic relationship.

Other writers have maintained that it is the unhealthiness of the female role itself that creates problems for women (Hare-Mustin, 1983; Miller, 1984; Sobel & Russo, 1981). This role includes the suppression of negative feelings, taking care of others before self, and exaggerated femininity. A recent study of depression in women conducted by McGrath and colleagues (1990) indicated that women's risk of depression exceeds that of men by 2:1 worldwide. These researchers related the higher depression rate to a number of factors including the socially endorsed passive–dependent personality style of women, the high rate of sexual and physical abuse of women, the inequity in marriage that protects men, but is detrimental to women (Broverman et al., 1970), and women's reduced capacity to earn a viable living. Therapists who persist in viewing female depression as a biological weakness or cognitive distortion without taking into consideration the depressogenic atmosphere created by a real world that devalues and oppresses women merely add to the distress women suffer.

Medical literature has demonstrated that women are hospitalized more often than men (Anderson & Holder, 1989; Chesler, 1972), that their complaints are not taken as seriously as those of men, and that they receive a disproportionately large share of the drugs prescribed for mental disorders (Fidell, 1980, 1981). Prescription drug abuse has been a serious problem for adult women (Mowbray et al., 1984). More recently, authors such as Gail Sheehy (1992), in *The Silent Passage*, and Carol Tavris (1992), in *The Mismeasure of Woman*, have reported a similar tendency toward overtreatment of gynecological problems.

Women at times have been the victims of sexual abuse by male therapists (Bates & Brodsky, 1989; Bouhoutsos, Holroyd, Lerman, Forer, & Greenberg, 1983; Gabbard, 1989; Holroyd & Brodsky, 1977; Mowbray et al., 1984; Pope, 1990; Pope & Vetter, 1991; Zelen, 1985). Between 5 and 12 percent of male mental health professionals admit to having had sexual intercourse with a patient (Bouhoutsos et al., 1983; Holroyd & Brodsky, 1977; Pope, 1987). This sexual exploitation has been extremely detrimental to clients, particularly in reinforcing their low self-esteem and damaging their trust to others. Feminists have proposed that the abuse mirrors the culture's view of women in general as inferior and the serious problems of their victimization (Committee on Women in Psychology, 1989).

It is important, at this point, to remind the reader that we do not intend to imply that all male researchers, psychotherapists, physicians, and theorists behave in ways that are destructive to women. On the contrary, many are effective in their contributions to women's health. Neither do we wish to suggest that when male professionals are harmful to their female clients they usually exhibit a callous lack of caring or a conscious desire to victimize women. Most professionals operate with the best knowledge available at the time. Even many of those who treated, operated, or prescribed unnecessarily were probably guilty at most of a benevolent patriarchal attitude, which may have prevented them from sharing their knowledge with the woman and allowing her to participate in the decision making about her own treatment. Of course, in every profession, there are those who are incompetent, callous, and self-serving, both male and female, but these have not been in our view, the majority. What we wish to point out is that the assumption that women were either dependent and uninformed, needing a professional to make decisions for them, or to be measured on a male scale of health has led to the unnecessary or detrimental treatment of many women for many years.

Men

Given the earlier critique of androcentrism in the mental health field, it seems peculiar to discuss hazards for men in psychotherapy. One might assume that the harm done to women generates benefits for men. In some ways this has been true. When women were being devalued for their passivity, dependence, and emotional vulnerability, men, by implication, were being celebrated for their relative assertiveness, independence, and emotional stoicism. Additionally, sexist family therapy practices tended to undermine women and support patriarchal leadership (Avis, 1988; Nutt, 1991).

Nevertheless, sexist psychotherapy has also harmed men, because neither women nor men benefit when therapists encourage clients to adhere closely to a narrow range of acceptable behaviors. Whereas role rigidity promotes depression in women, it also generates problems for men. Cleary (1987) noted that men are more likely to have problems with alcoholism and illicit drug abuse, antisocial behaviors, and suicide. Brooks and Silverstein (1995) argued that many aspects of traditional male socialization have encouraged the "dark side" of masculinity: a range of negative behaviors including violence, sexual excesses, social irresponsibility, self-abuse, and relationship dysfunctions.

Psychotherapy harms men when it fails to recognize the link between men's symptomatic behavior and their traditional socialization. Unfortunately, far too few programs for the treatment of substance abuse, wife battering, and sexual dysfunction include attention to gender issues. For example, Diamond (1987) pointed out that effective treatment of men's substance abuse demands expertise in special issues that affect men (p. 333). Long (1987) and Brooks (1992) made similar arguments for gender sensitivity in the treatment of male batterers.

Although men can be directly harmed by sexist therapy, they may be harmed more by therapy they do not receive. Vessey and Howard (1993) pointed out that women, by a ratio of 2:1, continue to outnumber men in therapists' offices. This statistic highlights the complexity of the matter; from one perspective, it could be seen as evidence that women continue to be pathologized and encouraged to take too much responsibility for relationship problems. Yet from another perspective, it can be seen as evidence that men continue to define their roles so narrowly that they are unable and unwilling to seek therapeutic help.

To some extent, men's avoidance of therapy is a product of the poor fit between the male role and the role of therapy client. Levant (1990) observed that "the male role requires that men be independent, strong, self-reliant, competitive, achievement-oriented, powerful, adventurous, and emotionally restrained. These characteristics . . . make it difficult for men to seek and use psychological services" (p. 309). Similarly, Osherson and Krugman (1990) cited emotional restrictiveness, ego boundedness, and emphasis on rationality as reasons that "male utilization of psychotherapy lags behind that of women" (p. 327).

Although men avoid therapy because they see it as unmanly, they also do so because it has usually been seen as not user friendly for men (Brooks, 1996). Several men's studies advocates have suggested that men will be more likely to benefit from psychotherapy when therapists become more sensitive to men's perspectives (Mintz & O'Neil, 1990), more knowledgeable about men's typical problem-solving style (Levant, 1990), or more aware of men's affinity for group environments (Brooks, 1996). In other words, men's failure to seek psychotherapy can be conceptualized both as a failing of men and as a failing of psychotherapy.

Psychotherapy also harms men when it fails to make allowances for men's typical methods of handling therapeutic impasses. Because men fear self-disclosure, are less aware of their feelings than women are, and express less affect in therapy than women do (Carlson, 1987; Heppner & Gonzales, 1987; Ipsaro, 1986; Maracek & Johnson, 1980), they are likely to be viewed as less desirable therapy clients (Mintz & O'Neil, 1990). Men's competitive style and intense homophobia interfere with their capacity to establish effective relationships with male therapists (Ipsaro, 1986). Men's difficulty relating to empowered women creates problems for male clients of women therapists. For example, because women are commonly expected to be nurturers of men, therapy often flounders when there is a need for the woman therapist to exert power and authority and the male client to experience emotional vulnerability (Mintz & O'Neil, 1990).

Finally, therapy harms men when it fails to attend to issues critical to men's emotional development. Osherson and Krugman (1990) held that "shame" plays a powerful role in men's lives and is too rarely addressed in their psychotherapy. Brooks (1990) contended that family therapy fails men when it does not challenge men's emotional stoicism, their overemphasis on work and career, their limited ideas about fatherhood, and their intense homophobia.

SEXIST ROOTS OF THEORY

Today the field of mental health recognizes that reality is always colored by the eye of the beholder and that therefore the social context of any theorist or therapist will have an impact on what is thought of as healthy or normal. For example, most students of psychology are cautioned to recognize the influence that living in the sexually repressive Victorian culture had on Freud's thinking about his psychosexual theory of development. Owing to the repressive cultural values, Freud most likely overemphasized the role of sexuality in human psychology and failed to address the important issue of social relationships, which was later discussed by his followers. Furthermore, although Freud admitted he did not understand what women wanted, he proceeded to explain the unhappiness and discontent he saw in his female clients in terms of the male value system; that is, women were unhappy because they lacked a penis. He did not consider the lack of power and autonomy women experienced in that culture as relevant because he assumed, as did many males, that a healthy women would be happy finding her meaning through marriage and children. Likewise, rather than believing that his female patients might have been sexually abused by their fathers or other relatives, Freud considered their tales of incestuous relationships to be fantasy and, often, wish fulfillment. His male perspective blinded him to the female experience and so influenced his theory that half the human race became pathologized. By calling attention to the social context and personal experience of the great theorists, educators hope to alert therapists to the dangers of believing their own expectations and value systems are the only ones by which to measure the functioning of others.

Many examples of sexist thinking occurred in the mental health profession in the United States during the 1940s and 1950s. At that time in the United States, the accepted model of a healthy family included a homemaker who was fulfilled through her loving service to her husband and children. For many women, this was indeed a rewarding lifestyle. But for others, as so well described in Betty Friedan's *The Feminine Mystique* (1963), such an existence was unsatisfying and occasionally even debilitating. Mental health professionals, who were mostly men at the time, did not understand what Friedan called "the problem with no name" (p. 13), partly because they had never been in the position of the 1950s traditional wife and mother and did not experience the negative aspects of that role. As therapists, they perceived their job to be that of helping their clients adjust to the realities of their lives, an understandable goal at the time but one that has been repeatedly challenged since then by many writers, both male and female. Today, therapists are encouraged to question the system to which they are asking people to adjust and not merely assume that what is, must be.

FEMINIST CRITIQUE OF TRADITIONAL THEORIES

In an attempt to understand and rectify what many people came to perceive as harmful psychotherapy, feminist therapists began formulating a critique of traditional theories and practices of psychotherapy. This critique began with a feminist analysis of individual psychotherapy and counseling in the 1970s followed by a reexamination of family and systems therapy in the 1980s. This line of thinking stimulated a similar, although less well-developed, critique from the male perspective. In the late 1980s and 1990s, writers on men's gender issues also began to question the gender socialization of males and its impact on men's health and therapy. Because the feminist movement was the stimulus that began the process of evaluation of gender bias in therapy and because the more fully developed feminist critique informs and influences the kind of therapy both genders receive, we summarize the feminist critique in the following sections.

Gender Bias in Developmental Theories

Feminist critiques of individual psychotherapy addressed both theoretical issues and evidence of bias found in research studies. Developmental theories were criticized for basing their descriptions on male models and then generalizing them to females (Belenky, Clinchy, Goldberger, & Tarule, 1986; Chodorow, 1978; Dinnerstein, 1976; Gilligan, 1982; Miller, 1986). In the early years of psychological research, most research samples consisted of white males, partly because white males were readily available as undergraduate psychology students. The problem with this approach, of course, is that men and women, in addition to having obvious biological differences, also undergo different life experiences and expectations, which result in different value systems, communication styles, problem-solving skills, and priorities. It becomes impossible, given these differences, to generalize findings from men to women or to measure them on the same scale. It is like comparing apples to oranges. For example, defining *maturity* as autonomy and independent identity without taking into account needs for connectedness and relationships discounts differences in male–female socialization. Because the male theorists considered autonomy and independence to be the highest goal of development, women who, owing to their role as caretaker and nurturer in the family, placed a high value on relationship were judged as less developed and mature than men (Gilligan, 1982; Miller, 1984). Instead of examining the strengths and drawbacks of each gender role, early developmental theorists judged both genders by a male value system.

Gender Bias in Personality Theories

Similarly, personality theories were criticized for describing women as innately passive and dependent, assuming these personality traits were inherent in biology rather than influenced by the social status occupied by the females studied. Later research (Hare-Mustin, 1987) has shown that individuals, both male and female, who are in inferior positions socially, economically, or politically are obliged to adopt characteristics of dependency and passivity as a survival tool. Women who were dissatisfied with the dependent and passive role were described by Freudian theory as suffering from penis envy, a pejorative description for a fairly reasonable desire to identify with the more powerful, rather than weaker, position in society. Women were caught in a bind, considered inferior if they were dependent and mentally ill if they were not. Another label in diagnostic manuals applied liberally to female patients is *histrionic personality disorder* (previously *hysterical personality*). This diagnosis describes an overemphasis of a set of characteristics and behaviors that were then and still are now taught to women as feminine behavior (Belote, 1981; Lerner, 1981; Wolowitz, 1972). Women again were placed in a double-bind position. If they did not have at least mild histrionic characteristics, they were not feminine. If they did, they were mentally ill. Finally, because women based so many of their moral decisions on what was good for their relationships, they were judged to be morally inferior to men, who more often cited abstract principles as the basis for their decisions (Kohlberg, 1969). In each of these cases, instead of viewing men and women as having different characteristics, behaviors, thinking patterns, and problem-solving techniques owing to the roles they each played in the present social structure, early personality theorists viewed women as inherently deficient by male standards. The role of gender socialization in women's development was essentially ignored.

FEMINIST PSYCHOLOGICAL THEORIES

To rectify the problem of sexist theory, feminist scholars have developed theories that are based on female experience and do not pathologize thought and behavior that are not in adherence with the traditional male value system. On the contrary, being different from men is seen as just that—different, not defective. These theories argue for a *revalorization* (French, 1985) of female values; that is, they ask society to hold traditionally feminine values of connection and relationship in as high esteem as the masculine values of autonomy and independence. A perspective such as that endorsed by these feminists, which gives equal respect to male and female experience, is one of the cornerstones of the gender-sensitive therapy described in this book.

Developmental Theories

Feminist scholars such as Dorothy Dinnerstein (1976) and Nancy Chodorow (1978) have attempted to explain the development and perpetuation of patterns in an industrial society that are destructive to both genders. According to both of these theorists, the conventional allocation to women of child-care responsibilities results in different value systems, relational capacities, patterns of communication, and experiences of power, solely on the basis of gender identification. Dinnerstein argued that the roots of misogyny are in the irrational infantile fears of the engulfing power of the female caretaker. This exaggerated fear is contrasted to a more realistic appraisal of the father's role in discipline formed through the eyes of the older child. Chodorow suggested that little girls can form their sexual identity while relating closely to and modeling themselves after their mothers, but that little boys must identify themselves as different and separate from mother. Because little boys do not have a present father with whom to relate closely, they develop a value system based on separation, autonomy, and abstract principles. Boys form their identity not through modeling, but by defining themselves as different from mother. By so doing, they reduce their capacity for intimacy and emotional expressivity. Little girls, on the other hand, place a high priority on relatedness, connectedness, and caring for others as modeled by their mothers. By identifying with mothers who often sacrifice their own desires and goals to serve their family, little girls reduce their capacity for autonomy and independence.

Personality Theories

Theorists such as Jean Baker Miller (1986), Carol Gilligan (1982), and Mary Field Belenky (Belenky et al., 1986) have proposed developmental models of mental health that are based on what they call feminine value systems rather than the traditional male values of autonomy and separation. Miller suggested that the capacity for nurturance and relationship seen in adult women is not a developmental lag but, on the contrary, a healthy mature manner of interaction necessary for society, which should be valued by males as well. Gilligan's research findings indicated that women often base their moral decision making on relational variables, such as caring and responsibility, instead of on rights and abstract principles. According to the levels of moral development proposed by Kohlberg (1969), such decision making would be representative of a lower level of moral development. Gilligan proposed that, on the contrary, relationships are important to a satisfying life, and decisions based on what is best for the relationship are not morally inferior but reflective of different priorities. Belenky and colleagues (1986) reported that women learn best when what they are taught resonates with their personal experience, as opposed to the traditional masculine method of not only learning through experience but also tending to accept or challenge the abstract principles taught by experts. Feminists are calling for a balance between connection and autonomy (Martin-Knudson, 1994).

FEMINIST CRITICISMS OF FAMILY THERAPY

Family therapy has also been strongly criticized by feminists for its fostering of traditional roles and for not alleviating the oppression of women. Hare-Mustin (1987) and others (Bernard, 1981b; Goldner, 1985) have written that after the Industrial Revolution, men became primary wage earners, and the home became for them a place of leisure and rest, whereas women, even those in the workforce, bore the major responsibility for child care and housework.

Research on marriage has shown it to have a positive, protective effect on men but a negative, detrimental one on women in terms of both physical and mental health (Gove, 1972, 1979; Gove & Tudor 1973). The pervasiveness of power inequities is evident in the fact that society still tends to expect the husband to be taller, older, more educated, and from a higher social class than his wife (Cowan, 1984; Gillis & Avis, 1980; Hare-Mustin, 1978). To the degree that family therapists are unaware of these inequities, they tend to reinforce the status quo, thereby hampering the growth of both marital partners (Hare-Mustin, 1978, 1987).

CRITICAL ISSUES OF FAMILY THEORY

Although early family systems theorists introduced a revolutionary new concept by considering the family context within which a patient developed and maintained his or her symptoms, they did not address the larger gender ecosystem any more than their predecessors had. Except for Virginia Satir, the pioneers of family systems theory were mostly male, and they were influenced as everyone is by the social context in which they lived. In the 1950s, when family systems theories were developing, the typical middle-class American family was thought to consist of a mother who was a homemaker, a father who worked outside the home, and two or three children. Systems concepts were developed from a middle-class male value system that was based on the ideal family of the 1950s in the United States, with virtual disregard for historical, cultural, or gender differences.

Luepnitz (1988) and others (Avis, 1988; Goodrich, Rampage, Ellman, & Halstead, 1988; McGoldrick, Anderson, & Walsh, 1989; Walters, Carter, Papp, & Silverstein, 1988) have identified several ways in which the pioneer family theorists' male construction of reality differs from a female perspective. Certain specific constructs of family systems theory are especially problematic with regard to gender equity. These are *circularity, complementarity, neutrality, hierarchy,* and *enmeshment.* The following sections provide the reader with the feminist criticism of these accepted foundations of family therapy.

Circularity

Circularity, like reciprocity, assumes that people are involved in recursive behavioral patterns that are mutually reinforcing. It results in making all family members responsible for events or, conversely, no one accountable for anything. Circularity assumes equality of power, but because wives do not typically have the same power or resources as husbands, they may end up falsely blamed. A commonly cited example is wife battering. Circularity assumes that the wife has some responsibility in causing the abuse and ignores the power inequity between the spouses. Although the wife may have participated in an interaction that triggered the husband's loss of self-control, from a feminist perspective, nothing justifies the use of violence to solve a disagreement. Circularity often results in blaming the victim. Furthermore, recent research (Jacobson, 1993) has indicated that what a woman does has no effect on whether or not she is battered.

Not considered in this criticism are the men who are physically abused by their wives and who are accused as wife beaters if they attempt to defend themselves because of the advantage their superior physical strength affords them in confrontation. The critique also does not consider the husband who is smaller and weaker than his wife, for whom a physical altercation is equally dangerous. Additionally, a man may be economically or physically dependent on his wife and without resources should they separate, or a father may sincerely believe that he would be the superior custodial parent postdivorce, but his plea is almost always ignored by the courts. In the United States, these cases are the exception to the rule, but they nevertheless exist, possibly in greater numbers than imagined. Perhaps a more gender-balanced criticism of circularity would simply take into account *power* differentials, regardless of the direction of the power.

Complementarity

Complementarity is another construct that is much more likely to disadvantage women. It assumes that at a deep level partners are fundamentally equal and that the observed inequality is only a matter of perspective. It suggests there is hidden strength in weakness or passivity. For example, in the traditional marriage, the competent, worldly husband who protects his helpless wife would be helpless himself if asked to cook their meals or sew on a button. However, this construct denies the reality of real-life oppression and power differential. The husband whose job provides the money that supports his wife and family can pay someone to cook a meal and sew on a button. The wife whose skills are not viable in the marketplace, by contrast, may have to receive welfare benefits without her husband's income (Morgan, 1991). This fact causes her to defer to his needs and wishes rather than risk her economic security. Were she equal to him in money-making potential, she might stand her ground on issues of importance to her.

Another example of complementarity involves the weak, sickly, or debilitated spouse and the overfunctioning caretaker. The theory would point out the power that the weaker spouse has over the stronger one: that of having his or her needs met by someone else merely by doing nothing. Although this situation can be seen in the relationship between the agoraphobic wife and her husband, it can also be found in the marriage of the physically disabled war veteran and his wife. Again, one must keep in mind the power differential and its relevance to the given construct—no matter which gender holds the power.

Part of the issue is one of respect and appreciation. If both spouses respect, value, and express appreciation of the contribution of the other, complementarity can work because a sense of equity exists. The problem arises when one spouse's offering is perceived to be less important or necessary than that of the other. At this point, the perceived lack of balance begins to take a toll on the relationship, resulting in poor self-esteem in one of the partners and resentment for the lack of equity in the other.

Neutrality

The systemic definition of *neutrality* requires the therapist to remain objective with regard to values as well as to refrain from taking sides within the family. Although laudatory in its attempt to keep the therapist nonjudgmental, neutrality has been challenged by feminists as an inappropriate therapeutic stance. If the therapist ignores the impact of gender-role socialization, a result may be a political stance of supporting the power differential and patriarchal structure of culture. The therapist whose neutral stance covertly supports the husband's view that children need their mother at home and therefore the wife should not work outside the home fails to understand how much power the husband's income and resulting independence give him over his wife. At the same time, this therapist does not acknowledge the positive effects on the father of more interaction with his children and less stress in the workplace. The therapist who does not raise for discussion the potential solution of the husband staying at home while his wife supports the family is endorsing a structure that does not open up possibilities that may alleviate the oppression of men and women.

Hierarchy

Systemic approaches that emphasize hierarchy often place fathers in executive functions within families and women and children at the bottom. They do not place a high value on the wives' role in the family and instead support the patriarchal assumption that males should be dominant. Therapists who adopt this approach automatically assume that dysfunction in the family is due to a reversal of the complementary pattern of male-up/female-down instead of questioning the value of that pattern in the first place. What message does the "father rules the roost" philosophy give to the female children in the family about their self-worth? In addition, the concept of father as head of the household does not leave much room for the more feminine style of decision making, that is, on the basis of consensual agreement and collective participation. Perhaps a more gender-neutral way of looking at hierarchy would be based on generation rather than gender. A collaborative arrangement between parents in decision making regarding their children would demonstrate the value of and need for both male and female parents as well as cooperative negotiation between the genders.

Enmeshment

Mothers have often been blamed for family pathology. They have been labeled as *enmeshed* or *overinvolved* without consideration of the importance of connectedness and relatedness in women's lives. Overemphasis on boundaries may violate this connectedness. The necessities of life over the centuries have made the father the person to go off and find food (make money) and protect the family (go to war). These duties reinforce separation, autonomy, and competition. Mothers have traditionally assumed the role of caretaker of children, a role that requires connection and cooperation. When mothers assume responsibility for children's welfare, it is because the larger society expects her to do so. However, these same mothers are criticized for being enmeshed and overprotective of their children when judged by the male norm of separation as healthy. Although there are cases in which a mother's symbiotic relationship with her child is detrimental and debilitating to the child, not all closeness is negative.

The devaluing of nurturance and overvaluing of autonomy provide yet another example of gender bias in family theory. A gender-neutral theory would recognize that both autonomy and affiliation are requirements of a healthy, fulfilling life and endorse the need for a balance between the two.

A NEW DIRECTION

Feminist family therapists are seriously questioning many of the basic concepts of family therapy and attempting to create new models for gender-fair therapeutic work. We agree that to ignore the differences in gender-role socialization and the power differential between men and women in the average family reinforces the status quo in the larger ecosystem. We demonstrate in chapter 4 that the status quo is often as detrimental to men as it is to women, although in a different way. The challenging of the present structure of society is believed to be important for the health and growth of both genders.

Thelma Jean Goodrich (1991) summed up the dilemma for family therapists in her daring book *Women and Power*:

> For family therapy to continue to accept as ideal the conventional model of family, with its gendered division of labor and its hierarchy of privilege and power, puts family therapy in complicity with the society to keep women oppressed. Fundamental to that oppression is the assumption that women belong in the home, so that even if we venture forth, we are still responsible for home. It is the knowledge that she is the unilateral provider of the experience of family for others—and the necessary years and years of thinking of others first and continually (because he will not)—that robs women of power. (pp. 18–19)

Many theorists, both male and female (Bly, 1990b; Goodrich, 1991), have written that it is in the *structure* of the traditional family that a misogynistic attitude is reproduced and perpetuated. When children see their mothers providing nurturance for their families without payment in a society that places the highest value on income, the implication is that child care and those who perform it are inferior. This might not be the case if money were not perceived as power and child care were not devalued. Indeed it is the *perceived implications* of the gender roles in an industrial society that are at the root of the problem. However, as long as the larger society continues to value dollars more than children and family, those who provide child care will continue to occupy the inferior position in society. We believe it will take a restructuring of the family, one in which men and women share equally the obligation to care for the children and provide the "experience of family," to elevate women to equal rank. Ironically, but not surprisingly, this same family structure reproduces and perpetuates the stereotypical male values and behaviors that are detrimental, even lethal, to men as well (see chapter 4). It is not our wish to suggest a particular family structure that would solve these difficulties but to call attention to the problem in a gender-neutral fashion that allows clients to work cooperatively toward their own idiosyncratic solutions.

CONCLUSION

It is clear that gender continues, even in this day of supposed enlightenment, to have a major impact on the lives of clients. Therapists who ignore the effects of gender socialization on the behaviors and thought patterns of their clients are unlikely to be effective in helping them reach their full potential as human beings. If the detrimental effects of gender socialization are not considered, therapists are likely to function as agents of social control, teaching their clients how best to cope with the limited and rigid roles that society has assigned. For psychologists, long noted for their tendency to question rather than accept "facts" at face value, such an approach should be unthinkable. Unless psychologists and other therapists and counselors are knowledgeable about the differing perceptions of reality for men and women growing out of differing biology, socialization, value systems, levels of moral development, role definitions, and political, economic, and legal power, they will unconsciously lead their clients to accept the status quo (O'Neil & Egan, 1992b). The first step in resolving many of the dilemmas brought to therapists by families, couples, and individual clients is an awareness of the gender differences that are often at the root of the problem. But that is only the first step. Therapists must also be able to translate knowledge into practical therapeutic interventions that move clients beyond their rigid roles to empathy and growth. The following two sections of the book provide information and techniques intended to facilitate this process.

PART ONE

The Gender Revolution

2

Process and Outcomes of Traditional Gender Socialization

Gender is one of the most basic constructs by which individuals define themselves. One's gender identity is his or her definition of self as a male or female person. Although biology determines the physical characteristics of maleness or femaleness, much of our experience of what it is to be male or female is a result of cultural forces and a process called *gender socialization*. The bulk of this chapter is devoted to a description of that process and a discussion of the results of traditional gender socialization for both women and men.

For centuries, men and women received cultural messages that are still deeply ingrained in American society. Despite the societal changes occurring today, the messages of past generations linger on. The clients we see in our offices come to us with a variety of ideas regarding what women and men are supposed to be. There are large generational differences regarding expectations and experiences. For example, someone who grew up in the 1950s might have an Ozzie-and-Harriet picture of family life, whereas today's young couples will have been influenced by Murphy Brown or Cybill. Middle-class clients in their fifties today are likely to have had a mother who was a full-time homemaker, whereas clients in their twenties are more likely to have witnessed a dual-earner partnership between their parents. Much of the literature discussed below examines the gender socialization messages of a decade or more ago. Because this is a transitional period, there will clearly be differences. Furthermore, there are regional differences. The cultural changes that are taken for granted in the metropolitan Northeast, for example, are still revolutionary in some, more traditional areas of the South and Midwest. Additionally, there are gender differences regarding the acceptance of change. The feminist movement is older and more developed than the men's movement and many men have resisted the changes, clinging to the traditional values of patriarchy. Cultures, like fast-moving trains, are slow to turn around. Therefore it is important to have a basic understanding of the centuries-old gender messages before we discuss the new, often contradictory, dictates of the gender revolution. This chapter addresses what we know about traditional gender socialization and its effect on both genders.

Before discussing the socialization process, however, we briefly address the contributions of biology, anthropology, and history to our understanding of gender identity. It is important that gender-sensitive therapists clearly understand how gender messages are transmitted by cultures and then absorbed by individuals so that they can explain this process to their clients. Because gender socialization does not occur in a vacuum, we delineate the female–male power differentials in the larger culture with emphasis on how the inequity in power affects individual male–female relationships. Then we describe the gender socialization process, including the elements and agents of gender socialization. A discussion of the developmental cycle of the gender socialization process from infancy to old age follows. This description points out how the gender socialization process is a continuous one and does not stop after early childhood. Finally, we suggest that, despite individual differences and much overlapping between the genders, the separate gender socialization experiences lead to misunderstanding and conflict that therapists can help to resolve.

BIOLOGICAL DIFFERENCES IN GENDER

There is no question that there are some biologically based differences between the genders. Obviously, men and women have different genital and secondary sex characteristics. The average male in North America is 5 inches taller than the average female (Doyle, 1989), although some women are taller than some men. Over the years, scientists have studied the biological basis for gender differences in areas such as aggression, visual–spatial ability, verbal ability, quantitative ability, hormonal effects, depression, intelligence, and physical strength, among others. Anne Fausto-Sterling (1985) has examined the evidence provided by many of these studies. She revealed the flaws of biological theories of gender that fail to control for the effects of socialization and pointed out how biologically based arguments have been used to promote the politics of gender in both directions. Furthermore, many scientists (Archer, 1987; Hyde & Plant, 1995; Lott, 1996) have argued that most biologically based gender differences found are too small to be clinically significant. Although this view has been disputed by Eagly (1995), the existence of differences in behavior does not necessarily implicate biological etiology alone. Thus, caution in interpretation is essential.

Recent advances in science have provided researchers with a noninvasive method for studying the live human brain at work—*magnetic resonance imaging*—that has led to the discovery of structural and functional differences based on gender. Cautious interpretation of these findings may help to explain such observed behavioral differences as women's apparent greater facility with language (Shaywitz & Shaywitz, 1995; Witelson, 1989) and sensitivity to the emotions of the other gender, as well as men's tendency to take action (Gur, 1995) or to compartmentalize. We say "may help to explain" because scientists do not really know the behavioral correlates of the thicker corpus collosum found in women's brains by Sandra Witelson (1989), although some hypothesize a greater ability to use both sides of the brain simultaneously. And although Ruben Gur (1995) reported that men, on average, have higher metabolic brain activity in the more primitive regions of the limbic system whereas women, on average, have more activity in the more complex parts of that system, he can only speculate that women might be more likely to use symbolic action while men may take direct action more often. In other words, although the ability to observe physical differences in the brain exists, researchers are not certain of the cognitive and behavioral consequences.

ANTHROPOLOGICAL DEVELOPMENT

Anthropology and sociology also have much to contribute to the understanding of why there appear to be fairly consistent differences between the genders. In her feminist treatise *Beyond Power*, Marilyn French (1985) has provided a scholarly review of anthropological and historical data regarding this issue. Another more neutral and very thought-provoking examination of anthropological evidence regarding the relationship between men and women in prehistory is supplied by Margaret Ehrenberg (1989) in *Women in Prehistory*. The interested reader is referred to these sources for a more detailed discussion.

For the present, suffice it to say that, at one time, some theorists hypothesize, men and women lived in harmony in egalitarian societies that were understandably organized around the reproduction and preservation of the species (Ehrenberg, 1989; Tanner, 1981; Washburn & Moore, 1974). Anthropological evidence suggests that for millions of years there existed an interdependency between the genders, in which men and women were equally valued as contributors to the tribe, and in which roles were often flexible and interchangeable (Ehrenberg, 1989; Lee & DeVore, 1976). Scholars (Doyle, 1989; Kelly, 1981) propose that, in an attempt to divide the necessary labor, early humans assigned roles to the gender most biologically suited to accomplish the task. Thus women took on the task of nurturing the young and men used their superior physical strength to protect and feed the family (Harris, 1977; Tiger, 1969). According to these theories, women and men then developed different skills and attributes that suited their assigned roles. These hypotheses have been challenged on the basis of "primitive" societies in which women are known to be hunters, fishers, and providers of food, and men are equally responsible for the care of the young (Dahlberg, 1981; Estriko-Griffin & Griffin, 1981).

HISTORICAL DEVELOPMENT

The Beginnings of Patriarchy

There are many theories as to why the egalitarian arrangement changed. One compelling hypothesis (Ehrenberg, 1989) argues that the shift from a forager to an agrarian society reduced the perceived value of women's contribution to the group while introducing the concepts of property and hierarchy based on ownership. Thus men, who were bigger and stronger than women, began to compete for property, not only for land, tools, and animals, but for women and children as well. Friedl (1978) believes that male hunters had two advantages that led to a social pattern of male dominance: (a) the power to control the distribution of meat to the tribe and (b) networking with other tribes. French (1985) suggests that adaptation to the needs of a larger population required a hierarchical organization based on abstract rules and principles rather than the anarchical, fluid, and cooperative structure of primitive societies. Alternatively, some scholars claim that fear of the reproductive power of women and the need for men to establish a *raison d'etre* provided the motivation for a male conspiracy to devalue and control women (Bettelheim, 1962; Horney, 1973). Others implicate the discovery of the male role in reproduction and the consequential desire to determine paternity as a root of the patriarchal value of control over women (Buss, 1995). Some anthropologists (Harris, 1977) suggest that male supremacy arose as a by-product of warfare that was necessary for survival in times when resources were scarce.

Patriarchy is frequently traced to the Greek emphasis on a division between mind (which they associated with male) and body (associated with female), Greek society's elevation of the noble male over the female, and their view of women as sex objects and servants for males (Doyle, 1989; French, 1985). The cause of patriarchy was further strengthened by the Christian religion, which emphasizes control over natural instincts, particularly sexual instincts that were associated with the less spiritually developed, but highly sexual female (Doyle, 1989; French, 1985). During the feudal period, aggressive and powerful men fought to capture and protect property, and the landed aristocratic class, for which the motto seemed to be "might makes right" was established. Women became part of the spoils to be taken. It was during this time that the practice of *primogeniture*, a process whereby property was passed to the eldest son, firmly established power in the male sphere. During the Renaissance, knowledge and creativity were highly valued, and were considered to be the realm of aristocratic men. Although several powerful and brilliant women emerged during this time, the common stereotype of women included a lack of intelligence or creativity. During the Victorian period of history, middle-class men began to focus on making money and gaining status; women were considered innocent, weak, and in need of protection.

The Role of Capitalism/Industrial Revolution

The advent of industrialized society further separated the realms of the male and female (Harris, 1977). Until the industrial revolution, most men and women worked together beside their children in the fields or shops as artisans, servants, and farmhands. The centralization of work during the industrial revolution required leaving the home, which made it impossible to care for small children while working. Although at first industrialists hired entire families, this became cumbersome and inefficient because young children distracted parents from production. With the invention of machinery, men, who were preferred for work with heavy machinery due to their superior strength, were forced to leave their families and work elsewhere while women and small children stayed home. Work hours were based on the profit motive and the machinery's ability rather than human need, so that some men were putting in 12 hours of work a day. Although unmarried women could continue to work in factories, married women were generally considered unreliable due to their child-care responsibilities and were hired less frequently. They became dependent on their husbands' salaries to feed the children and themselves, which further diminished their autonomy. Meanwhile, men also lost a sense of autonomy over their lives because their economic survival was dependent on the boss who controlled their every move while at work. Some theorists (French, 1985) believe that a need for some sense of control in their lives motivated men to dominate their wives and children, whereas compliance with male dominance became the only means to survival for women with small children. Thus capitalism and the industrial revolution further shaped the model of patriarchy that exists presently in the industrialized West.

Patriarchy Today

Whatever the influences, most civilized societies in recorded history have endorsed a patriarchal philosophy that, while often acting in a protective capacity, devalues women. That is, rights and privileges of economic and political power have been placed in the hands of men, which puts women in the position of dependents. The former egalitarian interdependency has been replaced in most organized societies by a hierarchical structure in which males are more valued, exert more power and control, and take more responsibility for the protection of the "helpless" female. Patriarchy takes many forms, and ranges from the male supremacist societies in which women are treated as property and may not even be allowed to be seen in public to the less severe situation found in the United States where many corporations fail to pay women equal money for equal work. There are also those patriarchal societies in which men are generally seen as superior, but some women actually exert a great deal of control (e.g., Margaret Thatcher in England, Indira Ghandi in India, wealthy widows like Rose Kennedy in the United States), either directly through economic and political realms or indirectly through the influence they have on husbands and sons. No matter what form it takes, patriarchy is a major influence in the gender socialization process because the origins of gender stereotypes are rooted in the division of labor present in society.

ROLE DEFINITIONS

A *role* is "a cluster of socially or culturally defined expectations that individuals in a given situation are expected to fulfill" (Chafetz, 1978, p. 4). Thus male and female roles are defined by their society and, as will be seen in the following discussion, are learned at a very young age through a variety of sources. Gender roles can refer to the actual job each gender is expected to fulfill, or a set of behaviors or characteristics that are typical of one gender rather than another. As we demonstrate, in American society, women are expected to be nurturing, emotional, and cooperative, and serve in the capacity of wife and mother and provide the sense of family for children and spouses. Men, on the other hand are trained to be aggressive, competitive, logical, and self-reliant and to serve in the role of protector and provider for spouse and children.

POWER DIFFERENTIALS

As is discussed in detail in later chapters, patriarchy has had detrimental effects on both genders. The power differentials discussed in the following sections put more emphasis on the effects of the women's lack of power in a patriarchal society. However, the "powerful" male role brings its own set of more subtle disadvantages, which will be covered in chapter 4. The fact that the rules and expectations of patriarchy have hurt both genders is a potentially unifying force for men and women as both struggle to navigate the turbulence of the gender revolution. The therapist can use this information to unite clients against a system that is detrimental to both.

In a patriarchal society, role definitions and gender socialization lead to a power differential. That is, in most aspects of life, men and boys have an advantage over women and girls. We have already mentioned the fact that, as a rule, the average man is taller, stronger, and heavier than the average woman—a fact that gives him a physical advantage over the woman in cases of domestic violence. But there are many other realms in which men hold the upper hand, including the economic, political, and legal arenas.

Economic

Only 7% of American families now make up the stereotypical family of employed husband, unemployed housewife, and two children.

In 1985, the U.S. Department of Labor classified 62% of mothers as employed outside the home, and found that the labor force consisted of 44% women. Most work due to economic necessity, and 40% are single, separated, divorced, or widowed and another 20% have husbands earning a poverty-level salary or less (U.S. Department of Labor, 1985).

In spite of their increasing numbers in the work force, women continue to work predominantly in low salary, low status jobs. In 1984, women held only 2% of top management post in large U.S. corporations and rarely sat on the boards of public companies (U.S. Department of Labor, 1985). In all realms of industry, women can rise to middle management positions but generally hit a glass ceiling above which they cannot climb; that is a fact often attributed to ambivalent attitudes of upper management regarding a woman's abilities and "place." It seems as though many CEO's continue to set policies and run companies with a value system based on the now almost nonexistent traditional family of male breadwinner/ female housewife. This hierarchal, profit-based attitude is one that is not friendly to most men, women, or families, and rejects such possibilities as day care, parental leave for mother and father, equal pay for women, flextime, no-relocation necessity, or shorter workday. Consequently, most women find themselves working in part-time or temporary work with no benefits, making three fourths of the salary of men for the same work (Decade of the Woman, 1992), and working in low-paying service positions with no chance for advancement. Furthermore, many women are single parents who must provide for their children with little or no help from the children's fathers (Morgan, 1991; Weitzman, 1985), which further reduces the economic status of women. In fact, almost two thirds of poor people over the age of 17 in the United States are female (Kamerman, 1984). Thus women are clearly at a disadvantage economically in our society.

Political

Although the last 3 decades have seen a marked rise in political activity by women, few have become governors or congressional representatives or senators, and to date, no woman has served as president or vice president of the United States (Center for the American Woman and Politics, 1984). The major barrier to women's power in politics may be the attitude of the voter toward women in general. That is, most men and women have been socialized to believe that (a) women should be occupied with their families, which leaves little time for politics; (b) women are more emotional than men and therefore unable to provide leadership in a crisis; and (c) women are too soft and will not "hang tough" in international politics ("U. S. Support," 1983).

The result of this imbalance is similar to its result in business. Women politicians as a group appear to be more humanitarian and public-service oriented than their male counterparts (Carroll, 1984; Merritt, 1982). However, because male politicians occupy the most powerful positions in government, the values of female politicians are often undermined. Political decisions often place a higher priority on defense and political favors to large business than on social welfare programs that help the poor, a population already overrepresented by women and children. Many established male politicians place "women's" issues like ERA and abortion rights low on their priority lists. Thus the lack of political power for women may prevent societal changes that could improve their lot.

Legal

Women are increasing their numbers tremendously in the field of law ("Change," 1985). However, even though more women are becoming lawyers and judges, they still only make up about 16% of the total number in the field. Furthermore, studies (e.g., Hanley, 1983) show that judges appear to give less credibility to witnesses, lawyers, and experts who are female than to those who are male.

Because men dominate the legal system, women are often at a disadvantage in legal matters. Unfair treatment in hiring practices, allocation of resources in education, and borrowing eligibility has existed for centuries. Recent legislation has addressed these issues, but even with nondiscriminatory laws in effect, enforcement has been difficult. In property law, women's contribution to the marital assets through housework and child care are often unrecognized, which puts many women at an economic disadvantage in cases of divorce. Social security laws discriminate against the woman who takes time out from her career to raise children, depriving her of a retirement plan. No-fault divorce laws disadvantage the "displaced homemaker"—the middle-aged woman who has devoted her life to caring for her and her husband's home and children but has not developed marketable skills.

Because many laws were written by men at a time when people were socialized to think of women as people who exist to serve men and chil-

dren in a nurturing capacity, but who should be protected, laws discriminate against men also (Basow, 1986; Hayman, 1976). For example, only
men were required to register for the draft. Unwed fathers have few rights.
Fathers are awarded custody less often than mothers. The vast majority of
those executed for capital crime are men. Nevertheless, in the majority of
cases, the legal system gives an unfair advantage to men.

For the most part women are disempowered and men are empowered
by virtue of gender differences, but there are a host of ways in which highly
gendered roles can be harmful to both women and men. Before discussing
the results of traditional gender socialization, however, we describe the
process itself and illustrate how people absorb notions of what it is to be
a man or woman in our society. We provide examples from many of the
elements of gender socialization, including cultural components such as
language and media, institutions such as work and school, and socializing
agents such as parents and peers.

ELEMENTS OF THE GENDER SOCIALIZATION PROCESS

There are several theories that attempt to explain the process of gender
socialization: among them are psychoanalytic, cognitive–behavioral, social
learning, and gender schema theory (Bem, 1974, 1981, 1982, 1983, 1984,
1987). The latter combines elements of the first three in that it recognizes
(a) that children play an active role in developing their concepts of masculinity and femininity, depending upon the developmental level; (b) that
differential treatment by socializing agents plays a role; (c) that children
will identify with same-sex individuals and model their behavior accordingly; (d) that affectional bonds with one or both parents will have an impact; and finally (e) that biological predispositions will also influence the
outcome. To the extent that a developing individual modifies his or her
behavior, thoughts, feelings, and expectations to conform to the gender
stereotypes he or she observes, that person will become a *sex-typed* or *nonsex-typed* individual. Those who do not process information on the basis
of gender are nonsex-typed; sex-typed individuals organize and process

information in terms of their gender schema. For sex-typed individuals, positive self-concept becomes dependent upon the degree of conformity to the gender norm. Thus people struggle to become more stereotypically male or female and cultural stereotypes become a self-fulfilling prophecy (Basow, 1986; Canter & Meyerowitz, 1984). The sex-typed individual whose identity becomes fused with the cultural stereotype of male or female will experience internal conflict and pain when conformity to that stereotype does not bring the promised satisfaction and fulfillment. This is the situation for people of both genders who are in the early stages of their gender role journey (see chapters 3, 6, and 9).

Children develop their gender schema through three processes: (a) modeling and imitation, (b) cognition and labeling, and (c) positive and negative reinforcements (Basow, 1986; Lott, 1994). There are many elements that contribute to the gender socialization process. These include such cultural elements as language, play, media, books, religion, school, parents, teachers, peers, and extended family. The following section describes how each of these cultural components influences an individual's concepts of male and female.

Culture

Children begin to absorb subtle gender messages through the common usage of language from the moment they begin to understand the spoken word. As automatic as it seems to most of us, the use of the generic terms *man* and *his* to refer to human beings in general encourages children to think of "male" as the norm and "female" as the exception (Briere & Lanktree, 1983; Fisk, 1985; Hyde, 1984a). Likewise, the use of common phrases such as *man and wife,* allow a man to retain his identity while the woman becomes a role. The standard placement of nouns and pronouns, such as *he and she, his and hers,* and *men and women,* which assign second place to the female sex, clearly connote women's actual place in society. And as is discussed in chapter 5, women and men learn different communication styles from their role models (Lakoff, 1975, 1990; Tannen, 1990) in a manner that reflects their status in society. In these ways, language plays a large role in gender development.

The type of play in which boys and girls engage also affects their gender identity. Children are more likely to play with toys that are labeled gender appropriate by advertisers, parents, and other children (Bradbard & Endsley, 1983; Cobb, Stevens-Long, & Goldstein, 1982; Downs, 1983; Schwartz & Markham, 1985; Ungar, 1982). Thus boys are encouraged to play with trucks, blocks, chemistry sets, and other stereotypically male toys, and girls are encouraged to play with dolls, kitchen sets, and makeup. This gives male children the opportunity to develop visual–spatial skills and contributes to the development of verbal skills among female children.

Boys are often encouraged to pursue competitive team sports like basketball, soccer, and football, whereas girls are encouraged to pursue more individual sports like horseback riding, skating, and swimming. Some researchers attribute male dominance in the workplace to the skills that men acquired while participating in team sports; these skills include competition, teamwork, and emotional detachment (Hennig & Jardim, 1977). However, overemphasis on success in sports can have negative consequences for men, such as an intense competitive, hierarchical view of the world that interferes with the ability to develop close relationships, cooperate with others, or admit vulnerability (Fasteau, 1974; Pleck, 1976). Certain male-dominated sports, such as football and hockey not only condone, but encourage violence. In fact, researchers have found that a sense of entitlement and a belief that violence is an acceptable method of goal-attainment is often correlated with athletes (Ogilvie & Tutko, 1971). Today, female participation in sports is approaching the level of male participation, although female athletes are still hampered by unequal funding and parental and societal suppression of competition (Basow, 1986). Some researchers have found that female participation in sports enhances women's and girl's sense of confidence and predicts greater success in the business world (Hennig & Jardim, 1977; Rohrbaugh, 1979).

Researchers (McArthur & Eisen, 1976) have demonstrated that children are affected by what they read. Women on Word and Images (1972, 1975a, 1975b, 1975c) published statistics indicating that not only do 75% of children's textbooks focus on male characters, but that male characters are depicted in achievement themes, whereas female characters are found in passive, restricted, or victim roles. Children quickly learn what behavior is most appropriate for their gender and often conform to the gender stereotype.

Stereotypical gender differences similar to those in children's books are evident in print media for adults. In the topics covered by popular magazines (e.g., *Playboy, Sports Illustrated, Road & Track* for men; *Good Housekeeping, Shape, Redbook* for women), areas of assumed interest are stereotypically divided along gender lines. Although since the 1970s there has been a modification in the manner in which women are portrayed in print that reflects the changes in women's roles, popular women's fiction such as the romance novel continues to portray women as dependent on a relationship with a man for fulfillment (Basow, 1986). At the same time, male fiction is dominated by themes of aggression, sexuality, and violence against women (Dworkin, 1981; Griffin, 1981; Weitz, 1977). The similarity between children's and adult fiction demonstrates a circular effect that reinforces stereotypical gender roles. Children learn from books what it is to be a man or woman, conform to that description, and then prefer as adults books that stereotypically portray men and women, thus perpetuating the gender stereotype. The written word both reflects the social reality and influences it. Similarly, women described in newspapers are often referred to as someone's wife or mother and their appearance is reported (Foreit et al., 1980). The message conveyed in these instances is that men are judged by what they do and women by how they look and to whom they are related.

Like those perpetuated in print media, gender images on adult and children's television are often stereotypical. The average child in the United States watches between 3.5 and 4 hours of television a day (Nielsen Media Research, 1985). Many of the shows that children see on television teach them that each gender is rewarded differently for various types of behavior (Feldman & Brown, 1984; Sternglanz & Serbin, 1974). That is, although things are slowly changing, children generally see male characters who are aggressive and direct and who are rewarded for achievement, and female characters who use manipulative, indirect tactics to get their needs met and are punished for being aggressive. In the 1960s and 1970s, child TV viewers saw men working outside the home and women occupied by homemaking activities (Bergman, 1974). This influence had a great deal of effect on children's gender schemas: In the late 1970s, the amount of time children spent watching television was directly and positively related to their acceptance of traditional sex roles by kindergarten age (Gross & Jeffries-Fox, 1978; McGhee & Frueh, 1980; Zuckerman, Singer, & Singer, 1980). In adult television during the same period, sexual stereotypes were abundant in dramas, situation comedies, soap operas, commercials, and network news shows (Courtney & Whipple, 1983; Dominick, 1979; Downs & Gowan, 1980; Downs & Harrison, 1985; U. S. Commission on Civil Rights, 1977, 1979). Such programs depicted women and men in traditional occupational and social roles, and privileged the male voice and male experience over the female.

In more recent years, television viewers have witnessed some changes in family structure and gender stereotypes. Old stereotypes persist and new ones have arisen. Today, men are often portrayed as Neanderthal (e.g., Married With Children, The Simpsons), confused by new roles (e.g., Home Improvement, Coach), or violently aggressive (e.g., Hulk Hogan). Women on TV now occupy professional roles and often are single parents (e.g., Cybill, Murphy Brown), but the emphasis is still on beauty and a relationship with a man. In addition to Bay Watch, which essentially serves as a showcase to display the female body, we see Grace Under Fire, a real woman struggling to be taken seriously in a traditionally male profession. In addition to male newscasters and talk show hosts, viewers do see highly successful women like Barbara Walters and Oprah Winfrey. Because these changes on television both reflect the changes in society and serve to reinforce them, future research in children's gender schemas may show a change in some gender expectations.

In American films, women have been traditionally depicted as either sexpots or homemakers. Although in the 1970s films began portraying women as more complex and realistic human beings (Mellen, 1978b; Wilson, 1977), since that time filmmakers seem to have reverted to the image of sexy bimbo and hooker. Movies continue to represent men as brighter and more competent than females, but many films distort the male character in a negative way by portraying him as too aggressive, violent, and sexually promiscuous (Mellen, 1978a; Weitz, 1977). Imagine the different messages regarding male and female behavior received by the women and men who watch these films.

Like print media, television and film, popular songs reinforce the gender stereotypes. Women are emotional, illogical, dependent, and passive, and men are sexually aggressive, demanding, nonconforming, and adventuresome (Reinartz, 1975). Of more concern, however, is the misogynistic treatment of women in rock music (Freudiger & Almquist, 1978) where women are seen as sex objects and victims of violence. Adolescents for whom this music is a mainstay are receiving a very negative message of male–female relationships.

Institutions

Institutions that contribute to the gender socialization process include school, religion, and the workplace. For children, a major socializing agent of the gender schema in which they spend a large portion of their time is the school system. Several aspects of school life are influential in the development of a child's gender schema. These include the teacher, textbooks, curricula, counseling, and school organization.

Teachers have a very strong effect on children's socialization (Honig & Wittner, 1982). They influence children's socialization in two ways: they serve as role models for same-sex children and they either positively or negatively reinforce children's behavior. Researchers (Sadker & Sadker, 1985) have documented that teachers tend to acknowledge and positively reinforce boys more than girls. Furthermore, girls are positively reinforced for neatness and obeying the rules whereas boys are reinforced for correct answers. These subtle differential behaviors convey to children the notion that boys are more important and should be smart, but girls, whose academic contributions are often ignored, should simply conform.

It is no longer legal to track female and male students into stereotypical curricula. Nevertheless, social pressure continues to exist for male students to take courses such as mechanics, woodworking, industrial education, and agriculture whereas female students are encouraged to take cooking, sewing, and secretarial courses (Alexander & Cook, 1982; Betz & Fitzgerald, 1987; Freiberg, 1991; Krupnick, 1985; U. S. Department of Health, Education & Welfare, 1979; Walker, Reis, & Leonard, 1992). Likewise, studies (Harway, 1980; Harway & Astin, 1977; Thomas & Stewart, 1971) show that high school counselors are less likely to advise female students—even those with high grades—to go to college. And finally, the fact that a large percentage of principals and school administrators are men (National Center for Education Statistics, 1983) although their subordinate teachers are most often women conveys a clear message of male dominance to children.

Despite its benefits to society as a whole and to the spiritual development of individuals, formal religion also plays a role in reinforcing patriarchal values. Because all the major religions of the world promulgate a belief that women are inferior to men and must obey them (Daly, 1974; Fiorenza, 1983; Ruether, 1983), children who get formal religious instruction or whose parents attend church regularly often learn that patriarchal values are the "right" values. Religions of the world insist that men and women act in ways that are consistent with the patriarchal view of the world—that is, that women serve God, husband, and children and that men serve only God and provide for and protect women. Thus religious influences have the effect of creating children's gender schemas in a way that conforms to traditional gender stereotypes.

Children see that more men occupy certain professions and more women other professions. This clearly indicates to them which occupations are appropriate for their gender (Franken, 1983; Kelley, 1981). When they see that women are more often in low-paying, low-status jobs, it may reinforce the notion that men are superior to women. However, it appears that girls are beginning to choose less sex-typed vocations, probably because of their exposure to more atypical role models that have emerged since the feminist movement of the 1970s. Boys, however, still tend to view work from a traditional gender schema (Basow, 1986; Franken, 1983).

Other Socializing Agents

Family of Origin

Sex-typing by parents begins at birth (Barry, 1980; Block, 1973; Condry, Condry, & Pogatshnik, 1983; Culp, Cook, & Housley, 1983; Frisch, 1977; Hildebrandt & Fitzgerald, 1979; Lynn, 1979; Rubin, Provenzano, & Luria, 1974). Fathers have been found to see their babies in more stereotypical sex-typed ways than mothers. As is discussed in the next section, parents treat their children differentially according to their own gender schemas. They also report having different expectations of male and female children, which influences their parenting style (Block, 1973; Fagot, 1981, 1985; Maccoby & Jacklin, 1974). Furthermore, parents model different behaviors based on the mother and father roles as defined by our society. This differential treatment reinforces stereotypical gendered behavior in their children and thus perpetuates the continuation of gender stereotypes across generations.

In addition to the subtle ways in which parents socialize their children, they supply children with not-so-subtle gender survival messages. These are both stated and modeled rules about how to be a man or woman. Following are illustrations of the sorts of gender role messages one group of young women received during their childhood and adolescence, which serve as examples of how this process works. A recent classroom exercise in a graduate-level course in the psychology of women produced a long list of gender survival messages received by the women enrolled in the class (Nutt, 1995). Most of these messages were some variation on the theme of being a good little girl whose beauty and servitude would attract a man who would provide and protect. Typical examples included:

"Marry rich, be quiet, and behave."
"You need to know that you are woman and therefore should be less aggressive."
"Behind every successful man there is a woman."
"Do not be overly ambitious because you are a woman. You need just a moderate education and a nuclear family."
"Be a nurse so you can meet doctors."
"Don't mow the lawn; it's not ladylike."

"You're weak, frail, and need someone to look after you."

"You can do what you want, but maybe you should curl your hair."

"Don't ask questions, do as you're told."

"Be pretty, be respectful, be polite."

"You should have no interest in sports or 'guy' stuff."

"Be a caretaker."

"Don't show anger."

"Men are protectors and you need to be protected."

"A man's word is law. Don't argue with it."

"Be sweet, neat, and organized."

"Don't get your clothes dirty."

"Conform. Be a follower."

"Get married."

"Dress up. Look feminine."

"Wear make-up."

"Don't beat boys in competition, especially ones you date."

"Be a good girl."

"Be asexual, do not demonstrate sexuality."

"You can do without college."

"You should look for a husband."

"Don't complain, and don't offend anyone."

"Serve others."

"Try to keep the peace."

"Always look at the positive side."

"Laugh and smile."

"Don't cuss."

"Have proper manners."

"Act like a 'lady.' "

"Always show respect."

"Marry someone 'smarter.' "

"Do not say anything unless you are asked."

Although this list represents responses from young women, one can imagine that men have received an equally restrictive, albeit very different, list of directives regarding their maleness. In the next section we review the effects of gender survival messages on both genders.

Peers

During the school years, and particularly during adolescence, peers may exert more pressure on each other to conform to certain expectations than either parents or teachers. For example, Fagot (1984) found that boys who played with feminine-sex-typed toys were more likely to play alone and were less socially acceptable to their peers than those who played with masculine-sex-typed toys. For both girls and boys, conformity to the gender stereotype is a major factor in peer acceptance (Hartrup, 1983; Parsons & Bryan, 1978). Children use terms *tomboy* and *sissy* pejoratively for peers who do not fit gender stereotypes. Boys and girls separate into same-sex groups in preschool and are particularly influenced by their peer group during adolescence. Some researchers (Hartley, 1959) believe that the peer group is the only source for boys of what it is to be male because many do not have an adult male available to them. Therefore the male conceptualization of appropriate behavior is often based on distorted and over-simplified views that boys get from media and each other.

DEVELOPMENTAL CYCLE OF GENDER SOCIALIZATION PROCESS

Since all people have experienced some degree of gender role socialization, the content of the role expectations should sound familiar. Less familiar, however, are differences in the process of socialization by which men and women learn their respective roles. The following section examines such phenomena across the stages of human development.

Infancy

Parents tend to dress girl and boy babies differently, in both style and color. Baby girl clothing tends toward dresses, ruffles, and the color pink and other pastels. Clothing for boys is either blue or bright primary colors and is often sports oriented. Many parents even tie a bow around baby girls' heads to identify their gender, which is an early acknowledgement of the importance of adornment in female lives (Hetherington & Parke, 1975; Shakin, Shakin, & Sternglanz, 1985).

Adults play with girl and boy babies in different ways (Huston, 1983). Boy babies are more likely to be handled roughly and played with aggressively. Girl babies are usually treated more gently, even though biological evidence demonstrates that girl babies are actually tougher and more hearty (Lerner, 1968; Williams, 1987). For example, despite medical advice to the contrary, boy babies are often tossed in the air or tickled, but girl babies are cuddled and serenaded. Mothers tend to withhold touch from boys at an earlier age (Goldberg & Lewis, 1969).

In patriarchal cultures masculinity is more valued than femininity. In the most extreme patriarchal cultures, the birth of a male child elicits celebration, and the birth of a female child elicits disappointment (or worse). There is clear evidence that in this culture and many other cultures boy babies are preferred over girl babies, especially for a first-born child (Arnold & Kuo, 1984; Hammer, 1970; Krishnan, 1987). In an *Athens News* (1995) press report, a Greek grandmother threw her newborn granddaughter out a two-story window because she wasn't a boy. This preference for male children has often subtle but vast impact on all girls, which affects their feelings of worth and relationships with others. It can cause them to devalue themselves and other women and girls, and feel that domination by males is just and proper. Many more girls express a desire to be male than boys express a wish to be female (Unger & Crawford, 1992; Williams, 1987).

In a patriarchal environment, masculinity comes with certain entitlements or privileges. However, all men and boys do not benefit equally from male entitlement. Some reap considerable privilege from their masculine status, but many others receive minimal benefit or are actually penalized for not being "manly enough," as we point out in chapter 4.

Childhood

In childhood, the differential treatment of girls and boys increases. Research by Gilligan (1982) and Chodorow (1978) illustrated that girls are kept closer to their mothers and are more likely to be protected by their parents, but boys are expected to separate and learn independence. For example, a boy of 10 might be sent on his bike to the store to get the ingredients to make cookies. A girl of the same age will most likely help her mother bake the cookies in the kitchen. This mother–daughter connection and protection for little girls often provides the opportunity for the development of good relationship skills and interests, but it often creates disadvantages for girls and women in arenas demanding autonomy, independence, and self-esteem.

In reverse fashion, little boys develop skills related to autonomy and independence (Lewis, 1972) but not those involved in maintaining good interpersonal connections in work, social life, and family. Researchers (Hartley, 1974; Weitzman, Eifler, & Ross, 1972) have found that boys are subjected to more physical punishment than girls, are less likely than girls to receive comfort for a minor injury (Lambert, Yackley, & Hein, 1971), and are more likely to be left alone (Fagot, 1978), all of which contribute to boys growing into self-reliant and "independent" men. Fathers, in particular, feel pressured to teach their sons to squelch any emotion that might make them appear weak or vulnerable (Choti, Marston, & Holston, 1987; Ross & Mirowsky, 1984; D. Williams, 1982). Male children are frequently exhorted to "Act like a man!," which essentially means "Don't be vulnerable and don't show emotion." These messages have negative consequences, particularly the induction of anxiety and an inability to express, identify, or deal with "soft" emotions as an adult.

Both children's toys and stories communicate society's expectations of their appropriate gender role (Caldera, Huston, & O'Brien, 1989; Huston, 1983; Liss, 1983; O'Brien & Huston, 1985a, 1985b; Perry, White, & Perry, 1984; Rheingold & Cook, 1975; Robinson & Morris, 1986; Roopnarine, 1986). Girls' toys are more likely related to home, nurturing, or appearance (e.g., kitchen appliances, doll babies, make-up, cooking utensils, etc.), whereas boys' toys tend toward sports, building, science, weapons, or vehicles (e.g., balls, chemistry sets, Leggos, cars, etc.).

Traditional fairy tales and more modern stories for girls usually portray women as passive victims or decorative figures (Dworkin, 1974). Take, for example, the story of Cinderella: A beautiful, young girl suffers abuse at the hands of her stepfamily, but she remains a good, hard-working, sweet little girl who serves her abusers kindly, until the charming prince—swept away by her beauty—takes her away from her unhappy circumstances. Events happen to girls, and they are often rescued by male figures (Purcell & Stewart, 1990). The more beautiful the girl, the more rich or powerful the male figure to whom they are attached. Girls are taught not to expect to be able to take care of themselves and to look good. This is the beginning of life-long messages to girls and women that they are primarily valued for their appearance (Coombs & Kenkel, 1966; Freedman, 1986; Hatfield & Sprecher, 1986; Nevid, 1984; Stiles, Gibbons, Hardardottir, & Schnellman, 1987; Wolf, 1991). Children's books depict males as adventurous and independent, solving challenges which require skill and competence (Weitzman, Eifler, & Ross, 1972).

Throughout childhood boys are taught to reject anything that makes them appear feminine. Boys are severely stressed by the inflexibility of masculine role mandates. Developmental researchers have validated this with their findings that role deviations in boys generate more severe sanctions than do those of girls (O'Leary & Donahue, 1978; Pleck, 1981). Young girls who experiment with other-gender behaviors are more likely to be encouraged, ignored, or mildly rebuked. However, young boys who experiment with behaviors that are even remotely "feminine" are subject to harsh negative responses. Fathers, more than mothers, are likely to enforce these narrow gender role expectations (M. Lamb, 1986).

Other developmental concerns that are central to childhood, such as the influence of school environment, play activities, and peers and parents have been discussed in previous sections.

Adolescence

Gender differences are even further accentuated at adolescence. Girls, who have done very well in school performance, often begin to pull back from academic achievement. Various writers attribute this to such factors as costs in social popularity for academic achievement, the bias toward male-type performance in the intellectually objective classroom, and the shift in focus toward dating and eventual family life (Belenky, Clinchy, Gold-berger, & Tarule, 1986). Whatever the cause, the shift has strong negative implications for girls' future career aspirations and achievements and their resulting satisfactions and impact on self-confidence and self-esteem.

As dating interests and behavior increase, girls tend to pay more at-tention to appearance and social popularity. For girls, peer status during adolescence depends upon their popularity with boys (Chafetz, 1978; Weitz, 1977). Large amounts of money are spent on clothing and make-up. Emphasis on appearance and dieting have taken a serious toll on fe-male health and created growing problems with eating disorders in fe-males of all ages, but especially adolescents. Adolescent girls who perform well academically are often criticized and made to feel different, inappro-priate, and unfeminine.

Adolescent boys, meanwhile, struggle constantly to achieve status with the community of men. In a wide-ranging study of cultures around the world, anthropologist David Gilmore (Gilmore, 1990) found that mas-culinity is almost universally an achieved status. That is, manhood is not granted automatically to boys as they age, but must be achieved through vigorous, and often terrifying and dangerous rites of passage. Fighting, sports, sexual activity, risk-taking, and alcohol-use are commonly seen as activities signifying virility (Fasteau, 1974; Gilmore, 1990). Passivity, aes-thetic interests, celibacy, caution, and alcohol abstinence are commonly viewed as shameful. In this hierarchical value system, boys are encouraged to compare themselves with each other and must always wonder if they measure up. As a result, they are prone to feeling envious of more "manly" peers and fearful of being overtaken, or surpassed, by those boys below them in the hierarchy. In this system, even the most hard-won sense of masculinity is jeopardized by even the slightest brush with role failure or weakness.

It is also during adolescence that male bonding, commonly under-stood as a need for men and boys to come together in all-male groups, plays an important role (Hartley, 1959), reinforcing a boy's identify as sep-arate from and superior to women and girls. Frequently, establishing dom-inance over females is accomplished by degrading anything female. This includes such acts as objectifying women and adolescent girls as sex objects, and using derogatory terms that label a woman by her body parts. As mentioned earlier, because male adolescents often do not have male adults available to serve as role models, their concept of what constitutes masculinity is often rigid and stereotyped, and frequently based on media presentation. Because gender-consistent behavior is a major factor in peer acceptance and peer acceptance is most important during this particular developmental period, the pressure to conform to stereotypical and somewhat distorted gender roles is extreme. Homophobia rears its ugly head at this time, so that any young male who shows the slightest sign of "feminine" preferences or behavior is ridiculed as being gay and degraded by his peers (De Cecco, 1985). Thus adolescent boys learn quickly to hide their anxieties and emotions from male peers with a veneer of bravado—the beginning of a lifelong emotional isolation from one another.

Toward the later years of adolescence, boys begin to think about a future career and suddenly become more serious about grades (Doyle, 1994). Although this is changing, girls feel pressured to find a mate, get married, and have children (Katz, 1979). High school guidance counselors add to the stereotypical gender roles by directing adolescents toward gender-appropriate career choices (Basow, 1986). Boys are given a larger diversity of choices, but girls are often directed toward teaching, nursing, and other traditionally female fields. Guidance counselors tend to view girls and boys with nontraditional interests as disturbed and less healthy than their peers (Betz & Fitzgerald, 1987; Fitzgerald & Cherpas, 1985; Fitzgerald & Crites, 1980; Robertson & Fitzgerald, 1990; Thomas & Stewart, 1971).

Young Adulthood

In young adulthood, the emphasis on relationships in women's lives and external achievement in men's lives continues to grow. As we discuss further in the next chapter, women are so strongly socialized to prioritize marriage and family above all else that many women cannot form an identity until they find a life partner (Kolbenschlag, 1981; Russianoff, 1981). Thus, even though women may be employed or even consider themselves to be on a career track, they often do not feel complete until they have formed a relationship (Russianoff, 1981). Therefore they often put their lives on hold—that is, they do not purchase a home or furnishings for themselves, do not put down roots in a particular geographic location, and make decisions based on potential for finding a relationship.

Even though American women are now waiting until later in their lives to marry, there is still pressure on them to marry and raise families. Young women in their late twenties often have the experience of family members asking pointed and intrusive questions about their marriage intentions. Some members of society begin to assume that there is something wrong with single women of this age because obviously no man wanted any of them. Research in the 1980s (Bennett, 1986) scared young women by telling them if they were single at 30, they were more likely to be killed by a terrorist than to marry.

During young adulthood, women get little encouragement for developing independence, abstract thinking, problem solving, risk taking, and career maturity. In fact, there is evidence to support the notion that women fear success (Horner, 1968, 1970, 1972; Sadd, Lenauer, Shaver, & Dunivant, 1978), perhaps not so much due to internal psychological variables as to the potential negative consequences of success to women (i.e., they will have a more difficult time finding a relationship). Much vocational research demonstrates that the career aspirations of young women are typically significantly lower than their abilities (Betz & Fitzgerald, 1987; Fitzgerald & Crites, 1980). These lowered aspirations serve to disempower young women in interpersonal relationships in the work force and larger culture. These societal pressures make it more difficult for women to develop the self-esteem necessary for truly healthy living.

For males, however, young adulthood is a time to select a career and thereby establish their identity (Levinson, Darrow, Klein, Levinson, & McKee, 1978). As they enter the adult world, young men take with them the competitive view of life they learned as children—a great deal depends on how high on the hierarchy they climb. Therefore, in the world of work, men choose competition over cooperation even if it costs them in the big picture (Ahlgren & Johnson, 1979). They do not share their fears or anxieties with one another because that would be giving valuable information to the enemy (Bell 1981; Ruben, 1981). Therefore, men isolate themselves from one another and often become dependent upon their female spouse for intimacy. Men take on the role of "good provider" (Bernard, 1981b), in which their very identity becomes equated with their work and their value equated with the amount of money they make. In the competitive spirit, then, "Families became display cases for the success of the good provider" (Bernard, 1981b, p. 4). An important part of the competitive view of the world is the idea that a successful man must be aggressive and "watch out for number one," even to the detriment of his friends and colleagues (Doyle, 1994). Thus young men often become absorbed with career success above all else. Gilmore's (1990) central thesis—that manhood ideology creates enormous insecurity and threat to almost all men—has major significance here. For American men, manhood is never guaranteed; it must be proven over and over for men to feel secure about their worthiness.

Middle Adulthood

In middle adulthood, the earlier established patterns continue. Women are primarily valued for their appearance and their care-taking abilities. As we discuss in the next chapter, women struggle against nature to maintain their "youthful" beauty, which is still considered to be their primary asset (Wolf, 1991). Women who have not married and had children often feel depressed, as though they have missed the most important goal in life (Bernard, 1981a). Women who have families often find their achievement satisfaction through the successes of the men in their lives (Lipman-Blumen & Leavitt, 1976). If a woman happens to be very successful in a career, but her children develop problematic lives, she is viewed as a failure because she has not succeeded at what is viewed as her most important life task (Public Eye, March 20, 1995).

At midlife, some women "wake up" to their socialization messages (Kolbenschlag, 1981) and begin to make changes. At this time, many women who have raised their families are entering the work force or attending school. They may be enjoying their new life-styles and accomplishments, but many are angry about the time they feel they have lost and at the internal and external barriers they feel to their new goals. These changes may also negatively impact heterosexual relationships because just as a woman may be developing her career and work life, her male partner may be nearing, or at least preparing for, retirement. This puts partners' interests and growth, at best, out of sync, and at worst, in conflict.

For men also, middle adulthood often brings a questioning of the values and rules learned in childhood and followed throughout a lifetime (Levinson et al., 1978). Men who have made it to the top of the hierarchical ladder reap the benefits of that success. However, because men's main identity is associated with their work, men who have not achieved what they expected to achieve by midlife often suffer depression and physical illness (Horwitz, 1982; Liem & Rayman, 1982). Unemployment results in high rates of illness for married men, which is probably due to the good provider sex-role expectations. Furthermore, the stress of competing in the world of business coupled with the male socialization to suppress emotion makes men more vulnerable to illness and reduces their life expectancy (Slobogin, 1977). Many men begin to question their life of toil at midlife (Friedan, 1993; Levinson et al., 1978) and resent what they have given up. Many begin to focus more on family and relationships at about the same time women are beginning to look outward.

The Senior Years

There is evidence that in the senior years, there is some tendency toward role reversal (Neugarten, 1964, 1968). Women tend to become more independent and aggressive and men tend to become more relationally oriented. There are some who believe the gender differences so strongly established in early life become less important as we age (Friedan, 1993). Ageism affects both men and women negatively because, in a culture that worships youth, elderly people are often seen as useless and incompetent. Nevertheless, some gender differences—such as those related to appearance and physiological differences—remain salient.

Because appearance is not perceived as a commodity that improves with age, women decrease in value in a culture that appraises women primarily on their appearance (Healey, 1986). Men's attractiveness is enhanced by career achievement, increased status, and grey hair; women's is not. Susan Sontag (1972) labeled this phenomenon the *double standard of aging*. It is, for example, much more socially acceptable for a man to marry a woman 20 years his junior than a similar action by an older woman. Terms and slang that refer to older women (e.g., old hag, witch, crone, old bag) tend to connote ugliness, evil powers, and repulsiveness (Covey, 1988; Payne & Whittington, 1976; Unger & Crawford, 1992). Older women receive a double dose of prejudice—sexism and ageism. Only recently have books such as those by Friedan (1993) and Jong (1994) begun to challenge stereotypes of older women.

Related to ageism is the culture's long-standing silence about the phenomenon of menopause (Unger & Crawford, 1992). The normal changes of midlife have been medicalized (Cowan, Warren, & Young, 1985; Goodman, 1982; Kaufert & Gilbert, 1986), couched in negative terms of loss, and considered embarrassing. Recent books by Sheehy (1992) and Greer (1992) have helped to debunk myths and give women support in making their own decisions about how to cope with physiological changes.

Because of difference in life expectancy and the tendency for women to marry men who are older than they are, there are many more widows than widowers in this country. Widowhood for many women has been a time of social isolation and poverty (Lopata, 1973, 1977). On the other hand, unmarried men who live alone have the highest mortality rate—twice that of their married counterparts (Kobrin & Hendershot, 1977). It has been suggested that the earlier age of death for men is related to a number of components of the gender socialization process (Harrison, 1978): (a) suppression of emotion, (b) inability to form intimate relationships and thus gain emotional support, and (c) coping mechanisms such as smoking, drinking, violence, and reckless driving which increase risk of death. Women's better skills at interpersonal relationships give them some advantages, but there are subgroups of culture that are rejecting to older, single women. For example, members of social groups containing married couples may not wish to include older, single women.

RACE, ETHNICITY, AND CULTURAL STANDARDS

Of course, class, race, and ethnicity play a role in how these different so-cialization messages affect men and women. For example, there is strong evidence that African American women do not suffer career–home con-flict the way middle-class White women do, because African American women have always been expected to both work and care for their fami-lies (Hyde, 1985; Unger & Crawford, 1992). Women in lower socioeco-nomic classes have always had to help provide for their families and have therefore often had more power in the family decision-making (Williams, 1987).

Race, culture, and gender interact and affect behavior in numerous other ways. For instance, Black men, suffering from racism as well as male-gender socialization, adopt what Majors (1986) refers to as the *cool pose*, an exaggerated version of the tough, self-reliant, aggressive male social-ization. Being "cool" and tough and refusing to back down in the face of challenge may contribute to the high level of violence among Black men that threatens to destroy them. For Black men who face economic dis-crimination and higher rates of poverty, the role of good provider dictated by male gender socialization is a difficult one to fulfill. However, Black men and women place even a higher value on career success for Black men than do Whites (Cazenave & Leon, 1987), perhaps because it is more dif-ficult to achieve in our prejudiced society.

In other non-European cultures, such as Hispanic or Asian American cultures, male dominance persists in various forms. Whether it becomes manifest in what is termed *machismo* in Hispanic cultures or in the con-servative gender-role attitudes found among many Asian Americans, some version of patriarchy is endorsed in most cultures world-wide. In addi-tion, the issue of violence toward women, which adversely affects female feelings of powerlessness and lowers self-esteem, cuts across all cultural groups (O'Neil & Egan, 1992a).

The valuing of women primarily for appearance also seems to be com-monly held in most groups. The standards for beauty may vary by class, race, and ethnicity, but there is always a standard. In fact, there is evidence in the day of satellite television and instant communication, that the Hollywood standard is becoming an international one. The prevailing cultural standard may put members of nondominant groups at a disadvantage by valuing a standard that they cannot achieve. For example, the ideal facial type for White models in the United States is not usually possible for African American or Asian women.

What is striking when one compares the cross-cultural literature on gender stereotypes, is that, despite the manner and degree to which it is manifested, the underlying foundation of gender socialization across cultures appears to be the same pattern of male dominance and power and female nurturance and beauty.

OUTCOMES OF TRADITIONAL GENDER SOCIALIZATION

Men and women live in two separate cultures because of the gender messages they receive throughout a lifetime that reinforce and reward different value systems, different personality characteristics, different communication styles, different problem-solving techniques, different perspectives on sexuality, assign different roles, and hold different expectations for relationships. Clearly, the roots for conflict between the genders are extant in this gender socialization process. This is not to say that there is no overlap in the perceptions of men and women, but that the genders emphasize and prioritize different aspects of the whole range of possible characteristics. This difference creates major misunderstandings and miscommunications as well as severe disappointment due to the failure of each gender to meet the expectations of the other. Often the problems that clients bring to our offices are rooted in their disparate experiences of gender socialization. The therapist's sensitivity to these issues can make him or her more effective and can potentially hasten the therapeutic progress. In chapter 5 we discuss the gender basis for conflict in detail. However, before addressing the areas of conflict emerging from traditional gender socialization, it is necessary to consider a factor that further complicates the problem—that is, the effect on both men and women of the social revolution our society is presently experiencing in the wake of the feminist movement.

3

Women's Gender-Role Stress and Changing Status

Women at the end of the 20th century are living lives very different from those of their predecessors in many ways. Today women make up 46 percent of the total workforce (Noble, 1993) and can be found in almost every occupation that was formerly male-dominated. Women make up 10 percent of active-duty military personnel (Hoff-Wilson, 1988), 15.3 percent of all lawyers (Briscoe, 1989), 17 percent of all physicians (Joyce, 1993), and 25 percent of all software specialists (Schmidt, 1985), and they earn 25 percent of all science and engineering doctoral degrees (Walsh, 1984). Sandra Day O'Connor became the first woman Supreme Court justice in 1981, and Sally Ride was the first woman astronaut in 1983. In the last 2 decades, there have been many changes indeed.

With these changes have come new requirements in terms of skills, education, workload, and personality traits. Many of the values and traits that were stereotypically considered male have been adopted by the "new woman" when faced with a male work environment and ethic. Despite the changes that have occurred regarding expectations of women in American culture, however, most researchers and writers still report different developmental expectations for girls and boys and different roles for women and men that are based on the centuries-old division of labor. As mentioned in the previous chapter, parents still tend to accept or expect different behaviors in both children and adults on the basis of gender. Even though most women are presently working outside the home, the traditional gendered behavioral expectations still operate. This situation causes major stress for women, because in many cases the traditional expectations and the "revolutionary" ones are in direct contradiction with one another. In some cases, this creates internal conflict; in other cases, women are stretched to the limits of their physical and mental endurance in an attempt to do all that is required.

This chapter addresses the issues that today's women face as they struggle with the coexisting conflictual messages of traditional gender socialization and the new expectations resulting from the women's movement. Because the area of the women's revolution is well known, we provide only a short discussion of this topic, following which we provide several case examples to illustrate our points.

THE WOMEN'S MOVEMENT

Recent history in this culture has shown a pattern of shifts in female roles and accompanying images. There have been several cycles of women moving from significant roles in the workforce, to traditional roles in the home, then back to the workforce, and back to the home, and so on. Many of these shifts have been driven by economic forces. During both world wars, while men were fighting in the military, women were needed to do civilian jobs. Hence, the birth of "Rosie the Riveter." When the soldiers came home, all forces in the culture, particularly the media, banded together to convince women that their appropriate role was in the home.

It has been only slightly more than 30 years since Betty Friedan shot an opening volley for the women's movement with her book *The Feminine Mystique* (1963). Friedan wrote eloquently about what she termed "the problem that has no name," describing "the strange dissatisfied voice" repeating, "Is this all there is?" (p. 13). At this time, many women had painfully given up their dreams of careers, higher education, political action, and independence in exchange for feminine domesticity. They were being taught

> how to catch a man and keep him, how to breastfeed children and handle their toilet training, how to cope with sibling rivalry and adolescent rebellion; how to buy a dishwasher, bake bread, cook gourmet snails, and build a swimming pool with their own hands; how to dress, look, and act more feminine and make marriages more exciting; how to keep their husbands from dying young and their sons from growing into delinquents. They were taught to pity the neurotic, unfeminine, unhappy women who wanted to be poets or physicists or presidents. (p. 13)

The average age of marriage for American women dropped from the late 20s into the teens by the end of the 1950s. Likewise, the number of women in the college population declined from 47 percent in 1920 to 35 percent in 1958, and most women who went to college did so to find an appropriate spouse (Friedan, 1963). The United States birth rate was overtaking India's, and "[i]nterior decorators were designing kitchens with mosaic murals and original paintings, for kitchens were once again the center of women's lives . . . . Many women no longer left their homes except to shop, chauffeur their children, or attend a social engagement with their husbands" (p. 14). Shortages in the traditionally female professions of nursing, social work, and teaching caused crises everywhere. Friedan stated that "[c]oncerned over the Soviet Union's lead in the space race, scientists stated that America's greatest source of unused brain-power was women" (p. 15).

Through her interviews and research, Friedan began to realize that many women suffered from the unnamed problem she had described. Because other women looked satisfied and fulfilled in their housewife role, any woman who felt troubled assumed something was wrong with herself. Women were so ashamed to admit their dissatisfaction that they never knew how many other women shared it. The psychiatric and psychological communities were also baffled by these women, who came to them feeling ashamed and hopelessly neurotic, and often sent them home with an overload of tranquilizers and messages to have another baby and appreciate their homes and husbands.

Sometimes "the problem" was blamed on the fact that housewives had too much education. Educated, bright women were dissatisfied with their role, which did not make use of their knowledge and did not challenge them intellectually. College educators suggested making women's education more relevant to the tasks they were "meant" to perform; that is, they should take cooking, sewing, and family health classes or learn how to use home appliances. At a time when there was a shortage of enrollment space in American colleges and universities, it was suggested that girls no longer be admitted because boys needed education in the Atomic Age more than girls, who could not use what they learned as housewives.

The questions set forth by Friedan and others led to the women's movement, which proclaimed that women had needs for more than home, husband, and children. Women needed broader choices that fit their individual needs and desires. Many women wanted a satisfying career. Some women might prefer to combine home and career, whereas other women might opt for a career and marriage, but no children. The relative importance of home and career issues might shift during different time periods in a woman's life. There might be times when a woman would want to focus on the housewife role, yet she ought to be free to make other choices at other stages. The bottom-line issue was and continues to be *choice*.

Since the present women's movement began, the number of women in the workforce has been rising steadily. Hochschild (1989) reported the following statistics:

> In 1950, 30% of American women were in the labor force; in 1986, it was 55%. In 1950, 28% of married women with children between six and seventeen worked outside the home; in 1986, it had risen to 68%. In 1950, 23% of married women with children under six worked. By 1986, it had grown to 54%. We don't know how many women with children under the age of one worked outside the home in 1950; it was so rare that the Bureau of Labor kept no statistics on it. Today half of such women do. Two-thirds of all mothers are now in the labor force.

These changes in women's lives have also brought on what Faludi (1991) has termed "backlash: the undeclared war against American women." In addition to the internal struggles women may experience with changing roles, there are external forces in the culture that criticize women who try to combine work and family, considering them to be bad mothers, selfish and self-centered, and unfeminine or masculine. The backlash has also impeded women's career progress through discrimination in opportunities and pay. Although recently it has been suggested (see, e.g., Helgesen, 1990) that women's socialization would give them advantages such as skills in consensus building (Helgesen, 1990) and there are books describing and helping to develop women's leadership ability (Cantor, Bernay, & Stoess, 1992; Wolf, 1993), women still often are not viewed favorably in powerful positions. Cantor and colleagues (1992) accurately reflected the dilemma of the modern woman caught between the old and the new when they stated that "the classical stereotype of women and femininity just doesn't include the idea of power, and although things are changing gradually, the stereotype is still hard to overcome" (p. 35).

ROLE PROBLEMS

The women's movement brought both new satisfactions and new problems into women's lives. Frieze, Parsons, Johnson, Ruble, and Zellman (1978) wrote that women suffer from three role issues: role overload, role conflict, and role discontinuity. As women have moved out of being exclusively homemakers and added on a career or job, few have given up any of their homemaker duties. Hochschild (1989) concluded that most married women with careers and families do "double duty," thus experiencing *role overload. Role conflict* refers to incompatible demands between work and home. The skills, strengths, and even personality characteristics demanded by one setting are often quite different from and sometimes even opposite to those demanded by the other. This is true, of course, for both women and men. *Role discontinuity* refers to the often-changing nature and balance of a woman's roles over a lifetime. At different life stages, different roles and behaviors are emphasized, and the discontinuity can cause stress. We discuss each of these issues as we examine how the messages of traditional gender socialization and the current demands on a woman's life combine to create severe gender-role strain. This conflict is particularly salient in the areas of women's relationships and families; the conflicting roles of housewife, mother, and career woman; society's continued emphasis on female beauty; and the mental and physical health problems resulting from a mix of the old and new demands.

IDENTITY THROUGH RELATIONSHIPS

Many of the childhood and adult patterns described indicate that (see chapter 2), women and girls are encouraged to form their identity through relationships with others. The developmental theorist Erikson (1964, 1968), in describing the developmental stage of "identity vs. role confusion," stated that a woman cannot fully form an identity until she knows what man she will marry and what children she will bear. Hence, he assumed that women must satisfy their relational needs before all others and that they could not independently define their own identity. Although Erikson responded to feminist criticisms of his assumptions, and newer theories have considered the strengths of female development in the context of connection (Jordan, Kaplan, Miller, Stiver, & Surrey, 1991; Miller, 1986), Erikson's original statements are still accurately reflected in the stance of many professionals, not to mention the general public. Many people still believe a woman finds her identity through her husband and children.

Kolbenschlag (1981), in her aptly titled book *Kiss Sleeping Beauty Good-bye*, described women as continually waiting: waiting for some man to fulfill their lives, waiting for some other person to provide them with identity, waiting for the completion of something missing. During such a waiting period, women are not fully living and developing their own lives. Even though more women are working and creating an identity that includes evidence of competence in their work performance, there are still many women who feel incomplete or unimportant without a relationship with a man (Russianoff, 1981). Our experience leads us to concur with the opinion of Russianoff: Many otherwise successful young women feel unfulfilled or incomplete unless they are in a relationship with a man. This fact is illustrated in modern comic strips such as *Cathy*, in which, despite the character's independent lifestyle, the focus is on finding the right man. This feeling has serious implications for a woman's commitment to a relationship, particularly the vulnerability of her commitment to a bad or unhealthy relationship. That is, if a woman believes that being in a relationship is vital to her positive self-concept, she is likely to stay in an unfulfilling relationship.

In *The Cinderella Complex*, Dowling (1982) suggested that women are kept in a somewhat childlike state of dependence. They do not feel free to make their own choices and believe that they need direction from another, usually a male. They are not confident in their own abilities to care for and support themselves. Sometimes this dependence is not obvious in the woman's behavior but exists at the emotional level and impacts what the young woman will allow herself to become and how she will relate to others. It may create internal barriers to her educational and occupational success and achievement, and it may cause her to invest in heterosexual relationships that are not in her best interest.

FEMALE–MALE RELATIONSHIPS

Clearly, the impact of gender-role socialization on women leads them to overvalue love relationships and gain an exaggerated amount of their self-worth from their connections (Horney, 1973; Russianoff, 1981). Women's tendency in heterosexual relationships to subsume their own personal needs to those of husband and family has not led to better mental health for women (McGrath, 1992). Pittman (1985) described the role of femininity as teaching women to give power to men to act in their behalf. As is pointed out in chapter 2, in the traditional culture, the male partner was expected to be older, larger, smarter, and better educated; to come from a higher social class; and to make more money (Cowan, 1984; Gillis & Avis, 1980; Hare-Mustin, 1978). When one gender is expected and trained to be dominant and one to be submissive, there will always be difficulties related to these inequities in their functioning (Hare-Mustin, 1978). The dominant one will tend to be egocentric and controlling, whereas the non-dominant one will be overly sensitive to the affect, needs, and behavior of the dominant partner to the detriment of personal needs and growth. These differences have important implications for the therapist in understanding the dynamics operating in heterosexual couples and in making use of strengths and weaknesses of each partner in the process of therapeutic change.

Because of the power differential, women, who hold lesser status, notice the disadvantages of their assigned gender role, and neither partner notices the disadvantages to men (see chapter 4). One result of the women's movement has been the rejection of the subservient role by many women who retain a desire for a committed relationship with a man. Because such a relationship would be impossible with a traditional, stereotypical man, who expects his wife to defer to him, the characteristics of the desirable man have also changed. Describing the changing status, Pittman (1985) noted the following:

> Not too long ago, the gender issues that came into therapy involved people who did not live up completely to their gender stereotype. Today, however, women who are totally and inflexibly Feminine are called "passive dependent" or "hysterical," while men who live up to the traditional Masculine ideals and are afraid to move beyond them might be called "workaholic" or "obsessive compulsive" or even "psychopathic." We may well have reached the point at which pure Masculinity or Femininity are considered pathological. (p. 26)

This change has resulted in confusion and conflict within and between the genders as they attempt to create relationships with new values and expectations. Pittman (1985) suggested that therapists function as gender brokers, who help clients sort out which traditional values and roles they want to retain and which they want to discard.

THE SECOND SHIFT

Role overload is most salient for women who try to combine career and family. Women who try to do everything have serious problems with exhaustion. Hochschild (1989) "averaged estimates from the major studies on time use done in the 1960s and 1970s . . . adding together the time it takes to do a paid job and to do housework and childcare . . . and discovered that such women worked roughly fifteen hours longer each week than men" (p. 3). "Studies show that working mothers have higher self-esteem and get less depressed than housewives, but compared to their husbands, they're more tired and get sick more often" (p. 4). Hochschild termed this work at home after work on the outside the "second shift."

Friedan (1981) called the family "the new feminist frontier" (p. 57) because of this work and role overload on women who were performing their outside job and most of the home functions. She expressed the fear that women will "shortchange their own personhood" (p. 57) if they do not find reasonable ways to combine needs and desires for work and family. She strongly supported both women and men examining their gender-role issues and being able to make broader and more satisfying choices.

Some writers have questioned whether it is possible for women to "have it all." This issue again underscores the need to reevaluate roles in the American family and possibilities in the work world such as flextime, part-time work that is respected, job sharing, on-site day care, reequilibration of the male and female contribution to work in the home, and split-shift work. (A more extensive discussion of the second shift and its effect on male–female relationships can be found in chapter 5.)

In addition to role overload, women are beginning to suffer, as men have, from role conflict. The skills and attitudes that are required in the workplace are often diametrically opposed to those required as wife or husband and mother or father (Farrell, 1987). Frequently, the work environment calls for a suppression of emotion, a critical eye for mistakes, a solution-focused problem-solving strategy, a competitive attitude, and aggressive self-promotion. The nurturant atmosphere of family life requires supportive listening, use of praise, expression of emotion, open communication, and cooperation. When a man or woman cannot shift gears between the two environments, career or family may suffer. When the workplace was male-dominated, it was assumed by some that work and family were separate, owing to the male tendency to compartmentalize (Clay, 1995). Recently, partly because of the increased numbers of women in the workplace, psychologists have discussed the "spillover theory" of work–family interaction; that is, the behaviors and attitudes of one realm affect the other (Clay, 1995). A woman who is under a great deal of stress at work may take out her frustrations on her family at home and therefore fail to provide the supportive, loving family environment traditional society expects women to provide. Because old gender messages and new role requirements are once again at odds with one another, both role overload and role conflict result.

WOMEN AND BEAUTY: THE THIRD SHIFT

The emphasis on women's identity through interpersonal relationships is tied to the emphasis on the value of female beauty. In her book *The Beauty Myth*, Naomi Wolf (1991) described in great detail how images of beauty are used against women:

> The affluent, educated, liberated women of the First World, who can enjoy freedoms unavailable to any women ever before, do not feel as free as they want to. And they can no longer restrict to the subconscious their sense that this lack of freedom has something to do with—with apparently frivolous issues, things that really should not matter. Many are ashamed to admit that such trivial concerns—to do with physical appearance, bodies, faces, hair, clothes—matter so much. (p. 9)

If beauty is the coin that buys the best relationships, then women will sacrifice much in terms of money, time, and esteem in the pursuit of beauty.

Complicating this search for beauty is the evidence that the current standard for beauty is one that no woman can achieve. The standard of beauty in the United States and Western Europe, with its criterion of extreme thinness, has become for most women an impossible goal (Stone, 1993). It has been suggested that the current ideal female figure is that of an adolescent male (Heyn, 1989). This impossible standard results in distorted body image, chronic personal dissatisfaction, eating disorders, and lack of self-esteem (Cash & Brown, 1987; Chernin, 1981; Freedman, 1986;

Jackson, Sullivan, & Rostker, 1988; Stake & Lauer, 1987; Unger & Crawford, 1992; Ussher, 1989). The struggle has been well summarized by Kaschak (1992):

> Since the body is never a finished product, but only as good as it is at the moment, only a work in progress, women must be eternally vigilant about appearance. More often than not, women become the enemies of their bodies in a struggle to mold them as society wishes. (p. 193)

Despite the fact that today women are expected to obtain an education, pursue a career, and raise a family simultaneously, they continue to be judged primarily on their looks (Bar-Tal & Saxe, 1976; Cash, Gillen, & Burns, 1977; Stake & Lauer, 1987; Wallston & O'Leary, 1981; Wolf, 1991). Naomi Wolf (1991) has called this focus on achieving attractiveness *the third shift* for women, coming after work and home. Women who wish to be successful must engage in exercise and dieting, use cosmetics, have their nails done, buy the right clothes, and even undergo surgery (Angier, 1993) to attain the image of beauty promulgated by advertisers and the media. (It is interesting to note that in the age of television, even male politicians are judged on their appearance.) To make matters even more complicated, although female physical attractiveness is correlated with high ratings on femininity and sexiness, it is negatively correlated with perception of expected job performance (Cash & Trimer, 1984; Cox & Glick, 1986; Dullea, 1985; Heilman & Stopeck, 1985). This correlation is higher for male than female raters (Holahan & Stephan, 1981). A woman who wants to be considered sexy and desirable by men risks losing credibility in the workplace. The demands of the old and new gender stereotypes are in direct contradiction. Even if the woman has the energy to do it all, one image undermines the other.

WOMEN AND HEALTH

Gender socialization messages, both old and new, have an adverse effect on the physical and mental health of women in today's society.

Eating Disorders

Probably the most salient health problems associated with women for which there is a strong basis in gender socialization are the eating disorders, specifically anorexia and bulimia. Many women regard their weight as an important index of attractiveness and become obsessed with maintaining an abnormally low weight in order to meet the criteria of beauty set by the fashion and movie industries. They binge and purge, exercise excessively, and use laxatives, diuretics, and amphetamines in an unrealistic attempt to achieve a body image that is more consistent with an adolescent male than an adult woman. According to Maria Root (1990),

> dieting appears to be a strategy women rather than men use to increase self-esteem, obtain privileges, increase credibility in the workforce, and contend with conflicting gender-role proscriptions. . . . Mythology, fairy tales, television, movies, and advertising lead women to believe that thinness is beauty, success, power, and acceptance, and therefore, dieting is a viable strategy. (p. 526)

Alcohol and Drug Abuse

As women begin to share more of the work stresses with men, they also seem to be employing some of the detrimental coping habits of men. For example, women's use of alcohol and drugs is on the rise (Brozan, 1985; Matteo, 1988). However, women's problems are more likely to go undetected owing to gender differences in usage patterns. Women are more likely to drink alone at home and are less likely to binge-drink. Consequences for women alcoholics and addicts are more severe than for men (Russo, 1985), because society does not tolerate this behavior in women as much as it does in men. Resorting to drugs and alcohol is gender-appropriate for men and not for women. The literature suggests that women alcoholics are less likely to receive support from their spouses and more likely to lose custody of their children (Russo, 1985).

Risk-Taking Behavior

It appears that as women are encouraged to be more assertive, they have become more aggressive behind the wheel of an automobile. For years, insurance rates for adolescent girls have been lower than those for boys because the accident rate of boys is so much higher. Recently, the accident rate for young women has increased as have their aggressive, risk-taking driving habits (Horvath, 1995). Although there is no clear evidence that the faster and more aggressive driving of young women is related to the women's movement, "death in the fast lane" has become a new health risk for young women.

Violence

In chapter 10, we discuss in detail the dangers of domestic violence and sexual assault to women in our society. Suffice it to say here that women suffer greater damage than men from incidents of domestic violence, are more often hospitalized, lose more time from work, and suffer more psychological difficulties as a result of their abuse (Gelles & Straus, 1989). Violence against women is seen by some (Hansen & Harway, 1993) as a direct result of the previously discussed power imbalance between men and women in a patriarchal society, and gender socialization plays a major role in the existence and perpetuation of violence against women in the family.

Although reviews of literature on aggressive behavior show no reliable gender differences in aggressive behavior (Frodi, Macauley, & Thorne, 1977) and the results of the National Family Violence Surveys of 1975 and 1985 indicate about equal numbers of incidents of male- and female-initiated violence in the home (Gelles & Straus, 1989), the stereotypical impression has been that men are more violent than women. Recently, however, violent women have been more prevalent in the media. A 1994 *London Times* article, for example, discussed the fairly recent phenomenon of all-girl gangs who assault and rob their victims in many of the major cities of the West (Burrell & Brinkworth, 1994). Movies depict violent women as heroines (e.g., *Thelma and Louise*); a female rock star (Courtney Love) assaulted members of the audience and was acquitted; and television programs feature women dressed in black leather who serve as human terminators (Xena, Warrior Princess). It is true that women have always committed murder (Weisheit, 1984) and participated in warfare (Rosenberg, 1984). The difference today appears to be that female violence is admired by the media as much as male violence always has been. Some writers (Burrell & Brinkworth, 1994) attribute this changing attitude to women's new autonomy gained since the women's movement and women's refusal to be "relegated to the status of 'ho's' and 'bitches' by the ugly misogyny of rap culture" (p. I-16). This hypothesis appears to be corroborated by Gelles and Straus (1989), who found that the most effective means at a wife's disposal to stop male violence was to fight back. In any case, violence has always been and continues to be a major threat to women's physical health.

Mental Health Issues

Depression and Suicide

As might be expected, the traditional socialization messages to women that they are not in charge of their own identity and are primarily valued for their appearance exert a cost on women's mental health. Hare-Mustin (1983) suggested that "the demands of traditional sex roles lead to more problems for women than men. Certain aspects of women's sex roles may influence the development of mental illness, such as holding in negative feelings, behaving to satisfy a male partner, passivity, learned helplessness, exaggerated femininity, and other-directedness" (p. 595). Women are socialized to attend to and feel responsible for the emotional needs of others and can easily fall into service as emotional conduits in relationships (Halas & Matteson, 1978). Women are often raised to speak the language of emotional connection, which shapes their understanding of who they are in relationships with other people. By virtue of this socialization, many women feel disentitled to set emotional and physical limits when relating to someone they perceive as having greater power than they have or to whom they feel a strong emotional connection. As summarized by Kaschak (1992), "since the esteem of many women is directly embedded in the success of their relationships, they must often sacrifice their own needs for the sake of a partner or children. Although they have enormous responsibility for these relationships, most women have little power to control them" (p. 161). Thus, it is not surprising to find that women have a higher depression rate than men by twofold (McGrath et al., 1990; Russo, 1985) and that women attempt suicide at a rate approximately 2.3 times greater than men (Kushner, 1985).

It is also telling that the mental health of single women and married working women has been found to be better than that of nonworking married women (Friedan, 1981; Hochschild, 1989). These results point to healthy aspects of experiencing a level of autonomy over one's life, a feat that can be accomplished by women only if they live nontraditional lives. Because traditional socialization messages coexist with the new ones, however, women who try to "have it all" suffer from severe stress and exhaustion.

Histrionic Personality Disorder

Thanks to the feminist critique of psychotherapy, most mental health workers are aware that the criteria for a diagnosis of histrionic personality disorder are merely exaggerations of personality characteristics and behaviors normally associated with femininity. They include such "symptoms" as dependency, exhibitionism, and manipulative behavior. Because traditional gender socialization teaches women to behave in these ways, it is no wonder that women outnumber men among people diagnosed with this disorder. These problems, like those associated with antisocial disorder in men, are now seen by most professionals as systemic issues, requiring systemic interventions; that is, the messages of gender socialization in the larger culture need to be addressed. Nevertheless, we continue to see many clients in our offices who have been well indoctrinated in "histrionic" or "antisocial" attitudes. For these clients, the changing expectations of men and women since the feminist movement are confusing and conflictual.

Women in Therapy

The advantage of women's socialization can be seen in women's greater willingness to seek therapeutic help. More women than men are recipients of psychotherapy services (Anderson & Holder, 1989; Gove, 1980; Gove & Tudor, 1973; Lewis, 1983; Rieker & Carmen, 1984; Unger & Crawford, 1992) because the role of patient or client is more compatible with the female gender role. Women are not criticized for seeking assistance; therefore, when couples or families are seeking therapeutic help, it is often the woman who makes the initial contact and, at least at first, is the most willing to work in therapy.

AIDING CHANGE

It is clear that women's roles have changed during the past 30 years from total emphasis on the homemaker role to increased opportunities for combining career and work roles. With these changes, new stresses and problems have resulted. These changes have a serious impact on both the individual woman and her relationships. Old models of being a woman are no longer relevant for women who want a nontraditional lifestyle, and not enough new role models exist. Similarly, there are few new models for heterosexual marriages and relationships built by partners who eschew traditional, stereotyped roles. Therefore, an important consideration for a therapist working with individuals or couples trying to make their way through these changes is to consider the progress of each person and couple on her or his (or their) gender-role journey (O'Neil & Egan, 1992b).

Both Downing and Roush (1985) and O'Neil and Egan (1992b) have proposed stages of development related to gender issues and gender awareness. Downing and Roush (1985) proposed a five-stage model of feminist identity development that includes "passive-acceptance, revelation, embeddedness-emanation, synthesis, and active commitment" (p. 698). In *passive-acceptance*, the woman is "either unaware of or denies the individual, institutional, and cultural prejudice and discrimination against her" (p. 698). *Revelation* is "precipitated by one or a series of crises or contradictions that the woman can no longer ignore or deny" (p. 698) and results in questioning of old role assumptions. *Embeddedness–emanation* is "characterized by connectedness with other select women, affirmation and strengthening of new identity" (p. 699). Women in *synthesis* "increasingly value the positive aspects of being female and are able to integrate these qualities with their unique personal attributes into a positive and realistic self-concept. They are able to transcend traditional sex roles, make choices for themselves based on well-defined personal values, and evaluate men on an individual, rather than stereotypic, basis" (p. 702). Active *commitment* "involves the translation of the newly developed consolidated identity into meaningful and effective action" (p. 702).

Their model overlaps with Rebecca, Hefner, and Oleshansky's (1976) earlier three-stage theory of sex-role transcendence. Similarly, the gender-role journey described by O'Neil and Egan (1992b) consists of five phases, labeled "(1) acceptance of traditional gender roles, (2) ambivalence about gender roles, (3) anger, (4) activism, and (5) celebration and integration of gender roles" (p. 112). Detailed descriptions of these phases are included in chapters 6 and 9.

It is critically important for a therapist working with a couple who are negotiating changes in their relationship that are related to their gender-role socialization to understand the differing awareness according to stage and the suitability of different therapeutic strategies to varying stages or phases of the couple's gender-role journey. Strategies must match issues and awareness, and these vary by stage. There are additional therapeutic needs if each member of the couple is at a different phase or stage. These strategy differences are further discussed when the concepts of gender inquiry and gender coevolution are developed later in this book.

CASE EXAMPLES

Following are case examples of women who have dealt with problems in counseling or therapy that have a gender-role-socialization foundation. Although there may be other issues contributing to the problem, it is our belief that many clinicians are naive about the important contributions of gender-role socialization. Overlooking this crucial source of information is detrimental to the growth and change process of clients.

Case 1

Deborah is a 29-year-old White woman who requests therapy for relationship issues. She is employed in a responsible position as an accountant in a large oil company, and she has never been married. She has had several serious dating relationships in her life, but they all ended when the man decided that he was not ready for marriage. Deborah has a strong desire to begin a family. She reports that she feels like there is something wrong with her because she is not yet married. She is being pressured by both her parents and her extended family to get married and settle down. Although she loves her job, she does not appreciate her success in it because of her perceived failure in her intimate social life. She feels deserted by all her friends from high school and college, who have already married, and finds herself becoming more and more depressed.

Deborah is an example of a woman who has been socialized to believe that her most important role is as a wife and mother. Like the women described by Karen Horney (1973), no matter what else she might achieve, she will feel like a failure if she does not meet societal expectations. A self-help book by Penelope Russianoff, *Why Do I Think I'm Nothing Without a Man* (1981), addresses the need for women to define success in broader terms. Gender-sensitive psychotherapy would aid Deborah in challenging the need for her self-worth to revolve around one traditional role.

Case 2

Martha is a 43-year-old woman who came to counseling complaining of fatigue, exhaustion, and lack of enthusiasm about anything in life. She is married; has three children ages 9, 11, and 15; and works as a social worker at Child Protective Services. She feels overwhelmed by the demands of her job and the activities of her family. Although she is strongly committed to both, she feels that there are not enough hours in the day to do either well. She entered the field of social work because of her strong need to be helpful to others, and she has received various promotions and community service awards for her accomplishments. She learned from her mother, however, that a woman's most important accomplishment is rearing healthy, active, achievement-oriented children, so Martha has always committed a large amount of time to her children and their activities and interests. She is also proud of keeping her family's large home attractive and well maintained without help.

Martha is an example of today's "superwoman." As women move into the workforce, most add on new roles and responsibilities rather than trading new tasks for old (Hochschild, 1989). This can result in many employed women with families working up to 80 hours per week in their two jobs.

Martha's primary identity comes from her role of wife and mother. Like Deborah in Case 1, no matter what other successes she has achieved, the role of wife and mother takes precedence. This situation is compounded by her career choice of social work, which puts her in a nurturing role in her employment and creates a large drain on personal and emotional resources. Martha would benefit from therapeutic work to understand her gender-role socialization and to begin setting personal boundaries.

Case 3

Sandy works as an executive assistant in a large corporation. She is 34 years old and has been married for 6 years. She came to counseling because she is afraid of her boss of the past 8 months. He has begun making unwelcome sexual comments to her, and she fears that the remarks will escalate into sexual behavior. She knows that she should report him, but she is afraid to. Her husband has just returned to school to earn a law degree, and she is the major support of the family. Her income is critical. Even if she did not lose her job, she fears her boss's retaliation if she should report him. He is careful to make his remarks only when no one else is present, so there are no witnesses. Sandy is fearful, anxious, and having trouble sleeping at night. She is also afraid to tell her husband for fear that he will blame her. Her husband and boss sometimes play golf together.

Sandy is an example of a victim of sexual harassment in the workplace and suffers symptoms of posttraumtic stress disorder. Her workplace is personally unsafe, and she feels helpless to effect change. Additionally, she feels trapped as the primary breadwinner in her family and by her socialized programming to take care of her husband's needs. Sandy could benefit from both individual and group psychotherapy to support her learning to take care of herself, to be assertive in reporting the harassment, and to set personal boundaries. Group therapy with other women who have experienced harassment would be a particularly useful, supportive, and validating intervention.

Later case examples in this book consider the impact of gender-role socialization on heterosexual couples and their relationships. Before assessing and dealing with its impact on couples, however, it is important to consider the individual gender-role journey of each partner.

Traditional gender socialization has not caught up to the sociological and political changes in our society. This situation has resulted in internal and external conflicts for both men and women. This chapter has discussed gender-role strain as it applies to women. In the next chapter, we discuss the effect these changes have on men, particularly men's struggle with gender-role strain and their confusion as they attempt to redefine masculinity.

4

Men's Gender-Role Strain

Because of the recent challenges to the historical devaluation of women, American culture has begun to address the ways in which gender socialization constrains women's lives. By giving greater voice to women's experience, theorists have subsequently been able to speculate about what is unique to the "male" experience and about possible role constraints for men. In this chapter, we describe the prominent components of the traditional male role and the most obvious elements of gender-role strain in contemporary men.

In Arthur Miller's *Death of a Salesman,* Willie Loman struggled to convey to his son the conviction that a "man's gotta be somebody . . . gotta amount to something" (p. 1). Fasteau (1974) characterized the male machine as "different from other beings—women, children, and men who don't measure up" (p. 29). Tom Wolfe described the world of the early Mercury astronauts as one preoccupied with determination of which of the test pilots had "the right stuff." In the theater, Professor Henry Higgins questioned, "Why can't a woman be more like a man?" Apparently he meant women should be more rational, reserved, and emotionally controlled.

Each of these illustrations provides some answer to the question, "What is a man supposed to be?" Despite minor variations of time and context, there has been a well-established traditional conception of masculinity. In fact, there has been so much consensus that "masculinity" never received much critical attention. After all, don't we all have a pretty clear idea of what a man is supposed to be like? Recently, as feminist theorists have examined the critical place of gender-role socialization in the lives of women, some scholars have begun to ask similar questions about its importance in men's lives.

It has been easier to understand the need for women's studies, because women have long been marginalized by the androcentrism of patriarchal culture. On the other hand, because men have historically received advantages from patriarchy, it has been harder to see how gender socialization could also harm them. Yet, over the past 2 decades, the field of men's studies has emerged to make a compelling case for a more complex view of gender, a social constructionist view that recognizes how both women and men are constrained by role limitations. Proponents of men's studies have argued that there is more to the movement than simple celebration of male virtues and heroic men. They insist that although there may be considerable advantages granted to men as a group, there are significant penalties for individual men. The overly narrow construction of the male gender role has always been problematic for many men, creating a sociocultural distress that Pleck (1981) labeled *gender role strain*. Pleck, and many other men's studies writers, have posited that in the past few decades gender-role strain has become a formidable problem for all men, as the rapidly changing culture has demanded new role behaviors from men and has been increasingly intolerant of rigid and antiquated ideas of proper male behavior.

CONTEMPORARY ISSUES

A defining cultural feature of the late 1980s and 1990s has been the enormous amount of attention directed at the unsettled state of contemporary American manhood. Partially, this has been a direct outgrowth of the modern women's movement, with women less willing to function as second-class participants in homes, workplaces, or relationships. But the women's movement has not been the only social pressure for men to change. The gay liberation movement has challenged rigid and heterosexist ideas about men's sexuality and relationship possibilities. Gay leaders have argued that traditional definitions of manhood are rooted in a hierarchical power structure that encourages White, heterosexual males to oppress minorities, gays, and women (Kimmel, 1994). The workplace, the most meaningful setting for most men, has also changed markedly. Women have entered the workforce in unprecedented numbers, making dual-earner families the rule rather than the exception (Gilbert, 1993).

In addition, the nature of the work itself has changed, as the economy has changed from industrial- to service-based. No longer are male workers valued primarily for their strength, stamina, and endurance. Instead, they increasingly are expected to develop the interpersonal communication skills needed in the new marketplace (Brod, 1984). In short, it seems that we have entered another historical era in which men have become exceptionally anxious about their masculinity. (See Rotundo, 1993, for a fascinating account of the changes in ideas about American manhood.)

In the face of these dramatic shifts in expectations of them, men have had a range of reactions. At one extreme are men who have reacted angrily and have bitterly demanded a return to traditional gender roles and values (Faludi, 1991). Other men, taking their lead from the women's movement, have joined together to develop a coherent response to cultural changes: the men's movement. Although there have been multiple branches of this contemporary men's movement (Brooks, 1991a; Clatterbaugh, 1990; Shiffman, 1987), all share a common objective: helping men make sense of the vital question, "What is a man supposed to be?"

WHAT IS A MAN? THE SOCIAL CONSTRUCTION OF MASCULINITY

A prominent theme in much of men's studies scholarship is the belief that the male gender role is a social construction and not a biological or moral imperative. That is, men, for the most part, act the way they do because of social programming and reinforcement, not because of their biology. (See Clatterbaugh, 1990, and Fausto-Sterling, 1985, for a thorough review of this issue.)

With their argument that masculinity is a social construction, men's studies scholars have been faced with the task of identifying and elucidating the core components of the male gender role—what the culture expects men to be like. Since the first appearance of writings about men's studies in the late 1960s and early 1970s, scholars have proposed numerous typologies of the male gender role.

David and Brannon (1976) presented one of the earliest descriptions, which remains one of the most popular and most empirically supported. According to these writers, men have tried to follow four primary behavioral tenets. The first, the Sturdy Oak, refers to the expectation that men will be emotionally stoic and will deny vulnerability. The second, the Big Wheel, calls for men to be preoccupied with work status, achievement, and success. The third, Give 'Em Hell, emphasizes the need for men to be forceful and interpersonally aggressive. Finally, No Sissy Stuff encourages men to reject anything that is considered feminine.

Another influential conceptualization of the male gender role was provided by O'Neil (1982) in his description of the *masculine mystique*. According to O'Neil, the masculine mystique programs men toward (a) restrictive emotionality; (b) health care problems; (c) obsession with achievement and success; (d) restricted sexual and affectionate behavior; (e) socialized concerns for power, competition, and control; and (f) homophobia. Doyle (1989) identified five primary elements of the male role that seem highly consistent with those noted by others: (a) The *antifeminine element* calls for young boys to avoid, and ultimately dislike, anything connected with what society considers feminine. (b) The *success element* refers to the belief that the world should be constructed along competitive lines, with manhood associated with being a "winner." (c) The *aggressive element* emphasizes the need to defend oneself, commonly through physical means, against other men. (d) The *sexual element* refers to a belief that men should be preoccupied with sex and sexuality. (e) Finally, the *self-reliant element* calls for men to be independent, emotionally self-sufficient, and reluctant to ask others for help in any realm.

In addition to observing and analyzing the male gender role, men's studies scholars have approached the issue from a number of other academic perspectives. Thompson and Pleck (1986) conducted some of the earliest empirical research and have been followed by others who hoped to develop greater rigor in defining masculinity (Eisler & Blulock, 1991; Good, Wallace, & Borst, 1994; O'Neil, Helms, Gable, David, & Wrightsman, 1986). Historians (Rotundo, 1993), anthropologists (Randolph, Schneider, & Diaz, 1988), and radical feminists (Kaufman, 1987; Stoltenberg, 1989) have enriched the discourse by adding temporal, cross-cultural, and political analyses. Although these lines of study introduce complexity and considerable controversy, there has been a fairly clear consensus emerging about what a late-20th-century North American man is supposed to be like. In its briefest version, the formula is as follows: First, he should place great emphasis on his capacity to serve as a breadwinner. In family life, he should provide leadership but not expect close relationships with his children. He should approach other men from a competitive stance and avoid emotional intimacy. He should maintain the upper hand in relationships with women and expect women to be the gatekeepers of sexuality. His emotional style should be rational and stoic, although anger will be allowed, or even expected, in certain situations. He should treat his body as a machine or instrument, exposing it to high levels of danger and generally ignoring its nurturance.

MAKING BOYS INTO MEN: THE PROCESS OF MALE SOCIALIZATION

In chapter 2, we discussed in detail the process by which little boys are taught to become men. As a result of their socialization, little boys come to see the world as a hierarchical one in which their status is constantly in question. Therefore, they learn to value competition, power, stoicism, and aggression, and to hold emotionality and vulnerability in disdain. Although the emphasis on autonomy and independence is beneficial to men in many ways, there are many aspects of the male gender role that are extremely detrimental.

How Gender-Role Strain Harms Men

Considerable attention has recently been given to the crisis of masculinity, that is, to the role stresses of contemporary men. Although the issue seems new, more than 25 years ago, one author (Ruitenbeek, 1967) suggested that men's losses in traditional roles of father, lover, and provider have produced "emasculation." Robert Bly has attracted an enormous national following with his men's retreats designed to help men deal with relationship losses inherent in postindustrial and high-technology cultures. Bly has lectured widely about the dangers to manhood from "female energy" and has called for greater sensitivity to "male modes of feeling" (Bly, 1987, 1990a). Promise Keepers, a socially conservative group of Christian men, has become alarmed about women's changing role in the family and has called for a return to traditional values and a restoration of men's leadership role in the family. In February 1994, *Time* magazine ran a cover story entitled "Are Men Really That Bad?" suggesting that "the prestige of masculinity is in steep decline" (p. 1).

Embedded within each of these perspectives is the mistaken idea that times were once simpler for men—that rules of manhood were once clear and coherent, only recently becoming confusing, contradictory, and stressful. A persuasive challenge to this point of view has been the "sex role strain paradigm" of Pleck (1981), which posits that the male sex role has always been contradictory and inconsistent. Pleck has made a compelling case that men not only experience distress when they violate male roles, but also are harmed even when they *do* perform according to role expectations. In what he referred to as the "socialized dysfunctional characteristics theory" of sex-role strain, Pleck argued that "certain characteristics prescribed by sex roles are psychologically dysfunctional" (p. 147).

What we see then is a situation whereby men are increasingly in distress trying to live up to a male gender role that (a) is inherently stressful, (b) has always been poorly defined, and (c) in spite of its inconsistencies, is undergoing sweeping changes owing to a variety of cultural pressures. As a result, men suffer in a number of realms.

Men and Physical Health

Perhaps the most obviously toxic component of the male gender role is its health-diminishing, life-threatening aspect. Men live shorter lives than women (8–10 years); experience a higher incidence of stress-related physical disorders; have higher rates of alcoholism, motor vehicle accidents, and suicide; and are more frequently the victims of homicide (Herek, 1987; Verbrugge, 1985; Waldron, 1976). Waldron estimated that three-fourths of the difference in life expectancy between men and women can be accounted for by gender-related behaviors.

Consistent with the Sturdy Oak tenet of masculinity, men are far less likely than women to perform routine preventative health behaviors (Nathanson, 1977). Because they are taught to reject femininity, many men feel discomfort with the passivity and dependency of the sick role and are disposed to ignore warning signs of illness and avoid bed rest during periods of illness (Skord & Schumacher, 1982). Men are taught to venerate "heroes" (Betcher & Pollack, 1993; Gerzon, 1982) and, as a partial result, are more prone to high-risk behaviors such as high-speed driving, recklessness in sports activities, and excessive consumption of alcohol and food, and they are subject to higher rates of all types of accidental injury (Harrison, Chin, & Ficcarrotto, 1989). Many observers have agreed with Harrison (1978) that the male sex role is hazardous to men's health.

Men and Mental Health

In addition to having a highly adverse effect on men's physical health, the traditional male role also hampers men's mental health. Most recent research on the interaction of gender and mental health has focused on how the culture and the mental health system interact to produce emotional problems in women. For example, the work of Nolen-Hoeksema (1990) and McGrath et al. (1990) has been exemplary in demonstrating how learned helplessness may engender depression in women. There has been much less study of masculinity and mental illness, but some research

(Robins et al., 1984; Widom, 1984) has found that men are more likely to receive antisocial personality disorder and substance abuse diagnoses, and generally have a lower threshold for aggressive or violent coping behaviors. Given that young men are commonly presented with highly contradictory messages about violence (Miedzian, 1991) and that physical activity, cognitive distraction, and alcohol abuse are socially sanctioned methods for men to reduce stress (Nolen-Hoeksema, 1990), these findings are not surprising. It would be consistent with the work of Williams and Spitzer (1983) to argue that sociopathy and alcoholism are principal mental health costs of the traditional male role.

Male–Female Relations

Because young men are exposed to limited, narrow, contradictory, and often denigrating images of women, they are disposed to have considerable difficulty in male–female relationships. Many feminists writers have noted this problem and have attributed it to the misogyny they see as deeply rooted in Western culture (Bullough, 1973). For example, Williams (1977) analyzed popular mythology and concluded that the most available roles for women were those of "temptress-seductress, earth mother, mystery, and necessary evil" (p. 3). In brief, she argued that these roles prevent women from being seen by men as full human beings and instead placed them on pedestals as overseers of sacred family values or vilify them as mysterious, treacherous, or inferior beings. Women's bodies have been objectified, and their sexuality has been constructed as a prize to inspire men's competitive efforts. Although they are generally deprived of full participation in many aspects of the culture, women have usually been entrusted with a measure of sexual leverage through their role as gatekeeper of sexuality in relationships (Farrell, 1987). Women's "power" as dispensers of sexuality, coupled with their tendency to be stronger than men in relationship skills and emotional expressiveness (Pleck & Pleck, 1980), make them seem indispensable to men.

Although men are presented with varied ideas about women's intrinsic nature, they are presented with one principal idea about proper male–female relationships: that men should control and provide leadership. O'Neil (1982), in his description of the masculine mystique, noted that proof of masculinity usually depends on men's display of power, dominance, and ability to control others, particularly women.

Male–Male Relationships

Men are raised to think hierarchically (Brooks & Silverstein, 1995). They tend to view the world as having limited resources, necessitating interpersonal relationships characterized by endless competitive interactions, resulting in survival of the fittest (Doyle, 1994; Kohn, 1986). In areas ranging from job performance to sexual functioning, athletic skill, or mental alertness, they are prone to compare themselves with other men and to remain continually concerned about their ranking. Men's self-esteem is rarely based on inherent self-worth but on their ability to outperform others. Although this competitive value system may have many cultural benefits, particularly in a free-enterprise economy, it has a major downside for men. The benefits and entitlements accorded to men in patriarchal culture are more generously granted to "real men"—men who live up to male role standards. As a result, men become preoccupied with their relative standing in this hierarchical value system, often feeling envious of those above them and fearful of those below them. This environment is profoundly toxic to male–male relationships, because emotional openness and vulnerability, essential ingredients of intimate relationships, cannot be allowed by men fearful that another man may gain a competitive edge (Nardi, 1992).

If the competitive nature of male–male relationships is not constraining enough, homophobia adds another significant impediment to intimacy and friendship among men. Since the coining of the term by Smith (1971), *homophobia* has been somewhat loosely applied to a variety of attitudes, behaviors, and beliefs. In brief, homophobia includes a general aversion to homosexuals, a fear that male–male intimacy may cause one to be considered gay, and a terror that a man might discover himself capable of physical attraction for another man. O'Neil (1982), who argued that homophobia is one of the defining features of the traditional male role, has been joined by numerous men's studies writers who see it as having a suffocating influence on men's friendship potential (Doyle, 1994; Herek, 1987; Nardi, 1992).

Men as Fathers

Of all the changes in the lives of contemporary men, none has been more noted or applauded than the trend toward new models of fatherhood. Pleck (1987) noted that "the new father is clearly on the rise in print and broadcast media" (p. 93). According to Pleck, the new father differs from earlier models in several respects. First, he is present at the child's birth, often serving as a coach during the delivery. He is emotionally and physically involved with infant children, not just older ones. He actively and willingly participates in the day-to-day work of child care, not just play. He is broadly involved with the lives of his daughters, not just his sons. In general, he strongly asserts himself as a coparent, avoiding the easy trap of slipping into the role of auxiliary parent à la "Mr. Mom."

Even though there has been enormous popular endorsement of this new father role, the older fathering role of distant breadwinner remains highly salient for many men. When one examines the actual behavior of fathers as opposed to the ideology of fatherhood, one finds that the new father is still slow in arriving (DeLarossa, 1989; Jump & Haas, 1987; Pleck, 1993). For example, some observers make the pessimistic claim that mothers still perform two-thirds of child care (Hochschild, 1989), although others are more optimistic and see a slow but unmistakable trend toward greater father involvement (Pleck, 1993).

Many factors have been cited to account for the relatively slow rate of change in the conduct of fatherhood. Bronstein and Cowan (1988) partially attributed this slow progress to culture-wide institutional resistance, including resistance at the workplace (Doyle, 1994) and in the legal system (Kiselica, Stroud, & Rotzien, 1992). Levant and Kelley (1989) implicated traditional male socialization, with its minimal emphasis on development of the emotional skills critical to parenting. Other factors constraining fathers are male inexpressiveness (Balswick, 1988) and the paucity of child-care experiences available to male adolescents. Because fathers typically feel entrusted with "toughening up" their children (especially sons), they are more likely to interact with children in a nonnurturing and authoritarian manner. These patterns frequently produce family structures in which mothers are more in tune with children's lives and fathers are relatively disengaged or alienated.

Men and Psychotherapy

Although many psychotherapists are now reporting greater numbers of men in their offices (Betcher & Pollack, 1993; Bograd, 1991; Kupers, 1993; Meth & Pasick, 1990), women continue to seek therapeutic help more frequently. Even when they do seek help, men are likely to be less than ideal psychotherapy clients. There are several aspects to men's socialization that account for this situation.

First, because men generally have been taught to seek interpersonal independence, they seek help as little as possible (Scher, 1990). Examples of this are plentiful: One need only call on popular images of men who spend hours searching for a destination, rather than ask for directions, or who injure themselves carrying heavy objects, rather than ask for help.

In part, this disinclination to seek help may be an outgrowth of how young children are taught to solve problems. Traditionally, girls have been given help quickly when encountering problems, but boys have been expected to persevere (Basow, 1986). Sometimes, this is a useful pattern that encourages boys to overcome obstacles and to develop confidence in their capacity for independent functioning. At its worst, however, this pattern has the major downside of teaching boys to associate help seeking with weakness and unmanliness, that is, with being "feminine."

As noted earlier, men are taught to interpret the world in hierarchical terms, to see life as a series of competitions with clear winners and losers. Unfortunately, many men come to view therapy as a sign of weakness, which is the worst thing one can reveal in an intensely competitive world.

Because therapy generates high levels of interpersonal intimacy, it requires scrupulous discrimination between desires for emotional intimacy and sexual desires. Because men commonly sexualize their intimacy needs (Brooks, 1996; Silverberg, 1986), they can become highly stressed in the therapy relationship. Heterosexual men who have experienced traditional socialization are destined to struggle with sexual desire for female therapists and to experience homophobia with male therapists.

More than any other relationship, psychotherapy calls for men to be sensitive to their internal affective experiences and to translate those experiences into verbal realm, that is, to be emotionally expressive. This is usually a difficult process for men, because suppression and emotional stoicism have been taught, whereas verbal communication has commonly been delegated to women. Many men have come to accept the idea that women communicate by talking and men communicate by doing or performing. It should not come as a surprise, therefore, that men have generally viewed therapy as women's way of solving problems (Silverberg, 1986).

In brief, psychotherapy calls for many skills and attitudes that seem to be foreign to many men: asking for help, experiencing vulnerability, relinquishing interpersonal control, becoming sensitive to distress, and expressing feelings. As a result, men tend to avoid therapy, participate guardedly if they are desperate enough to be involved in it, and terminate as soon as possible.

ETHNOCULTURAL VARIATIONS IN MALE GENDER-ROLE STRAIN

Although it is useful to speak of a male experience, it must be remembered that there is no single male experience. Men's experiences vary greatly, depending on their social class, race, ethnicity, age, and sexual identity. According to Kimmel and Messner (1992), male gender roles vary from race to race and from culture to culture. It is more accurate to think in terms of many masculinities than of a single masculine experience.

For example, considerable attention has been given of late to the special problems of African American men (Lazur & Majors, 1995; Majors, 1986, 1994; Majors & Billson, 1992). Lazur and Majors (1995) wrote the following:

Constrained by economic roadblocks and societal discrimination, men of color are frequently considered foreigners by the dominant culture. . . . Power, success, and even providing for his family are defined within the context of the dominant racial and cultural belief systems. Reconciling cultural and male identities with economic and social obstacles is critical for men of color. (p. 337)

Whatever component of the male role one chooses to examine, there will be variations dependent on ethnocultural differences. For example, Brod (1988) noted that Jewish masculinity and Asian masculinity place a greater emphasis on intellectual aggression or competition than on physical aggression. In contrast, Majors and Billson (1992) described how aggressive physical posturing (the "cool pose") is adopted by African–American men to cope with the damages of inferior economic opportunities. Likewise, there are extreme variations regarding the expression of affection among men between the Asian and Latino cultures (Ramirez, 1988; Sue & Sue, 1990).

Needless to say, the topic of ethnocultural variations of masculinity is an important one. Kimmel and Messner (1992), Lazur and Majors (1995), and Levant and Pollack (1995) have offered excellent resources for further exploration of these issues.

CASE EXAMPLE

Many of the men we have seen in psychotherapy have been totally oblivious to the fact that their gender socialization has in some ways endangered and constrained their lives. Frank was just such a man.

Things had always seemed to go well for Frank. A bright and ambitious management analyst, he had made positive impressions on senior management from the moment he entered the prestigious telecommunications corporation. Far more quickly than most, he had earned promotions and gained a powerful position within upper levels of the company.

Frank and Lorraine married while Frank was still in business school, sharing financial hardships and a dream that Frank's career would bring success, comforts, and fulfillment to them both. Like so many of her friends, Lorraine had put aside her own professional ambitions to play the role of corporate wife: emotional caretaker, entertainer, mother of model children, and symbol of Frank's domestic stability. After a few years of devotion to wifely and motherly duties, Lorraine realized that she was taking little pleasure in her role and was feeling smothered by the demands of Frank's career. Eventually, she insisted on a chance to pursue her own career interests.

Frank did not respond well to Lorraine's distress. Initially, he dismissed her pleas as "one of Lorraine's phases" and made token efforts to help her find "a little something" for herself. When Lorraine's initiatives did not go away, Frank became irritated. When Lorraine suggested a divorce, Frank was shocked at first but soon became infuriated. To him, Lorraine's behavior was an outrageous affront, a complete rejection of his tireless efforts to provide her with "everything a wife could want."

Although he was greatly upset, Frank continued to carry on as usual, until he experienced a minor stroke. For several days he lost complete motor control on his right side and was only able to speak a few words. A perceptive speech therapist insisted that Frank's neurologist refer Frank to a psychotherapist.

Frank entered therapy with as much guardedness and resistance as humanly possible. Although he claimed great respect for psychologists and psychotherapy in the abstract, he was dismissive of their potential usefulness for him. He was quick to acknowledge his "sins": "Hey, I admit I should have done a better job of taking care of myself. I know I need to drop a few pounds, quit smoking, and take a little more time off. Look, I appreciate your time Doc, but frankly, I think I know exactly what I need to do."

After 30 minutes of condescension, Frank began shuffling in his chair, looking at his watch, and making comments about the therapist's busy schedule. When the therapist commented on Frank's low level of interest in therapy, he hesitated but eventually admitted that he had great misgivings. The therapist commented that Frank's reservations were not unusual in that many men view therapy as abstract, impractical, and a little embarrassing. Some men, the therapist continued, are even annoyed at the inconvenience, because God knows, they are heavily pressed for time already.

These comments seemed to fall on receptive ears. Frank looked directly at the therapist and pointed his index finger, saying, "You know, you hit it on the head there, Doc. Frankly, I'm getting just a little bit tired of all this crap!" Frank stood and began pacing about the room. "Here I kill myself trying to make a better life for everybody, and all I get is unhappiness and a major lack of appreciation."

It was at that point that the therapy really began. Frank quickly catalogued a range of disappointments and frustrations. Behind his bitterness, he discovered many other, more painful feelings and unsettling questions. Why was Lorraine so unhappy? How had he failed? Why was he having so many powerfully sad feelings about his daughter's imminent graduation? Why was he losing his edge at work? Why did he feel disappointed, even when experiencing unprecedented levels of success? Why did the old family videos evoke unexpected tears? Why was he constantly feeling a vague sense of loneliness? What had happened to his male friends?

In the very first session, Frank realized that therapy offered something for *him*. Rather than getting the expected pop-psychology lectures about self-care and slowing down, it gave him a chance to identify the strains of the contemporary masculine role.

Before beginning couples therapy, the therapist referred Frank to a men's group. In that group, Frank discovered that he was not alone. He encountered other "successful" men, as well as men he normally would have considered "losers." To his amazement, he realized a connection with all of them.

One member of the group, Phil, struggled with a painful career decision. Should he enter the lucrative family business or enter art school to pursue the career that truly interested him? To complicate matters, Phil was "lucky," in that Kimberly, his marital partner, was a successful physician. Kimberly supported Phil, giving him unbounded latitude to make a decision independent of finances. Frank was engrossed as he listened to Phil's struggles over issues of financial success versus personal gratification. He was surprised, yet supportive, when Phil confessed, "Actually, my greatest fear is that Kim will lose respect for me. Hell, she may take up with some high-powered physician stud she works with."

In a later session, Frank confronted his intense homophobia. Carl, a middle-aged junior college professor, challenged Frank with an observation that he seemed aloof and arrogant. As the encounter played out, Frank realized that he had, in fact, been contemptuous of Carl, primarily because he thought him "faggy." As Carl and Frank explored their relationship (or, more accurately, lack of relationship), Frank gained insight into his habit of rating other men. Frank tended to admire (and envy) men who seemed more successful than he, whereas he tended to scorn the losers (blue collar men, gay men, and some minority men).

Space prohibits further descriptions of Frank's gender-role journey. In general, it can safely be said that Frank has continued to explore the multiple sources of gender-role strain in his life. These positive steps were instrumental in preparing him for couples therapy, where he and Lorraine began the difficult process of constructing a new, more empathic, marital relationship.

CONCLUSION

Thanks to the increased attention feminism has brought to the female experience and to the emergence of men's studies, psychologists have recently had the opportunity to identify the critical aspects of the male experience. Men's studies scholars have pointed out that young boys are rigidly socialized to aspire to a standard of masculine conduct that is inherently unrealistic and unattainable. They are commonly bullied to avoid any behaviors that appear "feminine" or "faggy." They are pressured to prove their masculinity through masculine rites of passage that may include behaviors that expose themselves and others to danger. Through this process, many men come to feel entitled to the patriarchal privileges of manhood but simultaneously reap substantial penalties in the form of constricted interpersonal relationships, impaired physical health, and diminished psychic well-being.

Because of their limiting socialization, men typically are reluctant to enter psychotherapy, often feeling suspicious of its usefulness and of therapists' intentions. Often, they enter therapy under pressure from loved ones and expect to suffer in the therapist's office. It is imperative, therefore, that therapists be intimately familiar with the characteristics of men's gender world and be adept at translating this knowledge into gender-sensitive psychotherapy for men.

5

Clash of the Genders: When the Two Worlds Collide

The hopes and concerns that men and women bring to relationships are extremely deep-rooted, having been passed down through the generations over thousands of years across many cultures. No matter what couples may think they believe and tell each other about their commitment to new gender ideals, there exists at a deeper, unconscious level, many almost archetypal expectations both of the other gender and of a committed relationship. These expectations have great impact on any modern relationship. Although many of the stereotypical gender roles and characteristics that have persisted throughout the centuries may have emerged from biological differences, they have been translated in each succeeding generation and culture, thus becoming distorted and, in some cases, irrelevant. For example, the male upper-body strength that placed men in superior positions in agriculture or industry is no longer required for many of the most prestigious occupations in the United States, but those occupations are still predominantly male (see chapter 2). And modern technology allows a woman to control when and if she has a child, but women are still seen as unreliable in employment outside the home because of their capacity to bear children. Regardless of technological advances that make the traditional division of responsibility and characteristics unnecessary and irrelevant, certain personality traits and roles continue to be more often associated with one gender than another (Eagly, 1995), and deviance from these expectations often creates conflict and discomfort. This chapter discusses potential conflicts between the genders that appear to be the result of traditional gender expectations.

WHAT ARE GENDER EXPECTATIONS?

The gender socialization process essentially indoctrinates women and men to expect stereotypical characteristics and behaviors of each gender (see chapter 2). As evidence that this phenomenon still exists, recent research (Canter & Meyerowitz, 1984; Del Boca & Ashmore, 1980; Spence & Swain, 1985) indicates that men and women continue to distinguish between masculine and feminine traits in a stereotypical manner. Likewise, most women and men conform to some degree to the gendered expectations society has taught them. That is, they see the world through their gender schema and modify their behavior to fit the stereotype. Or, on the contrary, they rebel against the stereotype and don't fit it, thus generating increased role dissonance and, sometimes, discomfort.

The pressure to conform to rigid gender expectations results in the formation of two separate cultures that are often in conflict. Heterosexual marriages and relationships often seem to be formed between two persons who come from different worlds, each bringing very different expectations and skills to the relationship. To the extent that men and women are insecure about how well they are meeting their role mandates or feel compelled to rigidly adhere to all aspects of their gender role programming, they will be constrained from achieving the emotional intimacy which comes from self-disclosure and mutual understanding.

AREAS OF GENDER CONFLICT

The roots for conflict are extant in the socialization process we described in chapter 2. The gender messages received throughout a lifetime result in the genders having different values, different personality characteristics, different styles of communication, different problem-solving techniques, different roles, and different expectations for relationships. Add to this the changing rules and roles introduced to our society by the feminist movement, and the complexity of and potential for gender conflict increases exponentially. Simply educating clients to gender-based differences can be a major step toward gaining empathy and understanding for the other gender.

As we discuss gender differences throughout this chapter, we highlight the gender differences, rather than similarities to make our points as clearly as possible. We want the reader to understand, however, that we recognize that at times we are overstating the case. We know that nothing is absolutely true of all women or all men. In some areas, some men's behavior is more like that of most women; in other areas, some women's behavior is more like that of most men. Our point is although traditional socialization doesn't create totally opposite gender groups, it does produce behavioral preferences that cannot be ignored. Because, in our experience, psychological theory and therapeutic interventions have neglected to address these issues, we risk overstating our case. We want to be absolutely certain that critical gender differences are never again dismissed as insignificant and that cultural difference is not equated with psychopathology.

Value Systems

For an elucidation of the development of separate male and female value systems—the *masculine principle* and the *feminine principle*—the reader is referred to Marilyn French's *Beyond Power* (1985). (Also see Exhibit 5.1.) For the purposes of this discussion, suffice it to say that sometime during the process of social evolution, men began to place a high value on transcendence over nature and one's instincts. As mentioned earlier, mind/body philosophy is often traced back to Plato, but it is clear that organized religion, particularly Western theological belief systems, and the continued development of civilized societies reinforced the need for transcendence over natural impulses for the survival of the human race. How women came to be associated with body and men became associated with mind in the mind/body dichotomy is subject to debate, but is usually attributed by anthropologists and sociologists to women's capacity to give birth, which in ancient times appeared magical and mysterious. The point is that over the centuries men placed a high value on control, competition, reason, power over others, hierarchy, domination, autonomy, instrumentality, and the use of abstract rules and principles to govern one's life. Women, on the other hand, were associated with what, adhering to the transcendence philosophy, came to be considered lesser values: spontaneity, cooperation, compassion, emotion, affiliation, submission, nurturance, expressivity, and a pragmatic application of rules based on affiliative needs. Today some women and men recognize the desirability of these qualities, and many women work toward what French calls the *revalorization* of the feminine principle.[1]

Exhibit 5.1
Characteristics of Traditional Masculinity and Femininity

Masculine principle	Feminine principle
Control	Spontaneity
Competition	Cooperation
Autonomy	Affiliation
Power over others	Empowering self and others
Reason	Emotion
Instrumentality	Expressivity
Hierarchical organization	Equalitarian organization
Domination	Submission
Abstract rules and principles	Compassion
Aggression	Nurturance

Note. Characteristics summarized from *Beyond Power: On Women, Men, and Morals,* by M. French, 1985, New York, Ballantine Books.

[1]The reader is also reminded that feminist writers Chodorow (1978), Dinnerstein (1976), Gilligan (1982), and Miller (1986) have contributed more current psychological theories to explain male and female value differences, based on the developmental task of gender identification with mother as primary caretaker. See chapter 1.

Both men and women are capable of the whole range of values that can coexist despite their apparent contradictory stances. Indeed the man who uses compassion and cooperation with his allies during war tempers the level of atrocity that war brings with it. At the same time, the woman who uses reason to find a solution to a catastrophic problem while being aware of the emotional reaction she is having is more effective than the woman who collapses into tears in total helplessness, responding only to her emotional side. In other words, both men and women are more effective when they can access both so-called feminine and masculine values. Unfortunately, gender socialization often has the effect of training out values stereotypically associated with the other gender to the point that many men and women become half people. Those who can and do demonstrate their so-called other-gender side are often denigrated by society for not being a "real" man or woman.

The effect of this imbalance in value systems in a marriage can be very disturbing to the couple. An example may help to illustrate the point. A husband and wife in therapy arrived for their session in the middle of a heated argument regarding a cellist they had just heard at a concert. The cellist was female and the couple had encountered her coming down the stairs of the concert hall lugging her cello case. The wife wanted her husband to offer to carry it for her, but he refused to do so. To the wife this meant that he was an unfeeling, hard-hearted, selfish bastard who never thought of anybody but himself. She felt that a cooperative, compassionate person would have wanted to help. He countered that he respected the cellist's ability to cope, and stated that if she needed help, she would be assertive enough to ask for it. To him, offering to carry the cellist's case was putting her one down on the hierarchy and was an insult that implied that she was weak. He would not have offered to carry the case for a man and, if he respected her as an equal, why should he offer to carry the case for her? This man was one who had been touched by the rhetoric of the feminist movement and who no longer responded with a knee-jerk gentlemanly reaction. The fact that he had been criticized for opening doors for women and standing when they entered the room had made an impact on his thinking. His response was a rational one given the cry from many women in his office to be treated equally, which he interpreted as treated "like a man." Now he felt attacked for taking precisely the stand that his feminist consciousness required. But the incident does serve to illustrate the difference between men and women in interpreting a situation based on different value systems, and the added complexity of interpretation during a time of social change.

A second example illustrates the priority men place on hierarchy and competition and the concerns women show for affiliation and cooperation. One therapist worked with a couple who was in conflict over how the wife should handle her employees. She was the owner of a small business and was having trouble getting her employees to get their work done in a timely manner. Following traditional feminine values, she had befriended the employees and had even listened attentively to their personal problems. But when their performance was very important to her personal success in the business, she found herself extremely uncomfortable criticizing their work and demanding a faster turn-around. She complained to her husband nightly about being caught between her friendship with the employees and her desire to keep her business competitive. Her husband did not understand her problem. As far as he was concerned business is business. She should call them individually into her office, tell them why she is dissatisfied, give them a specific deadline by which they need to get their projects done, and impose some sort of penalty if they fail to make deadline, whether that was working overtime without pay, relinquishing a potential bonus, or losing their job altogether. Good employees should be able to separate friendship from business and if they cannot, he reasoned, the business she had invested capital in was more important than their feelings. After all, his wife *is* the boss and that's her job. The frustration the husband felt over his wife's being stuck and her frustration over his not understanding her need to prioritize the relationship, was a direct result of different value systems. (In a later section we address the issue of his offering advice she won't take.)

Personality Characteristics

As a direct result of placing higher priorities on certain values, especially with regard to the affiliation/autonomy dichotomy, men and women develop personality characteristics that are more likely to be found in one gender than the other. For example, women tend to be more nurturing and expressive (both verbally and physically), more in touch with their emotions (except anger), more cooperative even when it is not in their best interest to be so, and more likely to avoid confrontation and smooth things over in relationships outside the family (Chodorow, 1978; Gilligan, 1982; Miller, 1986). Men are more competitive, aggressive, assertive, and logical (David & Brannon, 1976; Doyle, 1989; O'Neil, 1982). They are also instrumental; that is, men prefer to do something, rather than talk about something (Doyle, 1989; Gray, 1992). They are comfortable challenging the ideas of others and often enjoy activities in which they can compete for the "top dog" position. Men seldom show tender emotions, which are considered weak and unmanly, but are very likely to express anger.

Of course there are emotional men and logical women. There are nurturing, supportive male bosses and aggressive, angry female bosses. Again we wish to stress that men and women have the capacity for a wide range of personality characteristics, and indeed we believe that the wider the range available to each individual, the more healthy and fulfilling a life that individual will have. Unfortunately, as we have previously stated, gender socialization encourages only personality characteristics that support the masculine principle for men and the feminine principle for women. Men and women who step outside those bounds are often considered in a negative light and pay the consequences.

So what effect does this have on a marriage? Both women and men often not only expect but demand at least a certain quota of gender-appropriate personality characteristics in their partners. Otherwise, a spouse may be rejected as unsuitable. Men and women seem to be intuitively aware that they need the full range of personality variables to live a satisfying life or that they need the attributes of the other gender to complement their own. But men and women who require the opposite-sex traits in their mates often become frustrated when the negative side of those attributes interfere with the realization of a satisfying relationship.

For the sake of illustration, we offer two brief examples here. As we point out later in this chapter, many women want men to protect them from harm. As is reinforced in military training, a man must have all of the gentle, soft emotions programmed out of him in order to be a good protector. He must not give in to fear, pain or compassion. He must be aggressive. He must be able to access anger. He must place a high priority on physical strength or the use of weaponry. He must be action-oriented and decisive. He must be able to assess the weaknesses of his enemy and attack. However, when a man does not share his anxieties, fears, grief, and depression with his wife, she may feel shut out or distanced from him. When he prefers to go out and putter in his woodworking shop or work out in a gym rather than sit and chat with her, she may feel rejected. When he provides a quick solution to a problem instead of providing her emotional support, she may feel unheard. When he criticizes the way she does something in an effort to problem-solve, she may feel devalued. When he gets angry in response to what he perceives as attack from her, she may feel hopeless. However all of these characteristics were required for the protector role.

A man expects his wife to be his nurturer and his friend for life, supplying him with the emotional side that is undeveloped within him (Pleck & Pleck, 1980). In order for her to do so she must be in tune to emotions (both his and her own), she must be expressive so that he will feel appreciated, she must be accommodating so he will feel supported, she must draw him out so that he will have permission to talk about things that are "unmanly," and she must be careful not to criticize him or demand too much from him because it will hurt his ego. Often, when she wants to talk about emotions, he feels inadequate and confused. When she cries in the middle of an argument because she is in touch with feeling hurt and because she does not hold back on the expression of her feelings, he may feel stymied and manipulated. If she becomes resentful and begins to take digs at him, he may wonder why she didn't say what she wanted in the first place. When she asks him what he is thinking or feeling, he may feel annoyed and want to be left alone. When she talks to him in indirect ways about changes she would like, he may not get the message. When she finds indirect methods of getting him to do something she wants, he may feel manipulated. However, once agains her actions are merely the talents she has developed over time in order to be a "good wife."

Of course, not all men and women are programmed to behave in the ways we have described above. Enough are, however, to make the above-described·interactions common concerns that couples bring to therapy.

Communication Styles

Recently, gender studies have added interpersonal communication to the growing list of human endeavors mediated by gender socialization (Tannen, 1990). Instead of studying how people communicate, it is now becoming possible to study how men communicate and how women communicate. Recognition of key differences will provide insights into the gender basis for miscommunication in a relationship. Several factors contribute to these differences, including relative power in a relationship, the stereotypical value systems, the language skill, and the uses of communication (Gray, 1992; Lakoff, 1975, 1990; Tannen, 1990).

Watzlawick and colleagues (1967) discussed how power differences are played out in interpersonal communication and described the differences in communication between *equals* (symmetrical interactions) and communication between *non-equals* (complementary interactions). Healthy relationships are those in which the participants are able to move freely between complementary and symmetrical interactions, dependent upon the demands of the situation. For example, each marital partner should be able to nurture the other during times of adversity. Neither should be frozen into either a protector/savior posture or a protected/saved posture. Likewise, when legitimate differences of interest occur, each partner should feel comfortable entering into negotiations with the other. The unhealthy relationship then is one in which healthy conflict is not possible.

It can be seen through this framework how rigid socialization that differentially imbues men and women with power sets the stage for unhealthy communication patterns between genders. Traditionally, men have had far greater political, socioeconomic, and physical power. Women usually have had more relationship and communication skills because their position as the dependent and subservient gender has required that they develop these skills for survival. When there are cases of these power imbalances, major communication problems ensue. For instance, a woman who fears physical or financial retaliation obviously will be reluctant to engage in symmetrical interactions (i.e., to push her position too far). Instead, she might be likely to resort to more indirect communications. Men, socialized to view dominance and leadership as the male entitlement (and the male responsibility), may be distressed when women interact symmetrically (i.e., get too pushy) and may feel the need to "keep her in her place."

Women's greater affective communication skills and "relationship power" also create communication problems between the genders. In situations requiring interpersonal relationship skills (e.g., nurturing children, dealing with extended family, interacting with friends), men typically defer to women, putting themselves in a one-down position. In the critical area of relationship maintenance, however, men may be highly threatened by women's greater verbal skills and ability to identify affective states. Gender differences in stress reactivity have been documented (Gottman & Levenson, 1986). Men are more physiologically reactive to stressful stimuli than women. As a result, men frequently avoid emotional conflict, or, in all too many cases, may try to suppress the pressures to communicate by exerting their superior physical and financial power. Men's avoidance of intimate communication likely results from their greater arousal and subjective discomfort in the face of interpersonal conflict.

Authenticity and appropriate self-disclosure generally enhance interpersonal communication. It seems logical then that communication between men and women should be characterized by abundant sharing about differences in backgrounds and experiences, as well as by efforts to describe accurately gender-based reactions to all situations. Unfortunately, this is nearly the opposite of what actually takes place. Men are taught that they are not supposed to tell women (or other men, for that matter) their innermost thoughts and feelings because women will either see them as weak and reject them or misunderstand and criticize them. Women often assume that men see the world the way they do, and are surprised and offended to find that is not the case because they tend to believe their way is the right way. Thus men and women often hid their private lives from each other because these gender role pressures are so restrictive and unforgiving (Cahill, 1986). However, this process is problematic when the norms of one gender world are kept secret from members of the other and when it prevents authenticity and self-disclosure. For example, a man faced with a devastating personal loss, trained to believe that masculinity requires a Sturdy Oak facade (David & Brannon, 1976; see chapter 4), may neither communicate his pain to his partner nor be able to explain why he is emotionally constricted. Likewise, a woman who sees nurturing, caretaking, and self-sacrifice as an integral part of her femininity will have great difficulty acknowledging the part of herself that is enraged by the need to care for a husband with a debilitating illness such as Alzheimer's Disease.

At the root of the dissimilar communication styles used by men and women is the socialization process that causes the genders to set different priorities in their value systems. Communication patterns reflect these different value systems. Male communication is designed to establish independence and a favored position within a hierarchy, but female communication is meant to provide connection and support. The result is, at its best, a complementary communication pattern that leaves women in a one-down position. In the worst case, both genders feel frustrated, misunderstood, and helpless.

Deborah Tannen (1990) has accumulated and published linguistic research that provides support for these widely observed stylistic differences in her popular book, *You Just Don't Understand*. A brief summary of her findings is important to provide a foundation for the therapist working with couples and families. Typically, women use language to provide understanding and support, give praise, validate experiences, illustrate with personal experience, and connect with others emotionally—all of which encourage the sharing of intimate experiences, including personal problems. Women are often tentative and indirect in their speech patterns, use tag questions to encourage further discussion, qualify their statements, deprecate their own contributions, speak in a quiet voice, and avoid eye contact in public meetings. They tend to support the positions of others, listen attentively and empathically, wait to be invited to speak, and do not interrupt. In reaching a decision, women prefer consensus to the use of hierarchical power. All of these communication patterns reflect women's desire to connect and their fear of offending others, as well as their role as nurturer and their lower status in society.

According to Tannen, men, on the other hand, use language to offer advice, provide solutions, share information, and impress others with their accomplishments, credentials, and ideas. They see verbal conflict as a contest and so will challenge and criticize the opponent's position, interrupt, change the subject, compete for the floor, obscure communication with intellectual verbosity, listen critically to find the flaws of their opponent's argument, and frequently pull rank or offer ultimatums. They often speak more loudly, directly, and assertively than women, and maintain eye contact in public. They may dismiss certain problems as unimportant and often divert talk away from personal issues that might show weakness. These communication patterns are a direct result of the value many men place on hierarchy and power, on the need to save face and be in control. The value system many men endorse, in turn, stems from the societal role of protector they have assumed in most recent cultures.

It is important to reiterate the fact that although the male style of communication gives them the advantage in the public arena, they are at a disadvantage in communicating about interpersonal relationships. Their typical style does not foster self-disclosure, provide emotional support, or serve as a vehicle to emotional intimacy. Therefore they will often shut down and avoid intimate communication altogether, which then angers their isolated spouse even further.

The miscommunication between the genders because of these differences can even occasionally be somewhat amusing. For instance, one male client shared his solution to the double-bind experiences he often found himself in when communicating with his wife. When, for example, she asks him how he likes a new dress, he has learned after 20 years of marriage that he is not really looking for his honest response, but neither will she trust his automatic approval. Rather than spend the time and energy it takes to provide her with the emotional assurance she is looking for, he has learned to respond by saying, "That's a trick question, isn't it? I don't do trick questions!" Sadly, in many instances, such miscommunication leads to conflict and disappointment for both spouses.

Although some popular authors do not recommend that men attempt a new style of communication (Gray, 1992), it is our opinion that verbal styles are learned, just like languages. Women are starting to modify their stereotypical communication patterns in order to be more effective in the workplace. Although the research indicates that when men or women adopt a style that is more typical of the other gender they are likely to meet with criticism (e.g., Basow, 1986; Cann & Garnett, 1984; Costrich et al., 1975; Shinar, 1978), women gradually are becoming more assertive, direct, and even confrontational when appropriate in a work setting and men are adjusting to this change. Men, too, can learn to shift gears and make use of new communication techniques—most importantly, active listening—in order to facilitate communication in their homes. In the experience of these authors, it is not that men don't want to learn to communicate better in their relationships, but that they don't know what to do. Sometimes men are more responsive when they have worked through their problems and learned new skills in all-male psychotherapy groups (see chapter 4). But it is not just men who need to learn; women will profit from becoming more direct and assertive at home, while maintaining their supportive listening skills. Not surprisingly, it is actually a combination of male and female communication patterns that allow for greatest potential for intimacy in a relationship. Both genders, however, must be prepared to deal in a constructive manner with the negative feelings that arise when their spouse starts to communicate in a "gender inappropriate" manner. For change to occur, it is helpful if it is encouraged and rewarded by the spouse. In the meantime, an understanding of the communicational style of the other gender at least lessens misinterpretation and de-escalates distancing behaviors.

Again we wish to remind the reader that we are well aware that not all men or women communicate in the styles that Tannen has described.

There will always be exceptions. But a knowledge of typical communication patterns will aid the therapist in identifying when gender socialization might play a role in communication difficulties experienced by her or his client.

Problem-Solving Techniques

We have already discussed the tendency of men to be action-oriented and to engage in instrumental behaviors and the female preference to talk about issues in order to sort things out (Tannen, 1990). Due to the fact that men have been socialized to hide insecurities and doubts, they generally prefer to think things through in solitude until they have found a solution to a problem (David & Brannon, 1976; Doyle, 1989). They are likely to make use of their critical thinking ability to define the problem and brainstorm for possible solutions, most of which probably require that they do something—work harder, make more money, but a gift, get some flowers, take a spouse out to dinner, move to a better climate, and so on. Women, on the other hand, will probably want to discuss the problem and look for someone to commiserate with and support them emotionally, perhaps coming to a consensus on the best way to deal with the issue. Once women have received that support, they may or may not actually do something to change the situation. For many women, the feeling that they have been heard and understood gives them the energy to either take action or merely cope with the situation.

It is easy to see in the following scenarios how the different problem-solving approaches create conflict in a marriage: A woman shares her difficulties with her husband for several reasons, but the most important one is to make an emotional connection with him. She is looking for his support and validation. The man, used to solving problems in a different manner, gathers information, examines her handling of the situation critically, and provides a solution. She feels that he thinks she is stupid, inadequate, and in need of a caretaker. She does not feel supported or emotionally connected at all. She gets angry and does not take his advice. He feels set-up and betrayed. If she didn't want his advice, why did she tell him her problems? Did she do that simply to make him feel inadequate? If his advice is no good and he cannot make her happy, he is not being a very good husband.

A man becomes quiet and brooding, verbally noncommunicative, as he chews on a problem he is dealing with. Or he goes out for a drive. Or he works out at the gym, engaging in physical activity that clears his mind and allows him to attack the problem afresh. His wife, in her emotion-monitoring role, knows something is wrong and begins to ask him questions in hopes of getting him to talk. He does not want to share his worries with her because he is perfectly capable of handling them independently and he should protect her from his problems. So he avoids her questions and she feels shut out. She wants to feel close to him and, from her female friendships, she knows that sharing problems is one of the ways to develop intimacy. She begins to badger him, so in order to avoid a major conflict, he withdraws physically. She is hurt and angry, which merely compounds his frustrations. Now he has two problems to solve. Both spouses feel inadequate and unappreciated.

The reader is reminded once again, that men and women come in varieties. That is, not all men and women solve problems in this stereotypically gendered fashion. However, because the gender training we all receive is so pervasive, simply understanding and acknowledging the different coping strategies that most men and women use goes a long way toward preventing the misunderstandings resulting from gender differences in problem-solving skills.

Sexuality

Both biology and socialization are at the root of the gender clashes in sexual expectations and desires. For example, men, in general seem to want sex more often than women, in general. They are more likely to use erotica to become aroused. They are more likely to fantasize about multiple partners and enjoy recreational sex (Carnes, 1983; Zilbergeld, 1992). Women, on the other hand, are more concerned about the emotional relationship they have with their partners and more often desire a monogamous relationship. They most often want verbal communication, gentle touching, and cuddling (Zilbergeld, 1992).

Recent articles (Buss, 1995) have suggested that these differences are explained by *evolutionary psychology*, a metatheory that considers the different adaptive demands faced by men and women throughout human evolutionary history. Essentially, this theory suggests that for the reproduction of the human race, men needed sexual access to many reproductively valuable women whereas women needed men who could commit to the protection and nurturance of mother and children during their vulnerable years. The theory then points to the development of psychological differences between men and women that were perpetuated by mate selection and intrasexual competition.

Whatever the reason, men and women frequently come to the bedroom with widely divergent needs and desires (Gray, 1995; Zilbergeld, 1992). Unless they understand and respect these differences they will have difficulty finding the common ground between them on which they can build a sexually satisfying relationship. The problem is compounded by the media bombardment of false ideas about human sexuality, which both reflects and influences cultural values.

Most media represent the male role in the sex act as one of technical expertise, and leave out the emotional aspects so vitally important to many women. The unenlightened man who buys into the James Bond mythology of ever-ready sex is burdened with beliefs counterproductive to a satisfying sexual relationship. Such men, for example, may believe any of the following myths of male sexuality: that the size of his penis is extremely important, that all touching should lead to sex, that the verbal expression of emotions is unmanly, that the goal of sex is orgasm, that only intercourse is real sex, that an erection is absolutely required and is a sign of a true man, that he should move the earth for his female partner, that he should always be interested in sex, that he should take the lead and know what he is doing, and finally that even if a woman doesn't want sex, he should proceed and make her enjoy it (Zilbergeld, 1992). Thus men may come to the marital bed with unrealistically high hopes, a host of destructive myths about sexuality, and a great deal of anxiety regarding their ability to please the woman.

Many men feel that it is not only their sexual skill that proves manliness: They must also seduce many women because the more women they have "bedded," the more virile they are (Pittman, 1989, 1991). This proof of manliness is in direct conflict with a committed, monogamous relationship. So men often enter marriage with a hope for readily available sex with a comfortable partner and a simultaneous regret for giving up the fantasy supplied to them by the media (Farrell, 1987).

In our professional experience, however, we have found that for women, there is a different list of requirements for a satisfying sexual relationship. Primary among these is a sense of emotional intimacy with her partner that comes from the verbal communication of feelings, the sharing of joys and fears, and the trust that comes from being safely vulnerable with one another (Hite, 1987). Secondarily, she looks for an appreciation of her as the focus of his life, the most important ingredient around which his plans revolve. She wants to be honored, respected, desired, and valued by him. She desires to be touched and caressed in a way that communicates his love for her, but does not necessarily always lead to sexual intercourse. Given the fact that men are taught that the expression of emotions is sissy stuff and women may crave that very thing for arousal, it is clear that expectations can clash in the bedroom.

In order to help clients improve their sex lives, sex therapists often ask the couple to write down their sexual fantasies. Gender differences regarding sexuality are often more clearly delineated in these descriptions. So often the woman will write about a romantic picnic by a lake under a tree complete with food, wine, music, and proclamations of undying love from her handsome suitor while her male partner will write about black leather, fishnet stockings, garter belts, and the perfect body ready for him to do anything he wishes from a massage with hot oil to oral sex (Heiman & LoPiccolo, 1988). Clearly the woman is more focused on the emotional relationship, the man on the physical.

In many societies throughout history, women were not expected to enjoy sex, participating in it only for reproductive reasons or because it was their marital duty. Men believed they were entitled to sexual relations with a marital partner upon demand, without consideration of her wishes. The sexual revolution of the sixties and seventies challenged these basic assumptions by publicizing the capacity for sexual pleasure in women and freeing them to explore their sexuality within or outside of a committed relationship. One result of this revolution was the greater demand put on men to perform sexually and be concerned about his partner reaching orgasm. This applied pressure to both men and women; his anxiety about performance and manliness detracted considerably from his pleasure and she often faked orgasm to keep him from feeling badly. More recently men have begun admitting that they don't always enjoy sex either and sometimes fake orgasm as well. Measuring up has become an issue for both genders, which greatly reduces the pleasure experienced by either (Zilbergeld, 1992).

There is also evidence (Schnarch, 1991, 1995) to suggest that some women are eager to explore what are often thought of as traditionally more masculine sexual impulses and interests, and that some men are equally interested in taking a more passive and traditionally feminine role. As men and women talk more honestly about their relationship in general, these ideas also become more open to exploration. A frequent result of such exploration is an end to fights about who initiates sexual encounters, as each member of the couple begins to take more responsibility for her or his own sexual interests and needs.

Today, partly due to the change in both men and women's roles in society and partly due to the spector of AIDS, experts in male sexuality (Brooks, 1995; Zilbergeld, 1992) are recommending a move away from the male emphasis on performance and "scoring" with the perfect body to the traditionally more feminine model of sexual activity, mutual pleasuring, and emotional closeness with the total human being. (For in-depth discussion of changing attitudes and behavioral and psychological interventions, the reader is referred to *The New Male Sexuality* [Zilbergeld, 1992].)

A gender role conflict that has potential for violent and criminal results is the female role as sexual gatekeeper/seducer and the male role as sexual initiator/aggressor. As previously stated, women have been taught that their physical attractiveness is their most important commodity (Wolf, 1991) and that they can use this power to facilitate social interactions and obtain what they want in indirect ways (Williams, 1987). Thus they will often send out subtle messages that men interpret as sexual invitation even when the women have no intention of expanding such innocent flirtation to sexual encounter. To make matters worse, even when women are interested in sexual encounter, they have been taught that direct sexual approaches are "unladylike" and might threaten men, thus they are likely to make use of the same subtle tactics that they use in everyday social intercourse. Men can be confused by such messages and, in the worst case scenario, feel set-up by a "tease."

On the other hand, it is men who are taught to be the initiators of sex in a direct manner and so they take the risks of rejection (Zilbergeld, 1992). Men have also been taught that the number of sexual encounters they have is a measure of their manliness and that it is the woman's role to stop them (Farrell, 1987). When this attitude is compounded by the media-fed belief that women say no when they mean yes, many men find themselves accused of rape or sexual harassment in today's society. This can even be the case in a marital relationship, once viewed by the judicial system as a private domain that should be exempt from such laws. Today, the accusation of rape in a marital relationship stands up in court in several states. Men and women who have different views of their role in the sexual relationship may be headed for serious problems.

Infidelity

Over 40 years ago, the well-known Kinsey report (Kinsey et al., 1948, 1953) stated that 50% of husbands and 26% of wives had engaged in some sort of extramarital relationship during their marriages. More recent data (Smith, 1993) indicates that this percentage has lowered somewhat to 21% of men and 12% of women. This reduction in reported infidelity may be due to changes in accepted social values or the potential lethality of sexual encounters in the day of AIDS, among other possibilities. However, given that both men and women expect fidelity from their partners in a relationship, the existence of extramarital relationships appears to constitute a clash in stated expectations— not between what men and women say they want, but between what they want and what they do. Because we see gender socialization as a major contributor to marital infidelity, we wish to address it at this point.

Various authors (Brown, 1991; Lusterman, 1988; Pittman, 1989) have described typologies of extramarital affairs and their causes that range from one-night stands to long-term emotionally involved relationships. Gender socialization plays a role in most of these situations. For men, there are multiple operatives at work. Some men do not move beyond the adolescent stage when "scoring with women" and "putting notches on their belt" defined success and determined their hierarchy among their peers. Even men who reach a level of maturity that allows them to appreciate the potential for true intimacy in a committed relationship frequently feel some regret at marriage because commitment to a permanent relationship with one woman constitutes a forfeit of the dream of multiple sexual relationships with the perfect female body, an image the media has promulgated successfully (Brooks, 1995; Farrell, 1987). This reaction is reinforced by peers who tease men about being trapped in the "marital yoke," as though their lives were over. Other men intensely feel the weight of responsibility for providing financially for their wives and children. For these men, the Sturdy Oaks, the need to be self-reliant, self-assured, and protective of their spouse may preclude their sharing true intimacy with her and results in their feeling isolated, alone, and unappreciated. Because men are taught to avoid any kind of intimacy ("no sissy stuff") except for sexual intimacy, they may retreat to a sexual affair to feel connected and close (Lusterman, 1988). Sometimes these men allow themselves to be vulnerable with the other woman because the rules for the masculine role require only that the husband protect and provide for the wife, not the affairee (Lusterman, 1988). Other men, having accepted the value of autonomy as the most supreme, fear being swallowed up by closeness in a marriage, and use an affair to maintain some distance and boundaries (Pittman, 1989). There are many motivations behind the infidel's behavior, many of which can be traced to the dysfunctional lessons men have learned from their gender messages.

Women too have affairs, and for them also these affairs are usually an effort to fill some missing aspect of their lives (Brown, 1991; Pittman,

1989). As in the case of men, some women never grow beyond the adolescent years in which their power to attract and seduce men establishes
their worth. These women miss the romance of being worshipped and
adored, feeling life to be meaningless unless some romantic pursuit exists.
They have accepted the notion that a woman's worth is in her beauty and
that her purpose is to catch a man. Once she has done this, what is next?
Often she must catch another man in order to feel alive. In many cases,
however, women are looking for the emotional intimacy (Glass & Wright,
1985) that comes from the verbal sharing of thoughts, feelings, fears, concerns, and even the petty details of daily life and they find themselves terribly disappointed by a husband who "never talks." Here the previously
described clash in gender expectations regarding communication set the
woman up to feel isolated and lonely, which will result in her searching
elsewhere for the connection she craves. If she finds a man who can listen the way her women friends can, she may be very vulnerable to having
an affair. In other cases, women feel put down, disrespected, and discounted by their spouses due to behaviors and attitudes that are a direct
product of gender socialization (see chapter 2 and elsewhere this chapter).
The woman who feels unappreciated and ignored will seek appreciation
and attention elsewhere. This is particularly true if she is seen by the other
man in terms other than her role as wife and mother, which is sometimes
the only way her spouse seems to be able to view her. Receiving respect
and recognition for being herself will provide the right atmosphere for an
affair. And finally, due to the existence of inequities in the larger culture
(see chapter 2) that reduce their influence and choices, many women feel
powerless to bring about change in their relationships. Having an affair
may be seen as a way of gaining power. In a world in which men compete
for women, having the attention of another man may be a wake-up call
for the oblivious spouse. In each of these cases, the gender socialization
of men and women contribute to the dynamics of the affair.

Although a clash of expectations regarding infidelity does not exist
between the genders, the expectations regarding the relationship's benefits and the role each spouse must play in order to obtain those benefits
are often in conflict. Therefore gender socialization plays a large role in

marital dissatisfaction and the resultant existence of infidelity despite the fact that both genders express desires to the contrary.

STEREOTYPICAL MARITAL EXPECTATIONS

Given the above conflictual expectations regarding the genders, what do marital partners expect of one another in the marital relationship?

In a recent informal survey (Philpot & Howze, 1994) of 30 college and graduate students ranging in age from 18 to 46, the most frequently mentioned expectation of marriage by men was that of (a) having one's best friend for a mate, followed by (b) a desire for emotional and physical intimacy, (c) total acceptance, support, and loyalty, and (d) emotional security forever. Women listed (a) deep emotional intimacy more frequently than any other expectation for marriage, followed by (b) good communication, (c) equal sharing of problems, parenting, and housework, and (d) someone to do things with. Although the responses sound very similar, it must be remembered that male friendships and female friendships are based on different behaviors; that is, emotional intimacy for a man is often linked with physical intimacy whereas for a woman it is often verbal communication. For a woman, total support and loyalty could mean an abandonment of one's own goals and beliefs for the sake of one's spouse. Emotional security forever may have an unhealthy dependent sound to it, and women and men tend to handle problem solution in different ways. Furthermore, communication and equal sharing of roles such as parenting and housework were only mentioned by women. In fact, only three out of 29 male participants referred to parenting at all—two in reference to their fear of that role and the third expecting a spouse to handle it for him. No men referred to housework or communication. On the other hand, no female participants, but several male ones stated that marriage would be a major financial responsibility for them that would cause sacrifice and loss of "freedom and fun." Both genders stated with equal frequency that fear of abandonment or fear of being stuck in a bad or boring relationship were their most dreaded expectations of marriage. Both genders feared a change in personality after marriage. In chapter 9 we show how adherence to rigid gender stereotypes appears to bring about these very results.

Although this is a very limited sample (undergraduate and graduate students of psychology, low N) and was not scientifically conducted, it is nevertheless interesting to see how responses to open-ended questions evoke conscious responses that, in many ways, still reflect gender stereotypical expectations. Obviously, as with any face-valid survey, the tendency of the respondent to give politically correct, acceptable responses could have affected the results. For example, only one female participant mentioned the desire for financial support and only one male participant said he was looking for physical beauty. Whether that is due to actual differences in this sample, or the fact that these desires are unconscious or politically incorrect, or yet another factor remains unknown.

No matter what the particular set of circumstances each individual brings to marriage, his or her experiences are shaped by the larger culture, which, as we have pointed out, continues to endorse and proselytize certain roles and characteristics that have pervaded many cultures throughout history. It is possible, then, to predict (while allowing for individual differences) some of the more common marital expectations and resulting problems one many have. These common expectations can be broken down into functions each gender performs for the other. That is, many men are looking for an attractive woman with whom they can have readily available sex, a nurturing and loving woman who will take care of their emotional needs, a competent mother for their children, and a partner who will handle the domestic responsibilities of the home. Many women want emotional intimacy with a man who will provide for and protect them and their children. Certainly not all men and women have the same set of expectations. There will always be those who do not fit the stereotype. Nevertheless, a large proportion of the clients we seen in our offices will have similar expectations of their relationships. In the following section, we discuss how these societally reinforced stereotypical expectations play out at the end of the twentieth century.

ROMANTIC LOVE/SEXUAL LOVE

Romantic and sexual love is an area in which it is not uncommon for men and women to have drastically different expectations. Although not all people's expectations conform to those offered to them by the media, many do. Thus, gender-specific expectations are linked to the media socializing agents, as we illustrate in the following discussion.

What Men Expect

Beauty First

In many ways very little has changed regarding gender expectations. Even today the most valuable commodity a woman has with regard to attracting a desirable male is her beauty and sexuality (Lott, 1994; Wolf, 1991), despite the struggle of the women's movement to emphasize other attributes, especially competence to provide for oneself. The most beautiful women seem to attract the most powerful (i.e., richest) men. The first thing a man notices about a woman is whether she is attractive (Bar-Tal & Saxe, 1976; Deaux & Hanna, 1984; Farrell, 1987; Garcia, Stinson, Ickes, Bissonnette, & Briggs, 1991; Howard, Blumstein, & Schwartz, 1987), and very often he will not pursue an acquaintance if she does not approach his ideal of beauty, which, of course, is frequently based on such unrealistic images as airbrushed photographs of naked 20-year-old female bodies found in *Playboy* magazine (Brooks, 1995). Clearly, whether consciously or unconsciously, the man expects beauty and sexuality from the woman in marriage.

Therefore women are preoccupied with the accoutrements of beauty, which include everything from makeup, clothing, and diets to face-lifts and hairdye (Lott, 1994; Wolf, 1991). Keeping up with American beauty standards can be a very expensive proposition. Women worry about men finding other women more attractive and tend to scan the competition to try to keep up. They take more time to get dressed than men because it takes longer to apply makeup and style their hair. Some men may find the amount of time and money their wives spend trying to maintain beauty annoying, and may not have an understanding of how male emphasis on female beauty contributes to this problem. No matter what other qualities a woman may have, she probably feels that she must maintain a certain level of attractiveness if she expects to keep her husband interested (Wolf, 1991).

One of a man's fears about marriage is that once the woman has secured him in a marital contract, she will let herself go and he will be committed to someone he no longer finds sexually attractive. In fact, Zilbergeld (1992) lists loss of physical attractiveness in a sexual partner as one of the main causes of reduced sex drive in a man. Additionally, the man who marries a beautiful woman feels he has elevated himself in the eyes of other men (Farrell, 1987; Howard, Blumstein, & Schwartz, 1987). As we know, of course, men and women of fairly equal intelligence and attractiveness tend to marry (Bowen, 1978). However, attractiveness often means different things depending on whether one is male or female. A woman's beauty may function as a sign to others that he has something of value, whether it be his own physical attractiveness, political power, money, or sexual expertise.

Readily Available, Eternally Passionate, Sanctioned Sex

Physical attractiveness in his spouse is of particular importance to his sexual pleasure, which is a primary expectation for men in a relationship. Most men cite the ready availability of a safe sexual partner as a major reason for marriage, although they often fear that the passionate sex of courtship will disappear after marriage (Farrell, 1987). They come to marriage with the hope that their sex lives will remain vital and exciting and that their marital partners will fulfill the sexual fantasies that they bring with them from the media. Unfortunately, as so well-documented by Farrell (1987), the media has filled men with the unrealistic fantasy of the perfectly shaped young female body, hungry for sex, always responsive, ready to experiment, and easily satisfied. To make matters worse, one of these perfect sexual partners is not enough; variety in partners and multiple partners is part of the fantasy. The reality of a monogamous relationship with a life partner, even when that sexual relationship is satisfying, pales in comparison to the stimulation offered by the "girlie" magazines, books, and movies that some men enjoy (Brooks, 1995).

At some level, most women are aware of this and feel the need to be both the seductive harlot and the pure wife at the same time (Radway, 1984). Women may fear abandonment if they cannot fulfill both roles simultaneously, which is often a difficult task. Because women have been taught by media that men are supposed to be sexually aggressive and are turned off by sexually assertive women, they are often reluctant to play the sexual tigress for fear of emasculating a man (Halas & Matteson, 1978). On the other hand, a husband may go elsewhere if she does not behave seductively. Because keeping her spouse happy is a measure of her femininity in the eyes of society, a woman tends to take responsibility if her husband does go elsewhere and may feel that she has failed as a woman.

We have discussed previously the many potential conflicts between men and women which can emerge in the sexual arena. Gender socialization plays a major role in these often contradictory expectations.

What Women Expect

Appreciation, Attention, and Romance

Women, too, expect sexual satisfaction in marriage, but the fantasies presented to them by the media are somewhat different. In spite of the sexual revolution, the romantic fiction formula novel remains extremely popular among women. As discussed in chapter 2, the basic premise of these books is the rescue of the beautiful woman from whatever conflict is complicating her life by a handsome, rich, and gallant man who then pursues her forever for her sexual favors (Cartland, 1995). She remains the center of his life, an object of great devotion, and she may count on him to solve all her problems. Her identity and self-worth come through the love of a man (Gilbert, 1984; Lamb, 1985). (This is not unlike the favorite childhood fairy tales of Cinderella and Sleeping Beauty.) Notice the lack of specific sexual content. Her sexual satisfaction is assumed because he is her protector, her provider who honors her and makes her the focus of his life. She needs this focused attention because it is through him that she achieves her own identity. Such adoration is obviously impossible for the husband who has his hands full dealing with the daily tasks of living, which leaves her disappointed.

The Man Who Can Be Fixed

An alternate formula for these romantic novels is the one in which the heroine is the one person in the world who is able to reach a man with a tragic flaw and save him from his fate, for which he remains ever devoted to her (Radway, 1984; Spacks, 1975). Women who follow this example are left with the unrealistic expectation that through a magical combination of sensuality and care-taking instincts (Radway, 1984), she can fix whatever is wrong in the man's life. Once she changes him for the better, he will reward her with a lifetime commitment. The reality, of course, is more akin to "what you see is what you get", so women should be happy with a man before deciding to spend a lifetime together. Not only can a woman not change a man, her attempts to do so may very well destroy any feeling he ever had for her. After all, men, like women, want to be loved for who they are and not criticized and remade into something else.

Note the lack of any reference to specific sexual material. It is not the sexual expertise of the male that wins the woman—although that is often assumed—but his adoration of her above anyone or anything else in the world. (See the section on sexuality, this chapter, for an understanding of how these fantasies affect sexual expectations.)

Of course not all men and women act in the ways consistent with gender stereotypes of sexual expectations, but it is often said that men give love to get sex and women give sex to get love. Given the fantasies fed to men and women in the media, it is likely that there is much truth to this adage.

Man As Protector/Woman As Nurturer

The Warrior Expectation

One expectation that has not changed for men in most cultures since recorded history is his role as protector. In his latest work on the male condition, *The Myth of Male Power*, Farrell (1993) documents in detail how men have been trained to be the warrior—the soldiers, the policemen, the CIA agents, and the firemen—in service of the "weaker sex" and children. Although this pattern probably developed due to man's superior physical strength, that physical characteristic is much less relevant in today's world of sophisticated weapons. Nevertheless, both genders continue to expect men to sacrifice themselves for not only their own families, but all women and children. In order to provide this service, men must be trained to deny weaker feelings such as fear, sadness, loneliness, and rejection and must embrace anger, aggression, and even hatred and be otherwise stoic. From early childhood, men learn that they must not cry or run away, but must stand up to other men, win competitions, endure physical pain, always be ready to come to the assistance of a woman or child in trouble, and so on (Doyle, 1989). (See chapter 2.) The result of this training is that many men really cannot identify their feelings, much less express them to their wives and loved ones. They may spend a great deal of energy in competitive endeavors, trying to one-up each other, measuring themselves on the male hierarchical scale (Doyle, 1989). Men often test themselves against other men even to the point of risking physical harm in ways as innocuous as playing eighteen holes of golf in the pouring rain rather than admitting physical discomfort or, worse, nearly suffering the loss of a limb from frostbite when snowmobiling or risking killing themselves in a drag race on a beltway. Sometimes measuring up on the hierarchy can lead to cruelty or violence when all else fails in proving their manhood or their superior position, whether it be in relationship to other men or to their wives and family. Men who have been fortunate enough not to have been too thoroughly trained as warriors—men who have struggled to maintain some sort of balance between their tender side and their protector role—walk a very fine line. To be too emotionally responsive, to back down from aggression at the wrong time, to compromise one time too many, could be tantamount to losing manhood (Gilmore, 1990).

Many women find the results of this warrior training to be frustrating and even depressing, leaving them with mates who cannot let down their guards and be emotionally intimate. However they often automatically expect the male to play the protector role within the family (Spacks, 1975): Who usually gets up and investigates a strange noise in the house at night? Who will probably run through the rain to get the car parked a block away? When a dog lunges at a man and woman walking on a street, which person is most likely to throw himself in front of the other to ward off the attack? And if a man fails to do what was expected of him, what will women think of him? The male role as protector is so automatically accepted by both genders that a reversal of roles, even if a woman is better skilled in a given endeavor, may shame him in his own eyes.

Nurturer/The Relationship Expert

Because his training to be the protector often incapacitates a man's gentle side, the woman is usually expected to be the nurturer in the family. It is usually up to her to monitor the emotional state of each family member, to be tuned in to the signs that indicate needs, frustrations, and hurts (Chodorow, 1978). Additionally, it is her responsibility to draw out those individuals who cannot express themselves to be sure they have an opportunity to ventilate and resolve their problems. If a child begins to have difficulty or if her marital relationship is not going well, the woman is likely to blame herself, as will society at large. She is seen as the relationship expert; she should be able to make it work.

Women who enter a marital relationship hoping to have the emotional intimacy they have had with other women in their lives are likely to find that many men will not understand the level of communication for which they are looking. Many men do not share the woman's view that talking about the tiny details of daily life builds closeness (Tannen, 1990). And many times, men's warrior training makes them uncomfortable sharing their personal struggles and internal conflicts, which is the very glue of relationships to many women. Often women feel alone and distant from the male spouse who works all day and watches TV all night. Unlike men, they do not usually feel that parallel play builds intimacy.

Men, on the other hand, frequently crave the nurturance and intimacy that their public image does not allow them to accept (Farrell, 1987). When they marry, they often hope for someone who will love them as they are, and let them express their weaknesses, their anxieties, and failures, and still stand by them. They are looking for a cheerleader, not a critic. Criticism is particularly difficult to take from the person you count on for nurturance. If they do not get the support they are looking for they may close down and stop sharing their innermost thoughts altogether (Gray, 1992).

Men want the emotional sustenance they cannot openly admit needing, but they often simultaneously fear that if they show too much weakness or need, they will lose the woman, who will no longer see them as desirable. Or, even worse, they will come under her control, which is unmanly (O'Neil, 1982). If they appear to be too responsive to a woman's demands because of their emotional dependency, their peers label them with derogatory terms in an effort to refocus them on what is important to manhood, that is, autonomy. Therefore men both desire the woman's nurturance and rebel against it.

In our clinical experience, we often see that the woman who has been taught to nurture may enjoy that role to a point, unless she begins to feel she is carrying all the weight and getting nothing in return. Although she enjoys the role of confidante and supporter, at the same time she wants her protector and provider to do his job: protect and provide. And while he is at it, she would appreciate a little nurturance from him. However, many times men cannot reciprocate with nurturance, having been taught to fix problems with action, rather than with words.

These contradictory desires within the woman seem as conflictual as the man's desire to be nurtured but remain strong and independent. In other words, a man can be strong and independent but enjoy being nurtured, whereas a woman can enjoy providing emotional nurturance, want to be protected, and still be an independent individual. When both partners are able to maintain a balance in the traditionally male and female aspects of their personalities, they understand that what appears contradictory is not contradictory at all. It is not an either/or proposition, but rather a both/and situation.

Man as Provider, Woman as Homemaker

Career as Obligation for Man, Housework Optional

Many young adults today would say that they no longer view the man as the primary provider for the young couple, that making money to support them is a cooperative enterprise (Bernard, 1981b). And with so many dual-career couples, indeed it is. However, in many subtle ways one can easily detect the traces of the old value system that divided the tasks of financially supporting the family and doing the necessary domestic labor to maintain a home between the sexes. Although this is evident in some of the internal conflicts the relationship pioneers experience when there is a role reversal, it becomes clearly manifest when children enter into the equation. It is also clear in the judgments (both formal and informal) made by the larger society on the individuals involved.

A number of years ago a study conducted at Yale and Harvard Universities (Bennett, 1986) created an uproar among single women in the United States. This was partially due to the distortion by the media of the results, which is not an uncommon occurrence. The hypothesis of the study (Faludi, 1991) was that because women tended to marry men 3 to 4 years older than themselves (a trend that was already changing at the time) and there were fewer men available in that age range (at the particular time the study was done), there would be a reduction in the opportunities for marriage for these women. As it turned out there were many criticisms of the study that essentially invalidated the results, but the message that reached the public was that unmarried women over 30 had very little chance of getting married, particularly successful, educated women. One implication was that if a woman was bright and financially independent, no man would want her. Although there are some men who are threatened and uncomfortable with successful women, this was not even a factor investigated by the researchers. Additional studies (Farrell, 1987) did indicate, however, that successful women were often interested in marrying men who were even more successful than themselves. Considering this criterion, the higher up the career ladder a woman got, the smaller became the pool of eligible men. According to these results, although a woman does not expect the man to be the only breadwinner in the family, she still thinks he should be as or more successful than she is. And men also often feel like a failure if they do not make as much money as their wives. Although they may talk a good equality game, both sexes have absorbed the notion that the man should provide for his family, and many become uncomfortable when that is not the case (Bernard, 1981b; Deaux & Hanna, 1984; Gould, 1974).

By itself, a couple might come to grips with the old messages and rewrite the rules. But, unfortunately, no couple is an island unto itself. Relatives, friends, the workplace, and even the court system continue to deluge the couple with the old value system. A husband who is not working outside the home and "allowing" his wife to support him receives many subtle and sometimes direct messages regarding his failure to be a real man. After all, a man is his work (David & Brannon, 1976). That is how he has been defined for the last few centuries. Most of our interviews with men of working age indicate that they feel an obligation to provide for their families, especially when there are dependent children involved. Although they often support the idea of their wives working and even appreciate the help, they see it as just that—help. They believe, sometimes resentfully, that their wives have a choice they don't have—to work outside the home full time, to work part-time and stay home part-time, or simply to stay home and be a homemaker (Farrell, 1987). Interestingly enough, recent research on career women indicates that they are much more likely than men to change jobs if they do not feel fulfilled in their work or do not like the work atmosphere (Gallos, 1989). Although one conclusion might be that women are more sensitive to the work environment than men, this does not seem to be the only factor involved. Instead, it appears that married men with children feel a greater obligation to endure a negative work environment in order to provide for their families, and will often base their career decisions on how much money they can make, rather than whether they like what they do. Although the study did not look at differences between single women who were the sole support of the family and women who were married or had no children, it is likely that a similar result would be found for any adult who was the only source of support for the family. But for purposes of this discussion, the results of this study support the notion that women who are married feel a greater freedom with regard to career choices than do men. Simply put, society does not expect them to carry the burden of financial support if they have an able-bodied husband around.

In the experience of the authors, many family courts still base their appraisal of a father's worth on whether or not he supports his family, not whether he can change a diaper. On the other hand, women are judged by their childrearing abilities. Some women who are successful in their career or schoolwork and hire babysitters to take care of their children may even be considered neglectful and lose custody ("Public Eye," *Time*, March 20, 1995). The father who does the same is making the best of a difficult situation. Clearly society continues to endorse the idea of man as provider.

Homemaking as Obligation for Women, Career Optional

Obviously the corollary to the principle of husband as provider is wife as homemaker. Today women make up 46% of the total workforce (Noble, 1993). And yet, in spite of the fact that, in two-parent families, 71% of mothers are employed outside the home (Hoffman, 1989), the vast majority of housework is still relegated to the wife in the family, as was clearly documented in Hochschild's (1989) *The Second Shift*. Many men simply do not see dusting, vacuuming, scrubbing toilets and bathtubs, washing dishes, doing laundry and ironing as their job. Sometimes even when men help with the housework, wives continue to carry executive responsibility over the home, deciding what needs to be done and when, parceling out jobs to their husbands. Cooking, which some men regard as a creative hobby and respect as appropriate work for a man, is often the woman's responsibility on a daily basis. She most likely must plan the meals, shop for the groceries, and provide the basic three meals a day for the family, whereas men prefer to grill out or cook gourmet meals on special occasions. (See Division of Labor Within the Home, later this chapter for further discussion of this issue.)

Of course, the fact that women make 75 cents on the dollar for the same work as men (Decade of the Woman, 1992) is a disincentive for any couple to support the woman's career if it will in any way inconvenience the smooth running of the home. For example, when a woman wishes to contribute to the family income and finds that the cost of child care is half her salary and that she will still have to do all the housework after working an 8-hour day (Hochschild, 1989), it is easy to see how she might get discouraged or how her working might come to be seen as a futile enterprise. The economic system does not encourage the wife as provider or career person.

DIFFICULTIES OF DUAL-CAREER FAMILIES

In the last decade more and more families can be classified as two-earner families. Only 7% of American families consist of the unemployed house-wife and employed husband with two children that was prevalent among the middle-class during the 1950s. The stereotypical expectations that evolved during the period of time when gender roles were clearly divided between workplace and home still influence the thinking of modern cou-ples who face an entirely different set of circumstances. Because of this, conflicts about the division of labor are particularly stressful in the cou-ples we see in our practices today. Of course, not all couples are caught in power struggles over who does the housework or cares for the children. Many young couples have been flexible in their role definitions and have formed an equitable partnership. Nevertheless, for many families, issues of career importance, labor division within the home, and care of chil-dren are salient.

Which Career Is More Important

One of the most difficult issues with which dual-career couples must come to grips is locating in an area where both partners can continue to advance in their careers (Sekaran, 1986). In the past, the wife followed her husband wherever his career took him, which short-circuited any chance for her to build a career of her own. Today, couples often com-promise by, for instance, taking turns, or insisting that a company find a good position for the spouse, or going where the partner who makes the most money needs to go. Many patriarchal companies still punish employees, male or female, who do not put their company first above their relationship in cases of relocation by failing to promote them, clearly endorsing the notion of a one-bread-winner family (Pleck, 1993; F. Schwartz, 1989). Although these companies are motivated by a bot-tom-line mentality rather than a particular choice of male or female provider, their position nevertheless has the effect of contributing to the reinforcement of the one-primary-provider-per-family ideal.

Division of Labor Within the Home

One of the most common conflicts experienced by young, dual-career couples involves the maintenance and cleaning of the home in the hours after work. Many men resist the idea of doing housework, partly because there exists a belief based on their gender socialization that housework is beneath them; they may believe that they are not as good at it as women, or they may not find it a lot of fun. Many men today were raised by full-time homemakers who saw to it that their bedrooms were clean, clothes were washed, and meals were made, and that the house they lived in was orderly and well-kept. Men often have not been trained to see the defects in a dirty home because they have not been expected to take on those chores as children. Therefore, even when men do help out with housework, the woman takes executive responsibility; that is, she is the one who assigns tasks and decides what needs to be done and when (Hochschild, 1989). It is often helpful to point out to frustrated women that men are more likely to take executive responsibility for the yard, the cars, and the maintenance on the outside of the house because they have been trained by their traditional-role fathers so to do. Lack of attention to housework is not merely obstinacy of the part of their husbands, but a matter of early training. It is illuminating to some women to discover that due to their own early training they are not as willing to attend to trimming the hedges or painting the garage as they are to dusting the furniture.

If a man notices that something in the home needs to be done and waits for his wife to do it or points it out to her, this may be a product of the socialization messages he has received regarding man's work and woman's work. Most men are less reluctant to cut the grass, get the oil changed in the car, fix broken appliances, take down storm windows, put up the screens, take out the garbage, and vacuum the swimming pool. And in fact, in our clinical experience, female clients often expect their spouses to know how to do these things and are disappointed if that is not the case. In other words, the male/female division of labor between the inside and outside of the home, between labor supposedly requiring physical strength and mechanical ability and that which does not, seems alive and well.

When men are actively engaged in some form of home maintenance, even that labelled as masculine work, women are likely to feel more supported and part of a team. It is most likely that when the husband has time to watch television after work and she must cook dinner, do the dishes, put the children to bed, and finish the laundry that the inequity of the workload becomes overwhelming. Many men believe their wives have standards of cleanliness that are too high, having been trained by full-time homemakers who could maintain such standards and still have some time for leisure activities. Obviously one solution to this problem would be to lower those standards. Secondly women often define themselves through their homemaking skills and do not accept their husbands' contributions when they are forthcoming. Frequently they will criticize the way a husband has done some task, which serves to discourage further efforts on his part. In our experience, we see that often the male contribution to this dance is a curious inability to do a task well which does not require any skills he hasn't used in other settings (i.e., cleaning his automobile).

On the other hand, there are men who, because of their own need for cleanliness and order and their childhood training, contribute equally to the housework without monitoring or nagging. The fact that they exist gives hope to the multitude of women who feel desperately overworked, putting in approximately 80 hours of work a week (Hochschild, 1989) and, at the same time, supports the notion that early training and socialization lie at the root of the problem rather than some innate, biological drive. (As an aside, it is suggestive that Gottman [1991] found a positive correlation between men who did housework and men whose marriages were happy and long-lasting.)

At one time the division of labor between provider and homemaker made sense, at least in terms of the amount of energy and time each put into the partnership. At the time of the Industrial Revolution, men were pulled out of the home to work and women were left in charge of the hearth (Bernard, 1981b). However, one clear message coming from the women's movement was that housework and child care were not part of the gross national product and therefore not valued and that women would only be treated with respect when they made equal money (Friedan, 1963).

Indeed recent research shows that women who work have increased power and influence in their marriages and higher levels of self-esteem (Betz & Fitzgerald, 1987). Nevertheless, men, who did not ask that their wives go to work, continue to prefer the old division of labor that results in the second shift for women (Hochschild, 1989).

Taking Care of the Children

The fact that men expect women to be the homemaker becomes even clearer when children are introduced to the picture (Hochschild, 1989; Jump & Haas, 1987; P. Schwartz, 1994). In spite of the fact that men are expressing much greater interest in being involved in the raising of their children than in past decades, many men still feel uncomfortable caring for and holding a newborn infant. Research (Schwartz, 1994) shows also that men are less comfortable with their daughters than with their sons, even when the children are old enough to talk to and participate in games. According to Schwartz, the reason for this is that men, not having had the experience of being a little girl, are not sure how to relate to her. They often regard infancy and the raising of the opposite gender as a mysterious province of the female world (Schwartz, 1994). Many traditional fathers believe that women have more patience and understanding to deal with a child's world, and seem unaware that she too might feel frustrated, bored, or stymied. In clinical practice, we have often encountered families in which the woman has had difficulty dealing with child behavior and the husband's response is to lecture her rationally about what needs to be done, implying that she has failed somehow as a woman because she can't handle her children. In these cases, the husband usually does not take over the responsibility but, however, if he attempts to, the woman feels even worse—as though she is inadequate. After all, they both believe she is supposed to know how to raise children automatically. On the other hand, a traditional man, suddenly tossed into the mother's usual parenting role who struggles with caring for his children, is often seen by others as a hero, someone very special who is able to function outside his normal domain, because traditional lore holds that children are a woman's territory, not a man's.

For a variety of reasons, the younger generations appear to be doing a better job of sharing parenting than previous generations. Research (Levinson et al., 1978) indicates that as men age, they become more interested in developing close ties with their families and become less concerned with success in business, either because they have already done well, or they are looking outside of their careers for gratification. Others (Friedan, 1993; Neugarten, 1964, 1968) believe that as men and women reach midlife, they get more in touch with the aspects of their personality that are generally associated with the opposite gender. Regardless of the reason, many men in earlier generations since the Industrial Revolution became aware of the fact that they not only were isolated from their families because of their devotion to work, but that they didn't even have the relationship skills they needed to try to connect. Seeing their fathers feeling cut off and lonely as they aged, and feeling the loss of a present father during their childhood, young men have become much more interested in building close relationships with their children (Kimmel, 1987; Levant & Kelley, 1989). Young fathers now participate in the birthing process and are encouraged and supported by new socialization messages to take a major role in parenting from infancy through childhood. Additionally, due to the high divorce rate in the United States, many single fathers have developed a new sort of relationship with their children that is not mediated by the mother. In response to these trends and contributing to their continuation, parenting courses for fathers (Levant & Kelley, 1989) have sprung up all over the country.

In the last decade, fathers have been encouraged to be in the delivery room, to hold the baby and care for it immediately after birth, to be involved in taking the child to the pediatrician, to participate in school conferences, and to be active in the daily care of the child in order to enhance bonding (Jump & Haas, 1987; Levant, 1994; Levant & Kelley, 1989; Pleck, 1987). This has been somewhat successful for the younger generation. Unfortunately, being an involved father is not an easy task in our culture. Businesses may not look kindly on a man or a woman who puts the family first. Interruptions to the workday due to the illness of a child or attendance of a school conference are frowned on if the employee is a woman, but intolerable for a man (Gerson, 1993; Pleck, 1993; Schwartz, 1994). When employers and colleagues alike consider men who prefer to be involved in the daily activities of their children at the expense of their work schedule as "slackers" or otherwise ridicule them, the pressure on men to devote their entire lives to earning money increases.

At the same time, the pressure on women to stay home and take care of their children is equally strong. Society is not reluctant to condemn a woman who puts more effort into her career than she does child care ("Public Eye," *Time*, March 20, 1995). In recent political discussions of family values, there have been some calls for a return to the days when mothers stayed at home, implying that much of the perceived deterioration in societal values is due to mother absence in the home. In much the same way that many psychological theories overemphasized maternal influence in a child's life (see chapter 1), conventional social wisdom holds that if a family has problems, the mother's neglect is at the root. It is assumed that a real woman will want to be with her children; a real man will want to provide for them financially.

Occasionally, a man would prefer to reverse roles, staying home with the child while his wife supports the family. When a husband expresses this desire, he may run into major objections from his wife. She could cite his higher income as the reason for her staying home, but in many cases she too believes it is her prerogative to take care of the children. This also becomes clear in cases in which a man takes initiative in disciplining or otherwise caring for his children and the woman feels that her territory has been threatened or goes so far as to sabotage the efforts the father has made. Although women and men may give lip-service to the need for two involved parents, they both are likely to let Mom do it. Just as men have traditionally identified themselves through their work, women have identified themselves through their children, and that unconscious claim to the child care territory does not die easily.

Despite recent changes in attitudes toward parenting, women and men are still struggling with the inability of corporate America to provide the kind of child care and flex-time necessary for the working parent (Silverstein, 1991). Because it is such a complex and costly issue for business, progress in that area is slow, but at least the issue is now in the public awareness. In the meantime, when a parent must take time off work to parent, socialization messages say that it is usually the mother who is expected to do so. This can be an area of conflict for young couples, as the man feels the pressure to succeed as the primary provider and she resents the implication that her career and work are less important. On the other hand, many women wish for an extended postpartum leave and feel pressured to return to work prematurely, struggling against a strong urge to stay home while the child is young. The husband may resent it when women have the choice to stay home with a child, which he may not even express because of society's pressures on him to provide. The internal confusion this issue creates for both spouses can also put strains on the relationship. Allowing both husband and wife to express their internal conflicts in an accepting, nonblaming atmosphere, opens the way for creative problem-solving. Focusing the couple on forming a united front against a system that does not usually support family issues and child care over business interests can do a great deal to prevent their blaming one another when this conflict occurs.

WHY GENDER EXPECTATIONS CLASH

Why *do* gender expectations clash? The problem is manifold. First of all most men and women are not aware of how very differently they have been socialized. Although they probably know vaguely that men and women are different, they do not anticipate all the clashes resulting from their gender training. Men and women basically expect to get the same kind of understanding and responses from the other gender as they get from their same-sex friends. They do not enter marriage expecting to be disappointed and frustrated by reactions that do not make sense to them.

Secondly, women and men are often unconscious of many of their expectations about marriage, even those stereotypical expectations delineated earlier in this chapter. They may be especially unaware of the emotional power of age-old rules and taboos regarding the roles and behavior of men and women, even when they intellectually disagree with them.

And, by definition, men and women are not conscious of the underlying dynamics that may have been passed down through the family projection process or that they may be unconsciously working out through projective identification. So, in many cases, married men and women simply do not know what they are getting into.

However, even when they are fully cognizant of some of the things they do want from their relationship and their spouse, couples very rarely talk about these things before marriage. Part of the reason for this is that they may not want to risk conflict around hot issues, even though those very issues have the potential to create the most open conflict once they have settled into the marriage routine. The topics that can often create conflict as a couple adjusts to the marital union revolve around sex, religion, money, extended family, friends, time use, recreation, household maintenance, work, and children (Barragan, 1976; Sager, 1976). These are the issues that would be raised as a matter of course if a couple was to get some premarital counseling, but couples who are in love and feeling good about each other don't believe they need premarital counseling. They unrealistically believe that as long as they love each other, they will find solutions to the problems. Usually these hoped-for solutions require one spouse to give in to the other in order to avoid fighting, a situation that only leads to resentment and eventual corrosion of loving feelings.

Certainly not all of the conflict that occurs around these topics is gender based. In fact, much of the disagreement comes from differences in family-of-origin patterns, which may or may not follow traditional gender lines. However, as we have pointed out, expectations for women and men around many of these issues are different simply due to gender socialization. For example, as the reader will recall from the previously cited survey results, a fairly important requirement for women of a spouse was reported as the sharing of household chores and parenting, something none of the men mentioned. This is an issue that is very conscious, but avoided by couples, because of its potential for heated conflict. A concern mentioned by many men, but not by women, was their loss of freedom to have fun once the financial responsibility of marriage was upon them. This may be one of the major reasons men are uncomfortable committing to marriage, but it is not something they share with their potential spouses. Many do not share these thoughts because they don't want to appear "unmanly," because, after all, the provider role is a major component of manliness in our society. Unfortunately, couples often don't talk to each other about this or other important problems in their relationship.

The Role of the Family of Origin

Of course, the assumptions people have regarding relationships with the other gender are also very much influenced by their own particular set of experiences in life, especially their observations of the marital relationship between their parents in their family of origin. Family psychology has very clearly described the family projection process, multigenerational transmission process, and projective identification exchanges, which, unless recognized and corrected, produce generation after generation of similar marital relationships. One familiar example of this process is the daughter of an alcoholic who marries a man whose alcoholism is not apparent at first, but develops later, and who repeats her parents' marriage, despite her vows not to do so. Certainly this is not accidental but the result of unconscious processes and behavior patterns that determine the choices each partner makes (Bowen, 1978; Dicks, 1967; Scharff & Scharff, 1987).

Earlier in the chapter we delineated some of the more common expectations that men and women have of marriage and each other due to gender socialization. Which of these particular conflicts or relationship patterns a couple may be susceptible to depends a great deal on the relationship they observed between their mother and father. There are as many permutations of family relationship patterns and conflicts as there are families, even if most models are traditional. The great number of possible family influences makes it important to do a gender inquiry (described in chapter 8) with particular attention to specific family-of-origin messages with every couple who comes to therapy. For example, a woman whose father was unfaithful to her mother and left the family for a younger woman, may be particularly susceptible to concerns regarding her attractiveness and sexuality compared to that of other women. She may expect her husband to be unfaithful and act in insecure jealous ways that actually bring about what she fears most. The man who witnessed his father being constantly criticized and denigrated by his angry mother will be particularly sensitive to criticism and suggestions even if they are expressed softly. He may fear being dominated by a woman so much that he passive-aggressively resists any suggestion for compromise or engages in open conflict to that end. Although many of the themes are the same because they come from deep-rooted gender messages passed down throughout history, each marriage must be understood within the context of the individual families of origin and the projective identifications each partner uses.

On a more conscious level, however, men and women come to a heterosexual relationship hoping for the best and fearing the worst. What constitutes for them the best and the worst is a combination of dreams and fantasies arising from literature, television, movies, plays, magazines, and other media forms (Cantor, 1987); formal teachings of religion; and the actual models from people's life situations (Basow, 1986). Although these may be healthy and realistic models, they are more often detrimental both to the growth of the relationship and to the growth of the individuals within it. When a couple does not allow for possibilities other than those that feel familiar, they are in danger of living a life that may be plodding and stultifying, or worse, self-destructive. Only when people are open to new possibilities will they be able to develop vital, rewarding relationships.

Unplanned Role Reversal

Our clinical experience shows that most couples who marry are ignorant of potential clashes due to gender socialization are unconscious of their potential conflicts of expectation, and avoid existing areas of conflict that they do recognize. As if these stumbling blocks weren't bad enough, external events can often influence the couple in such a way as to cause a shift in the value system and expectations of one or the other spouse, which unbalances a once-unified marriage.

Perhaps the most dramatic of these shifts occurs when the primary breadwinner and protector (usually the male) in a traditional complementary marriage is by some accident, unable to work or care for himself. (See case example at the end of this chapter.) At a time like this, the spouse who had been in a dependent position must now take the responsibility for providing for the family, a role that brings with it many changes in behavior and thinking. Such a role reversal is sometimes even more difficult for the formerly independent provider than it is for the newly responsible spouse, especially when the former believes his masculinity depends on his provider and leadership roles in the family. A husband in this position may feel that a wife who no longer defers to his opinion, who no longer has time or energy to nurture him emotionally, whose work puts her in contact with other men who are not disabled, or who begins to get a sense of her ability to take care of herself is a wife who could choose to abandon him. Although the role of provider may have felt to an incapacitated husband at one time like an unfair duty, the power, security, and esteem that he experienced in that role are now gone. And on top of all of this, his gender expectations require that he be the boss, that he be in control of his wife and family, and that his wife play the submissive role. Similarly, his wife may feel angry that he has abandoned his primary role in the family and left her to struggle with the financial needs. Her gender expectations may have been that her husband would take care of her forever and he has not done so. Despite the fact that circumstances make it impossible for them to play out the expected roles, they may find themselves in conflict because their new positions do not feel right.

Another similar situation occurs with some frequency in this information age in which automation and immediate communication allow businesses to operate with fewer people. As a result, the middle-aged, high-income manager may be laid off before he can collect his pension; the effect of his unemployment on the middle-class marriage may be drastic. He finds himself suddenly in the position of not being able to find a job due to age discrimination and economy-minded businesses who believe he is overqualified and too expensive for their open positions. Whether or not his wife is employed, he has been the primary wage-earner, and the family's sudden loss of income takes its toll on the relationship, partly due to mutual expectations that he should provide for the family, and to the added stress of financial strain. Again shifts in roles with their accompanying changes in behaviors and perceptions clash with long-standing gender expectations, resulting in conflict, depression, and often dissolution of the relationship.

Cognitive Shift

A different type of disruptive influence results when outside forces cause a cognitive shift that brings with it a change in values, behaviors, goals, communication styles, and attitudes in one of the spouses. This was the case with the women's movement, which has had a powerful impact on the thinking of millions of women in the United States over the last 30 years. It appeared to many men and the larger culture in general, although there is much evidence to the contrary (Friedan, 1963; Lewis et al., 1976), that women who had once been "perfectly contented" as homemakers and mothers suddenly became dissatisfied with their roles and began to branch out by returning to school, going to work, putting off having children or not having them at all, preferring to cohabitate with a significant other rather than commit to marriage, lashing out at men whom they perceived to be sexist, competing with men for positions of power, and in general disrupting the American status quo. For the man and woman who married under the traditional contract of the 1950s, this change in her often felt like a betrayal to him. Suddenly all of the gender expectations that they both had taken for granted at marriage were discarded by her, leaving them confused, hurt, and angry. Many men resisted the new demands place on them and struggled to restore the status quo. Clearly, a major clash in gender expectations created chaos in interpersonal relationships.

In the generation since the women's movement, many young women have absorbed, with some mellowing, the new feminist attitudes. However, many of the young men who have had confused and frustrated fathers as role models have not caught up with this change in society. For this reason, many of today's marriages struggle with the new woman and the confused man suffering from gender role strain (Pleck, 1981).

The Parental Emergency

New women also suffer from gender role strain in the wake of the feminist movement. Women who crave a marriage that combines career and motherhood may feel oppressed when they consider the possible consequences of staying home with a newborn child. From their point of view, loss of income and delay in career advancement due to temporary absence from work is equivalent to a loss of power in the relationship. This creates internal conflict for the woman who prefers to stay at home with her child, but is afraid of what that might mean in terms of the relationship.

There are numerous other cases to consider. For instance, some husbands do not want their wives to stop working and have children because they are afraid of the deepening commitment accompanying the arrival of children. Such a man wants a "boy marriage" in which all of her attention is focused on him. In this case, he uses her desire for a career to avoid having to share her with children and face the fears of responsibility and sacrifice that come with parenthood.

The gender clashes in the modern marriages do not involve a sense of betrayal, as do those in which one member of a traditional marriage has decided to change the rules. Gender clashes in modern marriages are more of a process of evolution. That is, both genders are making an effort to find new ways of relating in response to the gender revolution and do not have much of a roadmap to follow. Nevertheless, gender clashes often bring couples into therapy as they struggle to find solutions to the conflict.

Gender Politics

The women's and men's movements both have been formed in response to perceived injustices and inequities in the present structure of our society. Their primary goal is to further the psychological and social understanding and to improve the political status of the gender each represents. In that process, both groups sometimes lock horns, each seeing the other as the oppressor or abuser who must be changed or controlled. The inflammatory rhetoric, statistics, and advice often escalate conflict in male/female relationships. In an effort to make sweeping sociological changes, both genders are sometimes encouraged to take aggressive, almost militant stances on conflictual issues, rather than trying to understand and consort with the "enemy." This becomes quite problematic when a man and woman wish to resolve issues revolving around gender in order to reduce conflict and build a warmer, more intimate relationship. Because they are encouraged to do so by their same sex friends, the media, the organized gendered political groups, some men and women find themselves in entrenched positions, escalating a disagreement into a major disruption of their relationship rather than looking for common ground. This is tragic for the couple, because many times they truly want their relationship to work, but cannot see their way around the political stances they have taken in order to compromise.

The politics of gender also affect the therapist. Although we therapists endorse a belief in neutrality in therapy, in reality none of us is truly neutral. Very few therapists, for example, can feel neutral when we see a child beaten to death by a parent, no matter how much we understand that the parent was also an abused child and has no emotional resources or parenting skills to help him/her deal with the demanding child. The case is the same with gender issues. If the therapist feels the structure of society is truly harmful to one gender or the other, she or he will be hard-pressed to prevent that prejudice from seeping into the therapy. Indeed, the feminist critique essentially requests the therapist to bring up issues in such a way as to open up the possibility for societal change, which is an extension of the belief that the personal is the political. Although the men's movement has not yet resulted in a similar demand in support of men's issues, it has at least called our attention to issues of unfairness to men in our society. The only gender-neutral stance in our view, is to make our clients aware of both sides of an issue in a balanced manner, promoting an understanding that neither gender has total power nor takes total responsibility for the injustices that exist today (Pittman, 1985). By helping our clients walk in the shoes of the other and discover the role that each plays in maintaining the status quo, we can lead them to the common ground that will allow them to solve their own problems without merely endorsing the political platform of either gender.

FOLLOWER/LEADER OR PARTNERSHIP?

The therapist who is fully cognizant of the advantage and detriments of traditional roles in a relationship will be able to help his/her clients understand that with privilege comes responsibility. For every positive aspect of a particular role, there also exist negatives. The therapist can guide women and men in an exploration of the pros and cons of various potential roles they could play in their marriage, allowing them to decide for themselves what will best serve their needs—gaining informed consent, so to speak.

For example, the woman who expects her husband to fulfill the protector and provider role without taking on any of those responsibilities herself must be aware that certain consequences accompany that position. If she is unwilling to take the responsibility for providing for herself and taking care of her family, she is in a dependent position. Such a position requires playing the role of follower, deferring to the preferences and decisions of the leader. This is how the traditional marriage worked, often to the detriment of the mental health of the woman, who did not feel she was taken seriously (Chesler, 1972; Gove, 1972, 1979, 1980; Gove & Tudor, 1973). Many young women believe they should be heard and their opinions considered, but sometimes they also believe they should be supported financially and protected. They are still operating somewhat under the old exchange of beauty and sex in return for financial security. Many young men have come to expect the woman to carry her share of the financial burden and may begin to feel resentful if her offering is only her beauty. The old balance may be restored with the birth of children, if the wife does all of the housework and cares for the children. Nevertheless, she may expect the patriarchal attitude of the traditional husband who considers himself the head of the house if she plays the traditional wife/mother role. Her contribution to the relationship is to meet the needs of her husband and children in return for financial support.

On the other hand, the man who wishes his wife to be a major contributor to the financial security of the family must be aware that he then must shoulder a share of the housekeeping and child care responsibilities as well as consider her wishes in decision-making. He may have trouble accepting the fact that she may openly disagree with him and sometimes act in a unilateral manner. She may accept a job, for example, that takes her away from her family and he may have to provide the child care that she cannot. She may purchase something she likes without asking him his opinion. She may do as he stereotypically does, occasionally choosing to do something for herself instead of always deferring to the needs of the relationship. Likewise, the woman who wishes to take equal part in making decisions regarding the couple's life together must also be willing to take the lead, to make suggestions, to take risks, and to take responsibility when something goes wrong.

For women and men who have not had models of flexible, cooperative, and equal relationships, creating a balanced partnership feels very strange. They have to make up the rules for themselves while struggling with the internal conflicts generated from past models. Systemic family therapists often refer to expanding the cognitive map that clients bring to therapy in order to help them find possible solutions to the dilemmas they are facing. When we inform our clients of the effects of gender expectation on their thinking, we, in effect, remove the blindfold from their eyes and expand their cognitive map. The following case history is an example of how the messages absorbed through gender socialization can blind a couple to the resolution. This case example illustrates the role a therapist can play in facilitating a resolution to conflicts rooted in gender socialization by removing the gender blindfold.

CASE EXAMPLE

Jo, age 40, and Andy, age 47, had been married for 20 years. During the first 11 years of their marriage, they both worked in the electronics business Andy had established, having built the business together. They worked well together and found a certain synergy coming out of their interactions at work and the success the business was showing. They each spoke with respect and admiration of the abilities and contributions of the other in building the company. They travelled extensively during those years, mostly in the Caribbean, where they both enjoyed scuba diving, boating, and just lying in the sun. They had a passionate and rewarding sex life. They described their marriage during those years as vital, exciting, and extremely satisfying.

When Jo was 31-years-old the couple decided it was time to have a family. Both sets of parents had been pressing them for some time about their desire for grandchildren, and although their lives seemed full and happy, both Andy and Jo had assumed that someday they would have children. The business was doing well and Andy felt he could hire someone to handle Jo's role at work so that she would be able to stay home and care for a baby. The fact that Jo would quit work and raise a family was accepted by both of them without question because both had come from traditional families in which the father went to work and the mother played the role of housekeeper.

Andy and Jo had two children, both boys, two years apart. Shortly after the birth of the second child, Andy was in an automobile accident and broke his back. Although, fortunately, he did not lose the use of any of his limbs, he suffers from severe back pain most of the time. Because of the pain he is less mobile than he used to be and has gained a great deal of weight that exacerbates the back pain. About once every 6 months, Andy is confined to bed for about 5 days, unable to move. The doctors originally gave him pain medication, but he has tried not to use that very often because he is aware he could become addicted. He does use muscle relaxants and is very careful not to do anything that triggers his pain. He no longer engages in many of the physical activities Jo and he used to pursue as hobbies. Worse yet, sexual intercourse has become extremely painful for him, regardless of position. The exertion sex requires and even the pleasure of orgasm is marred most of the time by muscle spasms in his back, which do not subside for several days. He, quite understandably, has lost interest in sex. Jo, however, is still very much interested and misses their active sex life. She finds it hard to believe that Andy no longer enjoys sex because of the pain. Instead she thinks that he finds her unattractive now because she too has gained a little weight and, at 40, does not look like the sexy woman he married. In reality, Jo is attractive, despite being somewhat plump. Andy is quite overweight, however, and very gray, but has a pleasant smile.

At the time the couple came to marital therapy, the boys were 8 and 6. They were both very active, dynamic children like their parents. They tended to get into mischief constantly and both challenged Jo's authority daily. The children were doing good work in school, had many friends, and engaged in numerous activities. They were basically healthy normal children. Jo often found herself frustrated by the children and yelled at them a lot. She did not think this was a bad thing. Her mother had yelled at her. She was also annoyed with Andy because he did not seem to notice the bad things the boys did and was more upset with her for yelling than with the boys for their behavior. Jo was an only child raised by her mother and had little experience with little boys. Andy, on the other hand, was the oldest boy of four and had helped take care of his brothers when he was a child. His father had died when he was only 10, and he had become the "little man" of the family. He saw his sons' behavior as normal and acceptable and rarely raised his voice at them.

They came to therapy at Jo's urging because she was feeling depressed. She no longer felt loved and appreciated by Andy and, in fact, felt the whole family sided against her. She felt inadequate as a mother because the boys were always testing her and Andy seemed to think she yelled too much. His constant advice to her to relax felt to her like he didn't support her as a parent. She also knew Andy suffered a lot of pain and felt guilty for being angry with him much of the time. But the truth was that she did not like her lot in life anymore and blamed a great deal of that on Andy's disability. When Jo was feeling particularly frustrated and unappreciated, she would begin to confront Andy regarding his lack of interest in her sexually, which would cause him to withdraw, becoming a "couch potato" and watching the "boob tube" incessantly.

For his part, Andy only wanted her to be happy so he could have peace and quiet. He felt inadequate because he could no longer perform sexually in a manner that was satisfying to Jo. In fact, he avoided physical contact and affectionate embraces altogether so that Jo would not get her hopes up. He still went to work every day although sitting at his desk triggered pain and he no longer enjoyed the work. He wished he could spend more time with the boys because he had missed having a father and wanted that for his children. He expressed concern that his wife took the kids too seriously and let them upset her. He felt that she was a good mother, but just didn't know what to do with boys. Because he was gone most of the day and in pain at night when he got home, he did not do much to help Jo with the boys or the housework.

Although a great deal of the marital unhappiness expressed by Andy and Jo in therapy was due to the difficult adjustments they had had to make because of Andy's accident, there were some fairly obvious options which they had failed to see due to the messages of gender socialization. Before the birth of their children and before his accident, Jo and Andy had both felt good about themselves and each other. They were both competent in the workplace and as spouses. They had given each other a great deal of reinforcement and appreciation. Both of them now felt inadequate performing the traditional roles they had assumed. Andy wished he no longer had to work because he wanted to spend time with his boys and felt guilty for feeling that way. He also felt like he was no longer a real man because he couldn't satisfy his wife sexually. Jo felt like a failure as a mother because raising the boys was not "a piece of cake." She thought motherhood should come naturally to her because she was female. She also felt inadequate as a woman because she didn't seem to be able to stimulate Andy sexually. She was afraid her relationship would turn out like her parents' marriage—essentially a sexually dead companionship. She missed terribly the easy affection they had once shown to one another and blamed that on her "fading beauty." She also felt that she should be able to adjust to Andy's disability because he couldn't help it. The fact that she found the adjustment depressingly difficult made her feel a failure once again, because a good wife wouldn't ask to have her own needs met. She should accept her lot graciously because it was not as bad as experiencing physical back pain.

The gender messages abound in this case. This was a couple who had once had a very vital relationship and still had love and respect for one another. They had many good relationship skills that made them easy to work with. The use of gender inquiry and an exploration of the gender messages they had received throughout their lives allowed them to recognize the distorted thinking that made them both feel bad about themselves. Andy's negative evaluation of himself as a man based on his inability to bring his wife to orgasm with vaginal intercourse came from the messages he had received, particularly from the media, regarding the man's need to have an erection and perform the sex act in a traditional manner. Jo's belief that Andy's lack of interest in sex was due to her lack of physical attractiveness was a result of messages she had received regarding her responsibility for keeping the man interested and the importance of beauty to all men. Andy came to understand that Jo needed his touches and pets more than sexual intercourse and that by avoiding touching her, he actually increased her anxiety and unhappiness. He also began to compliment her on her appearance as he once had so that she would realize she had not lost her beauty. The combination of his displays of affection and attention to her looks increased her confidence in her ability to attract him and she stopped berating him about their lack of sex. Together they explored various positions and methods of sexual stimulation that might bring Jo some satisfaction. Jo stopped expecting Andy to get the same joy out of sex he once had, recognizing that he truly had painful spasms brought on by sexual excitement and started seeing his attempts to please her as acts of love. Andy was able to stop thinking about sex in terms of his performance and switch into a mode of mutual pleasuring, and was able to relax and actually enjoy their interactions.

Once Jo and Andy accepted the idea that raising children can be taxing and that women did not have a corner on the patience market, they were able to dispassionately look at how their individual experiences as children had prepared them to be parents. Jo, as an only child raised basically by her mother, had little understanding of what is expected behavior for boys. Furthermore, Jo's mother had demonstrated a model of parenting in which yelling was not only permissible but encouraged as the only means of discipline. Andy, on the other hand, knew what it was to be a boy and accepted the level of activity and noise that Jo found intolerable. In his family of origin, especially after the death of his father, parenting focused on the big things like providing food, shelter, protection, and love, rather than teaching children to put away their toys and eat the proper food. In some ways, he realized, he was probably over-indulgent with his children because of his childhood experience. When Jo stopped feeling like a failure simply because her boys challenged her, she was able to admit that she really wished she could go back to work part-time and share the parenting role more with Andy. This came as a pleasant surprise to Andy. It was something that he really wanted, but had felt it was his duty, as a man, to support the family completely as long as there were dependent children in the home. Because she knew the business well, Jo was able to start back to work part-time in their electronics business while Andy stayed home a few days a week with the boys. She found that when she had relief from them occasionally, she had much more patience with their boyish antics. Andy found, conversely, that when he was with them all day long, they sometimes got on his nerves, too. Now that they were sharing the parenting role, they were able to commiserate about the negatives and share the positives as a team. Andy was very happy not to have to go to work every day and greatly appreciated, as he once had, Jo's ability to spell him there.

The former sense of partnership and personal adequacy returned to their relationship and they were able to deal with the difficult adjustments to Andy's back injury with renewed hope. Jo was able to give herself permission to feel frustrated and deprived and still not blame Andy for it. She stopped adding insult to injury by no longer feeling guilty when she wanted their old life back. Indeed Andy also wanted it back. Gradually they were able to find ways of making their lives more satisfying despite his limited physical abilities. Rather than blaming themselves for being inadequate and attacking the other verbally, they supported each other in the face of challenges and found mutually satisfying solutions. They began to feel good about themselves and their relationship once more.

CONCLUSION: COPING WITH THE SOCIAL REVOLUTION

The clients we see today in our offices are living through a dramatic transitional period in family relationships. Some will have had both the luxury and pain of receiving and accepting clear gender messages regarding the roles they were expected to play and the advantages and disadvantages of these positions. Some will have rebelled against those very messages and may, like the adolescent, declare that red is green merely to define themselves as different from what they perceive as a totally detrimental arrangement between the genders. Others will have been raised by parents who, while struggling not to pass on the traditional values with which they disagreed, have failed to provide a replacement that is workable. Still others, the relationship pioneers of our age, will be attempting to create new, flexible methods of cohabitation with the other gender and find themselves struggling not only with the broader culture, but with surprising internal conflicts. No matter what their stage of development, these clients will have been strongly influenced by the gender socialization process we have described in Part I of this book. They all will benefit from an exploration of the gender expectations they each bring to the relationship as well as a conscious understanding of how these expectations affect their interaction. In Part II, we elaborate on the therapeutic interventions that we have found to be effective in accomplishing this daunting task.

PART TWO

Gender-Sensitive Interventions and Techniques

6

Gender-Sensitive Psychotherapy

The escalation of the battle of the sexes in the wake of the feminist movement can be viewed as *schismogenesis* (Bateson, 1935; Simon, Stierlin, & Wynne, 1985): a polarization on issues between the sexes in which each side becomes so invested in converting the other to the "right way" that any hope for resolution is lost. A second-order change is required to release the couple from their entrenched positions and enrich their cognitive maps enough to offer a two-winner approach. In systems theory, *first-order change* is defined as a change in the system that does not alter the structure. First-order changes follow the rules, so to speak. *Second-order change*, on the other hand, is defined as a change in the rules governing a system's structure, so that the structure itself changes (Watzlawick, Weakland, & Fisch, 1974). Rather than seeing the other gender as the enemy and feeling the need to justify the "right way" of being to one another, the genders must come to understand that they are both negatively affected by rigid gender socialization. The enemy, if one exists, is not the other gender but the inflexibility of gender messages that do not allow for growth. The instrument of second-order change suggested here is systemically defined gender-sensitive psychotherapy.

Gender-sensitive psychotherapy is the valuable by-product of the feminist critique of psychology and family therapy. It is frequently misunderstood as therapy that is sensitive to women's issues, although that alone was never the intent. In this chapter, we define gender-sensitive psychotherapy systemically; that is, the therapist must be aware of both men's and women's issues that might influence the effectiveness and outcome of psychotherapy. In the following pages, we discuss the most important concepts and principles of systemically defined gender-sensitive psychotherapy and introduce the techniques and interventions we have found to be most effective.

The Division of Family Psychology of the American Psychological Association has developed a list of requirements that therapists must meet if they wish to do gender-sensitive psychotherapy (Philpot & Brooks, 1988). According to these guidelines, gender-sensitive therapists

- Are knowledgeable about the differing perceptions of reality for men and women growing out of biological differences, male–female developmental theory, socialization in a capitalist–patriarchal society, value systems, levels of moral development, role definitions, and real power differentials in the political, economic, and legal arenas.
- Understand the implications of the current literature in women's studies, men's studies, and gender-difference research.
- Are familiar with the theoretical bases for understanding gender differences and are aware of the uses and limitations of the theories.
- Impose no limits on the roles to be played by males or females and impose no limits on the potential for growth by either sex.
- View the often predictable dichotomies of distancer–pursuer, expressive–instrumental, logic–emotion, and function–form as inevitable, but perhaps exaggerated, results of socialization rather than intrapsychic pathology.
- Approach therapy from as androgynous a perspective as possible, given the limitations of their own gender, maintaining an awareness of the special needs of men and women and of the techniques that will most facilitate treatment for each.

HALLMARKS OF GENDER-SENSITIVE PSYCHOTHERAPY

The preceding guidelines delineate only two of the necessary ingredients of effective gender-sensitive psychotherapy: (a) the psychotherapist's thorough knowledge of gender issues in our society and (b) his or her attitude regarding the freedom of the clients to break the rigid rules of gender socialization. For gender-sensitive couples therapy to be truly effective, the therapist must also educate the clients and facilitate their adoption of a similar nonblaming, flexible, and empathic attitude toward one another. This goal requires the clients to understand and accept several important concepts that might be considered the foundations of gender-sensitive psychotherapy. These include (a) the existence of a gender ecosystem, (b) the process of gender socialization, (c) androgyny, (d) empathic knowing, (e) gender coevolution, and (f) the gender-role journey.

The Effects of Gender Ecosystems

Therapists are generally familiar with systems theory and the process of socialization, but the clients frequently are not. It may be necessary to explain to them the meaning of the term *ecosystem*. Ecologists study the relations between living organisms and their environment. In sociology, *ecology* refers to the study of the relationships among the distribution of human groups with reference to material resources and the consequent social and cultural patterns. In family systems theory, a *system* refers to a group of interrelated individuals that has a boundary, like a family, a place of employment, or a school. Systems may be open or closed; that is, they may exchange information, energy, and material with the surrounding environment, or they may not interact at all with the surrounding environment.

When we speak of ecosystems, we are talking of large systems such as major religious, ethnic, or cultural groups that share beliefs, attitudes, expectations, and behaviors. The gender ecosystems are the largest and most basic of all ecosystems, because every individual belongs to one or the other. Gender is the first classification into which people are divided; it comes before age, ethnicity, religion, socioeconomic status, or any other category. Male and female gender ecosystems indoctrinate their members with values, expectations, and behaviors, many of which transcend even ethnic or national cultures. What we learn about how to be a man or a woman comes from these gender ecosystems interacting with one another. Men and women are indeed brought up in different worlds.

The Process of Gender Socialization and Its Results

In many cases, clients do not even recognize that there is any way of being other than what they have personally experienced. When men judge women by men's standards, they appear to be soft, emotional, illogical, indecisive, unassertive, and indirect. When women judge men by women's standards, they appear to be cold, insensitive, contentious, pompous, self-centered and selfish. This is a direct result of the gender-socialization process described in Part I. They have been enculturated with the value system, communication style, personality variables, and problem-solving skills of one gender ecosystem and do not understand or accept the culture of the other. Clients must first be educated regarding the different gender messages they have been taught and come to understand that both genders have valuable skills and attributes. The reality is that both genders can appreciate the qualities of affiliation *and* autonomy, cooperation *and* competition, control *and* nurturance, and reason *and* emotion, although they often prioritize them differently.

Common Ground Between the Two Genders (Androgyny)

There was a time when men and women believed the opposite sex was mysterious and unpredictable and did not even try to understand each other. Subsequently, a movement was afoot that suggested that women and men should have the same values, the same goals, the same needs, and therefore the same patterns of communication and interaction. As Hare-Mustin (1990) said, both an exaggeration of differences and a denial of them are errors of bias. The research clearly shows that differences exist, whether they are due to socialization or biology or both (Belenky et al., 1986; Fausto-Sterling, 1985; Gilligan, 1982; Tannen, 1990), but there is also a great deal of overlap. There is common ground for understanding and accepting one another without blame and criticism.

Men and women have the capacity to adopt *all* human values and attributes, whether they have been socially defined as masculine or feminine. Both women and men need to be connected to others but to have a large measure of control over their own lives. They need to be able to use both their emotions and their rational abilities. They need to feel competent and empowered but also safe to express their vulnerabilities and fears. They need to be able to take control and lead or to relinquish control and follow. They need to stand up for themselves in conflict and yet learn to compromise and cooperate. For a truly fulfilling life, they must feel free to access attributes that have stereotypically been defined as belonging to the other gender. Rather than rigidly complying with the dictates of gender socialization, they should be able to move flexibly back and forth between the gender worlds.

Most of this book thus far has dealt with gender differences. But it is important not to lose sight of the fact that, despite so many divergences, women and men are more alike than they are different. This is true as well of human beings of various ethnic backgrounds and from various cultures around the world, but it is especially true of men and women raised in the same culture. The anatomist and cell biologist Roger Gorski made a similar observation at the level of human biology: "There is so much overlap that if you take any individual man and woman, they might show differences in the opposite direction" (Kolata, 1995, p. C7). The universal human needs to be understood, validated, respected, valued, and supported form the bridge between the genders as they struggle with marital issues.

Empathic Knowing

Empathy can be defined as the ability to understand the experiential world of another without actually being a member of that world. When empathy exists, it allows for greater trust and commitment to relationships. People who understand the struggles of others are more likely to approach others from an accepting, nonhostile framework. People who are deeply fearful of altering customary patterns are more confident about experimenting with new patterns if they feel that their stresses are understood. People who appreciate the experiential world of their partner are more capable of experiencing interpersonal warmth.

At the core of gender-sensitive work with couples is the concept of *empathic knowing*. Empathic knowing consists of two ingredients: (a) a knowledge of gender socialization, including its systemic nature, and (b) empathy for the plight of both genders. Knowing what the other has experienced and how that experience has affected his or her perceptions, thoughts, and behaviors leads to greater empathy. When both spouses reach this point with regard to their personal gender experiences, they have achieved empathic knowledge of the other. It is this cognitive–affective shift from a position of angry egocentric entitlement to mutual understanding that allows a couple to work as a team to find their way out of the gender traps they experience. When they understand that neither gender has conspired to manipulate or control the other, and that the enemy, if there is one, is a larger system that reinforces and perpetuates a condition that is unhealthy for both of them, they are no longer locked in an accuse–counterattack relationship that prevents solutions to the problems. Instead, they can begin to rewrite the rules, at least for themselves and their children, and find innovative ways of meeting their mutual needs. At the very least, they can give each other emotional support to endure the status quo. At most, they can focus some of their energy on changing the larger system as well, through education, politics, religious institutions, business, government, and their personal example.

The goal of our particular brand of gender-sensitive psychotherapy is to create an environment in which the clients can discharge their own sense of entitlement and defensiveness long enough to walk in the shoes of their partner with true empathy. They learn to respect and value the differences in the other gender and participate in a cooperative effort to meet their individual and mutual needs. By doing this, they reach the highest developmental level of marital interaction as described by developmental psychologists (Bernal & Baker, 1979, 1980; Jurkovic & Ulrici, 1980;

Tamashiro, 1978), that of the interdependent, mutually enhancing, vitally alive couple relationship.

Creating a Positive Gender Coevolution Process

Another vital aspect of effective gender-sensitive psychotherapy is the creation of an atmosphere in which the partners can develop an understanding that not only are both genders victims of socialization, but also that both participate in the molding of the other over a lifetime. By modeling what previous generations have done and what they see in the world around them, men and women have automatically placed gender expectations on one another and either subtly or overtly discouraged what does not fit the model. Neither partner is the villain, but each of them has a great deal of effect on the development of the other through a simple process of choosing what behavior is rewarded and what is punished or ignored. This rather simplistic behavioral notion is often applied in a totally unconscious manner as one individual naively responds to the other, blindly following the programming of traditional socialization without much thought as to why it should be so or how it might affect either the partner or the relationship. Thus, they have participated in perpetuating the very characteristics and behaviors they now complain about. They certainly cannot be blamed for this, however, because they have only done what they have been taught to do. When they understand this, they can begin to listen to the experience of the other without feeling the need to defend themselves or counterattack. On the contrary, a concerted effort to understand the world of the other gender and to help the other nondefensively to find solutions to the gender binds imposed by society brings about mutual growth and satisfaction. Understanding the coevolution process has a liberating effect, because once one realizes that one's responses to one's spouse can have either a rigidifying or growth-enhancing result, one recognizes the potential for healthy change.

The Gender-Role Journey

The entire process of moving from being a thoroughly enculturated male or female, unaware of the restrictions and detriments of obeying gender survival messages, through an increasing level of dissatisfaction with the restrictive role of traditional male or female roles, to the thinking of a liberated woman or man, has been called the *gender-role journey* (O'Neil & Egan, 1992b; O'Neil & Roberts-Carroll, 1988). Shifting from egocentric entitlement to empathic knowing is not a smooth journey that a couple makes in perfect step. Most often, one partner has surged forward and is literally dragging a reluctant and somewhat recalcitrant spouse behind. The stages of the gender-role journey (O'Neil & Egan, 1992b; O'Neil & Roberts-Carroll, 1988; see Exhibit 9.1) are fairly predictable, beginning with a position of unconscious compliance with gender programming received in childhood, with all of its egocentricity and unrealistic expectations, followed by one spouse or the other becoming vaguely dissatisfied with things as they are and beginning to question the system. From that point, the dissatisfied spouse moves through a period of consciousness raising, which often leads to anger and blame. If the journey is to be completed successfully, however, individuals must move beyond blaming the other gender for their predicament and begin to take responsibility for their own happiness, making appropriate and often unilateral changes in attitude and behavior. Once people move beyond angry blaming, they are more open to gaining an understanding of the other and to seeing the entire system in which they both play a part. When a spouse gets to this stage in the journey, empathy for the struggle of the other spouse can facilitate the growth of the partner as well. In this way a couple will struggle through their gender-role journey, occasionally leapfrogging over one another as they work toward a coevolutionary relationship. In chapter 9, we provide case examples that illustrate interventions that are appropriate to each stage in the gender-role journey.

THE ROLE OF THE THERAPIST

Knowing the preceding concepts is vital to a therapist who wishes to conduct gender-sensitive psychotherapy, but also important is the therapist's ability to connect with and inspire confidence in his or her clients. In this section, we discuss the important qualities of therapists that serve as a foundation for working with individuals, couples, and families in therapy.

Before therapeutic change can effectively occur, it is necessary for clients to have confidence in their therapist. This confidence includes trust in the therapist as both a person and a professional and a belief that the therapist both can and wants to be helpful. Clients must feel assured that they can tell the therapist their innermost feelings and fears and will be understood and not betrayed.

Carl Rogers (1951, 1954, 1957, 1959) postulated early on that there were three necessary and sufficient interrelated conditions that must be met for therapy to occur. The first of these is empathy, a deep and accurate understanding of the other person, sometimes going beyond that person's awareness of self. The second is genuineness, or congruence, which refers to the therapist's ability to be genuinely him- or herself in the therapeutic relationship. Genuine, or congruent, therapists are aware of their own inner experiencing and allow their own true self to be apparent in the counseling session. The third condition is unconditional positive regard, a total acceptance of the individual. In the presence of these three conditions, people grow and release their own actualizing tendencies. In Rogerian theory, these three conditions make it possible for clients to have confidence and trust in the therapist.

Other theorists have described similar facilitative conditions such as that the therapist or counselor "be authentic, respect the client, and provide for a supportive therapeutic environment" (Parsons & Wicks, 1994, p. 87). Being authentic means being a "real" person and not hiding behind roles. Respecting the client means truly valuing and appreciating the person as a human being. Providing support is achieved through the counselor's use of active listening skills, which may include reflection, clarification, elaboration, and summarization.

Research data in counseling and therapy have consistently supported the same result, that the strongest predictor of therapeutic success is the quality of the therapeutic relationship (Bergin & Garfield, 1994). As practitioners tend toward integrated or eclectic theory bases (Norcross & Goldfried, 1992), the delineation of these core therapeutic conditions becomes even more important. Research has suggested that therapeutic benefit is associated more strongly with the identity and

171

characteristics of the therapist and the therapeutic relationship than with any specific type or theory of psychotherapy (Crits-Christoph & Mintz, 1991; Luborsky et al., 1986). Bergin and Garfield (1994) reflected the conclusion of Frank and Frank (1991) "that psychotherapy is a process of interpersonal persuasion in which therapist values, beliefs, and optimism serve to overcome demoralization, instill hope, and provide a believable meaning of life for clients" (Bergin & Garfield, 1994, p. 239). Controversy exists over what may be defined as "therapist personal values" versus their professional beliefs about what is good and healthy for their clients, but many authors have pointed out that a therapist's personal and professional values become so intertwined that in practice it is not possible or meaningful to attempt to distinguish between them (Bergin, 1980; Beutler, Clarkin, Crago, & Bergan, 1991). Therapists who value personal growth, expression of feelings, and autonomy and devalue submission to authority have more successful therapeutic outcomes (Bergin & Garfield, 1994; Bergin & Jensen, 1989), because clients tend to adopt for themselves the personal values of their therapists (Atkinson & Schein, 1986; Beutler & Bergan, 1991; Kelly, 1990; Tjelvelt, 1986). There is also evidence that therapist characteristics such as attractiveness, trustworthiness, and expertness lead to successful therapeutic outcomes because these qualities are related to persuasiveness (Corrigan, Dell, Lewis, & Schmidt, 1980; Heppner & Claiborn, 1989; Heppner & Dixon, 1981).

The research on therapist characteristics and values circles back to the original therapeutic premise proposed by Rogers (1957) concerning the three core necessary and sufficient conditions for successful psychotherapeutic change (Beutler, Crago, & Arizmendi, 1986; Lambert & Bergin, 1983). It is impossible to separate therapist characteristics and values from the characteristics of the therapeutic relationship. Patterson (1984) concluded that "there are few things in the field of psychology for which the evidence is so strong" as the research that supports the "necessity if not sufficiency, of the therapist conditions of accurate empathy, respect, or warmth, and therapeutic genuineness" (p. 437).

FAMILY OR COUPLES THERAPY

The bulk of the literature on therapeutic outcome and core conditions has focused on individual counseling or psychotherapy. The development of the same core conditions in couples or family therapy has added dimensions of complexity. In therapeutic work with a couple, the therapist works to develop trust with each partner, which can be difficult when the partners are in conflict and connection with the other may be seen as evidence of disloyalty. In addition, the therapist is actually working with three clients: each individual and the relationship. To balance the therapeutic session and communicate to all participants that they are heard, accepted, and understood can be a complicated but vital task. Success at this task not only allows therapy to progress, but also provides valuable role modeling to each partner regarding how to respect each other even when in conflict.

Feeling respected, accepted, and understood by the therapist allows each partner to explore personal issues further in the presence of the other. It is critical that the therapist also provide safety for that expression by creating ground rules that require partners to listen to each other and not misuse personal material then or at a later time. The therapist models active listening and acceptance of each partner's feelings. Only after acceptance and processing of feelings does the therapist question which behaviors from each partner would best serve the relationship. The therapist facilitates the open exchange of feelings and the negotiation of new ways of relating that replace old ones that did not work.

In a sense, what the successful therapist does in couples therapy is teach the partners to provide, as much as possible, Rogers's necessary conditions in their relationship with each other. A relationship in which each person is deeply empathic with the other, is genuinely present in the relationship, and truly accepts his or her partner is one in which each person flourishes. When each partner so flourishes in connection, so does the relationship. A therapist who demonstrates these conditions gains the confidence of her or his clients and helps them through teaching and modeling to nurture and strengthen their relationship.

GENDER ISSUES

One area in which the therapist specifically encourages expression of feelings, empathic understanding, genuineness, and total acceptance of the being of the other is in relation to gender roles and expectations of gender-based behavior. Most couples are not fully cognizant of the proportion of their behaviors and conflicts that are based on gender-role socialization. It is an appropriate task of the therapist to encourage each partner to describe what growing up in her or his gender role felt like and what expectations for self and others were created. As gender brokers (Pittman, 1985), therapists help clients analyze their gender-role stereotyping and then make informed choices about what characteristics to keep or discard. To allow clients to develop the confidence in the therapist necessary to accomplish this task, the therapist must be well schooled in the gender-role socialization of both sexes.

The therapist must be able to see through stereotyped behaviors that clients have learned from family and peers and aid them to reach below the surface to deeper feelings and desires. A gender-skilled therapist is not fooled by men who are stoic or women who do not display their competence and has the skills to guide clients to acknowledge and display their total beings. It is imperative that the therapist be fully aware of typical gender-role messages that clients have received and be skilled in helping clients identify and question them. Expertise in understanding how male and female gender-role messages interact and affect heterosexual relationships is critical. It is also crucial that the therapist be comfortable with clients' decisions about their own values and behavior no matter where they fall on a traditional–nontraditional continuum.

PRINCIPLES FOR GENDER-FAIR THERAPY

Nutt (1991) articulated a set of gender-sensitive principles for family therapists that can serve as guidelines in their work with families and couples.

Principle 1. Family psychologists are knowledgeable concerning sex-role socialization and biological and psychological development and their impact on men, women, boys, and girls and on their roles in the family.

This should include specific knowledge about issues such as sexuality, menopause, impotence, violence, eating disorders, and differences in psychological development, particularly concerning concepts of autonomy and connectedness.

Principle 2. Family psychologists are especially aware of the impact of the power differential between men and women on the family and on family issues such as division of labor, decision making, child rearing, financial issues, and career choices. The power differential in which men are expected to be taller, older, and better educated does not allow for reciprocity and equality in the family. An awareness of the power differential should also be extended to the relationships between therapist and family and between cotherapists.

Principle 3. Family psychologists are aware of the sexist context of the larger social system and its impact on the family and individuals. Everyone is the product of a culture that is gender-biased, with different expectations for women and men. Taking a stance of neutrality can victimize women who are in the lesser power position. Neutrality does not exist.

Principle 4. Family psychologists are aware that assumptions and precepts of systems theory relevant to their practice may apply differently to women and men and create further problems for the family system. Concepts such as reciprocity, complementarity, enmeshment, boundaries, hierarchies, and differentiation warrant careful examination for gender bias with every family one treats.

Principle 5. Family psychologists are committed to promoting roles for both men and women that are not limited by cultural stereotypes. Men should not be expected to achieve and gain primary life satisfaction through career advancement and women should not through relationships. Pittman (1985) coined the term *gender broker* to describe the nonsexist family psychologist who helps families sort out which values and roles they want to retain and discard. There are no preconceived limits on the choices of roles or direction of therapy.

Principle 6. Family psychologists acquire skills that are particularly facilitative for women and men in their sex-role journeys. This may include sex-role analysis, assertiveness training, consciousness raising, examination of concepts of masculinity and femininity and the interactive nature of gender-role stereotypes, and analysis of gender-role stress. They help empower women and develop intimacy skills in men. Equal spouses can better negotiate uniquely fulfilling relationships.

Principle 7. Family psychologists actively pursue their own gender-role journey (O'Neil & Roberts-Carroll, 1988). They actively examine personal and cultural assumptions about female emotionality, vulnerability, dependence, passivity, narcissism, depression, and nurturance and about male rationality, objectivity, self-control, success, career orientation, resistance to therapy, stoicism, sexuality, aggression, violence, and distance, and they examine how these assumptions impact their work with families.

Principle 8. Family psychologists use nonsexist language in therapy, teaching, writing, public speaking, and supervision. Terms such as *he* and *mankind* to refer to persons in general are not perceived by others as gender-free. Language creates images and assumptions.

Principle 9. Family psychologists are aware of the interactions of sexism, racism, heterosexism, ageism, classism, handicapping conditions, and all other forms of discrimination and prejudice and how they affect different family systems. The culture, experiences, and needs of a single-parent family headed by a Black woman, a gay or lesbian family, a middle-class Hispanic family, and a White family with a handicapped father are quite different.

Principle 10. Family psychologists work toward the elimination of sex-role bias as a source of pathology in all institutions of society. If as psychologists we are ethically bound to promote human welfare and if sex-role stereotyping has a damaging effect on individuals and families, then psychologists have an affirmative responsibility to be politically involved to benefit society.

Basic human needs and experiences link all peoples, no matter how different they may appear on the surface. Acceptance and respect for the differences between the genders is the goal. Rather than criticizing and trying to convert, the genders need to learn to understand one another. The therapist's job is that of the interpreter and diplomat, one who negotiates between separate gender worlds, teaching cultural differences to the clients so that they can learn to interact in a manner that results in satisfaction rather than frustration and conflict for both.

INTERVENTIONS AND TECHNIQUES

In this section, we briefly describe some of the most effective interventions we have used in helping our clients bridge the gender gap. Although for the purpose of explanation they are discussed as if each intervention were a discrete technique, this is not the case. They are all interrelated, frequently leading into and overlapping with one another. In the subsequent chapters, we elaborate on these models and interventions and provide case examples.

Validation and Normalization Must Come First

The first step in the process for the therapist is the somewhat delicate operation of making both husband and wife feel heard, understood, and validated simultaneously. This is particularly difficult when each is, as is often the case, rigidly defending his or her position as the "right way of being" and demanding that the other partner change. Connecting with and validating both spouses simultaneously can be a tricky process. Neither spouse will be able to hear the pain of the other unless he or she feels heard and understood. Therefore, it is important for the therapist to provide each spouse the opportunity to share his or her experience in a way that does not accuse or blame the other partner.

There are several ways in which this can be accomplished. First, it is important to avoid "toxic" issues as much as possible until the therapist has made a good connection with each spouse and they both feel supported and understood. When one partner expresses a frustration that has clear gender roots, the therapist can normalize this experience while demonstrating to the couple how the larger system has in some measure victimized them both.

Another effective method is to gain distance from the pain of the present by allowing the partners to discuss the gender messages they have received from parents, teachers, peers, and others in their childhood, connecting those old tapes to present attitudes and behaviors. Each partner must have an opportunity to do this. Usually the process begins naturally when a gender issue is brought up by one member of the couple. At that point, the therapist can explore with husband and wife, one at a time, what lessons they were taught in their family of origin around this issue. Both partners must feel that the therapist will give them equal time and is not taking sides. By focusing on messages from the past, the therapist can avert the tendency of each partner to blame the other for present difficulties. The spouses are more likely to be able to hear about and develop some understanding of the early origins of their partners' values or behavior patterns because they are not invested in defending their own entrenched position in the present.

It is also important to instill hope by pointing out how, now that they understand the origin of the problem, they can work on ways to change it. As is the case with most therapy, the client gains the insight that he or she can rewrite the rules; that is, each individual can choose to discard those messages from the past that do not work in the here and now while retaining those that have some value (Pittman, 1985, 1990, 1991). Together, they can brainstorm new ways of interacting that will meet their mutual needs.

Psychoeducation

All couples therapists face the challenge of moving the client from a position of blaming and attempting to change the spouse to one of self-examination and changing oneself. In the case of gender issues, the therapist has an effective and readily available tool to neutralize the conflict and reach this goal: psychoeducation regarding gender socialization and its systemic nature. As clients bring up issues that have clear roots in gender socialization, the therapist can identify this fact and educate the couple regarding stereotypical gendered behaviors. For example, a male partner who does not understand his wife's demand for communication can be educated as to the different purposes communication serves for stereotypical men and women. He will begin to understand that women use communication, even about trivial incidents, as a means to connect with another, not necessarily to impart or solicit information. When he recognizes that what seems like a waste of time to him is important to her sense of closeness, he can more readily engage in conversation that would normally take a back seat to the newspaper or television set. Likewise, when a husband appears to be trivializing his wife's problems, the therapist can educate the wife regarding the stereotypical male attempt to comfort through diminishing the problem. He is not discounting her so much as providing her with the response he would want—one that essentially expresses faith in her ability to handle the problem. Once the couple understands the intent of the behavior, they can develop responses that are more satisfying to both. Many more examples of the use of psychoeducation are discussed in the next chapter. As an adjunct to couples therapy, bibliotherapy and psychoeducational workshops can be used to speed up this learning process.

Uniting Against The Ecosystem as Scapegoat

Keeping the systemic perspective in mind at all times, the therapist responds to every complaint and frustration that has its roots in gender socialization by normalizing the experience and demonstrating to the couple how the larger system has in some measure victimized them both. As the therapist makes interventions that point out how both partners suffer and both partners contribute to the maintenance of a system that is not good for either because they have been trained to do so, it is a natural evolution for the couple to begin to view the gender ecosystem as the enemy. This gives the therapist a scapegoat toward which to direct their anger, which in turn unites them in a partnership against the system. They can then turn their energy toward making new rules for their relationship that do not necessarily follow the dictates of the larger society.

Reframing and Translating

As mentioned previously, the gender-sensitive therapist often acts as a gender broker, essentially explaining the male code to the female and vice versa. Much as the language interpreter occupies a central position in international negotiations, the therapist may find it helpful to serve as a communication mediator, a translator of the separate languages of the genders. After receiving input from one partner, the therapist "decodes" the message by placing it in the context of that person's value system. Then, before sending it to the intended receiver, the therapist reframes the message into the spouse's language, conveying the sender's efforts to enhance the overall relationship. Once the receiver of the input recognizes the positive intent of the message, he or she can respond concerning how well that behavior meshes with her or his needs. The process continues with the therapist helping the partners to see how traditional role patterns create problems and to negotiate new arrangements that more closely meet each other's needs. The use of reframing and translating is expanded and illustrated in the next chapter.

Empathic Interviewing

To empathize and connect with another person, it is often necessary "to walk a mile in his (or her) shoes." Don-David Lusterman's interview technique (1989, 1993) makes it possible for a couple to do just that. Essentially what Lusterman does is to teach the couple Interviewing Skills 101, coaching them in asking open-ended questions, active listening skills, reflecting what they hear, avoiding interruptions and defensive responses, and validating the needs, concerns, and hopes of their partner. This experience interrupts the reflexive patterns of accusation and defense that so often occur between partners who automatically interpret any unhappiness of the other as a criticism or deficiency within themselves. It then allows the couple to design solutions that can meet the needs of both partners. Even if the behaviors themselves do not change that much, often the very act of validation changes the emotional atmosphere so that what once was felt as an imposition becomes the opportunity to offer a gift.

The Gender Inquiry

The gender inquiry is a unique and effective contribution to gender-sensitive psychotherapy developed by one of the authors (Lusterman, 1989). This technique is based to a certain extent on gender-sensitive training models that have been developed for family therapy trainees (Roberts,

1991). Each of these models has, as a common goal, the insight that comes from understanding that gender messages are transmitted across generations and are part of a larger culture. This realization engenders greater empathy for the other sex and can be the genesis for a dialogue about how to change messages that appear to be detrimental to either spouse. Most relevant to the therapy session are the questions about gender messages that come from one's family of origin and, in particular, reflexive circular questions (Tomm, 1988) that give clients the possibility of choosing to be different.

The purpose of these questions is threefold. (a) They teach, through personal example, that the gender ecosystem is at the core of many of the misunderstandings and dissatisfactions the spouses are experiencing and therefore depersonalize much of the conflict between spouses. (b) They demonstrate how the sexes influence and mold one another within the family of origin and pass on similar destructive messages to future generations. (c) They expand cognitive maps and offer the possibility of change in the present to bring about change in future generations.

Because the gender inquiry is one of the techniques most integral to our work, we have devoted an entire chapter to an explanation and illustration of the method (see chapter 8).

Auxiliary Treatments

Many times couples come to therapy while they are also attending psychoeducational and therapeutic groups such as Alcoholics Anonymous (AA), Al-Anon, or men's or women's consciousness raising groups. Although sometimes, as mentioned in chapter 5, these groups can incite the clients toward angry, nonproductive, mutual accusation, often they can be used to advantage in therapy. For example, the focus in AA and Al-Anon on taking responsibility for one's own behavior and not trying to control, manipulate, or project blame on the significant other can be reinforced and examined in couples therapy. What men and women learn in consciousness-raising groups about gender socialization can be applied to their relationship during therapy but with the added understanding of the coevolutionary process. If therapists endorse the attitude that both men and women are victims of their gender socialization and that they do not deliberately conspire to hold down or abuse the other gender, they can use the knowledge the clients gain from the consciousness-raising groups to strengthen the coevolutionary concept. This allows the partners to move away from entrenched positions of blame and consider new behaviors that enhance their mutual growth.

The Violent Couple

There is one case in which the use of the techniques in this book is contraindicated. Many experts (Bograd, 1984; Goldner, 1985) have criticized the use of conjoint psychotherapy in cases of domestic violence. Indeed, bringing up the sorts of issues we have discussed thus far can escalate the violence between the partners by increasing tension and vulnerability in the batterer. Therefore, the techniques that we describe in this book are contraindicated until the batterer and victim have been successfully treated and the violence has ceased for at least 6 months. We discuss this issue in more detail in chapter 10.

CONCLUSION

In this chapter, we have articulated the most important principles, guidelines, theoretical concepts, and techniques of our brand of gender-sensitive psychotherapy. We have stressed the importance of the knowledge and attitude of the therapist in bringing about therapeutic change. We have explained the hallmarks of gender-sensitive psychotherapy: the acknowledgment of a gender ecosystem; the process of gender socialization; the concepts of androgyny, empathic knowing, and coevolution; and the gender-role journey. In the next chapter, we elaborate the interventions and models we use, which are illustrated by case examples.

7

Therapeutic Interventions

Although the authors practice and teach gender-sensitive psychotherapy separately in different parts of the United States and with different populations, our experience as therapists has resulted in a common
philosophy. We believe that when the therapist can lead the couple to a
point of understanding and empathizing with the gender world of each
spouse, a major cognitive–affective shift occurs, which leads to reduction
of conflict, more effective problem resolution, and greater emotional intimacy. Although we may reach this point by different methods, the goal
is the same.

In the previous chapter, we briefly described the techniques we have
found to be useful in treating couples whose problems appear to be rooted
in traditional gender socialization. We consider these interventions to be
part of an assortment of tools at the disposal of the therapist. In our opinion, there is no invariant prescription for every case. Because we work with
divergent populations and in different geographic locations, our experiences have been varied even though our goals are the same. Collectively,
we have developed a variety of techniques that appear to be effective in
bringing about empathic knowing and positive coevolution. The reader is

cautioned to recognize that some approaches may fit better with a particular case or population than others. Furthermore, certain interventions may not work well together with others. We do not view these interventions as a package that must be applied in a set step-by-step fashion. Instead, we offer the reader a cornucopia of techniques from which to select the most appropriate tool to bring about positive change. The only aspect of our work that *is* invariant is the knowledge base of the gender-sensitive therapist and his or her philosophy regarding the process of gender socialization.

In this chapter, we describe and illustrate three approaches to gender-sensitive psychotherapy and discuss the populations we have found to respond most positively to each. Because the fourth model, the gender inquiry, is unique to our philosophy of gender-sensitive psychotherapy, we have devoted an entire chapter to its elaboration (chapter 8).

PHILPOT'S PSYCHOEDUCATIONAL APPROACH

Description

Philpot (1991, 1995) has developed a psychoeducational approach to gender-sensitive psychotherapy that essentially unites the couple against a common scapegoat: a society that socializes people into rigid roles that are detrimental to both genders. This approach seems to appeal to well-educated, well-read individuals who enjoy analyzing situations from an intellectual perspective. The beauty of the psychoeducational approach with these couples is that it uses their defense mechanism of intellectualization as a door through which to introduce a new way of looking at the issues. With new insight comes the willingness to try new behaviors tentatively. If both partners are well educated regarding the cyclical nature of gender socialization (that is, the role they each play in molding the behavior of the other), they are careful to reward and encourage the new, preferred behaviors. The result is an escalation of positive, functional interactions to replace the former, negative ones.

The goal of therapy with a couple who have become entrenched in polarized positions over gender issues is depolarization through expansion of their cognitive maps. Most often, both spouses are locked into a repetitive, dysfunctional set in which each partner tries desperately to convince the spouse that his or her way is the right way. They have become submerged in an either–or, right–wrong, black–white dichotomous manner of thinking, in which one perspective must defeat the other. To this end, they attempt to triangulate the therapist as judge, each hoping to form a coalition with the expert to validate her or his position. It is at this point that the therapist can begin the depolarization process that consists of the following four steps.

Step 1. Reflection

The first step is simply *reflection* with some tentative amplification: merely restating what both husband and wife have expressed individually, sensitively restating the emotional stance and thought processes of each. When therapists are thoroughly familiar with the issues and typical gender perspectives, they can follow the clients' lead and with a high degree of accuracy predict the feelings and rationale that will follow. The correct and empathic statement of positions the clients have not yet verbalized fully, but recognize as resonating with deep-felt emotions, has the validating, bonding effect that creates the therapeutic "magic." Both genders feel heard, understood, and supported at once.

An example may help to elucidate the process. A couple were locked in a dysfunctional pattern of metacommunication; that is, they argued constantly regarding the way they communicated with one another. Her position was that she wanted to discuss the problem areas in their relationship and get some resolution. He avoided such discussions, much to her frustration. His position was that whenever they had such discussions they were angry at each other for weeks and it put a damper on their sex life. He found the talks to be detrimental to the relationship and saw no reason to engage in a painful interaction. Neither understood the position of the other.

The therapist bonded with the wife by reflecting her frustration at not being able to problem-solve with her husband because he found those discussions distasteful. If nothing ever changed, she would have to learn to live with a situation she found untenable or leave the relationship, neither of which was a pleasant thought. The wife responded in agreement and expressed her sense of helplessness in the situation. The therapist bonded with the husband by reflecting how his wife's desire to problem-solve sounded to him like a list of things he did wrong and expressed how painful it must be to listen to a laundry list of complaints, particularly if he did not understand those complaints and felt he was being criticized. The therapist asked the husband how he usually reacted when he felt criticized, and his response described a three-step process: (a) At first, I try to correct whatever is wrong, but if I can't, (b) I try to defend my position, and if that doesn't work, (c) I just avoid talking about it because we'll only get mad. The therapist then pointed out that his avoidance also made her mad and that therefore there was no way he could win. She stated that he too felt helpless in the situation, which he confirmed.

In this way, the therapist validated the experience and positive intent of both partners while describing the systemic interaction. Both felt heard and understood, although uncertain of how to proceed. The dysfunctional set was identified and described but not yet transformed.

Step 2. Psychoeducation

The second step is *psychoeducational* and somewhat didactic. The fact that the therapist simultaneously agrees with what the clients view as dichotomous and incompatible positions is disconcerting and stimulates curiosity. At this point, the therapist can teach the clients about the construction of reality along gender lines and the attitudes and values that can be expected to result from the socialization process. The educational component can be kept as simple or made as sophisticated as the clients' education and intelligence can appreciate. It is important for the therapist to connect with the negative aspects of gender socialization for both genders, so that motivation for change is bilateral. This step has the effect of enriching the cognitive map and opening new possibilities for perception. Additionally, it normalizes male–female positions and neutralizes toxic issues between the couple by clarifying their source as gender socialization and not deliberate personal demeaning directed at one another's value systems.

In the preceding example, the therapist subsequently discussed the issues in more depth. She identified the wife's role of monitor of the relationship as a product of her gender socialization and lauded her efforts to tackle problem areas before they became too large to handle. The clinician then turned to the husband and explained the research of Gottman and Krokoff (1989), which indicates that a wife's early accommodation to her husband's needs may correlate with marital satisfaction in the early part of the marriage, but sooner or later her resentment and anger will be expressed—openly, passively–aggressively, or psychosomatically—none of which would be a pleasant experience for either of them. Examples of how this might happen in this relationship were elaborated.

On the other hand, the therapist continued, most men have been taught that if they are adequate as men, their wives will be happy. Therefore, they feel somehow responsible if their wives are dissatisfied, as though they have failed in some way; they become defensive if their wives hit them with a laundry list of complaints, particularly if they do not know how to "fix" the problem. The result is uncomfortable emotionally and not productive. A typical learned response of men to uncomfortable emotions is distraction and avoidance. Of course he would not want to engage in this kind of discussion. No one would. But the result is a sense of isolation and the danger of losing his wife.

So we have a dilemma. If she does not talk about the issues that bother her, the relationship is at risk in the not-too-distant future. If she continues to approach the subject the way she does now and he continues to respond as he always has, the conflict is never resolved. The resultant painful emotions put the relationship at risk of either escalating conflict or increasing isolation from one another. What to do?

The therapist then informed the couple of the importance to a woman of verbal communication as a way to bond and feel close to her spouse. Sometimes, in fact, all the woman needs is a listener, and she is not asking for a solution to a problem or a change in her spouse. However, the therapist cautioned, the wife must be aware of the impact her words have on a man because of his gender training and interpret his responses accordingly. The clinician also talked about the very strong gender message men absorb regarding their loss of manhood if they let a woman tell them what to do. Although this may seem irrational, it nevertheless plays an important role in a man's emotional reaction to a woman's request for change. As the therapist talked about the various aspects of gender socialization, both clients chimed in with stories and examples from their own lives. In this way, the initial building blocks of empathic knowing began to be laid.

Step 3. Confrontation With Reality

Sometimes, as they face the massive task of dismantling centuries of gender training in an effort to improve their relationship, one or both partners in the couple express the belief that it is too difficult. They speculate about the possibility that another woman or man would be different, more expressive, more cooperative, more affectionate, and so on. Although this may be true to some extent, the problem is that all men and women have been exposed to the same gender socialization, and remnants of that training will show up in every couple. Therefore, Step 3 is *confrontation* with reality. It consists essentially of a short speech that points out that gender differences exist between all women and men to some degree and must be accepted. An example might be the following monologue, delivered after a discussion of Chodorow's (1978) theory concerning the etiology of priority differences between men and women with regard to autonomy and affiliation:

> Well, now that you understand where each of you is coming from, we need to find a way to communicate so that you can meet each others' needs. Because there is one thing I can guarantee you: If either one of you imposes your perception or value system on the other, you kill the relationship. Whenever one person dominates the other, both suffer, and eventually the relationship becomes bitter and unrewarding. And since you both tell me, by your very presence here, that this relationship is valuable to you, we need to start working on a two-winner approach to resolving these issues. It should also be clear by now that changing spouses (if either of

188

you has fantasized that solution) is probably not going to help too much with a lot of these issues either, because most men and women will have been socialized in the same way. Women will be like women, and men like men, whether we like it or not. I'm reminded of Rex Harrison's lament in *My Fair Lady*, "Why can't a woman be more like a man?" But then that would probably be boring as the devil. Anyway, what I would like for you to do right now is to think of yourselves as speaking two different languages, say French and Spanish, because there are similarities in your thinking, but also differences. And for the last few sessions, I've acted as an interpreter. Which is okay, but I don't plan to move in with you, so it would be much more efficient for me to teach you how to speak each others' language. Then you can communicate and work on solutions.

Step 4. Brainstorming

The fourth step consists of *brainstorming* for solutions. Before problem resolution can occur, however, the therapist must teach the clients the elementary techniques of empathic interviewing (see the next section). Both partners state their position, not with the purpose of converting the partner, but to inform the spouse about feelings and needs. Partners learn to listen to the experience of the other without feeling the need to defend or impose their own view. The therapist helps them clarify the most important underlying needs that must be met for the relationship to be satisfying to both. Creative two-winner solutions to problems emerge from the clients themselves. These solutions may require the therapist to do some skills training such as active listening or behavioral contracting, or the therapist may need to offer a ritual prescription, simply reframe, or employ any one of the many therapeutic techniques at his or her disposal to facilitate the clients' accomplishing their goal.

As therapy progresses, whenever such issues arise, the therapist continues to take responsibility for interpreting them systemically, treating both female and male perspectives as equally valid, and moving from reflection to education, normalization, and depersonalization to brainstorming. It should be emphasized here that violence by either gender inflicted on the other is never to be considered a valid solution to a problem (Geffner, Bartlett, & Rossman, 1995; see chapter 10).

In the case at hand, the therapist suggested that the clients interview each other to discover what would facilitate a discussion of their relationship; the technique resulted in some problem resolution rather than wheel-spinning accusations and defensiveness. For this particular couple, several ideas were adopted. First of all, the couple decided to set aside a time every day just to talk, and the wife agreed to bring up negative concerns about the relationship only once during the week. The result was that both spouses talked about their work, their children, their social life, their hobbies, their sporting activities, and the daily events of their lives frequently, resulting in a closeness they had not felt since they dated. Second, the husband practiced active listening and reflection skills as well as cognitive restructuring skills to interrupt his automatic defensive responses when his wife brought up an uncomfortable issue. Third, the wife refrained from accusing her husband of failing in some way, framing her concerns in terms of her needs and wants. Fourth, the wife remained open to suggestions from him of how these needs might be met, rather than telling him what she wanted him to do. Finally, both partners encouraged and rewarded the other when any small step toward change occurred. Whenever they slipped into the old patterns, they jokingly reminded each other that they were, after all, "just a man or woman."

Because these solutions emerged from this couple, they were effective. Other interventions might work better for another couple. The most important element of this approach is its nonblaming viewpoint, which unites the couple against a common enemy—*gender socialization*—in an effort to save their relationship. Couples develop creative teamwork to defeat this problem that is "bigger than both of them."

Case Example: The Benevolent Patriarch

A taciturn, well-dressed, balding real estate developer in his early 50s came to therapy for a "brief consultation" regarding his marriage. He and his wife, who was 10 years his junior, had been married for 15 years. Before they were married, she had been a loan officer in a bank, but as soon as their sons, ages 11 and 9, were born, his wife stopped work to become a full-time homemaker and mother. Mr. J. reported that he had been very depressed for several years because of the marital conflict he was experiencing. He described his wife as a wonderful mother and housekeeper but indicated that she was constantly angry at him, screaming and yelling, and never happy with anything he did. He said his home was a war zone from which he would stay away as much as possible except that he loved his sons and wanted to be with them. In fact, he had often thought of divorce because he felt his marriage was hopeless, but he did not want to leave his little boys. He indicated that he had lost his father when he was 5 years old, his mother had never remarried, and he felt the absence of a father was a major contributor to his unhappiness in life. He vowed he would not leave his children fatherless. His major defense against conflict was withdrawal, however, and he responded to his wife's yelling by closing himself in his home office after the children went to bed. When asked what his wife was angry about, he said he honestly did not understand. She complained about money, but she had everything she wanted. She complained about his work, but she profited from it. He was home every night, but she said she was lonely. She was more extroverted than he, but she knew that when she married him. He said he was baffled and therefore could never please her.

The therapist empathized with his discouragement but told him the situation was probably not as hopeless as it seemed. They probably needed a fresh perspective; they were both too close to the problem and too rigid in their positions to see the answer. After assessing the level of Mr. J's depression, interpreting his symptoms as internalized anger and a sense of hopelessness, and offering a few behavioral suggestions as a temporary bandage, the therapist suggested that he bring his wife in for marital therapy. Because the apparent cause of his depression was a relationship issue, therapeutic work would require both of them, particularly since he was invested in saving his marriage. He seemed doubtful that she would agree but said he would think about it. He did not return after the first visit.

Six months later, a vivacious, attractive, dark-haired woman came in for an initial interview. Fifteen minutes into the interview, she revealed that she was the wife of Mr. J. and that she had decided to come in and interview the therapist to see if she would like to continue. She also explained that she had been in therapy with several other therapists and requested that her husband join her, but he had never come for more than one visit. After she had given up on therapy, her husband suddenly informed her that he had visited a therapist by himself whom he liked. (He told her this several months after his initial visit.) She said her husband was "into control" and that she believed he wanted to select the therapist they would see so he would have the upper hand. She said she knew enough about therapy now to trust that he would only have the illusion of the upper hand and that if she liked the therapist, she would come to marital therapy because she knew they needed it.

When asked her perception of their marital difficulties, she responded immediately that her husband treated her like a child, which insulted her. For example, in spite of the fact that she had a degree in accounting and had been a loan officer of a bank before her marriage, her husband gave her money a little at a time, making her explain what she needed it for each time. Although he never refused to give her money and did not accuse her of being a spendthrift, he insisted that she come to him every time she ran out of cash. She had become so exasperated that she had gotten a job as a cosmetics salesperson (which she could do on her own time and still be an available parent) just to have money she could spend without accounting for every dime. She had no knowledge of their bank accounts, trust funds, insurance policies, or financial investments of any sort. Her husband never talked to her about his business, and she would often find out from his partners' wives that the firm had just won a large bid or just invested in some property in town. It was humiliating to her that her husband would share this information with others, but not her. He had even requested that she not come into his office. In the last several years, her husband had made things even worse by avoiding spending any time alone with her. He came home, played with the boys, and locked himself away. They never went on trips together, and although they socialized, they only did so with other couples present. They never talked about intimate, important things. The only communication they had either was trivial or occurred when she screamed at him. She felt like the least important person in his life. She would leave if it were not that the little girls loved him so much.

Mrs. J. made an appointment for conjoint therapy the following week, but she warned that they might cancel because Mr. J. had a habit of doing so. However, this was not the case. Apparently, the few behavioral suggestions and the message of hope the therapist had conveyed to Mr. J. 6 months earlier had made him feel better and given him confidence that this therapist might be able to help. Conjoint therapy began with an exploration of what had attracted the couple to one another in the beginning, which suddenly shifted the negative atmosphere to one of mutual excitement. Mr. J. had originally been attracted to Mrs. J. because she was outgoing, vivacious, bright, and very "emotionally generous." His own mother had been so busy making a living to take care of her children that she had been unable to give him much emotionally, and he saw Mrs. J. as very different. Mrs. J. had seen Mr. J. as a "rock": someone she could count on to steady her when she became overemotional, unlike anyone in her family of origin. Neither of them saw, at this point, how their partners resembled their parents. They agreed that the good qualities were still there but that the problems had gotten out of hand.

Although there were many issues in this case, including projective identifications and ethnic differences, the turning point in the therapy came about because of the use of a gender-sensitive approach. The therapist had discussed in the first session with Mrs. J. the need to "hook" Mr. J. into therapy if anything were to be accomplished and asked for her cooperation. She had also given Mrs. J. a gender-socialization explanation for some of Mr. J.'s behavior and suggested some bibliotherapy on gender issues. Initial sessions focused on hearing Mr. J.'s side of the problem, giving him time to ventilate and explore his feelings. When Mrs. J. talked about feeling like a child, she did so with coaching from the therapist, in a way that did not sound angry and accusative but sad and vulnerable. For the first time, her husband heard and understood why she felt badly in spite of the fact that all her material needs were met. At first, he insisted that men were supposed to take care of these matters, and as long as she got what she needed, why did his wife need to bother her pretty little brain with such things? But he admitted that he could see how this behavior would insult her intelligence, and he did know she was a capable woman. After brainstorming with Mr. J. all the logical, rational reasons Mrs. J. might need to know more about the business and their financial affairs and indicating that he had to be aware of these reasons, the therapist suggested that there might be another reason, perhaps of an emotional nature, that would cause such a reasonable man to not take the rational approach. Could he identify the gut feeling he had when he thought of sharing financial information with his wife? With patient and gentle prodding, Mr. J. was able to say that his mother had been very controlling and that he had vowed that he would never let a woman control him again. After all, a real man controlled the woman, not vice versa. And if his father had been alive, he would have prevented his mother from being such a domineering person. His fear was that if he gave his wife any information about their finances, she would take over like his mother had and tell him how to run his life, and that would mean he was not a man.

As is often the case (see chapter 9), the J.s were at different points in their gender-role journey. Mrs. J., owing partly to her several years of individual therapy and partly to life experiences, had advanced beyond blindly following gender-role programming. She also, with the help of the present therapist, had gained an appreciation of her husband's need to "catch up," as well as of her potential role as cotherapist in accomplishing this goal. With the help of the therapist and her reading, Mrs. J. was able to respond to her husband without anger, outrage, or disbelief, but with reassurance that she only wanted to be closer to him, to share his life, not to tell him what to do. They were able to see that neither of them benefited from the hierarchical approach; Mr. J. felt on guard, defensive, and isolated, whereas Mrs. J. felt put-down, devaluated, and rejected. They were able to empathize with the position of the other without accusing or withdrawing.

Once the cognitive–emotional shift had taken place, the therapist was able to suggest that Mr. J begin to share what he felt it was safe to share with Mrs. J. and see what kind of reaction he got. As might have been predicted, partially because Mrs. J. understood so well the dynamics of her husband, Mr. J. found it was safe to take Mrs. J. into his confidence and began to share more and more. Finally, he even asked her advice on an issue regarding a loan and asked for her input on an investment, fully aware that he could use her input but make the final decision himself. Because she felt respected and valued at last, Mrs. J. became once again the warm and giving person she had been when they met. Mr. J., rejoicing in her affection and positive attention, asked her to accompany him on a business trip to Paris, during which they were both amazed at the renewal of romantic love between them. One year later, Mrs. J. dropped in just to let the therapist know that things were still going very well and that they had never felt so close before.

Although this case had many underlying dynamics, several of which have not been discussed, the use of a gender-socialization explanation for Mr. J.'s behavior and coaching his wife in a new way of responding to him brought about a cognitive–affective shift that laid the groundwork for the major changes they both made.

LUSTERMAN'S EMPATHIC INTERVIEW

Description

In the previous section, we pointed out the necessity for therapists to teach certain skills to clients before they can find effective solutions to their problems. Probably no skill is as basic or vital as empathic interviewing. Although Lusterman works mostly with a metropolitan, educated, professional, and predominantly Jewish population, empathic interviewing has proved effective with couples from all walks of life (Stuart, 1980). The determining factor in the use of this technique has more to do with the emotional maturity and psychological functioning of the individuals than with their socioeconomic or educational status. A client who is incapable of empathy owing to an Axis II diagnosis or one who is psychotic would not be an appropriate candidate for empathic interviewing.

Lusterman inducts the participants into empathic interviewing with an opening request such as the following:

I am going to ask you to take the role of interviewer. You are to ask your partner to talk about how he or she feels about an issue that the two of you are in conflict about. You are to listen carefully and draw your partner out. Do not respond to what is being said. Your job is to develop a better understanding of what your partner is thinking and feeling. Stop from time to time to summarize what your partner is saying. Ask your partner whether your summary is accurate. You may be told that you were accurate with some ideas but missed others, or that you completely missed some point. If you understood only partially or not at all, ask some more questions and then try to paraphrase again. Once you are able to paraphrase accurately, try to imagine what your partner may be feeling. Be careful not to answer or correct the other person—this only causes defensiveness. Let's try now.

It is often difficult to hold each participant to the task at hand—that of entering into one another's worlds. It is necessary for the therapist to be extremely interventive and to prevent defensive responses or provocative questions. Participants are reminded to continue this same type of dialogue at home. Many report that, with practice, this way of communicating becomes a natural and useful practice, not merely in the therapy room, but also in their daily lives.

Lusterman then offers the clients guidelines as to which responses and behaviors engender empathy and which do not. For the interviewer, he suggests the following behaviors as productive:

1. Listening attentively to the content of what is being said.
2. Listening attentively for the feeling state that may underlie the content.
3. Looking directly at the person.
4. Being aware of what your own body is "saying" to the person, for example, nodding assent or dissent.
5. Repressing any "answering" thoughts.
6. Carefully avoiding comparing your thoughts and feelings to the other's.

7. Stopping after a few minutes to paraphrase the other and, if possible, imagining the feelings the other may be experiencing.
8. Drawing the other out as completely as possible; losing yourself in the other's experience.

For the interviewee, the following behaviors are recommended:

1. Speaking in "I" language, for example, "I feel worried and neglected when you are going to be very late and don't call," versus "you" language, for example, "You never call; you make me furious."
2. Reporting what you are experiencing rather than emoting it.
3. Being careful to avoid impugning the other, but carefully describing what is happening inside yourself.

Lusterman also provides a list of DO NOTs: behaviors that prevent the development of empathy for one another. These include the following for the interviewer:

1. Thinking ahead to how she or he will "answer" the interviewee.
2. Interrupting and criticizing the interviewee.
3. Saying, or thinking, "How about me?"
4. Explaining why the interviewee feels as he or she does.
5. Interpreting what the interviewee is saying, rather than paraphrasing it.
6. Saying, "You're wrong."

For the interviewee, the following behaviors are not recommended:

1. Attacking the other, rather than describing how the other's actions impact on you.
2. Showing very strong emotions, rather than finding words to describe what you are experiencing.
3. Emoting rather than reporting what you are feeling.
4. Saying, "You're wrong."

Lusterman instructs the clients to use empathic interviewing (a) when the other is speaking in an attacking manner, creating defensive feelings;

(b) when they notice a change of appearance in the other, such as tearing up or clenching of fists; (c) when feeling strong emotions and fearing an explosive expression of them; or (d) when feeling "unheard" by the other.

More recently, Lusterman has been providing his clients with a script, which he asks them to practice at home. This gives the clients an opportunity to learn the technique of interviewing and reflecting without tapping emotionally toxic issues. He also frequently cautions them not to try the empathic interview on their own issues until he gives them permission, thus implementing a paradoxical intervention that is very effective. Clients defy his wishes and successfully discuss painful issues using their newly learned communication skills.

Case Example: Gee, I Thought You'd Never Ask

By educating the couple in basic communication techniques and monitoring their process, the therapist can teach the clients to express themselves in a manner that is nonattacking, to draw one another out, to listen attentively, and to reflect what they hear, so that they can provide each other with a validating experience. The following case example illustrates this process.

After using the introductory remarks and instructions regarding interviewing described previously, the therapist began the following dialogue:

Th(erapist): Let's try now. You were just talking about Jane's going back to work. She was just saying how put down she feels by you. Why don't you try to find out what is has been like for her.

Jim: This is ridiculous. Why do we have to be so formal? Janie, why are you making such a federal case about going back to work? All the other women on the block work.

Jane: You're putting me down.

Th: If you want to know more about Jane, don't tell her about herself. Ask what she thinks and try to put all your effort into hearing her.

Jim: [smiling] Why are you resisting going back to work so much?

Jane: You see? You're criticizing me again. You want to tell me what I think—don't want to hear me.

Jim: [to Therapist] She doesn't make it easy.

Th: Ask her what she's thinking about going back to work right now.

Jim: Okay. What are you thinking about going back to work right now?

Jane: I'm thinking that, no matter what I do, somehow you'll find something wrong with the way I do it.

Jim: That's because you don't have any confidence in yourself.

Jane: [Glares at Jim and refuses to answer.]

Th: I'm going to stop you, Jim. If you keep telling her what's wrong with her, you won't know anything more about her. Why don't you ask her what she means about your finding something wrong with the way she'll do it?

Jim: What do you mean, I'll find something wrong with the way you'll do it?

Jane: From the beginning, you always had to be the leader. If you wanted to go skiing, we had to go skiing.

Jim: That's because you're not adventurous.

At this point, Jane slammed out of the room and spent several minutes alone in the waiting room. Jim expressed amazement at "the way Jane just blew up" and pointed out that this happened at home as well. The therapist pointed out that Jim had blocked every attempt that Jane had made to tell him what she thought, either by making a judgment on her or a defensive statement, and wondered if Jim could see any connection between this exchange and other, similar conversations at home.

When Jane returned, Jim was encouraged to continue the questioning. Jane began to describe the way Jim used money as a form of control. During this session and the next, Jim remained provocative and defensive, and it was difficult for him to paraphrase her words. After several sessions, he was finally able to paraphrase her.

Jim: You believe that I don't treat you like an equal. You feel that I put you down by criticizing the way you spend money and that I make you feel that being a mother isn't a real job. You feel angry with me because you think I want you to do everything to my specs and that I use the fact that I have a "real job," one that brings in the bucks, as a way of controlling and judging the way you spend money.

At another session, Jim mentioned a fight they had about the way he had taken care of the children one morning. He was very angry, because he felt unjustly criticized.

Jim: You always make a mountain out of a molehill. You'd think I had committed a major crime.

Th: Jane, this would be a good time to interview Jim.

Jane: Don't you understand that you could have hurt the kinds by letting them play around in the back of the station wagon instead of putting the seat up and putting them in the safety seats?

Jim: Any time I do anything with the kids, you undermine me.

Jane: That's because you never give them your full attention. Just like when you're home alone with them. You say you're watching them, but your mind's on something else.

Th: Jane, can you ask Jim what he means when he talks about being undermined?

Jane: Do you think you really give the kids your full attention?

Th: He's only going to defend himself if you ask him that. Try to just ask him how he feels undermined.

Jane: Okay, how do you feel undermined?

Th: [smiling] Gee, I thought you'd never ask. [Both laugh.]

Jim: Seriously, I feel like if I do something with the kids, you Monday-morning quarterback me. I have my way of doing things and you have yours. You make me feel like mine has no validity in your eyes. I feel that you get mad if I don't do something, but if I do it, it won't be right.

Later, the subject turned to Jim's attitude about work.

Jim: I really hate having to have two jobs while you stay home with the kids.

Jane: That's what I mean. You put me down and make being with the kids sound like it's nothing, because it doesn't make money.

Th: Jane, you're defending yourself. He's telling you what he's feeling. Try to find out more about it.

Jane: Tell me more about how you feel about work.

Jim: What I really feel is that it's unfair. I want to be as involved with the kids as you are. I don't mind splitting up work with you. In fact, I'm envious, I guess, when I'm working two jobs, you are at home, and I don't get the time at home.

This encounter led to a new understanding for both partners. Jane expressed surprise, saying, "It's incredible to me that it took you 7 years to tell me that you don't feel that everything I've done is nothing. I wish you could have said that along the way." Jim responded, "I think I am kind of jealous, and instead it came out as an attack on you."

This example illustrates the beneficial effects of teaching a couple how to interview one another. It also highlights the importance of an active therapist intervening frequently to stop defensive and attacking statements and supply appropriate one-ended questions. Eventually, because the rewards are so valued by the clients themselves, they learn to interview one another in a competent manner, which paves the way for empathy and understanding.

BROOKS'S INTERGENDER TRANSLATING AND REFRAMING

Description

Brooks (1991b, 1995) has described his efforts to improve communication in couples stressed by disequilibrium in traditional gender-role alignments. This approach is largely a product of a Veteran's Affairs Hospital work environment, a context in which the male partner commonly has had a traditional gender-role orientation and is resistant to relationship change. Because the impetus for change typically comes from the woman, who has become newly empowered owing to her husband's disability, this approach places extensive emphasis on the therapist as supporter of political change. This perspective holds that no in-session techniques are likely to be effective unless the political context of the relationship is managed, prochange pressures have been supported, and the antichange pressures have been neutralized. Only when that has been accomplished can the therapist move to the next phase: the estimable task of promoting compassion and understanding between the partners, serving as intergender translator and reframer.

Setting the Stage

The basic premise of this approach is that in "traditional" couple relationships (those in which both partners began the relationship with traditional gender-role expectations of each other), a common precipitant to therapy is the poor fit between traditional marital roles and contemporary pressures on men and women. Typically, the partner who seeks help is the woman, and the partner resisting change is the man. Given that the husband generally has more physical, financial, or political power, the change potential is dependent on the wife's empowerment. Brooks (1991b) suggested a six-stage treatment model for this situation: (a) The therapist becomes knowledgeable regarding the gender-role pressures and socialization of each partner; (b) the therapist maintains therapeutic lever-age by perpetuating homeostatic imbalance (i.e., resisting premature reconciliation); (c) the woman's empowerment is supported; (d) encouragement is given to the man for willingness to consider change; (e) consciousness-raising activities are provided to the man; and (f) the therapist monitors the situation regarding possible conjoint therapy for reconciliation.

Making Connections: Developing Empathic Knowing

This model, like the others described herein, places heavy emphasis on the need to make connections with each marital partner, that is, to convey deep appreciation of each partner's gender-role accommodations. In this stage, when each person becomes more attuned to his or her gender-role issues and experiences compassionate support from the therapist, the process of empathic knowing is begun.

Occasionally, this connecting and reframing process can begin in conjoint sessions, especially in the rare instances when both partners have become keenly aware of their own gender-role issues and have developed nonadversarial interest in the perspective of the other. More commonly, however, both partners have, at best, some awareness of their own issues and a fairly contentious attitude toward their partner's ideas. A further complication is the typical gender imbalance in preparedness; that is, women simply have been thinking about these relationship matters for a longer time. It is common, if not modal, for a man to see the problems as "coming out of the blue" or for him to feel "blindsided" by her dissatisfactions. In these cases, it may be necessary to do individual therapy with both partners before attempting conjoint work.

The sessions with the woman are usually easier because of the woman's interest in therapy as a mechanism for change. Although the woman may be distrustful of her husband, she is likely to view the therapist as a potential ally. This will be especially true when the therapist validates her by demonstrating familiarity with her struggles. Here, the therapist and the woman thoroughly catalogue the multiple ways that patriarchal culture has impinged on women in general and on her in particular. In this session, the woman's distress is placed in the context of the larger culture, and the woman discovers an understanding supporter.

Sessions with the male partner are likely to begin more stressfully, placing greater demands on the therapist's skills at "joining." Typically distrustful of psychotherapy, the man commonly enters the sessions with a variety of negative postures: hostility, resentment, fear, embarrassment, or shame. He may view therapy as a necessary price to pay to reestablish the marital relationship, or he may see it as a mechanism for manipulating his spouse. In brief, few men enter therapy with appreciable awareness of gender-role issues and strain. Even fewer men enter therapy wishing for significant gender-role changes.

The first manifestation of empathic knowing emanates from the therapist. To defuse a man's apprehensions about therapy, the therapist approaches the man with clear communication of acceptance and understanding of the male experience. As an informed guide, the therapist eases the client through an exploration of his masculine socialization experiences, discovering areas of pride and areas of strain. A gender-informed therapist usually has little difficulty helping a man discover formerly unrecognized areas of emotional pain. Education about the changing culture and the pressures of masculinity offers new avenues of exploration for men as well as alternative explanations for role failures.

For example, even the most well-defended and argumentative man may be relieved to find a therapist who does not begin from a critical stance but from a posture of validating the man's best intentions. In this more comfortable atmosphere, the male client is likely to be engaged by inquiries about his work (or inability to work), his social isolation or estrangement from his children's lives, his sexual disappointments or dissatisfactions, his need to ignore his physical discomfort and emotional distress, and his anxiety about his ability to maintain a stoic masculine facade.

A critical final element during this stage of therapy is preparation of women and men for the conjoint sessions yet to come. In the separate sessions, the therapist has helped each marital partner to discover personal gender issues. But the therapist should then begin to introduce "benevolent curiosity" about the positions of the other partner—the "flip side" of the issues. The therapist raises questions about what things must be like for the partner. "Wouldn't it be interesting and helpful to know what your partner thinks about this?" This stage of therapy ends with an introduction to the potential benefits of gender coevolution.

Conjoint Sessions

When the previous treatment stages have been completed and the marital partners seem confident that the therapist appreciates their respective positions (by demonstrating benevolent curiosity), conjoint sessions are helpful. In these sessions, the therapist may do well to be more active than usual in facilitating communication. Much as the language interpreter occupies a central position in international negotiations, the therapist may find it helpful to serve as a communication mediator, or translator of separate languages of the genders. After receiving input from one partner, the therapist "decodes" the message by placing it in the context of that person's value system. Then, before sending it to the intended receiver, the therapist reframes the message in terms of the sender's efforts to enhance the overall relationship, according to the logic of the receiver's gender world. Once the receiver of the input recognizes the positive intent of the message, he or she can respond concerning how well that behavior meshes with his or her needs. The process continues with the therapist helping the partners to see how traditional role patterns create problems and to negotiate new arrangements that more closely meet each other's needs.

In general, this approach is similar to most couples therapy approaches, except that it places major emphasis on how gender-based differences in communication style affect therapy. It differs in terms of (a) its preoccupation with power and relational politics and (b) the initially high degree of centrality of the therapist.

Case Example: Finding a New Path

Kathy called to make the appointment, but that seemed to be about all she felt willing to do. In the first session with the couple, Kathy was passive, almost sullen; Jerry was more active, but obviously apprehensive.

Kathy (age 29) and Jerry (34) had been separated for several months following a 10-year marriage. They had married after Kathy's first year at an out-of-state college. Jerry, who had stayed in the home community to continue working for an engineering firm, had great difficulty with Kathy's absence. Kathy had been anxious and ambivalent about returning to school. Jerry and both sets of parents lent support to the stay-at-home side of Kathy's ambivalence. Kathy abandoned her college plans, and she and Jerry were married that fall.

The marriage went reasonably well for several years. Jerry's work was challenging and his salary was lucrative, and Kathy found a reasonably tolerable administrative assistant position. Unfortunately, Kathy's job had relatively few challenges and no real advancement possibilities. As her work became more tedious, Kathy became more restive and frustrated. Tension mounted. Jerry could not understand Kathy's unhappiness and was frustrated that she seemed to take him for granted.

Several events pushed the marriage to the breaking point. Two years before the therapist met the couple, Jerry had become infatuated with a young woman he met on the job. Although the relationship broke off before an affair developed, bad feelings remained. Kathy was hurt; Jerry was only partially remorseful because he felt Kathy had lost interest in him.

At her job, Kathy encountered unexpected problems. Her boss, a married man in his mid-50s, began making sexual overtures to her. At one point, he suggested that Kathy become his personal travel assistant, accompanying him on his many international trips. Although she was outraged by his advances, Kathy was dismayed to realize that she was not totally uninterested: World travel seemed far more exciting than the routine of her current job. She flatly rejected her boss's advances but was left feeling even more dissatisfied with her situation.

Matters worsened when Kathy's father suffered a moderate heart attack, leaving him partially paralyzed and intensely aware of his mortality. Because Kathy felt that her father had lofty ambitions for her, she began to experience even higher levels of frustration and a greater sense of urgency about her career. Additionally, Kathy's younger sister announced that she was pregnant for the third time, and Kathy's mother escalated pressure for Kathy to enter the "grandbaby sweepstakes."

The final stressor was Kathy's chance encounter with Angela, her former college roommate, who had an exciting position with a firm in a nearby city. As they visited, Kathy recognized envy for Angela's lifestyle as well as her own growing feelings of emotional suffocation. In their conversation, Angela, who lived in a college town 60 miles away, offered Kathy a place to stay if her marriage ever deteriorated.

Not sure how to proceed, Kathy decided she needed a marital separation. She was not ready to take Angela's offer, but she felt she had to get away from Jerry. In the several months immediately preceding the first session with them, Kathy and Jerry had lived separately, seeing each other a few times each week.

The first session was confusing and disjointed. Kathy maintained that she wanted to save the marriage but seemed listless and discouraged. Jerry was hurt and anxious. He professed great love for Kathy and a willingness to make any sacrifice to save the marriage. He spoke emotionally about his dreams for "having a family and growing old" with Kathy. This made her intensely restless and seemed to harden her resolve to leave. The more Jerry expressed love for Kathy, the "meaner" she acted. She sniped about his habits, his friends, his language, his interpersonal clumsiness, his sexual crudeness, and his simplistic lifestyle. The session ended with Jerry near tears and Kathy more bitter than ever. Fearing even greater distress, the therapist opted to see them separately for a few sessions.

Kathy presented in therapy in a defensive posture, because she knew she had been a "bad wife." Everyone loved Jerry—both sets of parents, their friends (most of whom were Jerry's work associates), and the members of their small-town community. Kathy was a mystery to everyone. How could she be unhappy with Jerry, after all he did for her? On one level, Kathy entered the session claiming she wanted to learn how to love Jerry again, to become a good wife, to discover her "maternal instincts." On another level, however, she was ready to attack if the therapist made any movements in that direction. Fortunately, he just listened to her.

When she realized that the therapist intended to listen and support, Kathy found her voice. She eloquently described her role in her family of origin: pride of her father and competitor with her mother. For the first time, she recognized the intensity of the bitterness she felt toward her mother and Jerry for not supporting her college plans. She realized that the years had made her increasingly fearful and demoralized. She felt trapped and suffocated by Jerry's love and devotion, her fears, and her guilt.

As we talked, however, the therapist was able to raise some questions about Jerry's "love and devotion." He claimed a willingness to "do anything" to save the marriage, but when Kathy's career was discussed, he reversed stance. Kathy remembered that Jerry had always been careful to note that they were totally dependent on Jerry's job and that relocation was impossible. Kathy had always accepted this, but now she was not so convinced. As they talked, she realized that Jerry's love was far from unconditional and had substantial strings attached. Kathy realized that her insecurities had been fueled by the image that Jerry and her mother held of her—bright but "flighty" and unpredictable. As she heard herself talk, Kathy discovered that she was not silly, flighty, or foolish and that there was validity to her feelings of unrest. She vowed to take charge of her life and began to make the necessary plans. The empathic knowing of the therapist had helped empower her to begin destabilizing the old marital relationship. It was yet to be determined if "gender coevolution" would be possible. That depended on the outcome of meetings with Jerry.

By the time the therapist saw Jerry the next week, Jerry was in acute distress. He arrived 20 minutes early and was eager to get help in coping with his marital crisis. Although not an overly demonstrative person, Jerry was clearly upset and fearful. As he viewed the situation, he had always been highly reasonable and considerate of Kathy's needs. When she was unhappy, he exerted tremendous effort to make her happier.

Lately, however, Jerry had begun to be alarmed at the intensity of Kathy's unrest. Her conviction about pursuing a career, whatever the cost, had pushed him toward panic. He came to the session with multiple questions: What should he make of Kathy's new attitude? Where would this lead? More to the point, how could he change her mind? How could he get her back? Jerry's hopes for therapy were straightforward: "Please help me figure out a way to get my marriage back to what it was several years ago."

In the explorations of Jerry's concerns, one major fear was discovered. Despite his obvious competence and career success, Jerry knew that Kathy was, in many ways, brighter and more talented than he. His fear was simple: What if Kathy outdid him? What if she found herself surrounded by men who were smarter and more talented? Wouldn't she abandon him?

The session was immensely helpful in highlighting Jerry's reactions to Kathy. Jerry saw no benefit to Kathy's career. Her empowerment was fraught with dangers. From his perspective, any reasonable man would oppose it. Here the session had arrived at the crux of the matter. If the marriage was to continue, Jerry had to coerce Kathy back to her old role, or he had to confront his fears of a new, more equalitarian relationship.

First, we discussed the option of suppressing Kathy. Jerry wanted the therapist's ideas on the issue, and he gave him a twofold response. First, he told him that, in his view, suppression of Kathy would not work well, because she was determined to continue her career. Furthermore, even if he could hold her back, the price would be too high, with the risk of her returning to a demoralized and unhappy state. Second, the therapist advised Jerry that Kathy's career could be exactly what the marriage needed: a major plus for Kathy *and* for him. Jerry was skeptical but willing to listen and consider the process of gender coevolution.

*Gender Coevolution: Is It a "Leap of Faith" or
a Cautious Step?*

Jerry, like most men, had been taught to base his self-worth on his capacity to provide, to lead, and to protect. It was according to this value system that he took care of Kathy. The better he was able to perform in these areas, the more valuable and lovable he felt. But this lovability was conditional. Any disruption in his functioning, whether from disability, unemployment, or retirement, could jeopardize his sense of worth. "If I don't lead or work, how can Kathy possibly love me? Wouldn't she realize that she's better off without me weighing her down?"

But Jerry had a more intriguing problem. He *was* functioning as a provider. He wanted to lead and protect. But Kathy was not buying into that arrangement. She seemed to be moving toward emotional and financial self-sufficiency. To Jerry, this was functionally equivalent to *his* not functioning. If he were not the sole provider and relationship leader, Kathy would not need him and therefore would not want him. From this perspective, Jerry had to resist Kathy's plans. It was his only source of security in the relationship: As long as she needed him, he would have a place in her life. At this point, the therapist had to intervene.

A critical objective of therapeutic work with Jerry was the introduction of a new model of male–female relationships. The therapist had to show Jerry a relationship model that was based on cooperation, interdependence, and mutuality rather than on domination, rigid leadership, and control. He needed to convince Jerry that it might be possible for Kathy to love him because she *wanted* him, not because her welfare was dependent on him. He would have to realize that he could maintain Kathy's respect even if he did not keep meeting all the traditional standards of masculinity.

The problem is as follows: Although it is not always spoken about openly, this model flies directly in the face of what most men have been taught about women. Men are taught that biology and evolutionary programming cause women to be drawn irresistibly to the strongest, most powerful, and most highly functioning male of the species. After all, hasn't survival of the species been dependent on this elemental fact of nature?

The therapist knew he would have a hard time convincing Jerry that the alternative model would work. Not only was it contrary to his traditional male socialization, but to some extent it was unpopular and unproven. After all, if this model were so great, where were all the success stories? Weren't the same old male heroes still getting the women on television and in the movies? His male friends certainly endorsed the traditional "keep 'em barefoot and pregnant" model. Could the therapist produce compelling empirical evidence that this change would almost always produce greater happiness?

What could the therapist offer Jerry? First, he needed to tell him about what many women were beginning to say regarding their new expectations of men. He needed to tell him about the growing literature supporting the advantages of equalitarian relationships. To be more convincing, however, the therapist needed to describe the personal testimony of the many men who had successfully walked this path. In short, he had to persuade Jerry to consider the radical idea that the bulk of what he had been taught about male–female relationships might be false. Although the therapist could offer him some impressive testimony, on some level Jerry had to take a "leap of faith" against conventional male wisdom.

On one level, the therapist asked Jerry to take a revolutionary step when he asked him to consider a radically different way of relating to Kathy. On another level, however, their process of relating differently was much more tentative, cautious, and interactive. Jerry and Kathy would each take a step, observe the reactions of the other, and proceed from there. Progress was not a direct path from point A to point B but a much more irregular and erratic course.

In particular, Jerry needed to become more relaxed about masculine performance standards and more attentive to supporting Kathy's empowerment. But was this safe? Was Kathy ready for a less traditional man, or was she ambivalent, still fantasizing about a man to take care of her? Once the process was underway, the therapist had to work with both Kathy and Jerry to help them evolve together.

Men's Resistance to Gender Coevolution: Finding Jerry's Pain

Before couples will undertake gender coevolution, many traditional values, beliefs, and emotional impediments must be faced. We focus here on the specific issues faced by men like Jerry.

Jerry grew up believing that it is a man's duty to protect and provide for his family. He had done that and done it well. He felt proud of his success, but he was keenly disappointed that Kathy showed no gratification or appreciation. She seemed to have no trouble taking advantage of the opportunities his work made possible, but she never seemed grateful. He felt that he had not expected much, just a few signs of recognition and appreciation. He said that he hated to complain but felt that most men got better treatment than he; he was entitled to more in return for his efforts. He claimed that he even supported some career ambitions for Kathy, as long as she did not get "carried away with them." In brief, Jerry felt cheated. He married Kathy expecting that she would live up to their initial contract, but she was now changing the rules. He wanted the old contract back.

As a young man, Jerry had assumed that he would eventually recreate his family of origin. Although he knew that men liked to pretend to want independence, he realized that the *Father Knows Best* fantasy was his fondest dream. He wanted a home, a dutiful wife, and loving kids. True to his socialization, he yearned for a son he could teach and coach and a daughter who would love and admire him. Jerry admired his father and always expected to continue the family tradition. But Kathy seemed to be raising doubts about his dream family. Wouldn't her career destroy his dreams? The thought was deeply depressing to him.

Jerry's image of his father was that of a successful and utterly confident "master of the universe." Neither his success nor his wife's fidelity were ever a source of concern. Jerry had expected to follow that path and become a competent and indispensable provider. Because he was desperately needed by his wife, he would have nothing to fear. But Kathy threatened that security. If she did not need him, would she still want him? Wouldn't there be a great risk of her replacing him with a more competent, more highly functioning man?

Jerry was intensely secretive about his marital problems. Although he often held Kathy accountable for the problems, he privately suspected that the marriage failed because he was not manly enough. After all, hadn't their sex life gone to hell? Raised to believe that "real men" satisfy their wives, Jerry felt shame that Kathy was so unhappy. How did he fail? Was he too inarticulate? Too inadequate as a sexual performer? His self-esteem was devastated.

Finding A New Path: Helping Jerry Counter His Pain

Once the therapist had identified Jerry's pain, he could offer alternatives to the traditional male value system that supported it. It would have been foolish and arrogant to claim that Jerry had no justification whatsoever for his bitterness and anger. Even though his expectations may have been based on a patriarchal model, he had tried to play by the only rules he had been taught. From his perspective, he had a right to be mad.

The therapist's role was to help Jerry see the self-defeating aspects of his anger. Furthermore, the therapist wanted to help him see the world from Kathy's perspective and show him how traditional expectations of women had been suffocating Kathy and jeopardizing her long-term welfare. The therapist had to help Jerry understand how the world was changing, thereby helping him appreciate why Kathy felt she had to change.

Jerry's anxiety was based on his idea that Kathy thought in the same way that he had been taught to think. Kathy assured me that she had become less interested in Jerry's leading her and now wanted his support for her ambitions. She loved it when he validated her ambitions rather than her fears and insecurities. The therapist's role was to help Jerry recognize this new route to Kathy's affection.

Jerry's traditional dreams might not be realized, so he had a right and a need to grieve for them. Yet all was not lost. There could be new dreams and new satisfactions based on a relationship that offered satisfactions, intimacy, and mutual affirmation that were not possible in traditional arrangements. The therapist's job was to help Jerry begin to appreciate the possibilities.

Jerry thought he was alone in the struggle with new definitions of masculinity and that he alone could not "keep his wife in line." As the therapist helped him to overcome outmoded patriarchal role pressures, he needed to help him realize the magnitude and prevalence of the issue. It was not a matter of his failure as a leader but a profound alteration in the way women and men were looking at the world.

Outcome

Jerry and Kathy have taken many steps toward gender coevolution. Kathy has entered school and is living with Angela. Despite his fears, Jerry has agreed to provide financial support for Kathy and has developed enthusiasm for her career objectives. Kathy has found new affection for Jerry and has begun to consider a possible reconciliation.

The outcome is far from clear, however. Kathy is wrestling with ambivalence and sometimes considers abandoning her career plans. Jerry gets fearful and "slips," that is, initiates controlling maneuvers (calling her late at night to check up on her whereabouts or griping to Kathy's parents about her inattention to his needs). In general, however, both have recognized the benefits, and they have agreed to fight jointly the multiple impediments to the new relationship they are gradually creating.

CONCLUSION

In this chapter, we have provided the reader with a variety of techniques, all with the goal of empathic knowing, that can be employed to help clients understand and resolve gender-socialization issues. Case examples have illustrated the importance gender messages play in keeping couples stuck in unsatisfying patterns and what the therapist can do to lead the couple out of their pain into more fulfilling relationships. In each of these cases, the clients gained an understanding of how their gender socialization had influenced their relationship. They developed empathy for the plight of the other and dropped the defensive posture that had kept them in unproductive conflict. Instead, they began to experiment with new ways to relate that were not endorsed and supported by traditional gender socialization. They became aware that they could choose to deviate from traditional expectations when such deviation allowed them to have a more fulfilling relationship. In the next chapter, we discuss and illustrate the unique process of gender inquiry, which brings about the attitude change required to achieve such positive results in therapy.

8

Gender Inquiry

People seldom have the opportunity to sort out how they learned to be a boy or girl, a female or male adolescent, and later, a man or woman. We receive cues from many sources but are often unmindful of their meaning and influence on our growth. As we have demonstrated in chapter 2, we learn about gender from our parents, our siblings, our peers, our teachers, and our religious and cultural institutions, as well as from our reading, television, movies, and theater. This learning of gender roles has a powerful impact on later functioning and relationships. In chapter 5, we summarized the research concerning expectations, values, coping methods, priorities, communication styles, and personality variables of men and women, as well as the positive and negative impacts of gender socialization on both genders. In this chapter, we relate important questions that the therapist may use to explore this gender history. We see this exploration, which we call a "gender inquiry," as essential to the conduct of gender-sensitive therapy. It is a process that sensitizes not only patients, but the therapist as well. We find that when the therapist has done a number of such inquiries and has examined his or her own gender experience or gender-role journey (O'Neil & Roberts-Carroll, 1988), she or he becomes acutely conscious of gender issues that earlier would have been ignored or mishandled.

WHAT A GENDER INQUIRY ACHIEVES

The gender inquiry is consonant with gender-sensitive training models such as Roberts' (1991) that were developed for family therapy trainees. The aim of an inquiry is to clarify the variety of ways in which gender messages are transmitted across generations. These include transmission at the micro level by significant others in the inquiree's life (e.g., parents, siblings, extended family) and important adults (e.g., teachers, youth leaders, religious authorities) and at the macro level by the various media, including books, movies, music, theater, and school curricula, and all of the other ways in which culture is transmitted. Some of these messages are idiosyncratic; that is, they reflect the specifics of a given person or family. Others are nomothetic; they present norms present in the dominant culture or peculiar to the ethnicity of one or another member of the couple or family.

We are convinced that such an inquiry develops insight both for the person being questioned and for other family members who witness the inquiry. These new insights, we believe, produce greater empathy for members of one's own and the opposite gender. Increased empathy, in turn, can stimulate dialogue about how to change messages that appear to be detrimental to relationships between men and women. Such cognitive and empathic shifts can have a profound effect not only on relationships between men and women, but also on the ways in which parents and other significant adults interact with children of both genders.

QUALITIES OF A SUCCESSFUL GENDER INQUIRY

Many therapists, and certainly those trained in family systems, are aware of patterns of familial interaction that repeat from generation to generation. They are less likely to be conscious of the impact of gender socialization, which often is also embedded in family traditions as well as in ethnic and social class values transmission.

The most organized body of writing about gender was inspired by feminist theory and scholarship. H. G. Lerner (personal communication, August, 1995), for example, defined *gender* as "the predominant cultural meaning that the dominant group ascribes to being male or female at a particular time and in a particular place." This is a useful nomothetic understanding of gender. As therapists, however, our interest is directed also to the great individual variance in human behavior including the transmission of gender values. Although we must be aware of the most common patterns (see chapter 5), we should also preserve our curiosity about how a specific person has learned his or her gender role and remember that there is a wide divergence in this learning. We must begin an inquiry carefully, therefore, without allowing the most common constructions about gender to interfere with our ability to hear our patients in an open and unbiased manner. It is our responsibility to help our clients to understand, explore, and grow, rather than to impose our own values.

To maintain a nonjudgmental stance, it is most important that questions be phrased in a general way, in an attempt to avoid "leading" the respondent. Rhetorical questions (e.g., "Do you see how your father's orders put your mother at a disadvantage?") may cause the interviewee to become defensive, thus inhibiting the development of insight and blocking change.

We have developed an array of questions that we hope will stimulate conversation about gender and its role in people's lives and relationships. There is no one right way to use this inquiry, and each situation will suggest where to place the focus. It is our hope that the therapist will develop a great curiosity about gender issues and will ask still other relevant questions in the context of the therapeutic process.

In chapters 2 through 5, we discussed the research concerning how most men and women learn to live gendered lives. This information prepares therapists for some of the responses they may expect to hear while conducting the gender inquiry. However, the therapist is cautioned to remember that each person is unique and that although many of the experiences men and women have are common to their gender, some are not. It is best to conduct the gender inquiry with this idiosyncratic approach in mind, remaining sensitive at the same time to the relevant nomothetic issues.

Although we present a series of questions that are arranged in a logical and sequential manner, the therapist will probably choose to keep the issues raised by these items in mind for use as the opportunity arises, rather than presenting them in an organized and formal way. In whatever manner it is used, such an inquiry is valuable for individuals, couples, and families in treatment; for an understanding of normative gender development; and for training purposes. The promotion of an understanding of the ways in which gender affects feelings, thoughts, and behaviors also helps to create a new level of empathy and thus fosters improved communication.

WHEN TO INTRODUCE A GENDER INQUIRY

The opportunity to introduce an inquiry is recognized by the context. For example, a patient in individual therapy may mention difficulty in her relationship with her mother. Further conversation might reveal that she was uncomfortable with the subservient way in which her mother acted toward her father. This would be a useful time to begin a gender inquiry. Similarly, an opportunity arises when a couple is locked in a struggle about the division of labor in their relationship or as parents struggle with the reaction of their daughter to parental rules that are different from those imposed on her brother.

For the most part, it is probably wisest to proceed in a developmental fashion, going back to people's early learnings about gender rather than attempting to fashion an immediate intervention at the moment that one senses some gender issue arising. For example, if a couple is arguing about division of labor, an immediate intervention might take the form of an attempt on the therapist's part to help the couple to come to some new agreement about equity issues. A developmental approach would begin with a more leisurely examination of how each member of the couple saw such issues handled in their families of origin. A full understanding of the immediate problem usually requires an appreciation of the context of past gender-role socialization.

The therapist should be aware that when gender issues are raised, they are likely to arouse intense reactions. We are most likely to trigger strong emotional behavior if we begin with highly politicized questions, for example, who does the majority of household chores or who bears major responsibility for child rearing? We might make an analogy here to the common experience of family therapists, who find that rather than taking historical information and doing a genogram at the beginning of therapy, it is wiser to hold off on these activities until the therapist has developed rapport with the couple or the family and at least obtained a tentative and rudimentary sense of the system's toxic issues.

It is often just at the point that such toxic issues begin to arise in therapy, frequently in a highly emotionally charged and potentially destructive manner, that the cooler and more objective method of history taking may enable the couple or family to understand one another's experience.

WHAT SHOULD AN INQUIRY INCLUDE?

What follows is a broad series of questions from which the therapist may choose. These suggestions are not intended to be used as a questionnaire but as a source of stimuli to promote conversation about gender. A few questions may suffice to bring forth a wealth of information. Some of these questions are more appropriately explored when seeing a patient alone, because they might be embarrassing to discuss with other family members present. (See the appendix for a discussion of the ethical dilemmas such an individual interview may pose and methods of maintaining confidentiality.) The questions are phrased in a general way, in an attempt to avoid "leading" the respondent. As the interviewer draws out the respondent, it is equally important to proceed in a nonjudgmental way. We have divided the inquiry into developmental areas; we begin with the questions related to childhood.

Childhood

1. Do you think that your mother (father) treated you in some special or different way because you were a girl (boy)? How?

2. Do you remember anything that your parents did that strengthened your sense of being a boy (girl)? What was it?

3. Do you remember talking with either of your parents about being a girl (boy)? Which parent? What were some of the things you learned?

4. Were there things that you were forbidden to do when you were little because your mother or father didn't think that girls (boys) should do that sort of thing?

5. Were there things that you were specifically encouraged to do because of your gender?

6. Do you remember sometimes wanting to be like the other gender, for example, wanting to dress like that gender or wanting to change your name to one appropriate to the other gender? Did you speak about this with a parent, sibling, or friend? What was the response?

7. Did older siblings, peers, or teachers have very different ideas of what you should be like as a boy or girl? If so, how did this affect you?

Puberty

1. The transition from childhood to puberty is often a turning point in gender development. Do you remember some of the changes you experienced as a boy (girl) as you made this transition?

2. As a girl, how and by whom were you prepared for your first menstrual period? Did you feel that what you were told was helpful or that it made you uncomfortable? How do you feel you dealt with your first menses? What was the impact of breast development and other secondary sexual characteristics? How did other girls react to your breast development (too large, too small)?

3. As a boy, how and by whom were you prepared for the coming of puberty? Did the information you received help you to cope with wet dreams or with the fact that masturbation was now suddenly concluded by ejaculation? Were you worried about your physical size, penis size, and other secondary sexual characteristics?

4. As you entered puberty, what new expectations did you experience from parents, siblings, peers, teachers?

5. Do you think that you were particularly encouraged or discouraged in certain areas because of your gender (e.g., sports, intellectual pursuits, social activities, focus on appearance, artistic pursuits, vocational interests)? Did you receive similar or different messages from peers, parents, siblings, or teachers?

6. What did you learn about how you were expected to act with boys (if a girl) or girls (if a boy) and from whom? Did you get different messages from different sources? How did this affect you?

7. Did you sometimes wish you could have remained a child rather than entering puberty? Why?

High School Years

1. Moving from middle school or junior high school to senior high school is often a stressful time. What special challenges did this transition pose for you as a young woman (man)?

2. Did you feel that, as a member of your gender, there were particular expectations about the following:

Same-gender friendships
Participation in sports
Personal appearance
Intellectual achievement
Social interaction with "the other sex"
Sexual behavior
Personal reputation
Competitiveness
Friendliness
Career choice
Use of drugs or alcohol
Chores or responsibilities at home
Work
Curfews

3. Did you become emotionally involved with a member of the other gender while in high school? (If the client is gay or lesbian, similar questions should be raised about same-gender relationships. This should be done for all relevant questions for the remainder of the inquiry.) What did you most want out of this relationship (relationships)? What was the best thing about this relationship (relationships)? What was the worst? How did being in a relationship affect your relationships with same-gender friends? With other-gender friends? Did sexual or verbal abuse play any part in your other-gender relationships?

4. (If the person did not have an ongoing relationship:) What do you think stood in the way of your developing an ongoing relationship? Did you have brief relationships? What were you looking for in these encounters? Did you achieve your goals? Did sexual or verbal abuse play any part in these relationships?

5. Do you think that the expectations for you in the areas we have talked about so far were at all different because you were a girl (boy)?

6. Do you think that your own behaviors and values in these areas were like those of your peers or different? Do you think your parents, for the most part, approved or disapproved of your values and behaviors?

7. Think of the boy (for men) or girl (for women) whom you most admired in high school. Describe that person. In what way did that person seem to you to be an ideal representation of your gender? Were there ways in which that person fell short? How did you compare yourself to that person?

8. Was there a particular adult (e.g., teacher, family friend, coach, youth leader, relative) whom you most admired while in high school? Describe that person. In what way did that person seem to you to be an ideal representation of your gender? Were there ways in which that person fell short? How did you compare yourself to that person?

9. As you completed high school, did you feel ready for the next phase of your life as a member of your gender?

College or Early Work Experience

1. Did you begin working full-time right after high school? (If no, skip to the next section.)
2. Tell me something about your early work experience. Do you think that your gender had anything to do with the kinds of jobs that were available to you? Were there things you might have liked to try that seemed "off limits" because you were male or female?
3. Do you feel that the treatment you received at work was different because you were a female (male)?
4. Do you think your parents had differing expectations about work because you were a male (female)?
5. Did you sense any difference in the way men and women in general were valued in your work situation?
6. How did what you were seeing about the role of being a male or female at work square with what you had learned at home and in school?

If the person went to college:

1. Were your parents involved in your choice of college? Did gender considerations play any role in that choice?
2. Do you think gender had any effect on your choice of courses or college major?
3. Do you think that the treatment you received from advisors or teachers was in any way affected by your gender?
4. Did you see any difference in the way men and women were valued by faculty and staff?
5. What sort of social relations did you develop in college toward members of your own gender? Toward the other gender?
6. Did you develop an important relationship with a person of the other gender while in college? Describe the relationship.
7. How did your gender peers view this relationship? How did your parents react to it?
8. As you look back on the relationship, do you think that there were

aspects of the relationship dictated by gender that you now wish you could have done differently? In what way?

9. What were the qualities you most sought in a possible mate at that time? Have your ideas remained pretty much the same? If not, how have they changed?

Adulthood

Let's talk about your marriage now (or your current relationship or your current ideas about dating).

1. How would you compare your role as a woman (man) in this relationship with how your mother (father) acted?
2. Have your ideas about what you should be like as a woman (man) changed much as your relationship has progressed?
3. Do you believe that your mate takes an equitable share of responsibility in your relationship? (You might talk about this in terms of income or contribution in unpaid labor, household tasks, or child rearing).
4. Do you think that there are issues in your relationship that are hard to talk about with one another? Do you sometimes feel that there is no way to explain something to the other person because a man (woman) won't understand what you are feeling or trying to explain? Have you gotten better at breaking these impasses as the relationship has grown?
5. Have changing ideas about the roles of men and women over the last few decades had an impact on your relationship? Could you describe the impact?

A Few Final Questions

1. If you had asked your parents to tell you what kind of man or woman they had hoped you would become, what would they have said?

2. If your children asked you what kind of man or woman you would like them to become, what would you say?
3. If you could change one thing about how you function as a woman (man), what would it be?

CASE STUDIES

The method of inquiry we have outlined is of value not only as a therapeutic intervention, but also as a way of gathering data for the study of normal gender development. In fact, it is suggested that the clinician who seeks expertise in using gender inquiry begin by using the complete inquiry with a number of people who have no presenting problem. We begin with such an exploration, and then explore its use with couples and families.

Case 1. Application With an Individual

The Inquiry

Janice is a 40-year-old woman of orthodox Jewish background living in a large city on the East Coast. She is happily married and the mother of two young children, a girl age 10 and a boy of 8. She has a PhD in biochemistry and works part-time at a medical laboratory while she raises her children. Her husband is a well-established trial lawyer. She plans to return to full-time work in a more challenging job when the children are a bit older. She agreed to be interviewed out of curiosity. Following is a transcript of the interview. (*I* designates the interviewer, and *J* designates Janice.)

I: Thanks so much for consenting to be interviewed. I'm going to be asking you a series of questions that explore some aspects of your social development. Let's begin with your childhood—that is to say, before you reached puberty—from the time you were old enough to remember things until puberty. Do you think that your mom or dad treated you in some special or different way because you were a girl?

J: No, not really. It's kind of hard to tell, because my brother was so much older, so we never went through any stage of growing up together. I did have an older sister I was close with.

I: Do you remember anything that your parents did that strengthened your sense of being a girl?

J: Not really.

I: Do you remember talking with either parent about being a girl?

J: No.

I: Were there things that you were forbidden to do when you were little because of your gender?

J: I can't think of any in particular.

I: Were there things that you were particularly encouraged to do because of your gender?

J: I can't think of any in particular.

I: Do you remember sometimes wanting to be like the other gender, for example, wanting to dress like a boy?

J: Yes, I was a tomboy, big time, but I don't think that my folks minded.

I: Did your brother, sister, peers, or teachers have different ideas about how you should act as a girl?

J: No, I felt very accepted. Maybe my older sister was a little bother, because she was just the opposite, but nothing was made of it.

I: Let's go on to puberty. Do you remember some changes as you made the transition from childhood to puberty?

J: I began to be interested in boys, parties, spin the bottle, that kind of thing.

I: How were you prepared for your first menstrual period?

J: My mom was very prudish, and so she assigned my sister to tell me.

I: How did that work out?

J: I don't think it bothered me.

I: How did you feel about your changing body?

J: That went okay. I began to develop at about the same time as my friends.

I: As you entered puberty, what new expectations did you experience from your parents, sister and brother, peers, or teachers?

J: To do well in school. This was the most important thing, particularly coming from a strongly Jewish home. Interestingly enough, in our community the girls went to public school, while the boys went to Yeshiva [a religious day school, usually for boys]. Since I was a very good student, all of my teachers encouraged me.

I: Do you think you were particularly encouraged or discouraged in certain activities because you were a girl?

J: Mom thought I would be in trouble because I did things at the last moment. She especially worried about this.

I: What did you learn about how you were expected to act with boys?

J: Mom was very much a prude, so I couldn't talk about anything sexual with her. I got nothing. In fact, she expected me to know nothing, at least before marriage. My dad could be very open. Because he was a scientist [he was a biophysicist], he would talk to me about sexual things, but in a very scientific way, not so much in a personal way. If I had those kinds of questions, I went to friends.

I: Moving from junior high school to senior high is often a stressful time. How was it for you?

J: Not especially, maybe because of my older sister. I knew what she did before me.

I: Did you feel that, as a girl, there were particular expectations about any of these issues . . . ? [At this point, the interviewer explored the questions relating to the high school years. Only the salient replies are reported here.]

J: My personal appearance was important to me. I wanted to wear special things. It didn't have to be fancy, but it had to be "cool." I was still very motivated to achieve academically. I remember that I had a curfew, as did my sister, where my brother didn't. I was very competitive. I wanted to be best at whatever I did, whether it was school or athletics. In fact, I was a track star.

I: What about career choice?

J: My father kind of discouraged me from entering science as a career when I was in high school. Probably because he thought it would be hard for me to pursue a career, as a woman. But later, after college, he tried to push me toward medical school.

I: Did you become emotionally involved with a boy while you were a high schooler?

J: Yes, from 10th grade through most of college. He was good looking and intelligent.

I: What was the best thing about the relationship?

J: We were very similar. We shared interests in sports and science, and we were both good looking. We had the same goals.

I: What was the worst thing about the relationship?

J: He was selfish, egocentric. Everything of his came first: his exams, his track races. He became insulting; he spoke nastily in front of my friends. He was a sports "hero," and he got all puffed up with himself.

I: Think of the girl or woman you most admired in high school.

J: It's interesting. I had almost no female teachers. I think my only role model was really my father. It's only when I became a mother that I began to appreciate my mother.

I: As you completed high school, did you feel ready to move on to college?

J: Absolutely. I went to a woman's college, which went coed when I was a sophomore. I majored in chemistry. Only twelve out of about a thousand chem majors were women.

I: Did you see any difference in the way men and women were treated by faculty?

J: Quite the opposite. I felt that being in the sciences was very equalizing.

I: Did you develop a relationship with a man while in college?

J: I stayed in the same relationship. Little by little, my friends became aware that he was not treating me with respect, and they urged me to pull out. Maybe because it was a first relationship I stayed in it so long.

I: As you look back on the relationship, do you think that there were aspects of the relationship that were dictated by gender that you now wish you could have done differently?

J: I needed someone to treat me with more respect, put me first sometimes, give in to me sometimes. Someone who didn't have to win all the time; someone who could compromise.

I: Let's talk about your marriage now. How would you compare your role as a woman with how your mother was in her marriage?

J: My mom was a professional mother. This was enough for her. She didn't feel enslaved. She was very feminine. She didn't think she missed anything. I can't be home. I tried. I felt I was wasting time.

I: Have your ideas about what you should be like as a woman changed as your relationship has progressed?

J: Not really.

I: Do you believe that your husband takes an equitable share of responsibility in your relationship, for example, in household tasks, taking care of the kids, things like that?

J: He takes no role in those things. He is the main provider, but he is respectful of what I do and who I am. Not like my college boyfriend.

I: Do you think that there are issues in your relationship that it is hard to talk about with one another?

J: Sometimes. But the truth is that there are things that it's easier to explain to a woman, for example, having to take the brunt of home life, like having to cope with his need to eat at a certain time, having major responsibility for day-to-day things with the kids, things like that. Those I talk with my women friends about.

I: Is this a source of stress for you?

J: Not really. I think that, being in the sciences, I've felt an equal footing with men. It's just that I decided that, for now, my time would be divided between being a mother and a worker. But I feel respect from my husband in both my roles.

I: Just a few final questions. If you had asked your parents to tell you what kind of woman they had hoped you would become, what would they have said?

J: Mom would have said—the home, the family, and the children—take care of the kids, live through your children. I think, deep down, my father would say that he's sorry I didn't get my MD and only got my PhD. He wishes I was a PhD/MD. I won't do that, but I really want to go back to my career full-time when the kids are older. I guess, in a funny way, I am something of my father but also something of my mother.

I: If your daughter asked you what kind of woman you want her to be, what would you say?

J: I would tell her to do whatever makes her happy, what gives her self-respect. I think both my children have learned that women are supposed to do something very important with their lives.

Discussion

It is evident that Janice expresses comfort in her role and experiences herself as having achieved a balance between career and marriage. At the beginning of the interview, she reports herself as feeling treated similarly to her brother and sister, with no sense that she was receiving special gender messages. As the interview progresses, she seems equally unaware of the impact of her religious and cultural background on her gender development. It is interesting to speculate on the significance of the fact that, specifically because she was a girl, she was sent to the public schools, where her interest in the sciences was nurtured. It is also interesting that in many ways she fashioned herself more after her father than her mother. He was her model as a budding scientist; she could talk, albeit objectively, about sex with him. She was a tomboy, and it was accepted.

As the interview progresses, she describes her first major relationship. One senses that, were she a less integrated person, this relationship easily could have turned into a marriage with an underlying theme of domination and verbal, if not physical, abuse. Janice, however, used the experience to refine her ideas of what she wanted in a relationship. What is most important to her is that she feel respected by her mate and have the right to find her own way to integrate career and motherhood, with his approval and respect.

It is also interesting to note that, during her childhood, adolescence, and early adulthood, her primary model appears to be her father. She appears to have identified with the more worldly, rational, interesting, powerful, and effective parent. It is only during her adulthood, after the birth of her children, that she begins to sense appreciation for her mother's role in nurturing her and her siblings. In the end, she creates for herself a synthesis in which she finds fulfillment in work, relationship, and parenting.

Case 2. Clinical Application With a Couple

In exploring clinical applications of gender inquiry, we begin with the Farentinos, a couple whose presenting problem was a "sense of deadness" in their marriage. Despite their mutual complaint that after 25 years of marriage they both experienced a sense of "deadness" in the marriage, neither had thought of divorcing. Althea, a part-time salesperson in a dress shop, had been in individual therapy for some time for the treatment of depression. Having achieved little success, her therapist eventually suggested that martial therapy might be helpful. At the first meeting, Bill, an accountant, seemed equally depressed, although when questioned he said he was fine.

In the initial meeting, Althea expressed a great deal of bitterness toward an impassive Bill. She was angry because he was absolutely no help at home, because he showed little initiative (in her eyes) at work, and because he was "not a good friend." Bill said that things were fine and they would be perfect "if only Althea would stop pestering me about absolute bullshit." Now in their early 50s, finished with child rearing, their children "well launched," as Bill said, they seemed to have little to talk about without bickering.

It was difficult for the therapist to interrupt Althea's list of complaints. In fact, when the therapist intervened, Bill interrupted her and said, "Let Althea get it all out here." When asked whether he had any particular complaints about her, his reply was noncommittal. "So why are you here?" asked the therapist. "I'm Althea's guest," he replied. After a few sessions of this dance, the couple came in one day in a bitter argument, ostensibly about his refusal to help around the house.

The therapist felt that she needed to do something to break this cycle. Previous attempts had failed. As she listened, it was clear that the partners were struggling with their respective ideas of what men do and what women do. She thought of describing to them some of the literature about gender, but previous attempts along this line had been fruitless. Rather, she decided to explore with them what they knew about gender. She waited for an opportunity. Althea was complaining because she had been at work all day, and it had been a very hot day—a scorcher. Bill had come home from work early but did not prepare a light dinner for them, as she had hoped.

The therapist wondered aloud whether Bill had seen his father doing things around the house. "I sure did," he replied. "He was sick when I was growing up. In fact, he was on disability. My mother worked, and he was mostly at home, except for an odd job."

Th: Did you have brothers or sisters?

Bill: I had one sister, a couple of years older than myself.

Th: Do you think your mother or father treated you any differently?

Bill: Oh yes. My mother felt that we should help at home, you know, doing dishes, things like that. But my father was very adamant that was girl's work. Sometimes he would fight with my mother, that she would make me into a little girl. He would get especially angry if she would tell me to put on an apron when I did the dishes. It was strange, because he did dishes and things during the day, when she was out. But the minute she came home, he wouldn't do a thing. I think he was very angry because he couldn't work. I think he felt less a man. He had been a laborer and had loved his work. I think he liked the companionship with his friends also— he would go out drinking after work. All that stopped after the accident. He was really bummed out.

Th: So your mother and father really had different ideas about how to raise a boy.

Bill: Yeah. I remember, as I got older, my father was very strict about curfews and things for my sister. She was barely allowed out of the house, except for school.

Th: Did he have special rules for you too?

Bill: It's kind of funny. He didn't have real rules for me, like he did for Jeannette. But he had certain expectations for me. The most important was that I be a good athlete and, even more, what he called a "good sport."

Th: What's that?

Bill: Well, I was in Little League when I was a kid, and like if I got hit with

236

a ball or something and cried, he would get furious with me. Once he hit me because I cried when I got beaned. When I got older, it was very important to him that I made varsity. He bragged about that to his friends. I remember he would always kid my uncle Sal (whose son was interested in acting) that his kid would turn out to be a pansy, not like me. He never missed a game I was in.

Th: So he had very particular expectations for you.

Bill: Yeah, even about girls. It was almost like another sport for him. He wanted me to have lots of girls and (this is a little embarrassing) he wanted to know if I "banged" them too. I guess that was my major sex education: did I bang this girl or that. But there was more. He wanted me to get an athletic scholarship. He came from an immigrant Italian family. He wanted me to make something of myself. He told me he wanted to be sure that, no matter what happened, I would have a job. He pushed me to be an accountant, but I always hated it. I never even could get my CPA. That's why I still work as a comptroller, kind of a glorified bookkeeper. It's funny, because I loved high school. In fact, to this day, I'm an avid reader. But what I loved was English, social studies, languages, stuff like that. My father made fun of that. He would say, "Go with the dough." That's why he pushed accounting. He always insisted that I have a job in some kind of store in high school, so that I learned about business and brought in some money. But he wouldn't let my sister out of the house to work. She had to stay home to help with the chores Mom left *him* for the day and to help Mom at night. It pissed me off that he had so many expectations for me.

Th: How was your mother about this sort of thing?

Bill: She thought he was hard on me. She was the one who loved it when I picked up a book, just to read for fun. I think, if she'd had her way, I wouldn't have had to be an accountant. But she couldn't buck him. When she would try to fight him on something, he would say, "Here [meaning at home] I'm the man." I guess it was because he felt so lousy about not being able to work and that she brought home the bacon.

Th: Do you know how your mom felt about working?

Bill: I think that, secretly, she resented it, especially because she had to come home and do everything, but she never complained. She was wonderful. She took a lot of crap from him, because he was so mad, but she always made him feel good. Like he was a man.

Althea: Can I butt in here? Is that okay? [Therapist nods assent.] Bill, I don't think I ever told you, but you know how when Mom and I sat in the kitchen, she would talk to me a lot. She had a lot of bitterness. She felt that, if he hadn't felt so sorry for himself, he could have gone out and gotten some kind of work. But he refused. It made her angry. And she did show it, like she would "forget" to make him some food he liked, not iron his shirts right, things like that. There was a little silent war going on there.

Bill: I never saw that. It's funny, because sometimes I thought the same thing, that he could have done better, even after the accident. I can see her being angry, but I never thought of that. I certainly didn't see her show it directly.

Althea: It doesn't surprise me that you didn't see it, like your father. But it was there.

Th: What were your relationships with girls like when you were in high school?

Bill: I never stayed with one girl for very long. I would get angry and hurt quickly, think they didn't care. I also felt very screwed up about sex with girls. It was kind of strange. I think maybe because my father made such a fuss about it, I kind of didn't want to go too far. It was kind of a reversal thing. But underneath it, I was angry. I would get sarcastic and push them away.

Th: What about in college?

Bill: It was kind of the same, until I met Althea. I felt that she was kind and reassuring, like my mother. She was very supportive. She knew I hated the business courses and encouraged me to broaden myself. But she didn't push me like my father did. But I knew I had to do pretty much what my father wanted. It's kind of like, like a given. You have to figure out how you're going to support your wife and family, and like he said, it's a lot better to do it with your head than with your hands. It's just that [he starts to tear up], sometimes I hate it, I never liked the work. I really don't feel I ever made my mark, ever will, but—you gotta go on.

Althea: [Reaches for Bill's hand.] I never heard him talk like this. God, Bill, I'm always asking how your day was, things like that, and you always put me off.

Th: Althea, I think it might be helpful to you to know that the research indicates that men frequently avoid directly talking about emotionally significant issues. Maybe you'd like to ask him some more about this now?

Althea: Bill, it kills me to see you looking so sad, but to tell you the truth, it's kind of a relief for me. It's a part of you I've never really seen.

This exchange was an important turning point. For several sessions, the focus remained on Bill and his previously unexpressed pain and sorrow about his inability to meet the demands of the role in which he had felt imprisoned. During these sessions, the therapist pressed Althea to listen carefully as Bill talked about his discouragement with his work, which seemed so central and all-demanding to him. He learned that it was safe to talk with her about this, a possibility he had never considered. The therapist also suggested that Bill begin to do some reading about male consciousness. Bill picked up a little book in the waiting room called *What Every Man Needs to Know* (Pasick, 1994). This paperback contains a series of 365 ideas culled from things men have said in groups that the author worked with. None longer than a sentence, each seemed to jump off the page for Bill. These ideas seemed to open new worlds for him. They urged him to let up on himself as a man, to let himself experience his own vulnerability.

During these sessions, the therapist was tempted to move on to explore Althea's gender issues as well. Experience had taught her, however, that Bill would be much more receptive to Althea's issues if he were really in touch with his own. She waited patiently until Bill came to the topic of his perceptions of his mother and sister. It was only as he became empathically connected to himself as a man that he became more aware of the anger and hurt that were a part of their lives to which he had been numbed. The therapist continued to encourage Althea to draw him forth and to let him know that she could hear him and accept his feelings. As Bill began to feel better about himself, the therapist felt ready to shift to an exploration of Althea's gender history.

The exploration of Bill's feelings about his mother and sister seemed an ideal jumping point. Bill was now aware of how his father's disappointment in himself had shadowed the lives of his mother and sister. One day he said, "I wonder what would have happened if my family had come to see someone like you. Maybe we could have straightened some of this out."

The therapist said, "Maybe you can break the chain that your father was part of. One thing you can do in the present is to begin to really talk with Althea. A good place to begin would be to learn about how Althea learned to be a woman, just the way we've worked these last several sessions on how you learned to be a man."

The therapist then conducted a similar inquiry with Althea, enlisting Bill as her "cotherapist," encouraging him to ask questions that drew her forth. Althea had come from a "traditional" home, in which her father was the breadwinner and her mother was a "housewife" who devoted a great deal of time to church and other community work as a volunteer. Life had seem idyllic to Althea until she discovered, when she was in her late teens, that her mother was having an affair. This was never talked about in her home, and eventually the affair "blew over." Its effects shook Althea, however, calling into question everything she had learned in her home and church and leaving her feeling disillusioned about her mother and protective of her father. As we spoke, she expressed amazement that she had never spoken with anyone about this painful discovery. The issue of the affair, which occurred in the early 60s was explored in the context of the times. The therapist mused that it was curious that the affair happened at just about the time that Betty Friedan had written *The Feminine Mystique* (1963) and suggested that Althea read it. This led Althea to begin to think more empathically about her mother, to whom she had never felt close since the discovery. The therapy focused for several sessions on Althea's realization that her mother's affair was in part a reaction to her father's total absorption in work. A successful businessman, he seemed to work almost endlessly. As a child and adolescent, she had viewed her father's work schedule as "heroic." It was only now that she began to be aware of how his work had become a barrier between him and her mother. She became aware of how excluded she too felt from his life.

The therapist developed this theme of separation: In each of their families, their parents were, in a way, trapped in their genders and unable to reach across the gap. The gender inquiry enabled Bill and Althea to begin to talk with one another about what they each wanted from the marriage and to see how the gender stresses in their parents' marriages had affected their own relationship. Both agreed that, more than anything, they wanted to be able to continue to talk with one another the way they had begun to in therapy and not, as Bill expressed it, "to retreat into our separate corners the way we used to." They began to report that they were increasingly able to continue these conversations at home. They agreed that, as Althea put it, they were beginning to hear each other "with our hearts."

Case III. Clinical Application With a Family

Just as gender inquiry can be helpful in working with couples in a clinical setting, it also can be of value in family work. Mr. and Mrs. Levy brought their two adolescent children to therapy because of their concern about the children's frequent fights.

Mike Levy, a stockbroker in his early 40s, called the therapist. He said that the fights between his two children, Sean and Rita, were driving him crazy. During the conversation, he also mentioned that he and his wife, Ann, were having a lot of conflict about how to handle the kids. He described Ann as a housewife with a "very part-time job" as a boutique clerk at a friend's shop.

At the first meeting, the therapist met with Mike, a tanned, silver-haired man who exuded success; Ann, an attractive well-dressed woman in her early 40s; Sean, a well-built 17-year-old, who described himself as a very good student and a varsity wrestler; and Rita, his 16-year-old sister, who said that she used to be a good student but now, as a junior in high school, cared more about her social life. The following exchange occurred in the second session.

The Inquiry

Mike: I can't believe what a lousy week we had. Rita and Sean had a terrific fight. She was slamming around and throwing his stuff around, and he got so mad that he put a hole in the wall in the den. He told me that if he didn't put a hole in the wall, he was gonna put a hole in her head. I just can't believe it. And where was Ann? Off at the damned boutique with her friend.

Sean: I was just furious with Rita. We got into a fight about the dirt bags she hangs out with. I can't stand being in the same school with her. I'm so glad I'm getting out this year. She's a laughingstock. I'm just ashamed that she's my sister. She's got such a lousy reputation. People think she's a slut, and I was trying to tell her.

Rita: Who the hell is he to tell me who I am and what to do?

Mike: Maybe if you'd shut up and listen to someone . . .

Ann: Doctor, can you see how Mike and Sean gang up on her? It's always like this—it's no wonder she never wants to be in the house.

Mike: I'm only trying to help, and so is Sean. If Ann wouldn't protect her all the time . . .

Th: So, Mike, the way you see it, somehow Ann is doing something that's hurting Rita?

Mike: Yeah, and the fact that she's never around because of the boutique. I think she feels guilty and then she gives in to her.

Ann: It's been sticking in your throat from the minute I got this job. You can use it to pin anything on me.

Th: And the way Ann sees it—correct me if I'm wrong, Ann—you [therapist looks at Mike] hold her at fault for whatever problems Rita is having.

Ann: That's just the way I feel. It's like the boys against the girls around here.

Th: Mike, *does* Ann's job stick in your throat?

Mike: It's like from the time she got the job, the whole deal between us changed. I don't know—it's just . . . [He stares and says nothing more.]

Th: [after waiting for Mike to continue] What kind of deal did your folks have when you were growing up?

Mike: I don't see what that has to do with anything.

Th: Sometimes it helps me to help you all if I understand how you and your wife grew up.

Mike: Well, it was very different. My mom and dad had a candy store. We lived in an apartment upstairs. They worked 6 long days a week. I think it helped to kill my father. He died when I was about 20—heart attack [pauses].

Th: And what was the deal?

Mike: Well, Mom was always there if Dad needed her in the store, but if we came home, like for lunch, she was always upstairs. Or if we got into trouble at school, she went up to school. In fact, if we got into trouble, she never told my father. I just felt she was really there for him, and protected him, and she was there for us.

Th: So what exactly was the deal?

Mike: That she knew how hard he worked, that she was there for him, that she understood if he had it rough.

Th: And what was the deal for your father?

Mike: That he was to work very hard, to figure out how to support the family, and to know that he could count on my mom.

Th: Did you have any brothers or sisters?

Mike: I had one sister, Sara, 3 years younger than I am.

Th: When you were growing up, how do you think you learned what was expected of you as a boy?

Mike: Well, for one thing, my father assigned me all the heavy work, even when I was very little. I remember I was up at 5 in the morning with him, dragging in the bundles of newspapers. When I was a kid, it felt like the pile was bigger than I was.

Th: So you learned that it was important to be a hard worker?

Mike: Well, there was more to it. If I didn't do well in school, my mom would get very upset. She would explain that she didn't want me to end up like my father, who had no education. She would tell me that she didn't want me to have to work like a dog like he did and that education was the only way out. So I had to do very well in school. In fact, one of the big disappointments in my mother's life was that I didn't go to med school. But I remember, God help me if I got a bad grade or if she had to go up to school to see a teacher.

Th: How about your sister?

Mike: Oh, you mean Princess Sara? It was very different for her. I think she was always seen as the baby. About the only thing she ever did at the store was to jerk sodas and that was a rarity. And she wasn't very bright. But she was pretty.

Th: What was expected of her?

Mike: From my father, just to be adorable. She was the apple of his eye. By the time she was a teenager, she was a knockout. For my mother, she never made the fuss with Sara about school that she made with me. It seemed like she was being groomed to find the right guy. Mom used to say to her all the time, "It's just as easy to fall in love with a rich man." Which she eventually did. But it was weird. When she was a teenager, she seemed to be an expert in finding the scum of the earth for boyfriends. Mostly Mom kept this from Dad, but Mom designated me as Sara's secret policeman. I resented this enormously, and I don't think it made for a good relationship between me and Sara. It's only lately that we've gotten a little closer. I think she saw me as the enforcer, so my father got her love, and I got her anger.

Sean: The only difference between your story and me is that my enforcing Rita doesn't seem to make her the apple of your eye. You know what I mean?

Mike: No, I don't know what you mean. And I think it's an impertinent remark.

Ann: Can I butt in here? Mike, I think that Sean is saying something really important. I think you're still angry with Sara, even after all these years. And I think you take it out on Rita, and maybe on me too. It's like you expect me and Sean to make Rita right to your specs. It's not fair—and . . .

Th: Mike, I asked you before what you felt you learned as a kid about what it was to be a man. If I understood you correctly, you said that a man should work very hard, be the primary support of the family, and should be able to count on his wife's support in doing this. He should also be able to count on her to do the daily work of bringing up the kids and to be available to him and to them just about all the time. Do I have this right?

Mike: Yeah, that's just about on target.

Th: Am I missing something?

Mike: Not really.

Th: Ann, how does this correspond with what you learned about being a woman, growing up in your home?

Sean: What do we have to hear all this stuff for? What does this have to do with anything?

Th: It's a good question, Sean. Sometimes when we learn about how parents grew up, it helps us to understand things that are going on right now, even though it's so many years later. Let me get back to the question I was asking your mother. It might help us.

Ann: It's incredible how different it was in my home. My father was an auto mechanic, and he made pretty good money, because he was really good at it. My Mom was a college graduate. It was never mentioned, but I think that when she worked, she did better than he did financially, or at least as well. She didn't work when I was real little, but by the time I was 10 or so, she was an executive secretary for an important firm. By that time, they could afford live-in help, and by then Dad owned a garage. I really think that they thought of each other as equals. The only thing I didn't like was that my Mom wasn't around as much as I would have liked as a teenager. So I thought when I married Mike it would be great. He would want me to be at home, and then as the kids grew up, I could start getting into the work world.

Th: Do you think you were treated in any special way because you were a girl?

Ann: Being an only child, I had no standard of comparison with a brother. But I learned as a teenager that there were certain things it was better to talk to Mom about, and others, better to talk to Dad.

Th: For instance?

Ann: If it was stuff about guys, for example, always better to talk to Mom. Dad got nuts about almost every guy I went out with, until Mike. He loves him. But if I had school problems (I really didn't do great in school), Dad was much more understanding. It was really strange—even though Mom was the college grad, Dad really was more helpful about school problems. Also—this is funny—he encouraged me to be an athlete. I was a pretty good soccer player. It think he was, maybe, secretly disappointed that he never had a boy, but he certainly never showed it.

Th: If you had asked your folks to tell you what kind of woman they had hoped you would become, what would they have said?

Ann: I think each would say pretty much the same thing. "Be an equal partner, pull your weight in the marriage. But make something of yourself. Be a good mother." Stuff like that. In fact, that's something I'm mad about now. When we first got married, we both worked and made about the same amount. I always thought that, when the children were older, I'd take off from where I left off. But now, Mike, you really seem resentful. I feel like I supported you when you changed your job about 10 years ago, but I want to change mine now, in a way, and I think you're trying to stop me.

Rita: Dad, I really resent the way you make fun of Mom. I hate it when you call it her itty bitty job or stupid stuff like that. It's so demeaning. It's like you really think a woman's place is in the home. Do you think that makes me really want to try hard in school? It makes me think, what's the point? I don't know what you really want from me.

In the following session, the therapist was able to help Mike and Ann to understand how different their ideas about gender were. Ann's parents had a relatively equal relationship. By comparison, Mike's father, although he "wore the pants" in the family, was in fact dependent on his wife. She protected him, took care of the children almost entirely on her own, and took care of the home. It was hard for Mike at first to imagine that it might have been any other way. Times were so hard for them, and the store was such a burden. The therapist asked him to imagine how it might have been if his parents had handled the store differently, with each spending a little more time with the children and maybe Dad doing a little more around the house while Mother worked more in the store. Mike teared up and said, "Maybe my dad would have lived a little longer, if he hadn't felt so pressured." The therapist pointed out that maybe Mike himself felt some of the same pressure. Ann pointed out that it was her hope that she would really learn retail from the boutique and that she was thinking of it as a source of significant income within a few years. Wouldn't it be nice, she asked, if instead of putting it down all the time, he could see it as a way for him to slow down a bit as the kids got a little older?

As the therapist helped the family to focus on the role that gender played in the marriage, Sean and Rita's relationship improved. In another session, following a fight similar to the one that brought them into therapy, Sean apologized to Rita for blowing up and then tearfully demanded that his father release him of the burden of "being in charge of Rita." It wasn't long afterward that Sean and Rita went on a double date. At the following session, he said, "Listen, Mom and Dad, you don't have to worry so much about Rita. She's got pretty good social skills." Shortly after this, the family agreed that the fights between Sean and Rita had ended.

Discussion

We have demonstrated how gender inquiry can help clients to understand normative gender development and how it can be used in individual, couples, and family therapy. We have also pointed out that doing a number of structured gender inquiries can help the therapist to increase her or his consciousness of the powerful role that gender plays in everyone's life. Now we shift our focus to other ways in which therapists and students of therapy can improve their awareness of gender issues.

THE THERAPIST'S OWN GENDER AWARENESS

Just as people in treatment are affected by their gender socialization, so are those who treat them. For this reason, it is imperative that therapists examine their own history and belief systems with great care (Fitzgerald & Nutt, 1986; Nutt, 1991; O'Neil & Roberts-Carroll, 1988; Roberts, 1991). At this writing, most senior therapists lack both knowledge and training in this area. In the absence of such a curriculum, there are a number of actions that therapists might take to increase their own sensitivity to gender issues. One, of course, is to become familiar with the feminist critique of psychological theory and practice and, more specifically, the feminist critique of family theory and therapy noted in chapter 1. A similar examination of the growing literature of the men's movement and its critique (see chapter 4) is, of course, of considerable importance. Additionally, an understanding of the stresses experienced by both genders in the face of societal changes is required (see chapters 3 and 4). Tannen (1990) provided a linguistic analysis of communication between the genders that is quite useful. Attendance at workshops and conferences on gender is helpful, as is participation in an ongoing group that focuses on gender issues. Many national conventions, such as those held by the American Psychological Association (APA), American Association of Marriage and Family Therapy (AAMFT), and American Family Therapy Academy (AFTA), have developed both women's and men's groups, which provide an opportunity to deepen one's awareness of one's own gender issues. Some conferences also provide an opportunity for therapists of both genders to enter into dialogue concerning gender issues. Forming a peer supervision group to examine how perceptions of gender affect one's work is also valuable, as is insistence that supervision groups in general include a greater emphasis on gender issues.

A useful starting place might be to examine a number of cases through the course of one's career and discover changes in one's approach over time as a function of societal changes and increased personal awareness. In this regard, the therapist should think about such questions as the following:

- Did my intervention ease rather than entrench a gender problem?
- How would I have approached that case now, as I become more knowledgeable about gender?
- For therapists who are in relationships, dialogue with one's partner can provide both stimulation and enlightenment.

Systematic education and training, perhaps coupled with personal therapy with a gender-aware therapist, will produce a new generation of therapists sophisticated in gender issues. It is our hope that a thorough grounding in gender-role socialization will soon be a part of every training environment (Nutt & Gottlieb, 1993). This training would include the study of research and theory about both female and male gender issues. It would point out gender bias in research, theory, and practice and encourage trainees to analyze critically what they are taught through a gender-sensitive lens. A course in gender-role socialization emphasizing the effects of gender-role stereotyping on both men and women would be ideal.

Students in such a program would be encouraged to interview one another about their gender development and to study their own gender development and its effects on their value system. Roberts (1991) provided a list of questions for students of psychology to explore that provides structure to such a learning exercise. The inquiry method described in this chapter is likewise a useful training tool. Future therapists should be cautioned regarding blind spots related to their own gender-role socialization when working with a client of the same gender. For example, a woman in couples therapy might experience her husband and her male therapist as "ganging up" on her. A husband may have the same experience vis-à-vis his wife and a female therapist. Therapists must be aware that without training in gender socialization, they are likely to be oblivious to the experience of a client of the other gender and therefore ineffective and possibly even harmful. (See Nutt & Gottlieb, 1993, for a thorough discussion of gender issues in research, training, and practice.)

CONCLUSION

In this chapter, we have described the use of gender inquiry on several levels. We began by showing its application in the study of "normal" people. We believe that a structured questionary helps the therapist to learn about the normative power of gender socialization in shaping the lives of men and women. It is our hope that readers will attempt a number of such interviews so that they may become sensitive to both normative and idiosyncratic socialization issues. Through this process, the therapist becomes more conscious of how such factors as class, ethnicity, and religion all play a role in determining how gender plays out in the lives of individuals. It is also hoped that the reader will use this questionary to explore his or her own gender socialization, much in the way that students of family therapy chart their own genogram as part of their training.

We have demonstrated the use of gender inquiry with a couple in therapy, emphasizing the power of a careful, nonconfrontive exploration of each member's gender issues to help the couple reach new levels of mutual empathy. We then showed its application to family work. It is our belief that it is only as people become empathic to themselves and one another that deep and abiding change can occur.

At the conclusion of the case example of the couple, Althea Farentino described her "new" relationship as one in which she and her husband could "hear with their hearts." We believe that this ability to "hear with the heart" is an important shift in couples' relationships. This is a process that we term "empathic knowing" to remind the reader that the shift we seek is both affective and cognitive. In the next chapter, we describe the concept of gender coevolution, as we examine how couples fail or succeed in dealing with the gender barrier. We focus on what the therapist can do to promote the development of empathic knowing and lead the clients toward positive coevolution.

9

Gender Coevolution

Once a man or woman becomes aware of the detrimental effect of gender socialization on the quality of life experienced, it is natural to want to find someone to blame. The automatic tendency is to attack the partner as the culprit who made up the rules that oppress, endanger, or otherwise adversely influence one's life. Finding someone at whom to direct anger is one of the stages of dealing with trauma so well documented years ago by Elisabeth Kubler-Ross (1969). Heterosexual couples are in danger of getting stuck at this stage, which is detrimental both for the marriage and for each of the individuals within it. In this chapter, we describe and illustrate the process of *coevolution*, which is a process that has the potential to move couples and individuals beyond this plateau to a freer, more fulfilling life.

One of the hallmarks of gender-sensitive psychotherapy is the concept of coevolution. Men and women influence the socialization process of one another by rewarding certain attitudes and behaviors and punishing others. This process begins at birth and continues throughout a lifetime. The ways in which men and women mold each other can be blatant or subtle, direct or indirect, and person to person or societal. Through parental modeling, peer pressure, and the messages absorbed through the all-powerful media, children learn which behaviors, attitudes, values, and personality characteristics are desirable in men and which ones are desirable in women. They begin to find more attractive those members of the other sex who have the qualities deemed favorable by the larger society and to find those who differ, unattractive. By rewarding members of the other gender with attention and affection when they conform to society's norms, they reinforce their behaving in a stereotypical manner, even if they would prefer not to. It is only when men and women understand this interactive process that takes place between the genders that they recognize that they both participate in reinforcing the very rules they find oppressive.

Furthermore, Geis (1993) has even produced evidence that supports the idea of the self-fulfilling prophecy regarding gendered behavior. That is, the training we receive in the gender-socialization process so influences our expectations that we often perceive what we expect to perceive, despite evidence to the contrary. The way in which we interpret our observations depends on the gender of the person we are observing. Thus, when individuals deviate from the expected gender norm, we either punish their behavior with rejection, misinterpret it, or fail to see it at all.

The coevolution process exists at the historical and sociological levels as well as the personal one. For instance, when the ancient Celts waged war, their women and children attended the battle much as we would attend a football game today, cheering on the victors and booing the losers. In fact, the anticipated scorn of their women often prevented the surrender of the Celtic army, when they might have withdrawn otherwise (Ehrenberg, 1989). Thus, the women were influential in encouraging so-called male aggression at a societal level, because they needed male protection. Indeed, Buss (1995) even postulated that the existing psychological gender differences that are most prevalent have evolved through a process of sexual selection. That is, men have chosen women with the characteristics that suited their needs, and women have chosen men in a similar fashion, thus ensuring the continued procreation of men and women with these very qualities.

On a more personal level, both parents participate in the directing of their children's lives, thus influencing their automatic assumptions about how the world works (see chapter 2). Although the following example is not based on scientific research, it does provide an illustration of the circular nature of coevolution through the eyes of a layperson. A recent article in *The Washington Post* speculated that one reason so many men believe they know everything is that their doting mothers treated them as if they could do anything and gave them a false sense of competency (Kornheiser, 1995). If this is true, these women learned from their own family of origin and from media examples that the all-supportive, encouraging mother receives approval, whereas the critical mother does not. Thus, she is only doing what is endorsed by society, although her behavior perpetuates something she dislikes in the men in her life.

In a resort town where one of the authors lives during the summer months, 50- and 60-year-old men with lovely tans and gold chains around their necks can be seen parading million-dollar yachts adorned with bikini-clad, beautiful young women through the harbor. One may wonder what kind of gender messages the adolescents on the sidewalk are receiving from these images. Perhaps they are absorbing the idea that (a) if I'm female and I want the good life, I need to be beautiful and find a rich man and (b) if I'm male and want the beautiful women, I'd better make a lot of money.

There is a circular pattern of reward and punishment that perpetuates the socialization process. This begins at an early age and continues throughout a lifetime. Several examples gleaned from the following excerpts from two separate gender inquiries may help to clarify this point.

INTERVIEW 1: HOW A MAN CREATES A STEREOTYPICAL WOMAN

Therapist: The transition from childhood to puberty is often a turning point in gender development. Do you remember some of the changes you experienced as you made this transition?

Linda: When I was a little girl, I grew up in a neighborhood that was populated by all boys. I was physically strong and athletically inclined, and the boys accepted me as an equal. I played baseball, rowed rowboats and paddled canoes, swam in the bay, climbed flagpoles, built forts and blazed trails in the woods, went exploring in the cemetery, played Captain Horatio Hornblower on the docks, rode my bike with no hands, and played with cars and trucks in the dirt piles. I also got into a few fistfights, started by someone else, which I usually won. On the playground at school, when the boys and girls segregated themselves, I still played sports with the athletic girls and totally ignored those girls (sissies, I called them) who liked to stand around and talk or play house. I found that extremely boring.

The junior high school I attended was 12 miles from my country neighborhood in a city. It was very large, and my elementary school was only one of 12 feeder schools which supplied students to the seventh through ninth grades there. Junior high school was a traumatic experience for me but not because it was large or I was unprepared academically. I did very well in my courses, maintaining the A averages I had gotten in elementary school. My teachers liked me and encouraged me. What was traumatic for me was the reaction of my peers, especially the boys, to my athletic and academic abilities, which had once been a source of pride and identity for me. A particularly traumatic memory was the day I beat up Johnny Elder on the playground, in self-defense, I might add. But even though he started the fight and I won, I was ostracized by everyone because girls are not supposed to humiliate boys by beating them up.

Even before that incident, however, I found that the boys were openly hostile to me, while they seemed to be constantly looking at and trying to impress the girls who wore lipstick, curled their hair, and giggled incessantly about stupid things. Even the girls who had once studied hard with me to get good grades spent much of their time now talking about how cute the boys were and which movie stars or singers they thought were real hunks. They spent a lot of time worrying about what they should wear and making sure they all dressed alike. All of that seemed like a boring waste of time to me.

For 2 very long years, I was very isolated. The boys who had once been my friends were spending their time in sports activities with a much larger group of boys and did not want to associate with me. The girls were almost all "sissies" now, except for the nerds and the jocks. As much as I hated the derogatory terms, I had to admit I was a nerd and a jock. But like Groucho Marx, I sure didn't want to join any club that would have me as a member.

Finally, one summer day when he was far away from the other guys at school and safe from discovery, the boy who had been by best neighborhood friend for 7 years had a serious talk with me. He explained that I would always be his friend but that boys his age were interested in sex and so they wanted sexy girls with boobs who wore makeup and dressed like Sandra Dee. He explained that boys wanted to feel strong and tough so that they could attract the sexy girls, and when someone like me beat them playing pool or ping pong or could run faster than they could in PE, it was embarrassing, so they hated me for that. It was bad enough not to be the strongest, tallest, fastest guy in the class without being beaten by a girl. He told me if I wanted guys to like me, I should lose in games with them; I should pretend I didn't know the answers and ask for their help; I should wear makeup, shave my legs, and try to make myself look a little more like Annette Funicello. That way they would feel good around me and want me because I looked "hot."

I was outraged. Not because he had told me all of this, since I understood that he did it to help me and he was taking a terrible chance that he might be ostracized as well if anyone had seen him talking to me like this. But I was furious that the rules were so unfair. Why should boys have to feel stronger, smarter, better? Why couldn't they like me as they once seemed to have without my having to play dumb and helpless? And why did the girls put so much importance on looks, dating, and boys when there was so much more to life than that?

Well, I took his advice. I started the ninth grade with a definite calculated campaign in mind. I sat behind an attractive-looking new boy the first day of homeroom, and I laughed hard at his jokes, asked him for help in algebra, and praised him for his ability on the basketball court. I put on makeup at the bus stop (my mother had not let me wear it), began to show interest in dressing like the other girls so I'd fit in, and thrust my barely blooming chest out whenever I could. He asked me to the homecoming game, and from then on I was part of the in-crowd again.

I never stopped playing the game, really. I still worry about makeup and hair and my figure. I diet constantly. I still dress to match the models appropriate for my age. I am still very tentative when talking to a man I do not know, testing to be sure I can be frank or whether I must "watch out for the male ego." I still listen to men when they go on and on about something I find boring, because I "know" they need to feel important and attended to. I still laugh at jokes that are not particularly funny. And I still defer to a man's opinion, even when I think he is wrong, rather than argue him down. I will never again risk another Johnny Elder experience! And I am 55 years old.

WHAT IF?

Adolescence is, of course, a particularly vulnerable period of development, and most people mature beyond the years when belonging is the most important thing and everyone is so easily molded by the messages of culture, especially the subculture of the adolescent. But the preceding story is a good example of how males can influence the values of females simply by rejecting or accepting or, best of all, rewarding what they see. It must also be noted that the expectations of the females played a large role as well in influencing this girl's behavior. A confident and capable young girl learned that to be accepted by boys she must at least pretend to be incompetent and focus her energy, not on what were once meaningful activities to her, but on her appearance. She learned not to be direct and blunt with men but to approach them cautiously, in an indirect manner. She learned that although she might be perfectly capable of rowing the boat across the bay, she had better let him do it or he would feel bad about himself. She learned, essentially, that her ability to take care of herself had better be kept secret if she wanted to share her life with a man, because he had to feel needed by her or he would not stay around. Finally, she learned that nothing was as important to a man as the woman's beauty.

Suppose we create a fantasy world for a moment. Suppose the girl's athletic and academic ability were seen by the boys as valuable. Suppose they interacted with her as a respected competitor or, even better, as a friend whose cooperation would help them in whatever endeavors they chose. And what if, after they had developed a friendship with her that included direct and honest communication and mutual enjoyment of common activities, they discovered that she had developed a sexually attractive body. Suppose once the firm foundation of a genuine friendship was laid, they discovered their hormones responding to her as they would to any sexually desirable woman. Then, they would have true intimacy, mutual understanding, respect, *and* sexual fulfillment. They would have what most mature men and women long for in a relationship and only a few achieve after many years of struggle.

It is too much to expect a 13-year-old boy to resist the indoctrination he has received from parents, extended family, peers, media, teachers, boyhood heroes, rock stars, and religious leaders, much less the peer pressure of the moment. The point here is not that the boys in the preceding example were to blame but that they participated in the formation of a female with perceptions and priorities that fit the stereotype. These same characteristics would later become irritating and unfathomable to them, thus blocking the development of true intimacy.

INTERVIEW 2: HOW A WOMAN CREATES A STEREOTYPICAL MAN

Therapist: Were there things that you were forbidden to do when you were little because your mother or father didn't think that boys should do that sort of thing?

Mark: When I was really little, some girls threw snowballs at me and beat me up one time. I knew I couldn't hit back and didn't. My father told me boys should never hit girls. But it sure didn't seem fair. I remember that I vowed I'd never have anything to do with girls again. I hated them.

Therapist: What did you learn about how you were expected to act with girls and from whom?

Mark: When you're a teenager, your hormones take over and you need to do something about getting your sexual urges satisfied. It's just a matter of trial and error, really. You try various things, you watch other people, then you figure out what works and you do it. There will always be the Pete Alexanders, you know. The ones who are football stars and class presidents, who letter in all sports and belong to honor society, who go on to be J. F. Kennedy and President of the U.S. But most of us are just regular guys, and we do the best we can with what we have. For me, that wasn't getting mauled on the football or hockey team. I mean, in football the idea is to kill the guy before he gets you. In hockey, it's the same deal, except then they've got sticks! I didn't like getting beat up. *I just plain didn't like it!* No matter how big you are, no matter how good you get, there's always someone bigger. So I had to find another way.

But you have to star somewhere if you want the girls. They all went for the football quarterback, you know, or the guy with the great car. Well, I wasn't rich and I didn't like pain, so I tried to position myself so I was around girls. I played in the band, sang in Madrigals, was on the yearbook staff. I was in a few plays too, but never the lead. I just hung out with the cute girls in band and on yearbook staff and particularly in Madrigals. All the hottest looking girls were in Madrigals, which was a prestige singing group. Only the best singers got into Madrigals. But they really needed male voices because the macho guys didn't want to be singers, they wanted to be football heroes. So I tried out, and they took me because they really needed baritones.

I wasn't a total coward, you know. I had been indoctrinated enough to know I was supposed to take care of girls. One time a really pretty girl I knew jumped upon a beehive and the bees started stinging her all over her back. I told her to run for the swimming pool and began brushing the bees off her back as she ran. Then the bees started attacking me. I was stung 30 times before I hit the swimming pool. She only got 5 stings, but I'd do it again in a second. Especially since she tore off all her clothes when she hit the pool and clung onto me like I was her knight in shining armor. Those bee stings really hurt—it took a month for the swelling in my leg to go down. But she was so grateful and I felt so good protecting her, I wouldn't hesitate to do the same thing again. It feels good to be a hero. Not to mention the chance to see a girl naked.

Of course, the girls I hung out with never thought of me as a hero or even a boyfriend, just a friend. They always had me fixing them up with my friends, the ones with the cars. Then I watched Rick Hayes. He knew how to do cute. He knew how to just talk to girls. I mean the rest of us had no idea what to say to a girl, but Rick would just go up to them and start talking, laying on that Missouri charm, and it worked. He didn't have to bang his brains out on the football field, he just did cute. So I went to school on Rick, basically trying out things I saw him do, and then if they worked, I'd do them again.

But I really didn't start dating until my senior year. That's when the girls change. I don't really think the guys change. I think they go on playing by the same macho, tough-guy rules. But the girls stand back and watch, and they start noticing that this guy's smart, he's college material, maybe even med school. And they start going after the guys they think are going to make money. So suddenly, as a senior in high school, I turned into someone who had potential. That's when I started dating.

Therapist: Did you feel that, as a male, there were particular expectations about career choice and work?

Mark: Well, you find out that money is the major attraction for women. As long as you provide the house and car, and they don't have to go to work, you're okay. Although it's even better if you can give them trips abroad and diamonds. If a man has money, he can get the best-looking women. That's really what most women want. Which says a lot about what they think men are for. After a while, it pisses you off that all they want is your money. You start to feel used.

So I didn't really think much about what I wanted to do for a career. I just needed to make money. I don't think most guys think about personal fulfillment in their work until it's too late. Once you've got a family to support, you just better keep your nose to the grindstone, even if you hate your job. You don't have the luxury of changing jobs unless it means an increase in pay. Money is the number one consideration if you have a family. It just has to be.

Of course you pay a price for that eventually. You begin to feel like a meal ticket to the wife and kids, and after a while it wears on you. Especially if they take it for granted. Especially if they always want more. It seems like the only reason they want you is for the money you provide, not because they love you. You begin to resent the fact that you work hard every day at a job you hate so they can have life pretty easy. And that can ruin your relationship, if you're not careful. Believe me, I know.

WHAT IF?

Although he was probably not aware of the fact that there is a behavioral term for what happened to him, Mark clearly recounts how he was conditioned by women and society to devote the major effort of his life to making money. Describing his early motivation as hormonal, emphasizing his sexual needs, he relates the trial and error method he used to find a way to get his needs met. Unwilling to put himself through the most rigorous protector training (i.e., no football or hockey), he nevertheless was aware that as a male it was his duty to protect the female, for which he was highly rewarded. There are not that many opportunities, however, to rescue damsels in distress unless you are willing to choose a "protector" career, such as devoting your life to military service or police work. Mark knew he didn't like pain and was strong enough not to buckle under to adolescent peer pressure to prove himself in physical combat, disguised as sports. He was not interested in choosing a career that would put his life in danger.

The other important role of the male in society is that of provider, and for that, Mark had great potential. He was a good college-bound student with a friendly demeanor and many interests. The smart and attractive girls in high school saw his promise and suddenly began to shower attention on him. He was not unaware of the reason he suddenly became attractive. This was something he could do without enduring physical pain. He completed college and got a good job with potential for advancement, which was rewarded finally by the commitment of a wife who would provide for his sexual and emotional needs for the rest of his life. His side of that contract was to provide for her financially and for any minor children they might have.

The contract that seemed so natural and fair in the beginning of the relationship, however, had its downside. Mark became a slave to a career that consumed most of his life. It did not allow him to participate actively in the raising of his children, so that as young adults their relationship with him was distant and awkward, unlike the close and easy relationship they had with their mother. He and his wife lived parallel lives—his devoted to work, hers to the home, children, and friendships with women. They never had the time together to nurture their relationship. Neither did he feel free to move on to a new career when he became disillusioned with the first. His unhappiness at work began to feel oppressive, and it was hard not to blame his wife and family for that. It was, after all, his duty to provide for them.

The preceding story is probably the most common one heard from men, because the male role has not changed much since the Industrial Revolution began. But let us pretend we live in another world and another time, when the provider role is no longer designated as male. What if when Mark was a teenager in school, the girls had found him attractive because he was smart and fun and had a variety of interests that made him versatile and stimulating to be around. Suppose the girls planned to support themselves in exciting careers of their own and were not looking for a provider, only a companion with similar interests and values. Suppose when he had married, the contract had been: We'll both work for a while; we'll both take time off to be with the kids; we'll work out of our home so we can both be with the kids; we'll take turns working and staying at home; we'll support each other in career changes and geographical moves; we'll reduce our standard of living so we can both have more leisure time to spend with the family and to pursue our common interests; or any of the other permutations a couple with children can invent to prevent the development of rigid roles that result in dissatisfaction and distance. Would they not have given themselves a much better chance to develop the intimacy and vitality of a truly satisfying relationship?

Again, the point we make here is not that the women in Mark's life who gave him the impression that his only value was as a financial provider are to blame for his life circumstances. The point is that in addition to the pressures of the larger culture for a man to be financially successful, the women in his life, especially his wife, had major influences on the choices he made that molded him into the man he is at midlife. They participated willingly, albeit unconsciously, in his socialization process.

CREATIVE COEVOLUTION OR CALCIFICATION?

Potential Outcomes for Couples

In the preceding two examples, we have shown how, in the process of growing up, men and women participate in the shaping of each others' values, behaviors, and roles, without a clear awareness of the results they may achieve or their power to do so. The molding process is not restricted to roles alone but includes all of the characteristics, values, behaviors, communication styles, problem-solving styles, desires, goals, and hopes that go into what it means to be a man or a woman. The process does not stop at adulthood but continues throughout a lifetime.

Because this process is lifelong, one's spouse can have a major influence on how one's relationship evolves, whether it becomes a rigid and unsatisfying existence or a growth-oriented and vital one. Much of the direction it takes depends on the level of awareness each partner has of how his or her automatic responses are tied to rigid messages about men and women that may be unhealthy. Individuals whose consciousness regarding gender socialization has been raised, through the media, support groups, or therapy, are more likely to approach the issues in a spirit of cooperation and possibility. Although the broader culture plays a strong role in the socialization process, once the partners understand the interactive nature of this process, they can begin to change its direction. Positive coevolution is entirely possible; it requires, however, that women and men approach one another with understanding, respect, and openness regarding what is possible for both genders.

The Role of the Therapist

The major task of the therapist is to create an atmosphere of trust and openness so that positive coevolution can occur. The therapist who sees a couple struggling with gender issues may use the previously described interventions of psychoeducation, reframing and translating, empathic interviewing, and gender inquiry to help the couple move from a stuck position to one of mutual growth. The therapist uses her or his skills to teach the couple the following:

- To view their marriage systemically, taking responsibility for their own contribution
- To understand the impact of gender socialization on their interactions
- To communicate openly and honestly, using "I statements"
- To listen nondefensively
- To educate one another *gently* regarding gender issues
- To empathize with the role of the other
- To be open to possibilities for change, even when breaking gender messages
- To show appreciation and support for efforts toward change

The therapist can help the partners look inward and start to ask themselves the following questions:

1. Where is it written that it must be the way it presently is?
2. Why do I feel I must—?
3. What do I do or say that makes you feel you must—?
4. How else could it be?

5. How can I support you in reaching your goals? What sacrifices or changes can I make to facilitate that process?
6. What are the ways you can support me in reaching my goals?

With the help of the therapist, the couple can examine how their own fears, expectations, and desires keep the other in a deadlocked position, rather than pointing a finger of blame at one another for the dissatisfactions they experience in the relationship. They can transcend the lessons of socialization and create their own way of being that is more fulfilling for both.

In the following section, we describe a couple who began their relationship in the late '50s and early '60s, at a time before the feminist movement and the sexual liberation of the late '60s, when the traditional family based on complementarity was the model. The complementary relationship assumed that men and women have essentially different personality characteristics, capabilities, and areas of expertise. Acknowledging that both stereotypically male and female qualities were necessary for a complete and full life, the complementary model obtained that goal by dividing the responsibilities for a relationship between the genders according to assumed areas of strength. Although in some ways that model worked well, it tended to restrict the partners from developing aspects of their personalities that did not fit the gender stereotype. Often this resulted in rigid patterns of behavior that separated and isolated the couple from one another rather than fostering true intimacy. It also left those who did not fit the stereotype out of a relationship altogether.

The choice of a couple from this time period is deliberate, as it allows the reader to see the rigidification or coevolution that can occur over a 2- or 3-decade period of marriage. Understanding the role of gender socialization in a relationship and the part each spouse plays in accomplishing the process can come through the efforts made by the couple by themselves as their relationship evolves, or it can be introduced by a therapist when a rigidified couple presents in therapy. Either way, the effect is dramatic and liberating. Commentary regarding the interventions a therapist might have used had this couple presented for therapy anytime during their marriage follows the case study.

CASE EXAMPLE: JUST A-DOIN' WHAT COMES NATURALLY

Glenda and Allen met while they were in high school. Theirs was the fairy-tale relationship. Allen was the captain of the football team, a large and attractive physical specimen with the personality of an extrovert, like his father. He was the son of the president of the local General Motors dealership, a man who had started out as a car salesman and worked his way up to owner of the business. The family was well known in town, upper middle class, and involved in local affairs.

Glenda was a cute, perky, blonde girl who was popular in high school. She was on the cheerleading squad and in choir and was well liked because she was so friendly and outgoing. Glenda's father was an electrician, and her family might have been considered working class. When Glenda and Allen began to date, everyone thought they were perfect for each other. They were a popular couple, fun to have at parties and dances.

Neither Glenda nor Allen was a particularly good student, although Allen's teachers often complained that he did not work up to his potential. Because Glenda was basically a C+ student and never caused problems in her classes, her teachers essentially ignored her. To them, as to Glenda, her academic performance was not particularly important. She would probably get married shortly after high school and start having children. She needed only a basic education to survive in the world. Allen would need to make a living to support a family, however, and his teachers were disturbed that he was not making the necessary college-entry grades, given the fact that his father was a prominent businessman and perfectly capable financially of sending him to college.

After graduation from high school, Glenda got a job as a receptionist at a beauty parlor while waiting for Allen to "pop the question." She was hired as much because she was pretty and friendly as for any other reason, and she knew it. Glenda was good with the customers and on the telephone, but she knew this was a dead-end job—something for her to do temporarily until marriage, which was her real ambition. In the '50s, the image was that any woman who was not married by the time she was 30 was destined to a life as an old maid, which was perhaps the worst thing that could happen to a girl—certainly worse than having an unhappy marriage or getting a divorce or being widowed. In those circumstances, the girl had proved she could at least attract a man and get him to propose. An old maid, on the other hand, was a complete failure as a woman. Of course, this was not a concern for Glenda. If Allen did not make a commitment to her fairly soon, she would move on to someone else. Allen, however, had potential. His family had money and he was cute and fun, so she would wait for a while. Wait and plot with her girlfriends how to get him to ask for her hand in marriage.

Allen went to work for his father at the dealership. He was a good kid and the football star. He was personable and well liked, and was the old man's son, so he did well as a salesman. His father pushed him about getting more education and made him attend night school at the business college nearby, hoping to motivate him to go on and get a degree in business management. Allen was enjoying his life the way it was. He worked at a job that he enjoyed; went to school a few nights a week to keep the old man off his back; went fishing, hunting, and biking with his friends on the weekends when he did not have to work; and saw Glenda as often as he could, given his busy schedule. The relationship with Glenda had heated up sexually, and she was allowing him to take more liberties. Basically, all was right with his world.

Through consultation with her girlfriends, Glenda had come to the conclusion that the one thing that really motivated Allen was sex. She was not sexually experienced, having gained most of her knowledge through romance novels, movies, and TV and from her "more experienced" girlfriends. All of these sources told her that if she could keep Allen interested sexually, but require a commitment before consummation, she might be able to get him to marry her. She was careful to maintain a distance from her own passion so that she could keep him "hot" but never satisfied. She would often tell him, when he was begging for her to "go all the way," that she could not do that unless she was sure he really loved her, by which she meant, but never stated, that he would marry her.

Allen knew what she meant, but he was afraid of marriage. Marriage meant to him that he would spend the rest of his life working to support a family, and all the fun would come to an end. Marriage meant he needed to give up motorcycle and hunting trips with his buddies and spend his weekends mowing the grass. Marriage meant making enough money to buy a house. Marriage meant having kids, and he did not know how to take care of kids! Marriage also meant giving up the potential of having other women, although sometimes he thought that having readily available sex was better than always having to seduce women. That became work, and the success rate was not good enough to be worth the effort. Because he was a man, and men were not supposed to be afraid or unsure, Allen never shared these concerns with Glenda. He was worried she would take his concerns personally, and he was probably right.

It took Glenda about a year to wear Allen down. Finally, he gave her an engagement ring, they set a date for their wedding, and in return she began to have sex with him. For a while, they were both ecstatic. She loved planning the wedding; he loved sex. Suddenly the day was upon them, and all at once they were a married couple. Almost immediately, Glenda began to develop what Allen called the "nesting instinct." She wanted to decorate their little apartment and cook exotic meals, and she talked about having children someday and fantasized about the house they would buy when Allen made enough money. She seemed to be in heaven. Apparently, having a home and family was her dream come true, but it caused dollar signs to run before Allen's eyes. He knew she expected him to make the money to finance her dreams, and it scared him. In addition, he began to realize that he did not have a lot in common with Glenda. He knew she did not like motorcycles, hunting, or fishing, and he thought he had to give all that up now that he was married. He did not enjoy shopping or decorating the apartment, because that was women's stuff, and yet he thought he should spend time with Glenda doing these things. Allen began to feel trapped. After a valiant effort at pretense, his resentment grew, and he became sullen and withdrawn.

Glenda was aware of his mood and knew instinctively it was her job to get him to talk about it so that she could make their relationship better. She began to ask him why he was unhappy, but he would deny it, afraid to tell her and not wanting to hurt her. Her questioning began to sound like nagging to him, so he would avoid coming home, making excuses that he had to work late or study in the library. She knew better, but she could not make him tell her what was wrong. She began to worry that she was no longer sexy or pretty enough or that he had gotten sexually bored with her already. She bought magazines filled with self-help articles and consulted with her girlfriends about the problem. He immersed himself in activity, work, and school and had an occasional drink with a friend, with whom he would reminisce about the good old days but neglect to talk about his misgivings about his marriage. He knew that men did not engage in that kind of troubles talk unless they were desperate. Things were not that bad, but they were not much fun.

Glenda was growing more dissatisfied with her relationship every day. It was not the way she had expected it to be. Allen was nearly always gone, and when he was home he was quiet and noncommunicative. She tried to engage him in chitchat about decorating the apartment or what happened in the beauty parlor that day, but he seemed uninterested, burying himself in the television set. Occasionally, he would offer advice as to how she ought to handle a dispute with a fellow worker or customer, but she always felt that he was somehow putting her down, that he thought she was too stupid to figure it out by herself. After all, she was only telling him about it to have some connection with him. She began to feel lonely. The closeness she had hoped for with Allen was not there. He did not respond to her the way her girlfriends did when she shared the details of her life, and he never shared anything about his life with her unless she nagged him, which took all the pleasure out of it. They never did anything together any more. In fact, they never did anything at all. Something had to change!

She was not sure how it happened because she knew she did not consciously plan it, but one day she found herself pregnant. She and Allen had never discussed when they wanted to have children, although it was a tacit agreement between them that they would have children someday. Glenda knew Allen would be upset by the pregnancy because, he was not ready, but she was pleased when, after the initial shock subsided, he started making plans. For Allen, the fact of his impending fatherhood meant that he had to get serious about life. Suddenly, his night classes took on new meaning. He began to compete for best salesman at the agency, and he talked to his father about the potential for promotion. He developed a plan. Within 2 years he would have completed his degree, in 4 years he would be sales manager, in 8 years he would be general manager, and by the time his father was ready to retire in 12 years, he would take over the dealership. He stopped thinking with resentment about the loss of his fun time with his buddies and put all of his energy into work. He borrowed money from the bank with his father as cosigner to buy a small house and prepared to take care of his child. Glenda was joyful once again. The pregnancy seemed to give them a common goal and bring them closer together.

After their daughter was born, Glenda quit work and stayed home to be a full-time mom. She had a new house to decorate, a baby to care for, and friends she could talk to over the phone or have over for coffee; her life was full. Allen was working hard and caught up in the excitement of his own future. School and work occupied him 12 hours a day. His life was also full. That they were beginning to live parallel lives that touched only in bed at night or when they played with their little girl did not matter to them. It was better than what had been.

Allen and Glenda settled into the Great American Dream. Allen was successful in following his plan, and his financial success pleased Glenda immensely. They had two more children, which took much of Glenda's energy but gave her the emotional intimacy she had not found with Allen. As Allen became more successful and the children got older, Allen and Glenda became immersed in an active social life, essentially following the footsteps of Allen's parents. Allen's financial success also allowed Glenda the freedom to hire a maid to help with the housework and to buy "things," which she did with regularity and a great deal of enthusiasm. Indeed, both Allen and Glenda became a part of that consumer generation of the 1980s, delighting in owning the best stereo, the newest car, the fastest speedboat his income would allow. They were both pleased with the status they had achieved in their small town.

When Allen stretched himself too thin by trying to expand too quickly, he had a moment of panic that he never shared with Glenda because he did not want to frighten her. Besides, she would never understand, not knowing anything about his business at all. He had never talked to her about the details of his work because he was sure she would not be able to comprehend, which had guaranteed that she did not have enough knowledge to be able to give him anything but emotional support at a time like that. As the protector and provider of the family, he did not feel he should expose her to his concerns or ask for her support. Instead, he went to his father, long since retired, who gave him some advice, opened a few doors for him among banking institutions, and essentially stood by him while he pulled himself out of trouble. Glenda never even knew why her husband had become particularly cranky and started drinking more heavily during that 6-month period. But she had given up trying to get him to talk to her about anything important anymore.

As the children got older and did not need her attention, Glenda began to feel once again that something was missing. The intimacy she had wanted with Allen was not there. Their sex life was routine, and sex was infrequent. He was too tired, she was too tired, and they both knew they just were not interested any more. Buying things had lost its appeal. One of Glenda's friends (the consultants, as Allen called them) had gone back to school. Another had gone to work as a buyer in a department store. Glenda began to dream about the possibility of starting a small curtain and upholstery business. She had been taught by her mother how to do upholstering, and it was a hobby that she had developed during her years at home. She often helped friends with their couches and chairs and would make drapes for the cost of the material. All of her friends praised her work and told her she ought to go into business, so she decided to approach Allen about this.

His reaction was critical at first. He said she knew nothing about running a business, that she could not even balance a checkbook. He said she might know how to sew well enough to please a few friends, but doing it for money was another story. He began to lecture her on the percentage of small businesses that went under in a year. She felt discouraged and humiliated and withdrew from him emotionally. He complained that she always reacted emotionally, that he was only being practical and reasonable. He said all of her decisions were based on her feelings, and she never used her head. She was even more hurt and felt a cold anger overwhelming her. Then, all of a sudden, Allen came back from the accountant's office saying maybe it was a good idea for her to start a business, after all. The accountant had suggested it might be a good tax shelter for him, and besides, if it made her happy it was worth a few bucks. Glenda was furious. Allen would not take her seriously unless some expert told him it was a good idea!

Although Glenda felt discounted and unimportant in her husband's eyes owing to this interaction, she did not let that stop her from taking his offer to set her up in business. She worked hard, bypassing Allen and turning directly to the accountant for advice as to how to set up the business and the books. She focused all her energy for 2 years on the development of a little company, but just as it looked like she was about to break even, their youngest son began to get into trouble. He was cutting school, getting failing grades, smoking pot, and hanging out with kids who were on the fringe of the law. Allen blamed it on Glenda's absence from home. It was true that she devoted as many hours a day to work as Allen did and that their son was home alone unsupervised much of the time. But it seemed unfair that Allen did not have to take responsibility for the raising of their son and she did. Allen said it was a matter of economics. His business supported them in the style to which they had become accustomed; hers did not. She closed her business so that she could get her son under control, becoming one of the statistics Allen had quoted 2 years previously.

Although their son did get back on track, Glenda never recovered from the anger she felt about this issue. The fact that her life took a backseat to that of Allen and her children made her so furious that she could no longer be civil to him. Her cold hostility made their lives at home so painful that Allen was happy to be away as much as possible. Thus, when he was invited to run for city council, it was not just his sense of civic duty and ego that motivated him to say yes. It was also an excuse to be gone all the time.

The inevitable happened, of course. Allen won the election after working many long hours with his campaign worker, a pretty young woman who admired and respected him and who shared his views politically. They had an affair. Glenda found out and divorced him, exacting as much money from him as she could as revenge for her wasted life. They both emerged from this relationship hating the other. They both felt they had done what they were supposed to do to be a good spouse to the other and that the other one had "screwed them over." They both distrusted the motives of the other gender for a long time to come, and neither of them ever recognized the role gender socialization played in the destruction of their once-promising relationship; therefore, they never had a chance to save it.

IF ONLY THEY HAD KNOWN: WHAT THE THERAPIST CAN DO

Glenda and Allen are not an unusual couple. Their story is a common one in this society, because men and women have been taught to behave and think in ways that often bring about these results. There are many things that might have worked differently had they been aware of the detrimental socialization "spell" they were under. They would have had to struggle against the prevailing messages of the larger culture, which is never easy, but there were a multitude of times when an awareness of gender socialization could have turned their relationship around. Had they turned to professional help at any time during their relationship, the therapist could have introduced them to a new understanding of their frustrations through psychoeducation, the gender inquiry, empathic interviewing, role reversal, future-pacing, and the many other techniques at his or her disposal. The goal of the therapist throughout would be to bring about cognitive–affective shift by expanding their "cognitive maps" to include an understanding of the negative impact of gender socialization and the potential for change.

Premarital Interventions

It is rare for a young couple to present for premarital counseling in a first marriage. Usually, the two are very much in love, often controlled by their hormones, and actively repressing any negative thoughts they might have about their relationship. It would have been highly unlikely for Glenda and Allen to seek premarital therapy. Nevertheless, there are several areas in which a change in their cognitive–affective attitude could have been of benefit to their future marriage.

To begin with, Glenda could have placed more emphasis on how she intended to take care of herself, rather than devoting her energies to finding someone to take care of her. This is one of those cognitive maps that require a second-order change; that is, the client must be made aware of a path toward her goal of financial security other than the traditional marriage in which the male serves as provider. Today, the women's movement has done a great deal to change the attitude of young women. Most of them do have a career in mind, and some plan to work for a lifetime, although many still regard their spouse as the primary breadwinner and plan to stay home during their children's early years. What has not changed is the pressure on women to marry. Even the successful CEO of a large company is looked on by the society as a failure if she does not also have a husband and children. It takes a great deal of ego strength to stand up to that kind of pressure and, in the '50s when Glenda was making these vital decisions, there were almost no role models to show her it was possible. However, the encouragement of a parent or teacher, the example of an admired public figure, or work with a psychotherapist could have given her the courage to defy expectations and use her potential. Clearly, she did not get that. It was Allen who was nagged by his teachers, pushed by his father, and given an opportunity through the well-established male network to begin his career.

It is not just Glenda who would have benefited from a societal change. Had Allen been able to think of Glenda as a partner who would contribute equally to the financial coffers of their family, he might have felt less frightened of the responsibility of a family and less reluctant to get married. His decision may still have been to wait for a while, a decision that would have been better for both of them. Nevertheless, he might have made that eventual decision to commit more freely.

In the '50s, when this couple was making these decisions, there were no viable alternatives to the traditional male-provider, female-homemaker pattern, owing to the pervasive attitude of the larger society and a lack of lucrative careers for women. But today, when a therapist is confronted with clients who are strongly influenced by traditional gendered role assignments, he or she has the opportunity to use psychoeducation, gender inquiry, and guided future-oriented fantasy as a way of countering rigid gender socialization and expanding their lifestyle possibilities.

As it was, Allen was manipulated into marriage by the only power Glenda had. Forbidden by society to ask openly for his hand in marriage, pressured to marry immediately after school or risk humiliation, discouraged from seeking any goal other than marriage and family, Glenda used her sexual power to reach her goal. In a world where marriage was viewed as a trap females set for males, having sexual relations before marriage was tantamount to throwing free bait to the fish. If men could have sex for free, why would they ever enter that institution of marriage? Glenda withheld sex until she had the commitment. What the research teaches us, however, is that although males often continue to view marriage with some trepidation, they want that kind of lifelong partnership as much as women do and indeed benefit from the marital union *more* than women do (Gove, 1972, 1980). A therapist working with a man struggling with commitment issues could provide bibliotherapy, men's groups, or the stories of other men to validate his client's feelings, while offering him a more positive, male-sanctioned opinion of marriage. In this case, had Allen been aware of the reality rather than the myth, he might have been more enthusiastic about the union, and Glenda's power play would have been unnecessary to reach the goal.

The sexual revolution of the '60s and '70s was an attempt to change these dynamics by removing the moral judgment placed on sex and abolishing the double standard in sexual relations. It was only partially and momentarily successful in reaching that goal. As most movements go, it probably went too far, and society realized free sex was not the answer either. However, the attempt to make sexual relationships a matter of mutual pleasure rather than a power play between the sexually aggressive male and the gatekeeper female was laudable.

Early Marital Interventions

Allen had bought the idea, hook, line, and sinker, that he was supposed to be strong, capable, self-sufficient, sure of himself, and secure. Because he had learned that one does not show weakness to an opponent or even teammates (they are all competitors for the top dog position, after all), he never shared his doubts and concerns with Glenda, either before they were married or after. He maintained the image of the strong, silent type and later became brooding and inaccessible. Had he told Glenda why he was afraid to get married at that time instead of pretending he did not know what she wanted, they might have begun to build the foundation for intimate communication that Glenda craved and Allen did not even know could help him. Of course, this was one of those pivotal times, in which Glenda's response to his opening up would make all the difference in the world. Had she seen him as weak or immature; gotten angry, nagged, and whined; or even laughed his concerns off as invalid, she would have sabotaged his attempt to be close. What she needed to do at that time was understand the valid concerns he had and even ask how she might help with that. If she were able to get enough distance, she might even recognize the unfairness of the situation from his point of view without having to point out in some defensive manner all of the sacrifices and work of motherhood as an equalizer. Glenda needed to create a safe atmosphere in which Allen could be vulnerable and still feel loved and valued. Later, when Allen felt understood and validated, he might have been able to hear how the role of housekeeper and mother had its own pros and cons, although Glenda probably had not begun to experience those feelings yet. Sometime during the marriage they would arise, however, and at that point Allen would need to understand that although it might look to him like she had an easier life, there were sacrifices and frustrations that accompanied her role as well. In that empathic and validating environment, they might even have brainstormed ways in which they could lighten one another's load. They might still have lived a complementary lifestyle. At that time in history, that might have been the only viable alternative financially. But at least they would have felt like a team, both pulling their own weight, rather than feeling abused and isolated in their individual miseries.

If Glenda and Allen had presented for marital therapy in the frustrating early days of their relationship, the therapist could have facilitated the process just described by teaching them communication skills and empathic interviewing. By empathizing with Allen's need to be in charge and competent and simultaneous feeling of being overwhelmed by responsibility, a male therapist in individual work with Allen could have coaxed him gradually into sharing some of his fears with his wife, in a way that did not blame her but merely stated his feelings. It would also have been necessary to coach Glenda on how to respond, making sure she understood the need to reward Allen's attempts at being vulnerable, because in the long run this would lead to the intimate relationship she so strongly desired. This would have required her to put her own fears and expectations aside long enough to understand Allen as a person, not as an object that existed to meet her needs. If the therapist had framed Allen's concerns in terms of what he had been taught about how to be a man, Glenda would have found it easier to accomplish this. Because it is the male who is most uncomfortable with this sort of intimate talk, it often is up to the female to practice active listening and reflecting skills first, until the male feels more competent and ready to hear her story. The use of the gender inquiry would have been effective at this point in providing some distance from the hot issues and offering some systemic understanding for both husband and wife. Eventually, both Glenda and Allen would have reached a point of empathic understanding of each other.

This process is ongoing throughout the marriage. At 19 and 20, one does not have the experience to be aware of all the complications and their accompanying emotions that life brings. The important point, however, is that an atmosphere of mutual understanding, nonblaming, and nondefensive communication is the foundation for the teamwork needed to face whatever comes along.

This is not what happened. Glenda, trained as she was by society, knew something was wrong shortly after their wedding and somehow felt responsible for monitoring and nurturing their relationship. Had Allen been aware of how important it was to discuss openly the negatives in the relationship, had he not been so concerned about appearing in control, had he not been worried abut protecting Glenda from his unhappiness, he would not have resisted her attempts to get him to talk about his feelings of inadequacy and entrapment. At that point, Glenda might have recognized that every time she talked about a dream, he saw it as a demand, and they might have found some way to dream together. She might have been able to tell him that if he wanted to go motorcycling or hunting with the guys, it was fine with her. She'd go shopping with her girlfriends during that time. Had he not been so susceptible to male socialization, Allen might even have taken an interest in decorating their apartment with her, making sure his taste was represented in his own home. She might have suggested that they continue to go out dancing together like they had in high school. He might have asked her if she would like to learn to water ski or play tennis, activities they could learn together and share. Although Glenda tried to open this dialogue, Allen's belief in the male myth prevented him from participating.

Equally problematic was Allen's reaction to Glenda's chitchat. If he had been aware that Glenda's attempt at small talk was, for her, a stereotypically female way of connecting with him, he might have been more attentive or even turned the conversation to something of interest to him. He might have suggested an activity or project they could do together and explained that, for him, working on something together made him feel close. If he had understood that when she shared a problem with him, she was modeling what she wanted from him, not expecting a solution, he might have been less ready with the answer. In fact, he probably *did* understand, at least unconsciously, that supplying the answer made him one-up in the relationship, feeling needed and adequate. If he could have put himself in her shoes, on the receiving end of advice, he might have recognized that a constant dose of instruction makes one feel inadequate and disrespected. He might have become less interested in supplying solutions and more interested in empathizing and giving emotional support.

The preceding constructive changes in the relationship could have been accomplished in marital therapy. Psychoeducation through bibliotherapy, movies, consciousness-raising groups, or therapist explanation would have made both Allen and Glenda aware of how much of their frustration came from not understanding the world of the other. Empathic interviewing, gender inquiry, and role reversal exercises would have provided them with more personalized data regarding how gender socialization influenced their expectations and behaviors. Once the cognitive–affective shift occurred and empathic knowing was achieved, the couple could have designed their own behavioral interventions, which would have brought them a great deal of satisfaction. Their relationship could have begun a process of positive co-evolution. The gender-role journey would have begun.

Interventions in the Middle Years

Because none of the preceding interventions took place, Allen and Glenda both felt lonely and isolated from the other. Allen used the typically male method of coping with stress and loneliness: He put all his energy and time into work, a place where he felt successful and rewarded. Glenda turned first to female friends and finally to the ultimate female role of motherhood to fill the emptiness. They began to live parallel lives in separate worlds.

Many couples in a complementary relationship end up living somewhat parallel lives, because by the nature of the role requirements they spend most of their time in different universes. But that does not mean they have to feel isolated from one another. Allen did not share his daily stresses at work, the details of his plans for his business, or his fears and concerns about success with Glenda for two reasons. First, because he believed it was his job to protect her from worry, and second, because he assumed she would not understand. It did not occur to him that she might be interested and willing to learn and that by sharing his business concerns with her, he would simultaneously develop aspects of her personality that lay dormant and strengthen their relationship. Glenda did not share the daily drudgeries of housewifery and motherhood with Allen because she was not encouraged to do so. It was just more small talk, which did not interest him, or some other problem to which Allen believed he had the answer. Although she can hardly be blamed for doing so, her failure to include him in the daily activities of his children kept him separated and distant from them. It was only as Allen grew older, however, that he began to regret his lack of participation in the raising of his children in any direct and active way. He was a complicit conspirator in the absent-father syndrome. Had both Glenda and Allen realized the effect of father absence on the development of their children and had Allen been aware of the rewards for himself in a close father–child relationship, they might have shared the parental duties more equally. In so doing, Allen would have had the opportunity to develop the nurturing aspects of his personality while simultaneously feeling closer to his wife and family.

A family therapist seeing this family for any reason during this part of their life cycle might have suggested more father–child interaction, more time alone for Glenda to discover or develop her interests, more communication between the couple, and more sharing of their separate worlds. Although men in many healthier, happier families of this generation were able to spend time with family, it was not the norm for men of Allen's generation. Today, many men and women are trying to change the rules, struggling against a society that uses the almighty dollar rather than the raising of productive, happy children as a yardstick for success.

Interventions at Midlife

The final blow to the marital relationship came when Glenda, having almost completed her first career as mother of dependent children, began to search for something else to give her life fulfillment and meaning. Allen had long since given up thinking of Glenda as an individual; he saw her only as the role she played in his life and could not begin to take her struggles seriously. Over the years, because they were so distant from one another, they had become the roles they played for each other—nothing more. Glenda wished to step out of her role to do something that Allen could not imagine she had the ability to do. His lack of respect for her as an adequate human being was so blatant to her, so automatic to him, that it was the death knell to their relationship.

It is likely that Glenda would finally have presented for therapy at this time to explore her dissatisfaction with her decreasing role as mother and her desire to do something else. A therapist would have validated that need, encouraged her new goals, and given her confidence in herself. Perhaps most important, a gender-sensitive therapist would have provided emotional support in the face of the criticism and skepticism she would encounter from a family fighting to maintain homeostasis and a society that punished her for breaking the rules. Adjunct consciousness-raising groups, bibliotherapy, and the model of other women would have facilitated this process. Glenda would have successfully moved on in her gender-role journey beyond the point of dissatisfaction with the old roles to a unilateral change. This would have created a crisis in her relationship, as indeed it did.

It is possible that a therapist would have been able to engage Allen in the decision-making process regarding Glenda's career plans and convince him to provide emotional support to Glenda for the greater good of their relationship. The fact that the accountant had been able to enlist Allen's support by appealing to his financial interest infuriated Glenda, because it was not she who had convinced Allen to support her but someone else for whom he had more respect. It is likely that a similar dynamic would have occurred had a therapist intervened on Glenda's behalf at this time; it would have been a disempowering move that might have sabotaged the therapeutic relationship. Through empathic interviewing, Allen could have come to know his wife as a person again and gained empathy for her situation, and through gender inquiry, he could have begun to understand how he had contributed to the crisis they found themselves in at this point by blindly following his gender programming. These techniques might have helped Allen to have the kind of affective shift necessary to support his wife genuinely. Had he been able to see her differently, he could have supported her goals, enthusiastically helped her set up her business, listened to her frustrations and successes with empathy, gloried in finally being able to share the economic strain with someone else, and celebrated her new-found self-respect with her. This was highly unlikely at this point, however, because there was little motivation for Allen to attend therapy or work on these issues.

Because these events never happened, Glenda stopped looking for validation from him at all and began doing what she probably should have done at 18, prove to herself that she could do something valuable and productive that could support her economically. She felt like an adequate adult who could compete in the real world of commerce. She felt good about herself, not through the success of her husband and children but because she, herself, was accomplishing something respected by others. Then, the rug was pulled out from under her by a society that holds the woman ultimately responsible for the welfare of her children.

Had Allen respected Glenda's abilities, had he taken her work seriously, had he valued her need for meaningful work and self-respect, he might have worked with her at that time to find other ways of "getting their son under control." In fact, if he had been aware of the importance of father–son interaction, he might have taken time away from work to spend with his son: finding out what was bothering him, doing projects with him, taking trips with him, playing sports with him, and getting him professional help if necessary. Indeed, had he been doing most of these things all along, it is possible his son would not have been having problems at 16. He did not think about the father–son relationship, however; he thought only of the need for a good mother at home. Glenda, loving her son and socialized to accept that responsibility, buckled under, with hate in her heart.

At this point, a therapist would have been able to bolster Glenda's resolve to resist traditional gender-socialization messages that held her responsible for her son's behavior and help her to explore solutions to her son's problem other than giving up her business. The therapist could have enlisted Allen's participation at this time for the sake of his child and could have quoted research that indicates the importance of the male role model to a boy's development. It is possible that love for his son and his stereotypical masculine analytic approach to problem solving would have led him to become more involved with his adolescent boy's life rather than insisting that Glenda leave her work. Although this occurrence would have averted the loss of Glenda's business and her resultant hatred for Allen, it is unlikely that their relationship would have improved unless they stopped living in totally separate worlds.

If the couple had been motivated to improve their relationship, the therapist would have been able to work individually with Allen using Brooks' translating and reframing approach: (a) educating him regarding the changes in society since the women's movement, (b) pointing out how the messages he had absorbed concerning what it is to be a man no longer work in today's society, (c) conducting a gender inquiry, and (d) facilitating his exploration of his own fears and concerns, catching him up to Glenda in his gender-role journey, so to speak, before initiating couples therapy. The therapist would have continued to empower Glenda, encouraging her continued independence and movement away from detrimental gender socialization but also would have begun to educate her regarding the reciprocal nature of the process: the coevolutionary aspects of male–female relationships. Adoption of this new systemic paradigm would have made it easier for Glenda to hear Allen's side of the story and facilitate his growth. Together, they could have redesigned their roles to enable a better fit to their individual and mutual needs.

At this point in their marriage, it is improbable that anything short of a nodal event—a major crisis, such as threat of divorce, Allen's business failure, discovery of serious illness, or death of a loved one—could motivate them to pull together and begin reparation of their relationship. Indeed, from a family systems point of view, their son's acting out might have been designed to accomplish just that. If so, it did not work as planned.

When Glenda gave up her dream, she lost any positive feeling for Allen. Once she had crossed that threshold, there was little hope for their relationship to survive. It is easy to understand the events that took place after this occurred. How sad it is that sometime in their 25 years of marriage no one turned the switch that would put their relationship on a different track.

WHAT MAKES THE DIFFERENCE?

Many traditional marriages from the '50s that were based on clear-cut complementary gender roles were emotionally fulfilling to both partners.

In these marriages, the partners found their way to positive coevolution, often without professional help. How is it that with the same socialization messages, the same roles, the same dissatisfactions, one couple ends their marriage in bitter divorce and another emerges with a sense of deep satisfaction with their growth as individuals within a nurturing relationship?

Traditional relationships were based on an exchange of services. The woman was expected to provide the nurturance and support for her partner and to handle the domestic duties of home and hearth, including the major portion of child care. The men were expected to provide financially for the family and felt that responsibility to be a heavy one requiring major sacrifices. Generally, the men felt a sense of entitlement that came with that responsibility—essentially, an exemption from the daily routine of home maintenance and child care and a "right" to have time to relax or be away from the family for recreation. The husbands worked long, arduous hours and experienced the stress of potential financial failure without an awareness of the stresses experienced by their wives in parenting and housekeeping. The women felt the responsibility for the relationship and for parenting and resented the failure of their husbands to take their fair share. With the advent of the latest women's movement, women became aware of the connection between power, respect, and financial remuneration in a capitalistic society, often resenting the sense of powerlessness they felt owing to their assigned gender role. Despite advances, many residual expectations continue in the relationships of today.

Glenda and Allen were individuals whose physical and temperamental characteristics fit well with the socialization messages they received in childhood. Because they were successful in conforming to the rules of gendered behavior they had learned, they were rewarded in their early years for behavior that later became detrimental. They had been so well socialized in a gender-stereotypical manner that when their mutual growth and happiness depended on a departure from the old rules, it was an extremely difficult departure to make. Therefore, they began to live in separate worlds, blaming one another for their problems rather than attacking the problems as a team. Perhaps individuals who have not been as easily or successfully gender-socialized (i.e., sex-typed, see chapter 2) because of their personal characteristics are more likely to try atypical methods of resolving problems that open the door to growth and change.

Positive coevolution is entirely possible, with or without therapeutic intervention. Individuals whose self-esteem gives them the strength to move away from protective defenses and rigid gender stereotypes are able to support one another in growth, whether or not their growth receives approval from the larger society. From our work with couples who struggle with issues emanating from traditional gender socialization, we can speculate on what skills and attitudes "make the difference." Coevolved couples begin by using open and honest communication to solve their problems. They view their relationship systemically; that is, they do not project blame on one another but each take responsibility for their part in conflict. They learn that if they approach each other in a calm, nonattacking manner, they get a more productive response than if they allow their anger to be freely expressed. They learn to express their appreciation to one another for the efforts they each put forth in making their partnership work. Over time, they become more aware of and articulate about the individual dissatisfactions and stresses that are a product of their gender roles. They can see how the larger society and their families of origin have absorbed and continued to endorse rules that they do not like and want to change. They are able gently to educate one another about these issues and seek ways to resolve these problems. They become open to hearing the other person's story because they know there is mutual respect and empathy between them. Even when their relationship seems unbalanced in favor of one or the other, they keep the total picture in mind, remembering the sacrifices and stresses of the other spouse in the past and seeing their present situation as temporary as they work for a mutual goal in the future. They maintain a sense of respect and appreciation for one another and perceive their relationship as equitable. They accomplish all this through the process we call *empathic knowing*. It is the therapist's job to create an atmosphere of mutual respect and appreciation in which positive coevolution can take place.

THE ROLE OF THE THERAPIST IN GUIDING THE GENDER-ROLE JOURNEY

One of the previously mentioned cornerstones of gender-sensitive psychotherapy is an understanding of the gender-role journey (O'Neil & Egan, 1992b; O'Neil & Roberts-Carroll, 1988). The gender-role journey consists of five phases: (a) acceptance of traditional gender roles, (b) ambivalence about gender roles, (c) anger, (d) activism, and (e) celebration and integration of gender roles (Exhibit 9.1). Glenda and Allen are a couple who did not successfully complete the gender-role journey together. In fact, as far as we know, Allen never got beyond Phase 1, that of total acceptance of traditional gender roles, although the financial losses incurred after his divorce could have propelled him through Phase 2 and into Phase 3. Probably because the traditional relationship was less satisfying to her, Glenda worked her way through Phase 2, ambivalence, in her early years of marriage and reached Phase 3, the anger phase, by midlife. Partly owing to the support and modeling of some of her peers, Glenda moved into Phase 4, activism, for 2 years while she pursued her short-lived career. Her decision to give up her business and buckle under to the expectations of others threw her back into the anger phase, where she remained stuck. In the previous sections, we addressed the potential role of a therapist, had this couple presented for therapy during any of these phases. In the following section, we provide case examples for each phase of the gender-role journey, with suggested interventions. As in any developmental approach, an accurate assessment of the phase (or overlapping phases) of the gender-role journey will enable the clinician to address the appropriate issues to move the client forward to the next phase.

Starting With Entitlement: Stage 1. Acceptance of Traditional Gender Roles

The therapist must work both with the couple and with each individual, accepting each position in the gender-role journey and moving them gently through to the next. Each phase has its own challenge. For example, the 22-year-old woman who emphatically insists that if her handsome

Exhibit 9.1

Phases of the Gender-Role Journey

Phase 1. Acceptance of traditional gender roles

- Accepts traditional notions of masculinity and femininity
- Endorses restrictive view of gender roles
- Endorses strength, control, power, restrictive emotionality for men
- Endorses warmth, expressiveness, nurturance, passivity for women
- Experiences limited awareness of how restrictive gender roles limit human potential
- Lacks awareness of how sexism restricts and violates people
- Receives rewards for acting in stereotypical ways
- Fears questioning authority
- Lacks information about how gender roles are learned
- Feels powerless and dependent
- Feels anger when others violate gender-role stereotypes

Phase 2. Ambivalence about gender roles

- Experiences dissatisfaction with stereotypical notions of gender roles
- Questions restrictiveness of gender roles through exposure to new ideas about sexism
- Experiences increased awareness of how gender roles and sexism violate people
- Experiences some fear of what it would mean to change one's gender-role ideas or behaviors
- Vacillates between the safety of stereotypical gender roles and the excitement and anxiety of possible gender-role change
- Feels confusion about masculine–feminine identities
- Begins to recognize the lost potential from restrictive gender roles of Phase 1

- Experiences sporadic irritation about sexism
- Begins to contemplate making gender-role changes
- Needs support from others to make changes or may regress to Phase 1

Phase 3. Anger

- Experiences negative emotions about sexism and expresses them to individuals and groups
- Experiences limited outlets for negative emotions, isolation, and personal pain about sexism
- Expresses negative emotions in ways that produce conflict, anxiety, and depression
- Restricts circle of friends to those who accept and understand the anger
- Recognizes that sexism is a form of interpersonal violence
- Recognizes that sexism produces male and female victims
- Experiences more interpersonal conflict with others regarding gender-role issues
- Remains "stuck in the anger" and immobilized
- Experiences difficulties pinpointing the multiple sources of the anger
- Begins to use anger to make personal changes

Phase 4. Activism

- Pursues an active exploration of how gender roles and sexism have affected one's life
- Deals directly with the pain of sexism and gender-role conflict
- Increases self-communication and feedback about gender-role issues in one's life
- Makes gender-role changes in one's life that are less restrictive and conflictual
- Takes personal responsibility for reducing sexism in personal and professional life
- Uses anger about sexism in positive ways

(cont'd.)

- Commits oneself to social–political–educational courses of action
- Makes personal, professional, and political plans of action related to gender roles and sexism
- Feels confirmed or disconfirmed by activism regarding gender roles and sexism
- Needs role models and support from others to continue the activism

Phase 5. Celebration and integration of gender roles

- Experiences deep awareness and satisfaction by viewing self and the world as unrestricted by gender roles
- Integrates anger about sexism regularly with efficiency and effectiveness
- Works against sexism regularly with efficiency and effectiveness, not out of anger but out of commitment to positive change
- Understands other people's gender-role journeys and their views of sexism and gender roles
- Experiences increased "gender-role freedom" in personal and professional relationships
- Continues active efforts to educate the public about gender and the violence of sexism
- Experiences greater compassion for other people's gender journeys and transitions
- Experiences increased personal power, autonomy, and strength
- Commits oneself to gender-role egalitarianism in personal, professional, and political areas of life

Note. From Neil, J. M., and Egan, J. (1992). Men and Women's Gender-Role Journeys: A Metaphor for Healing, Transition, and Transformation In B. R. Wainrib (Ed.), *Gender Issues Across the Life Cycle* (pp. 114–115). New York: Springer. Reprinted with permission.

boyfriend really loved her he would buy her the $10,000 diamond engagement ring, even though he is only a manager of a pizza parlor, needs to get in touch with the source of that notion, what she really wants from a relationship, and what message she might be sending to her boyfriend. The therapist can help her reject the fairy-tale dreams of Sleeping Beauty and Cinderella by helping her to make a more realistic appraisal of her situation in the real world of today, including an exploration of the fate of modern-day relationships in which beauty is exchanged for money. When she understands the implications of that sort of relationship for herself, including its frailty in the face of aging, she may be ready to hear how much more permanent her financial security would be if she could provide for herself. This realization moves her through the dissatisfaction with a marred fairy tale to a certain amount of consciousness raising. From there, the therapist might uncover the gender messages she received that led her to believe she had to catch a rich man rather than rely on herself to get an education and pursue a career that would provide for her needs. Eventually, she will gain the insight that if she does not make financial security her top priority in a relationship, she expands the number of potential partners considerably and might be able to marry someone she loves. In this way, the therapist gradually moves her away from entitlement on the gender-role journey. Often, such explorations are better done in individual sessions until clients reach a point at which they no longer see the significant other only in terms of self-centered desires but as a complete person with needs and frustrations.

Dealing With the Angry Partner: Stage 2 and 3. Ambivalence and Anger

When couples marry, they are usually at the same developmental level (Bowen, 1978; Scarf, 1989; Scharff & Scharff, 1987). This is true for their stage in the gender-role journey as well. They essentially speak each other's language. They generally have an understanding of the roles they will play in the relationship, which fit like a lock and key. When one partner becomes dissatisfied with the role and wishes to change the unspoken contract by which their union is governed, the other partner invariably feels betrayed and angry. Since the women's movement that began in the late '60s, women have broken their contracts all over the nation, and men have understandably become angry (see case example, chapter 7).

It is not only women who move on in their gender-role journey and opt for a new understanding of what is right or wrong. Men, too, become dissatisfied with their role as "meal ticket" for a family that takes them for granted (David & Brannon, 1976). For example, after 25 years of a traditional marriage in which he functioned as sole provider for his wife and five children, Rich suffered several career setbacks owing to the downsizing of his company. He finally found himself without a job at age 52 with two teenaged children still at home. He asked his wife, Sue, to go back to work to help out, which she did but not without a great deal of complaining and blaming him for failing as a man. Rich tried to find work, but he was unable to obtain a job that paid even close to what he had once earned. He and Sue began to argue constantly—she feeling betrayed and abandoned, he feeling misunderstood, unappreciated, and unsupported. Finally, they divorced, and he pursued an entirely unrelated career that was less prestigious and earned him less money but had been a longtime secret fantasy. She was understandably furious, feeling she was left to take care of herself in her early 50s with no experience in doing that.

The first step for Sue's therapist was to empathize with her plight and validate her sense of betrayal and abandonment. It was only when she felt understood and supported that she was able to look at the situation more holistically. When she realized that her anger was nonproductive and that she indeed needed to learn to take care of herself, she stopped expending so much emotional energy on hating her husband and focused her energy instead into vocational training in the computer field. This eventually led to employment that did not provide the standard of living her ex-husband had been able to sustain but at least provided security in the present and a retirement plan for the future. As she spent more time in the workplace, she got in touch with the stresses that occur there, which the therapist was able to use as a bridge to connect her with her ex-husband's experiences. As time went on, Sue was able to understand that her ex-husband had also been betrayed and abandoned by an economic system that was unstable. She began to have empathy for his plight and realized that her bitterness over the change in rules in their relationship only served to drive him away from her. She had contributed to her own abandonment.

Although this insight was too late to save her first marriage, Sue did remarry. She and her present husband contribute equally to the financial coffers in this marriage, and she is amazed at how that promotes equality in their decision making. She no longer plays the role of a dependent child who serves and obeys her parent in exchange for security. She has discovered that she enjoys being an equal partner in the present relationship.

Use of Individual Work to Play Catch-Up: Stages 3 and 4. Anger and Activism

Individual sessions are often useful to catch one partner up with the other on the gender-role journey. For example, a 54-year-old engineer, father of two grown children, came to therapy depressed and confused. He reported that his wife of 25 years, a 50-year-old registered nurse, had been complaining to him for several years since the children left home that he never talked to her. Because he did not understand what she meant, he ignored her for a long time, hoping the problem would go away. Finally, she stopped nagging him, went to work full-time, and spent all of her free time with her coworkers or the members of a women's support group she joined in her church. Her husband felt lonely and deserted and demanded that she quit her job and spend time with him. She said she did not feel close to him any more and that she preferred the company of her friends. He threatened to leave. She said, "Go ahead." He called her bluff and moved out, but he was miserable. He wanted his old life back, but she would not cooperate.

The therapist empathized with his confusion and desperation while simultaneously providing him with hope for reconciliation with his wife, although the marriage would not necessarily be the way it used to be. The therapist asked him what he would have done if he had understood what his wife meant when she said he never talked to her. Would he have tried to correct that problem? He answered affirmatively, indicating that his relationship was important to him, but he simply did not know what to do. In this case, the therapist was able to use psychoeducation to teach the client what a woman meant by *talk*, what significance talking had for her, and what the pitfalls are between a man and woman who communicate in traditional, gendered ways. The client was assigned reading material and given a chance to practice with the therapist in session. Then, the client was encouraged to invite his wife to join him in therapy, letting her know he was willing to learn new ways of relating because the relationship meant so much to him. The wife was surprised and pleased to know that he was trying to make changes and willingly came to therapy, where as a couple they continued work on their gender-role journeys together.

Advanced Partner as Cotherapist: Stages 4 and 5. Activism and Integration

Occasionally, it is possible for the therapist to use the more advanced partner in the role of cotherapist, enlisting his or her help in responding to the spouse in a therapeutic, rather than accusing, manner. This was the situation in the case of Mr. and Mrs. J. described in chapter 7. Mrs. J. had already been in individual therapy for 2 years, during which time she had received a great deal of support for her desire to be treated as an adult and for her assertive behavior. She had also attained a level of understanding regarding her contributions to the problems in her marriage. She was psychologically sophisticated enough to understand the importance of engaging her husband in therapy and was interested in hearing the therapist's ideas on how this might be accomplished. After 2 years of individual therapy, she was ready and willing to try a new way of looking at her relationship—systemically.

Mrs. J. found the gender-socialization theory resonant with her experience and gained insight quickly into many of the problems she and her husband had experienced. Because her husband had always been controlling—even in marital therapy, where he had refused to participate—she was excited about the cotherapy role she was being asked to play by the therapist. Therefore, she was more than willing to squelch her emotions temporarily to provide her less psychologically sophisticated husband with a safe, nonaccusatory atmosphere in which to express the emotions he was barely learning to identify. She knew that she could vent later with the therapist and that when her husband was ready, she would have her turn. It turned out, as illustrated in chapter 7, that when she delayed her immediate response and listened carefully to her husband, she felt empathy for his position and was able to respond to him in ways that allowed for negotiation of the issues. She was so appreciative of the fact that he was finally communicating with her on truly important issues that she felt rewarded for her restraint. In addition, because she was more advanced than her husband in communication techniques, she was able to learn quickly how to approach him in a manner that did not provoke defensive reactions. She became a model for him, another role she relished.

In this case, Mrs. J. was twice rewarded for her changed behavior: first, by the prestige of being trusted by the therapist to play such a therapeutic role, and second, by the positive response of her husband. Mr. J. was truly pleased that he could say something that usually "sent his wife into orbit," discuss it logically, and discover that he could understand her viewpoint on the issue. This process was so rewarding for him that he began to share more and more of his inner world with her, which was exactly what she needed for her to feel connected to him. The positive spiral simply escalated until they shared a wonderful second honeymoon in Paris. The entire case was made much easier by Mrs. J.'s more advanced position on the gender-role journey.

CONCLUSION

We have discussed the importance of empathy, genuineness, and unconditional positive regard (Rogers, 1957) in bringing about therapeutic change. When a therapist works with a couple concerning gender issues, he or she teaches them through modeling and education to provide these conditions for one another so that they can each share their gender journey, both its frustrations and joys, in a safe atmosphere. Respect, acceptance, and understanding of the gender-role journey of the other opens the door for change.

The therapist can facilitate positive coevolution by his or her systemic understanding of gender socialization, knowledge of the detriments of rigid gender socialization, willingness to explore and support ideas that do not conform to gender roles, and ability to teach clients the skills they need to communicate intimately and effectively with one another. Positive coevolution does not refer to the difference between a relationship that stays intact and one that does not. Positive coevolution allows each individual to reach her or his full potential within the relationship with the full support and understanding of the other. It is that acceptance of one's true self by the other that constitutes the intimacy so much desired by most of the couples seen in psychotherapy.

10

Power and Violence in
Male–Female Relationships

Earlier in this book, we indicated that the techniques described should not be used with couples in whom abusive and violent behavior is taking place. In this chapter, we address the special case of domestic violence. There are many controversies and myths concerning violent couples. Most of these have to do with who is responsible for the violence, whether it can viewed as systemic or asystemic in nature, and whether or not couples therapy can be effective.

In addition, it is common for violence to be overlooked by therapists (Holtzworth-Munroe et al., 1992). It is important for therapists to be aware of these issues for the purpose of assessment and treatment, because treating violent couples in conjoint therapy can be dangerous unless the violence has ceased. This chapter provides an overview of the issues involved in the treatment of domestic violence and outlines some of the current treatment interventions for victim and perpetrator.

According to Gelles and Straus's (1989) Second National Violence Survey, conducted in 1985, 16.7 percent of American couples experienced an incident of domestic violence during that year. That same study reported that between 22 and 67 percent of dating relationships involved some kind of assault. Koss (1990) indicated that half of all dating couples sampled reported violence during dating. Most of the incidents consisted of minor assaults such as pushing, slapping, shoving, or throwing things, but in a projected 3.4 million households, the violence had a high risk of causing serious injury. The enormity of domestic violence in the United States is clear.

BATTERED WOMEN

Although both men and women suffer physical abuse in their intimate relationships, most of the data point to more severe abuse in greater numbers perpetrated against women by men. Gelles and Straus (1989) reported in their 1975 National Violence Survey that 3.8 percent of women were victims of physical abuse each year, 6 wives per 1,000 were beaten up by their husbands each year, and the average battered wife was attacked three times each year. The results of their Second National Violence Survey, conducted in 1985, indicated that although severe wife beating had declined somewhat, there were still 2 incidents of severe wife beating per 1,000 women. Browne (1987) indicated that 24 to 34 percent of American women will be assaulted by an intimate partner during their lifetime. Women constitute 76 percent of spousal murder victims (Straus & Gelles, 1988); this figure supports previous findings by Dobash and Dobash (1977–1978, 1979) that 70–80 percent of murdered women are killed by spouses, family members, or male significant others. Lethality in cases of wife battering is most likely to occur when a woman tries to leave a relationship. Dobash and Dobash also reported that husbands were assaulted by their wives in only 1.1 percent of the cases they reviewed, whereas in 64 percent of the cases, women were assaulted by their male significant others. Others (Barnett, Keyson, & Thelen, 1992; Jacobson, 1993; Kurz, 1993) have indicated that perpetrators of violence are most likely to be men and that the violence is most likely to be initiated in the home.

BATTERED MEN

On the other hand, Straus and Gelles (1986), reporting the results of the previously mentioned 1985 National Family Violence Survey funded by the National Institutes of Mental Health (NIMH) and published in the *Journal of Marriage and the Family*, indicated that 2 million men reported having been assaulted by a wife or girlfriend. This statistic is higher than that reported by women, 1.8 million of whom reported assaults from a husband or boyfriend. They also reported that men and women physically abuse each other in equal numbers but that women were more often the initiators of violence. Furthermore, women in this study reported using weapons in 82 percent of the cases (compared to 25 percent for men) to make up for their physical disadvantage. A recent article in *U.S. News and World Report* pointed out that whereas the rate of severe assaults by men on women fell by 50 percent between the 1975 and 1985 National Family Violence Surveys, the rate of female assaults on males remained static during that time (Leo, 1996). Steinmetz (1978; Steinmetz & Lucca, 1988) argued that there is also a battered husband syndrome that must be addressed.

WHO IS RESPONSIBLE?

Most researchers minimize the extent of women-perpetrated violence against male significant others. According to Straus and Gelles (1988), "the same study that found forty-six men in one thousand being hit also found that the vast majority of these men were hit because they had initiated the violence and abuse. By and large, women used violence to protect themselves" (p. 105). Although women commit 48 percent of the murders of spouses or close friends, women's violence is usually self-defense (Straus & Gelles, 1988). This statement is corroborated by Okun (1986), who found that 54 percent of the battered women he interviewed retaliated in self-defense, as well as by Browne (1987) and Walker (1989), who found that women who murder have been recipients of more serious battering than women who do not.

There are several other factors that may explain the greater emphasis on abuse cases in which women are victims. One of these is the simple fact that men, in general, are physically larger than women, so that when they strike, they are more likely to cause damage. Second, men are less likely to report an incident of abuse by a female intimate, either because it did not cause damage and they do not think of it as abuse or because they are humiliated by being beaten by a female, whom society views as weaker and therefore easily controlled. Finally, a third and most frequently endorsed reason for these results is simply that they reflect the reality of relationships between men and women in a patriarchal society that only recently granted women status above that of property. Men beat women more often because it is a socially sanctioned behavior and because they know they can win because they are bigger. As Hare-Mustin (1978) stated, "the family has been the principal arena for the exploitation of women" (p. 181).

IS DOMESTIC VIOLENCE SYSTEMIC OR ASYSTEMIC?

There are those who believe the plight of the male victim may be overlooked in the present political climate (Steinmetz, 1978; Steinmetz & Lucca, 1988; Straus, 1993). The theoretical understanding of violence that researchers and therapists endorse may have a major effect on whether or not these professionals are willing to address the issue of male victims. Systemic approaches to abusive relationships have viewed the abusive cycle as an interactive process in which the victim takes part. They view violence as gender-neutral; that is, the abuse can be initiated by the man or the woman. In therapy, they have attempted to modify the interactions between the partners, teaching them more effective means of resolving their problems to eliminate the abuse (Stuart, 1980).

Feminist writers (e.g., Bograd, 1984) have criticized family systems approaches for essentially "blaming the victim" rather than insisting that the batterer take responsibility for his behavior. Although the spouse may have participated in an interaction that escalated to violence, in this view nothing justifies the use of physical abuse.

The woman usually has less earning power than her spouse (Decade of the Woman, 1992), less access to external resources, less physical strength, less education, and less work experience. For most women, a divorce will result in a reduced standard of living for herself and her children, as well as the severe stress that comes from playing the dual role of provider and single parent (Morgan, 1991; Weitzman, 1985). Women are aware of the potential dangers in this society of attack on women who live without male protection (Gelles & Straus, 1989; Jacobson, 1993; McGrath, Keita, Strickland, & Russo, 1990). Finally, many women have been socialized to believe the maintenance of the relationship is their job (Chodorow, 1978), which means a divorce is indicative of a personal failure. Consequently, many women do not participate as an equal in the relationship.

The feminist writers view abuse as part of an unequal relationship. Women often yield to their male partner's desires throughout the marriage, even when this is detrimental to their own happiness. For most women, marriage is important to their social and economic survival in a patriarchal society, a fact that limits their ability to negotiate assertively as an equal with their spouses. This power differential between women and men invalidates the circularity principle that systems theorists frequently apply to abusive relationships.

More recently, theorists (Harway & Evans, 1996) and researchers (Jacobson, 1993) have begun to see domestic violence as asystemic; that is, the etiology of the violent behavior lies within the abuser and is not affected by the marital system. Those who endorse this model tend to see violence as a principally male behavior that must be addressed through legal and social means. In their conceptualization, it is the patriarchal system itself and male gender socialization that perpetuates the male-to-female violence in this society. From this perspective, men feel entitled to abuse women to get their own needs met. Because these researchers and therapists do not want to minimize the enormity of the wife-battering problem in the United States, they are reluctant to discuss the issue of female batterers, because it might detract from what they perceive to be a larger problem.

Yet the data from Gelles and Straus (1989) clearly indicate that in 1985, overall wife-to-husband violence was 116 per 1,000, a number that is only 5 per 1,000 less than that reported for husband-to-wife violence in the same study. How does one explain the fairly equal initiation of violence between women and men? Is domestic violence systemic or asystemic? A discussion of the prevailing models that attempt to explain the domestic violence patterns and the latest research findings may help to shed light on the systemic–asystemic question.

MODELS FOR UNDERSTANDING THE CYCLE OF VIOLENCE

Walker (1984) described a pattern that begins with a period during which tension builds between the partners and concludes eventually in a violent incident. The violence is followed by a period of remorse and active courting of the victim by the batterer, an interval Walker called the "honeymoon period." Because no energy is exerted on solving the problem during the honeymoon period, the tension mounts again, and the cycle continues. Because the wife is rewarded during the honeymoon phase and the husband gets relief from the tension by battering, the behavior is reinforced. Eventually, because denial of the violence becomes impossible for both spouses, the honeymoon phase disappears. Nevertheless, the woman is aware that taking action to remove herself from the relationship can be more dangerous than staying in it (Hansen & Harway, 1993); therefore, she is motivated to remain in the relationship, and the tension relief continues to reinforce the violent cycle in the batterer.

According to the Duluth Minnesota Domestic Violence Project (Pence & Paymar, 1990), the core issue in a violent relationship is control, with violence being the enforcer of the control. Harway and Evans (1996) described the cycle of violence from the batterer's perspective. In this model, violent behavior is seen as one of an armamentarium of defenses against unwanted feelings that the abusive person employs when overwhelmed with feelings of shame, guilt, inadequacy, and helplessness. The defenses the individual employs can include (a) blame and denial to justify attack; (b) control of everything, including other people, in his environment; (c) alcohol and drugs to relieve the pain, and (d) acting out. These behaviors, although defending against the painful feelings in the short term, bring about more problems in the long term that increase the bad feelings. The cycle repeats, with the episodes becoming more frequent and abusive, unless it is interrupted by external factors. The important fact is that the cycle exists *within the batterer* and is not affected by the victim's behavior.

RESEARCH FINDINGS

Extensive research has been done to identify personality correlates and life experiences that define the batterer. Researchers (Dutton, 1988; Gondolf, 1988) have formulated a typology of batterers, which includes emotional inexpressivity, rigidity in thinking, low self-esteem, alcohol–drug abuse, criminal acts, antisocial and sociopathic characteristics, and a violent subculture. A large percentage of abusers have been abused themselves or have witnessed abuse between their parents or against a sibling in childhood. Other researchers (Edleson, Eisikovitz, & Guttman, 1985; Hotaling & Sugarman, 1986) have speculated that there is no specific batterer profile; they have reported that batterers as a group do not differ significantly from nonbatterers.

Recent process research (Gottman et al., 1995; Jacobson, 1993) has shown that in some cases the wife's behavior has no effect on whether or not arguments escalate to violence. In one study, violence was unpredictable for some men and had little or no correlation with the responses of the women. Gottman et al. (1995) found two types of batterers: *vagal reactors*, who calmly responded to wives' perceived attempts to control them by becoming threatening, belligerent, and contemptuous and thereby obtaining partner compliance, and *Type II men*, who responded to perceived abandonment with loss of emotional control, jealousy, fear, and rage. The vagal reactor abuser dissociated his physiological response from the behavior; that is, he became calm and focused. By manipulating his partner's emotions through threatening behavior, he was able to suppress her anger. These men were more violent outside the marriage than the Type II men; they were often diagnosed as antisocial, aggressive–sadistic, or drug-dependent. They were more likely than Type II men to have witnessed physical violence between their parents. Their marriages were usually stable. The researchers hypothesized that their wives stayed in the relationship because of fear or their own psychopathology. Type II men, on the other hand, lost control of their emotions in response to perceived threats of abandonment. Their violent behavior was meant to keep their spouses from leaving. These men were not violent outside the relationship, and 27 percent of their wives were able to leave the marriage.

Although there are clear differences between the two types, in both cases, abusers used violence to control the spouse rather than be controlled or abandoned. Such results point strongly to the importance of male gender socialization in the etiology of domestic violence.

THE ROLE OF GENDER SOCIALIZATION IN ABUSIVE RELATIONSHIPS

In the process of socialization, women and men receive messages regarding what is expected of them, and these messages help to explain domestic violence. Little boys are generally taught at an early age that they should show no emotions, allow no weakness, be powerful, win competitions, control their surroundings and other people, be interpersonally aggressive, and reject anything that might be identified as feminine (David & Brannon, 1976; O'Neil, 1982). As adolescents, many males measure their status on a hierarchy that is based on fighting, sports, physical strength, fast driving, consumption of alcohol, and sexual "scores" (Pittman, 1985, 1991). As a result, many men believe that they should control and protect women while simultaneously seducing them sexually. They tend to reinforce each other in considering anything feminine to be inferior and therefore frequently reject qualities that might help them find other ways to deal with stress and failure. Often they do not consider negotiation and cooperation as a means to problem solving but focus on having the power to control those who fall beneath them on the hierarchy. Furthermore, the society sanctions the use of alcohol and physical activity to reduce stress in men (Nolen-Hoeksema, 1990) and condones the use of violence (Miedzian, 1991), especially in sports (Lipsyte, 1994) and the military (Farrell, 1993) as well as when, in some subcultures, enforcing dominance over their wives (Dobash & Dobash, 1979).

The process research cited previously (Gottman et al., 1995) supports the effect of gender socialization on the behavior of the batterer. Because many men are socialized to believe they are superior to women, there is usually tremendous humiliation associated with the threat of being controlled or abandoned by the lesser sex. Men socialized in this manner do not have the intellectual, social, or emotional resources to problem-solve in a more appropriate manner. They may resort to violence rather than suffer this humiliation, especially if they have learned violent patterns of behavior in childhood or in their subculture. Because such men are taught to view women as clearly inferior and they measure themselves on their ability to control their surroundings, they are set up to use any means at their disposal, including violence, to keep their women in line.

It is easy to see how a man who has accepted these teachings would engage in violent behavior toward his wife in an effort to control her or to avoid the painful feelings of humiliation and shame that come from seeing himself too far down the hierarchical ladder that arises from male competition. But why does the woman take it?

Most women are socialized to adapt and cooperate, to take responsibility for the health of their relationship, and to sacrifice their own needs for those of their partner and children (Chodorow, 1978; Gilligan, 1982; Hare-Mustin, 1983; Miller, 1986). They are usually less prepared to support themselves financially than their spouses because they have placed their emphasis on their physical beauty (Wolf, 1991) as opposed to education and the obtaining of skills for the workplace (Betz & Fitzgerald, 1987). They often lack confidence in their ability to make decisions and feel incomplete without a spouse (Dowling, 1982). This helpless dependency is reinforced by the abusive spouse, who constantly points out his wife's inadequacies. For many women, relationships take precedence over everything else in their lives, essentially identifying who they are (Chodorow, 1978; Erikson, 1964; Gilligan, 1982). Therefore, these women often struggle to save even a painful and dangerous marriage rather than face the hostile world all alone. Of course, as previously cited, they may risk death if they attempt to leave an abusive spouse (Dobash & Dobash, 1977–1978).

The prevailing models of domestic violence and process research on batterers and abusive relationships suggest that violence is asystemic; that is, it is a problem within the batterer that is partially a result of traditional gender socialization in a patriarchal society. If this is the case, how does one explain women who initiate violence?

IS THERE MORE THAN ONE TYPE OF DOMESTIC VIOLENCE?

Perhaps systemic and asystemic violence coexist in society, and different types of violence call for different treatment interventions (Lipchik & Geffner, 1994; Ornduff, Kelsey, & O'Leary, 1995). It is clear from the preceding research that there are batterers who do not react in a systematic, predictable way to interactions with their spouses. There are men who feel entitled to use violence to control women or to relieve their stress without regard or empathy for the victim. In these cases, the asystemic conceptualization is valid.

But there are also men and women who get caught in systemic disagreements that escalate to physical violence, frequently complicated by drug or alcohol abuse. Gender socialization plays a role in these cases as well. For example, research (Gottman & Levenson, 1986) has shown that men have greater physiological reactivity to conflict than women and often use withdrawal or passive resistance to protect themselves against these feelings—a process Gottman terms *stonewalling*. When women are frustrated in their efforts to be heard by a spouse who stonewalls to avoid feeling controlled, they sometimes escalate their efforts to get a response by crying, screaming, shouting, throwing things, or even hitting. Because traditional gender-socialization messages teach men and women that women are expected to be emotional, this behavior is less a cause for alarm than male violence. Many women are also taught that a slap on the face is an appropriate method of showing disapproval to a male in response to an insult or affront. Because most women are smaller and weaker than their male spouses, they often believe it is acceptable for them to become physical in a disagreement. Gender-socialization messages that teach a woman that she has the status and responsibility of a dependent child, whereas the man must take the more powerful, controlling, and (one hopes) benevolent parental role, sanction her acting-out behavior and demand that her husband remain "adult." When her husband does not restrain himself physically, she may be not only surprised but injured as well.

For a man caught in a relationship with a woman who resorts to physical violence, a dilemma results. If he fights back, he is in danger of being charged with battering. If he runs away, he is not a *real* man, because his gender socialization messages have taught him that *real* men control their women. If he reports the incident, he is publicly humiliated because men are supposed to be bigger, stronger, and better than women and certainly not afraid of them. He can get out of the relationship, but it may take many such incidents to convince him the marriage is not salvageable. Seldom is he able to trace and understand the origin of her acting-out behavior.

In other cases, men and women who do not have good problem-solving and communication skills may trigger each other to anger, and the disagreement may escalate to physical violence (Stuart, 1980). This cycle is often facilitated by the use of alcohol or drugs. In these cases, both spouses are responsible for the interaction and both must make an effort to learn more functional methods of resolving disagreements. Learning skills such as anger management, communication techniques, and negotiation may be more effective when the violence is systemic in nature. The gender inquiry can also be used to uncover many of the dysfunctional cognitions that men and women bring to their relationships. The advantage of this approach is that it allows men and women to feel understood and validated but challenges them to change the rules by which they govern their interactions with the other gender. What they have been taught is dysfunctional, creating pain for themselves and their partners, and they must make up new and healthier rules by which to live in relationships.

On the other hand, asystemic violence requires different interventions. Because the profession has not yet developed highly effective methods of treating batterers such as those found in the Gottman et al. (1995) study, often the only recourse of the therapist is to empower the woman to leave the relationship and protect herself. Recommended treatment methods for both batterer and victim are discussed in greater detail in the following pages.

CONTRAINDICATIONS TO CONJOINT THERAPY

Although we believe that the gender-sensitive approach described in this book can be used to move a couple from an egocentric position of entitlement to an empathic understanding that promotes mutuality and respect (see chapter 9), when physical violence is present, these techniques are contraindicated. Despite the fact that gender socialization plays a large role in the cycle of violence (Hansen & Harway, 1993; Harway & Evans, 1996), *conjoint therapy is not recommended unless and until the violence has ceased for at least 6 months.* Therefore, when violence is discovered, we recommend that couples therapists make appropriate referrals to local domestic violence programs: domestic violence shelters, survivor support groups, therapists who are expert in treating survivors of domestic violence, and group treatment programs for batterers. Both gender inquiry and psychoeducation regarding the role of gender socialization in the development of belief systems are of benefit to both spouses in an abusive relationship; however, when violence is present, these techniques are most useful in individual or gendered group sessions, as described later in this chapter. Neither partner will be psychologically ready to share his or her gender-role journey in the presence of the other, much less hear the other with empathic understanding, until each has been treated separately. The batterer must first learn to acknowledge responsibility for the violent behavior, recognize that it is wrong, and learn alternative methods of resolving disagreements. Likewise, the survivor must be treated for "battered woman syndrome," with the goal of correcting cognitive distortions and empowering her to take charge of her life.

THERAPEUTIC INTERVENTIONS

Importance of Assessment

Experts in the treatment of people involved in domestic abuse (Hansen & Harway, 1993; Harway & Evans, 1996) have warned that therapists often are not aware of the violence occurring in the relationships of the couples they are treating. Citing Holtzworth-Munroe et al. (1992), they point out that 43–46 percent of supposedly nonviolent couples recommended by therapists as a control group for that study had experienced a violent episode within the preceding year. This finding indicates that the incidence of marital violence in distressed couples seeking treatment is likely to be even higher than the statistic of 1 in 6 in the general public reported by Gelles and Straus (1989). Recent research (Hansen, Harway, & Cervantes, 1991; Harway & Hansen, 1990) has indicated that therapists are not well trained to deal with battering in a distressed couple and often fail to address violence even when it is clearly delineated. Harway and Hansen have warned that the therapeutic interventions many of these therapists recommend can exacerbate the violence by raising painful issues for the batterer. For this reason, accurate assessment is vital.

Part of the problem is the therapist's understanding of what battering really is. Many people, including professionals, regard physical violence such as beating with fists, using guns and knives, or trying to run over the spouse with a car as evidence of domestic violence. Some experts in the field use a much broader definition of battering, however, holding that "battering is an act of control by one intimate partner over another" (Harway & Evans, 1996, p. 358). They define *battering* as abuse, whether or not *physical* violence is present. This definition would include holding a person down, unplugging the phone, giving intimidating looks or gestures, voicing humiliating put-downs, and threatening violence or otherwise using one's words to control another (Harway & Evans, 1996; O'Neil & Egan, 1992a). In the control model of understanding batterers' dynamics, any controlling behavior is predictive of physical violence. Therefore, Hansen and Harway (1993) recommended using a checklist (see Exhibits 10.1,

Exhibit 10.1

Examples of Domestic Violence

1. Verbal and emotional abuse as manifested by the following:

   Threats of divorce, suicide, or reporting to police
   Intimidation
   Stalking
   Accusations of infidelity
   Tracking time
2. Physical violence including the following:

Bodily	Trying to run over with car
Pushing or shoving	Using weapons
Slapping	
Biting	*To objects*
Kicking	Breaking personal property
Spanking	Tearing clothing
Hitting	Throwing objects
Holding down	Punching walls or doors
Twisting arms	Breaking windows
Pulling hair	*To control departure*
Choking	Blocking exits
Carrying against her will	Taking car keys
Kneeing	Taking money or credit cards
Burning	Unplugging phone

Note. Examples are from *Battering and Family Therapy: A Feminist Perspective*, by M. Hansen and M. Harway, 1993, Newburg Park, CA, Sage.

10.2, and 10.3) for assessing the capacity for physical violence as well as identifying any actual battering that is occurring and the lethality potential of that violent behavior.

A second problem is the unlikelihood of the victim revealing the domestic violence in the presence of the partner for fear of retaliation. Batterers who are aware of the legal ramifications of their behavior and who use denial and projection of blame as defenses are certainly not going to divulge their violent behavior. This possibility underlines the importance of having at least one individual session with each of the partners early in the treatment process. Although neither the batterer nor the victim is likely to admit readily to violence, signs of unreasonable jealousy, projection of

---

Exhibit 10.2

Signs of Potential for Physical Violence

1. Controlling behavior such as
   a. Tracking time
   b. Controlling finances
   c. Accusations of infidelity
   d. Prevention from attending school or work
2. Disguised emotional dependency such as
   a. Quick involvement
   b. Demand for fast commitment
   c. Unrealistic expectations that partner will meet all needs
3. Hypercriticism
4. Hypersensitivity
5. Projection of blame
6. Public humiliation
7. Verbal abuse
8. Isolation from friends and family
9. Use of force in sex
10. Cruelty to animals or children
11. Destruction of personal property and sentimental items
12. Threats of physical violence
13. Past battering
14. Use of force during argument

Note. Signs summarized from *Battering and Family Therapy: A Feminist Perspective,* by M. Hansen and M. Harway, 1993, Newburg Park, CA, Sage.

Exhibit 10.3

Potential for Lethality

Existence of any of the following indicates potential for killing:

Threats of homicide or suicide

Acute depression

Possession of weapons

Rage

Drug or alcohol consumption combined with hopelessness and despair

Obsessive rumination about partner and belief he cannot live without her

Easy access to intended victim or relatives

Note. From *Battering and Family Therapy: A Feminist Perspective,* by M. Hansen and M. Harway, 1993, Newburg Park, CA, Sage.

blame, pressure to make a quick commitment, isolation of the woman from outside resources, and hypersensitivity can cue the therapist that abuse is probably present (see Exhibit 10.2).

A third problem is the failure of many training programs to prepare the therapist to deal with abusive relationships, and therapists who are ill prepared to work with violent couples sometimes inadvertently collude with the couple's desire to hide violence by failing to assess for violence. Training in treating violent couples will lessen the potential for denial on the part of the therapist.

Treating the Batterer

Because most of those identified as batterers are men and because women sustain the most severe damage from domestic violence, most of the treatment interventions that have been designed to work with those involved in domestic violence assume that the perpetrator is male and the victim is female. Although we have acknowledged that this is not always the case, in describing the most current interventions, we refer to the victim as female and the abuser as male. We caution the therapist to remember that the use of these pronouns does not preclude the possibility that females can be physically violent as well.

Because individual therapy does not appear to be effective with this population, group therapy is highly recommended. There are several widely used treatment methods available that appear to bring about only superficial change (Geffner et al., 1995; Holtzworth-Munroe, Beatty, & Anglin, 1995). These include (a) anger management; (b) skills-building psychoeducational groups that teach communication skills, stress reduction, conflict management, cognitive restructuring, and gender roles; and (c) direct confrontation of men's tendency to seek power and control. The latter technique understandably has a high dropout rate because male socialization pressures men to believe they are always right. Any technique that prematurely demands that men admit wrongdoing elicits shame and is counterproductive. Although the skills-building and anger control methods teach the clients useful competencies, they do not reach the heart of the matter. The male gender survival messages that are at the root of the dysfunctional behavior need to be addressed.

A relatively new model of working with male batterers that takes the preceding concerns into consideration has been developed by Harway and Evans (1996). Because, in their conceptualization, so much of the batterer's thinking is a result of the socialization he has received with other males, they recommend resocialization in the company of other men. Because batterers define their *maleness* as being different from and dominant over women, they are uncomfortable talking about feelings, admitting wrongdoing, walking away from a fight, or giving up their perceived power (Harway & Evans, 1996). In this model, men who are more advanced in the resocialization process confront the behavior of newcomers and serve as role models. The process is not unlike that of Alcoholics Anonymous.

Counseling for batterers can be divided into three phases. The first of these is *crisis intervention,* during which the goal of the therapist is to educate men about violence and violence control, help with the identification of feelings, teach socially acceptable channeling of feelings, and develop a danger management plan. During the second phase, *short-term counseling*, the therapist begins to address issues of a deeper nature. It is during this phase that he or she teaches the client to channel his power needs into socially acceptable channels, explores fears of abandonment with the client, and helps him to work through feelings of guilt and shame. In the final phase, the therapist works with the client on healing the abuse of the past and developing relational skills with other men, women, and the spouse. The Harway and Evans model of therapy (1996), ANOTHER WAY, uses the previously described cycle of feeling avoidance to connect with men. By attributing batterers' behavior to their gender socialization and pointing out its negative impact on them, therapists help them to reduce their sense of shame and guilt and motivate them to make changes for their own sake.

Batterer groups that address the effects of gender socialization and the avoidance of feelings, such as the Evans model, are the most effective in providing the supportive atmosphere the batterer needs to deal successfully with his sense of shame and humiliation and avoid his tendency to resort to violence. In the company of other men who (a) have learned to identify and cope with their feelings, (b) recognize the detrimental effects of gender socialization and have rejected the objectionable messages, and (c) have developed skills in communication, problem solving, conflict resolution, and anger management, these batterers can begin to change their lives. Ideally, they can learn how to relate to women in more fulfilling ways that will allow them to enter new relationships without replaying the violence.

Unfortunately, outcome studies (Gondolf & Foster, 1991) have reported an extremely high dropout rate from batterer treatment programs, with as few as 6 percent completing 3 months of a 6-month treatment program. Of those who complete programs, there is evidence that physical abuse ceases at 6-months but verbal abuse continues. It would be naive to assume enrollment in such a program will solve the problem of domestic violence.

Treating the Survivor

Survivors develop the *battered woman syndrome*, a set of faulty cognitions that are coping mechanisms adopted to survive the battering while remaining in the abusive relationship. This faulty thinking consists of denial of the abuse, self-blame, and denial of emotional or practical options; involved also are an external locus of control, a desire to save the batterer by helping him overcome his problem while enduring the abuse, and a need to endure the violence owing to some higher commitment, such as religion or tradition (Hansen & Harway, 1993). This faulty thinking must be addressed before the relationship can be treated.

Survivor therapy is also divided into three phases (Dutton, 1994). In the *crisis intervention phase*, the therapist must assess for the existence of violence and the level of danger the woman is in. During this phase, the therapist's goals include educating the woman about battering and domestic violence, validating her experience, and helping her develop and practice a safety-management plan. The second phase, *short-term counseling*, may be done in individual therapy, but it is usually more effective when done in a group. In this phase, the therapist continues to educate the client about domestic violence using a feminist analysis to look at the social, political, and economic contexts. Additionally, the therapist may help the client to examine family patterns using a genogram and to label and validate her emotional and physical experiences concerning the abuse. Other goals of this stage of therapy include (a) working on empowerment issues, (b) developing independent living skills and attitudes, (c) addressing grief issues, and (d) encouraging self-nurturance. In the long-term psychotherapy phase, the therapist works individually with the client to facilitate the reexperiencing of specific traumatic events through the use of hypnosis, drawing, retelling the story, keeping a journal, and imagery. In this stage, the therapist continues to help the client express affect and facilitates new experiences of trust. It is during this last phase of therapy that the clinician may wish to work from a trauma model to eliminate symptoms such as self-blame, learned helplessness, depression, denial, external locus of control, rationalization, and delusions of grandeur.

Is There a Place for Couples Therapy?

The problem with many of the treatment programs designed for abusive couples is that they assume the marital relationship must end. In some cases, this may be true, but often couples wish to stay together and may drop out of therapy if it requires that they separate permanently. Furthermore, some experts believe family therapy is more effective than individual therapy in cases of abuse because the family structure plays such an important role in maintaining the abuse (Geffner et al., 1995). Additionally, conjoint therapy affords the opportunity for the couple to try out new skills with one another in front of a therapist, who can defuse and reduce emotion while coaching both partners in effective communication and problem-solving techniques.

Some authorities (Geffner et al., 1995; Hansen & Goldenberg, 1993) have recognized that there is a place for conjoint therapy in abusive relationships—after the violence has stopped. The program called AMEND (Abusive Men Exploring New Directions, 1990) recommends couples therapy when there have been no reports of violence for over 5 months, the abuser has accepted responsibility for his acts, and the clients have cooperatively participated in treatment groups. Hope is renewed and motivation to work in therapy is strengthened for these couples if the therapist indicates that after the violence is eliminated and individual therapy is deemed successful, marital therapy to address other issues within the relationship is possible and desirable.

Geffner et al. (1995) described a 26-week program of couples therapy divided into four stages. The first is directive, behavioral, and psychoeducational and deals with safety plans, anger management, behavioral controls, and education regarding the social roots of aggression. The second stage teaches communication techniques and effective expression of feelings. The third stage addresses assertiveness skills, problem solving, and negotiation techniques, and the final stage focuses on intimacy issues and relapse prevention. Principles that apply throughout treatment include that (a) each person is responsible for his or her own behavior, (b) batterers have the ability to stop battering, (c) violence and intimidation are *not* acceptable, (d) clients can change their relationship and their own behaviors, and (e) the therapist can facilitate this process.

After the violence is under control, according to Hansen and Goldenberg (1993), the first task of conjoint therapy is to understand the reasons the couple were initially attracted to one another (using such conceptualizations as the family projection process, multigenerational transmission process, and object relations theory) and to determine whether the marriage is adaptive or should be terminated. If the marriage is to continue, Hansen and Goldenberg (1993) work toward the following goals: (a) elimination of any violence or threat of violence, (b) reduction of emotionality, (c) expansion of the perception of choices and repertoire of behaviors of each spouse, (d) provision of corrective emotional experiences by teaching the couple to express the vulnerability and pain behind the anger, and (e) reinforcement of the social expectation that violence is unacceptable.

Once the violence is controlled and boundaries set, the gender-sensitive therapist can begin the process already described in this book, taking a gender-socialization perspective and using the techniques delineated in previous chapters. Gender-sensitive couples therapy allows the clients to try out new ways of interacting with one another using their new paradigms for understanding men and women in the presence of a therapist who can act as a gender broker, facilitating their journey from helpless anger to empathic understanding. (For more in-depth discussion of conjoint therapy with abusive couples, see Geffner et al., 1995; Hansen & Goldenberg, 1993).

WHEN A RELATIONSHIP MUST END

Whenever a couple presents for marital therapy, the object is positive change, which may or may not mean the maintenance of the marital relationship. Whether the partners wish to remain married or wish to divorce is their decision. The therapist's job is to facilitate that process and make it a healthy learning experience, whichever direction it takes.

In cases of physical abuse, however, some experts (Hansen & Harway, 1993) recommend a more proactive stance. Most authorities (Geffner et al., 1995; Hansen & Harway, 1993) stress that the safety of the battered woman must be addressed above all else in cases of domestic violence. This generally requires that the woman be removed from the home and separated from the abuser until both have received treatment and the violence has stopped for 6 months. Gottman et al. (1995) found that 20 percent of their sample of abusers suffered from psychopathology such as antisocial personality disorder that is fairly intractable to treatment; therefore, there are times when the woman's safety requires an end to the relationship. This step can be dangerous because it is when women attempt to leave that the partner is most likely to attempt to kill them. In fact, the therapist who supports his or her client in leaving might also be in danger at this time.

Hansen and Harway (1993) discussed the necessity of the therapist's acting "as a political change agent in ensuring the client survives" (p. 233). This may require acting as an advocate for the client, reporting the abuse to the authorities, finding shelter for the victim, and working with the victim in developing an "escape from the relationship" plan. Survivor support groups are helpful in reinforcing the message that the victim must save herself at the expense of the relationship. Once the survivor's distorted thought processes have been successfully treated, she will be better able to develop and carry out a plan to live independently.

CONCLUSION

Gelles and Straus (1989) stated their belief that socially sanctioned inequality is the prime contributor to domestic violence. Other experts in the field (Hansen & Harway, 1993) have agreed, suggesting that steps must be taken on the legal, treatment, and social levels to enforce the message that violence will not be tolerated. This approach is clearly necessary as a beginning step to reduce violence in the home; however, this step is like the safety-first intervention used in treatment programs for batterers and victims. It is a beginning, but the deeper issues of gender inequality and detrimental messages of gender socialization must be addressed and revised to bring about enduring change on the domestic violence front.

11

Applications to Parent–Child and Work Relationships

This book focuses primarily on bridging gender-based differences that create barriers between heterosexual marital partners. This emphasis is appropriate because these relationships are profoundly important and strongly impacted by traditional gender-role socialization patterns. But other important relationships are also greatly hampered by traditional gender constraints.

To appreciate the pervasive influence of gender socialization on all relationships, we need to look at critical relationship processes and examine how women and men have been taught to approach them. In this exploration of gender patterns, we make frequent references to (a) value systems, (b) communication patterns, (c) personality characteristics, (d) problem-solving skills, (e) sexuality, and (f) gender-role assignments. In particular, we address issues concerning interpersonal communication, autonomy and connectedness, male instrumentality, intimacy, sexuality, relationship maintenance, and power. In this chapter, we examine two other types of relationships—parent–child and coworker relationships—to illustrate how our ideas about gender coevolution can address common difficulties and set the stage for more rewarding interactions. Although a case example of gender inquiry with a family has already been given, this chapter provides a more in-depth discussion, along with a case study.

PARENT–CHILD RELATIONSHIPS

Many fathers approach parenting with a hierarchical value system. Because they tend to see the world as a place where only the strong survive, their interactions with their children are commonly characterized by pressure for achievement and success (Biller, 1971; Pleck, 1987). Fathers are especially pleased when their children are intensely competitive and are prone to boast about their children's accomplishments (Chafetz, 1978; Pleck & Sawyer, 1980).

Mothers may also appreciate their children's competitive successes, but they are more likely than fathers to place significant emphasis on cooperation and popularity. When children face the dilemma of pursuing a goal that might jeopardize a friendship, fathers are more likely to encourage their children to "go for it," whereas mothers are likely to have misgivings. Fathers typically emphasize the pursuit of excellence, whatever the sacrifice in emotional well-being, whereas mothers are more likely to temper pursuit of success with concern for their children's emotional comfort (Biller, 1971; Gilligan, 1982; Miller, 1984).

Because fathers grew up needing to develop the self through differentiation from the other-gender parent, they are more attuned to children's needs for autonomy and independence (Chodorow, 1978). They often urge their children to "cut the apron strings." Mothers, who experienced a sense of self in connection, are more likely to place greater emphasis on emotional attachments and the development of substantive long-term relationships (Gilligan, 1982). They are likely to criticize fathers for their detachment and lack of emotional connections to their children, whereas fathers are likely to be critical of maternal overprotection.

Boys are typically raised in authoritarian environments and grow up in subcultures that maintain conformity through threat and intimidation (Arkin & Dobrofsky, 1978; Doyle, 1994; Messner, 1992). Whether exposed to the sports subculture, fraternities, the military, or the corporate world, men have had to adapt to patterns of interpersonal environments characterized by power, threat, and emotional and physical intimidation. Not surprisingly, the parenting styles of fathers are more likely to be coercive, authoritarian, and power-based (Jacklin, Dipietro, & Maccoby, 1984; Pleck, 1987). The phrase "just wait till your father gets home" has struck terror in the hearts of many children.

Girls are typically raised in environments emphasizing interpersonal responsibility and acute sensitivity to the affective state of others. Therefore, when they become parents, women are more likely to appeal to a child's interpersonal sensitivity and empathy as a means of shaping children's behavior. A mother is far more likely to use statements such as "it hurts me to see you behave that way" or "think how you would feel if someone treated you that way."

No one needs to be reminded that each parenting style has its strengths and weaknesses. For illustration of the weaknesses, one need only remember the multiple examples of abusive fathers or guilt-inducing and overly psychologizing mothers. (Of course, both women and men are capable of both areas of excess. The point is that socialization creates a tendency for women and men to err in opposite directions.)

Gender-Based Dilemmas in Parenting

We have pointed out a few of the most general differences in the parenting styles of women and men; we now provide a few illustrative examples of how these gender preferences can be played out in the interactions between parents and children.

Fathers and Sons

Fathers' general preferences for achievement, success, and competition markedly influence their interactions with their sons (Doyle, 1994). Because they are not as accustomed to thinking of women as career-oriented, fathers are more tolerant of passivity, laziness, or indifference in daughters, whereas they are likely to be obsessed with promoting achievement motivation in sons (Fox, 1978). To ensure that their sons are independent and tough enough, they are sometimes prone to push and drive them mercilessly. Tears may become cues for punishment, because fathers feel it necessary to teach sons to suppress their fears and insecurities.

Fathers not only push and goad their sons but also withhold praise, fearing that they may make them "soft" (Osherson, 1986; Wagenvoord & Bailey, 1978). Love is expressed indirectly through material goods, rarely through direct praise, and almost never through physical touch. A firm handshake or whack on the arm is far more likely than a hug or kiss. Discipline is usually rooted in the father's superior strength and power. In the worst cases, violence occurs when the father's felt need to maintain hierarchical control clashes with the adolescent son's need to establish his personal power and autonomy (Hartley, 1974).

Fathers and Daughters

According to conventional wisdom, fathers always have a soft spot in their hearts for their daughters (e.g., she's a "daddy's girl"). There are many positive aspects to this situation. Relationships with daughters sometimes permit fathers access to their capacities for nurturance, tenderness, and compassion (Cowan, 1988). They can be a man's most meaningful noncompetitive and nonsexual relationships. Daughters can have opportunities to learn how to nurture a man and can gain powerful experiences of unconditional positive regard.

When stretched beyond their mildest forms, however, these gender-based patterns can be stultifying to daughters and severely restrictive to father–daughter relationships. Daughters who feel overly responsible for the emotional well-being of fathers cannot pursue their own developmental needs. When daughters are dependent on pleasing traditional fathers, they are more likely to replicate family patterns and less likely to seek their own careers. Fathers who require adoration from their daughters seek to perpetuate their elevated status, never revealing the authentic man beneath the heroic facade (Secunda, 1992).

Mothers and Sons

The mother–son relationship has had a troubled history in psychology. Concepts such as the oedipus complex and "schizophrenogenic mothering" have helped to create the idea that relationships between mothers and sons are inherently problematic. Of late, as feminist scholarship has challenged the androcentrism of traditional psychological theorizing, the society has become less tolerant of "mother blaming" and less pathologizing of the mother–son dyad. Thanks to this feminist corrective, one no longer is required to emphasize the negative effects of mothers and we now celebrate the multiple benefits of maternal influence. It is possible to see how mothers teach their sons about intimacy and connectedness, how they promote tenderness and compassion, how they soften their sons' traumatic confrontations with "boy culture," how they nurture in times of intense emotional crisis, and how they promote self-esteem and inculcate aspirations for emotional and psychological growth (Fagot, 1984).

This is not to suggest that there are no conflicts that are based on the differing socialization programs of mothers and sons. In particular, mothers and sons are likely to have problems with the autonomy–connectedness dialectic. As boys become immersed in traditional masculine environments, they experience intense pressure to distance themselves from their mothers and from anything remotely "feminine." They must reject their little-boy needs and adopt the facade of a tough and fearless little warrior (David & Brannon, 1976; Doyle, 1994). This is a painfully ambivalent time for sons and mothers, because at some level, both realize the absurd aspects of the manhood charade. In best-case scenarios, each recognizes the pain of the other and makes an accommodation to the other's distress. More commonly, however, both are threatened by the other's position and overplay their own position: Sons adopt a stance of repugnance for mother's hovering intrusiveness, and mothers become wounded by their son's distancing.

Mothers and Daughters

Mothers and daughters reap benefits and confront issues resulting from shared values and perspectives (rather than from clashing of gender-based perspectives). Socialized as women, mothers and daughters are taught to value connectedness over autonomy, relationships over achievement, other-focus over self-focus, and interpersonal cooperation over hierarchical influence (Gilligan, 1982; Miller, 1986). This value harmony has many positive outcomes for mother and their daughters, particularly in terms of intimate and enduring relationships. When contrasted with the father–son pairing, the mother–daughter relationship stands out in terms of its empathy and depth of relatedness (Miller, 1986).

Because of its greater degree of interpersonal connectedness, however, the mother–daughter dyad faces its own issues. Daughters often have difficulty achieving autonomy from their mothers. This is manifested in many ways: Some girls have difficulty setting boundaries with their mothers in terms of personal privacy, and some find themselves unable to say no to a request by their mothers, even when their own lives are full of other responsibilities. Many young women are reluctant to move away from home, feeling the need for physical proximity to their mothers.

The emphasis on connectedness also inhibits a woman's level of achievement. When women move toward greater involvement with work roles and careers, they sometimes need to place greater emphasis on personal career needs, to become less reactive to the needs of others, and to suppress their emotional sensitivity. Mother–daughter relationships, as traditionally structured, are poorly equipped to provide the emotional skills needed for these new environments.

Case Example

The Problems

The Brown family entered treatment because of the repeated clashes between the stepfather, John, and the younger son, Justin. The Browns were a blended family: John and Sherry had each been married previously. John was abandoned by his first wife, who, in John's words, took the two children and "ran off with some high-dollar doctor." Sherry was also abandoned by her first spouse, but he left Sherry with sole responsibility for the three children. When they were seen in family therapy, Jessica was 18, Len was 16, and Justin was 13.

John's emotional reactivity was identified as the primary problem, because he was continually angry and frustrated when Justin defied his parental injunctions. Although John had never struck Justin, familial tension was extremely high. After an especially scary bout of screaming between John and Justin, John disappeared for 2 days. After returning to the home, he refused to discuss the matter.

When invited to discuss this situation, each family member revealed a markedly different perspective. Sherry was annoyed by John's flight but seemed relatively less concerned with the problem than the others. She claimed to be frustrated and impatient with Justin but admitted that she had been ambivalent about how to address his occasional defiance.

Jessica seemed to be the family member experiencing the most intense distress. She was overwrought about the tension and potential for another family dissolution. With great anguish, she voiced her fear: "This family is falling apart, and I'll do everything in my power to keep that from happening!"

Len's demeanor was in dramatic contrast to Jessica's. Not only was he blasé about the situation, but also he was contemptuous of Jessica's "hysteria" and "mothering" of Justin. He chided Jessica for making a mountain out of a molehill, encouraging her to relax and mind her own business. All family members quickly supported Len's criticism of Jessica. John reminded her that he had advised her to quit being a "little mother" and to learn to ignore Justin's behavior. Feeling supported, Justin goaded Jessica: "Who says I have to listen to you? You're just a kid like the rest of us."

John continued the attack on Jessica by praising Len's "maturity." He directed a pointed comment to her: "Jessica, you should be more calm and composed like Len; he's the bedrock of the family." Sherry offered only meek protest of John's assessment. She admitted concern that Len might do better to express himself occasionally, but she generally felt no need to defend or support Jessica.

Enraged by the taunting from Justin, Len, and John, Jessica broke into tears, saying, "How can you ignore this situation? I'm acting like this because nobody else takes this seriously!" Looking to her parents, she continued, "This is your job, not mine!" Justin rolled from his chair with mocking laughter, and Len rolled his eyes heavenward.

Gender Analysis

The Brown family wrestled with several parenting problems rooted in gender socialization. Although John and Sherry had differing concerns, they managed to convey fairly traditional parental expectations to their children. Jessica had learned that she was the primary person deputized to look after the emotional well-being of the family. Despite pronounced adverse consequences to her own emotional comfort and long-term plans, she had dutifully taken on the utterly thankless task. Len had been encouraged to separate from family affective life. Although he was expected to be a leader, he was to provide leadership only through detachment and emotional stoicism. Justin, through his license to act out, had become the lightning rod for family anger and resentment. Like many adolescent males, he was presented with endless mixed messages about defiance of authority: "Boys will be boys."

Many of the aforementioned parent–child gender binds were well illustrated in the Brown family. Father–son binds took two qualitatively different forms. The relationship between John and Len seemed positive and respectful, yet it required that Len accept his stepfather's mandate for him to become a strong and stoic family leader. The relationship between John and Justin was tumultuous and threatened to become uncontrollable as Justin's autonomy needs clashed with John's need to maintain hierarchical control.

Father–daughter problems were apparent as John and Jessica played out another common theme between women and men. Although she was only a teenager, Jessica had taken on a nurturing and protective role toward her stepfather. She felt his pain, but she was rebuked for her efforts to reach out to him. In the family, she had become the repository of male resentment against female control. The distant relationship between Len and Sherry exemplified a common problematic pattern of the mother–son dyad. Sherry realized that Len was repressing considerable emotional distress, but she was reluctant to challenge his facade of imperturbability. In a common masculine manner, both John and Len assured Sherry that everything was fine. She was unconvinced.

Sherry and Jessica were caught in a painful mother–daughter bind. Each had been devastated by many years of emotional distress, distance, and abandonment. As Sherry had become overwhelmed by the emotional burdens, Jessica had moved into the role common to many women. Without authority or power, she had taken on emotional responsibility and the role of the family's emotional barometer. This loyalty to "women's work" exacted an enormous price: She was resented and ignored by her mother, criticized by her stepfather, and taunted by her younger brother.

Interventions

Amidst the overall family therapy plan, several interventions focused on gender-based parenting binds. In meetings with John and Sherry, gender inquiry helped each to explore the origins of their gender value systems and the translation of their values into parental expectations. They were encouraged to analyze their relationships with their parents, identifying critical gender mandates.

John was eager to describe his painful relationship with his father, who was an emotionally aloof, physically imposing, and "larger-than-life" figure. He admitted yearning for signs of approval from him and tearfully confessed that he never told his father he loved him. He admitted that he wanted to get closer to Len, especially because he had lost touch with his own son through divorce. But Len had seemed to need emotional distance, and John was completely lost about how to proceed.

At one time, things had gone much better between John and Justin, but John had become terrified of how Justin provoked him to rage. Justin's refusal to acknowledge paternal authority left John frantic. He pleaded, "Help me break that defiance before I end up hurting him!"

John became especially awkward when recalling his relationship with his mother. He recounted a relationship in which his mother had provided the only validation and love he had ever received. He had tried to repay his emotional debt to her, but she had always been a melancholy person, and he felt he probably had never given her enough happiness. He realized that he had always been torn about relationships with women. Although he craved the emotional support, he felt ambivalent about intimacy.

For John, Jessica had been a special challenge. He was overwhelmed by her capacity to care for him but was terrified to acknowledge the needier parts of himself. He admitted that he had been inconsistent with her.

Sometimes he welcomed her affection, but her insight and perceptiveness caused him to back away.

Sherry had greater difficulty recounting her childhood experiences with cultural messages about gender. Her father had died when she was young, leaving her feeling mystified about men and the masculine world. Her mother had taught her to maintain a strong sense of independence and general distrust for men. She remembered feeling relieved that her first child had been a daughter. Jessica had been delightful but maddening. As much as she tried, Sherry could not feel fully comfortable with Jessica's need to emulate her and continually seek emotional connection. Sherry was relieved, yet anxious, when Jessica turned her attentions to other family members. She admitted to a vague sense of guilt about her mothering of Jessica, particularly because Jessica had taken on so much child care responsibility when Sherry had felt emotionally drained.

Sherry was also uneasy about her relationships with her sons. She was proud of Len, but she worried that she had not done enough to maintain emotional connection with him. She knew that he must have had problems when his father left the family, but his apparent composure had been reassuring and comforting.

Justin was a mystery to Sherry. Even as an infant, he had been more energetic and less tolerant of physical comforting than the other children. He had grown up at a time when Sherry was a single parent, and Sherry had had no idea how to harness him or relate to him. In many ways, he had come to represent the masculine world that confused and worried her. When John had come along, she was eager to turn Justin over to John's authority.

After completing an extensive gender inquiry, John and Sherry were far more prepared to approach the task of developing a conjoint strategy for parenting Jessica, Len, and Justin. Each parent had become more appreciative of the gender-based origins of their partner's parenting philosophy and predisposition for parenting impasses; that is, they had achieved empathic knowing, which allowed them to coevolve as parents.

The insights gained through gender inquiry with parents can be used in many ways to further the overall therapy effort. Sometimes, the parents can be seen alone, and they can be educated and coached about how to develop more gender-sensitive parenting styles. Sometimes, parents can be joined with others in parenting groups designed to explore the interactions between gender and parenting style.

At other times, however, the gender-inquiry process can be extended into a larger family therapy intervention. For example, special meetings can be arranged for all male family members and for all female members to explore the messages of gender throughout the family's history. Follow-up intergender dialogues can be used to foster greater appreciation of the role of gender in each family member's value system and behavior within the family context. As with all attempts to bridge gender worlds, the specifics of the meetings are less important than the overall philosophical goal: the development of "empathic knowing" among persons who already thought they knew everything about each other.

WORKPLACE RELATIONSHIPS

The critical relationship dimensions we identified previously—interpersonal communication, values (autonomy and connectedness, power), problem-solving styles (instrumentality vs. expressiveness), sexuality, and roles (relationship vs. task maintenance)—are equally relevant to relationships between women and men on the job.

Men in the Workplace

Because they have been taught to be instrumental, men are prone to place great emphasis on task accomplishment. This value preference serves men well in many traditional work settings where there is almost exclusive emphasis on completing the mission. In the military, for example, loyalty to duties is paramount, even if it requires personal risk, neglect of family, or loss of life (Ridenour, 1984). Similar mission-first attitudes are prevalent in other high-risk environments more commonly populated by men: police work, firefighting, and athletics. Although few work environments are so extreme, this preference for task-focus usually characterizes men's approach to their work. In the corporate world, profit has always been the "bottom line," with all other values a distant second.

The management styles most commonly adopted by men in these traditional settings have been those that rely heavily on authoritarian hierarchy, power, and coercive influence (Grauerholz, 1987; White, 1988). American history is replete with adoration of these white male power brokers—Rockefeller, Carnegie, Vanderbilt—men once referred to as "masters of the universe" (Wolfe, 1988).

Because success is the sine qua non of most traditional male approaches to work, rivalry, competition, and "number oneism" dominate men's interactions with one another (Kohn, 1986). All other men may be seen as adversaries, so that tenderness and compassion between men is generally seen as risky or foolhardy. Men are prone to adopt a competitive stance toward each other, compete to attract the most desirable women as symbols of success, and simultaneously rely on women to nurture them or prop them up during times of failure or self-doubt (Brooks, 1995).

In the industrial era, men have functioned with rigid barriers between their work lives and their family lives. A principal theme of men's movement leaders has been the tragic loss of connection between men and their families (Bly, 1987). Although a great deal of attention has been given to men's public lives, secrecy has historically characterized their private family lives (Filene, 1987).

Although there has been considerable stress and pressure associated with the traditional male work role, it has come with compensations. In patriarchal culture, men are granted privileges and entitlements simply because they are men, and they expect women to place men's needs first (Gilbert, 1993; Hare-Mustin, 1990). The especially keen sense of entitlement experienced by successful men has been indicated as a fundamental cause of sexual harassment in the workplace (MacKinnon, 1979).

Women in the Workplace

Over the past several decades, women have found success in work environments formerly reserved for men and have shown the capacity to accommodate to the mission-first value system of the high-risk work environments. At the same time, however, women have not lost their interest in interpersonal connection and teamwork. When all other factors are equal, women can be expected to place greater emphasis than men do on interpersonal harmony and team moral.

Ironically, just as women are entering it in greater numbers, the workplace itself is undergoing dramatic shifts. Whereas power and authoritarian influence were once primary, now collaborative management styles have become necessary as the economy becomes more dependent on service and information technology. Because their socialization has traditionally emphasized collaborative and relational skills, women have advantages in these new work environments.

Women are less likely than men to make the sharp distinctions between work and personal roles. This has been partially because women have usually been saddled with the "second shift" (Hochschild, 1989), that is, continued family responsibilities even when taking on greater involvement in outside work. Women also have a greater likelihood of integrating multiple roles rather than seeing them as sharply distinct.

Because of their socialization toward connectedness, women in supervisory roles tend to handle conflict differently than men do. Whereas men may base decisions on abstract principles, with minimal consideration of relationship history, women may attempt greater accommodation to relational context in their decisions. Women may experience greater anxiety about how power or authority may jeopardize established relationships, whereas men are prone to jettison relationships to seek career advancement (Granleese, Trew, & Turner, 1988; Kuhlenschmidt & Conger, 1988). In managing conflict, women are prone to negotiate and seek consensus, whereas men are more likely to make arbitrary power decisions. Women may avoid conflict; men may seek it out (Doyle, 1994).

Finally, the female corollary to men's sense of entitlement may be women's sense of deference. Whereas men have been taught that work and leadership are their sacred duty, women have been taught to support and defer to men's needs. Although they have been encouraged to seek indirect power by appealing to men emotionally or sexually, they have been discouraged from seeking power for its own sake (Cantor et al., 1992). These socialization messages create considerable difficulty in the workplace, particularly when circumstances warrant that women take charge and men defer or provide emotional support.

Gender-Based Dilemmas in the Workplace

Traditional gender socialization restricts options and sets the stage for gender-based conflicts between women and men.

Male Boss–Female Employee

The dyad of male boss and female employee has been the most common workplace pattern, and its problems are the most familiar. The most obvious problems are those resulting from women and men being socialized to have differing approaches to the conflicts between "task-focus" and "people-focus." As we noted, men are taught to be instrumental and place mission above all else, whereas women are taught to be especially sensitive to feelings and team morale. In high-risk environments, when women may be constrained by the moral or psychological consequences of an action, male bosses may become disdainful of them for their "softness" or indecisiveness. To the female employee, the male leader may appear ruthless or insensitive.

In work environments where interpersonal sensitivity and communication skills are paramount, men may be particularly handicapped (Brod, 1984). Although expected to be team builders and environment experts, they have had little preparation and are clumsy and ineffective, eventually calling on formal or informal consultants to guide them through the confusing tangle of human relations. Recognizing the superior relational abilities of many women, male bosses are likely to be defensive as well as envious of and threatened by their women employees.

Because men have been taught to favor hierarchy and use of power, they frequently have difficulties with women employees who desire greater negotiation and sharing in decision making. Male bosses are frustrated that female employees seem to want more time to talk about upcoming decisions and to rehash past events. Female employees are hurt and angered by their male bosses' refusal to consult them, keep them informed, or review past problems.

Male bosses have been taught that competition brings out the best in people (Doyle, 1994). Therefore, they are likely to favor highly competitive work environments, with many employees vying for a few cherished positions. Workers may be divided into "insiders, or winners" (those having the boss's favor) and "outsiders, or losers" (those not considered worthy). Female employees, probably trained to prefer more group-focused environments, are intensely uncomfortable in such "cutthroat" environments and are inclined to back away to leave the field to the "old boy network." Male bosses interpret their aversion as weakness.

A classic dilemma of this traditional work arrangement has been the clash between needs of the workplace and needs of the home. Because of their socialization (and the reality of the double shift), women have been much more likely to weigh the demands of work *and* home, whereas male bosses have wanted them to think *only* of their job pressures. As a result, men in power have tended to think women are less committed to their work and needy of a "mommy track" (Schwartz, 1989). Women employees have taken action against the "heartlessness" of patriarchal bosses and have demanded more humane workplace policies. Although legislative changes have helped, many resentments and misunderstandings remain.

It is only recently that significant attention has been given to the most egregious problem of the male boss–female employee dyad: sexual harassment and abuse of power (MacKinnon, 1979). When male bosses interpret their positions of power as granting them sexual entitlement, female employees are placed in impossible binds. Should they accede to their bosses' advances or should they resist, jeopardizing their job or advancement potential?

Although they are not nearly as vulnerable as their women employees, male bosses also have some difficulties with this situation. As noted earlier, most men are needy of masculinity validation from women. Most men are also prone to interpret any attention from a woman as sexual interest (Gross, 1978). Therefore, many male bosses are unusually susceptible to losing their objectivity to a woman whom they perceive as being sexually interested in them. No one—male bosses, female employees, or male employees—benefits from this vulnerability in male bosses.

Female Boss–Male Employee

Once highly irregular, this dyad is becoming increasingly common. Because it runs counter to so many strains of traditional socialization, it has offered multiple challenges (and multiple benefits to those broadening their adaptive capacities to accommodate to it).

The most obvious issues with the female boss–male employee dyad is that it violates the traditional patriarchal power equation. For most men, the central theme of their struggle to achieve manhood has been their effort to reject the "feminine" and overcome the female authority they remember from boyhood (Hartley, 1974). As illustrated by Tom Sawyer's efforts to escape the oppressive control of his Aunt Polly and his female teachers, boys are taught that manhood and independence are synonymous. Needless to say, the reappearance of female authority in the workplace has seriously upset men's applecart.

At some level, many men hate the idea of women bosses (Cantor et al., 1992; Faludi, 1991). They see it as unfair and a violation of natural order. But this is not the only problem; in addition to anger, men may feel guilt or shame. Has this happened because I wasn't man enough? What will other men think of me when they see me taking orders from a woman? Another significant problem results from men's tendency to think hierarchically and see women as able to respect only *strong* men. If I am subservient to her, will she see me as weak or pathetic? Feeling "emasculated" already, men are prone to adopt a facade of overcompetence or invincibility. Asking a female boss for technical help or guidance is extremely difficult for most men. Finally, men who are experiencing emotional distress will be especially angry at a female boss who refuses to nurture or support and tells him to "suck it up and stop acting like a whimpering child."

Women also have been socialized to have problems with this women-in-power dyad. They have been taught to be overly self-critical and encouraged to avoid taking risks. They have been taught that when problems arise, they should look at themselves, and not others, to find the guilty party (Nolen-Hoeksema, 1990). Because authority and entitlement are not syntonic with female experience, women underuse their coercive power or influence. Taught to be sensitive to the feelings and well-being of others, they feel a need to provide rational explanations for their actions, even when the needed response is, "Do it now because I'm the boss and I'm telling you to do it!"

Finally, as is so frequently the case in male–female dyads, the sexuality issue needs to be resolved. How can a female boss praise and appreciate the work and talents of a male employee without inspiring his sexual fantasies and performance anxieties, as well as the competitive jealousies of other male employees?

CASE EXAMPLE

The Problem Situation

The mailroom of Diskettes International was in turmoil following a series of employee conflicts and threats of unfair labor practice lawsuits. An organizational consultant was called to try to resolve fallout from recent shifts in management structure in the small (12 men and 4 women) mail unit. After decades of male leadership, a veteran woman employee (Rachel) had been selected as the new unit supervisor. Although there had been disappointed grumblings, no overt problems surfaced for several weeks. After controversy over the assignment of choice overtime hours and the possible filing of a sexual harassment complaint, however, the lid blew off with a rapid series of angry charges and countercharges.

For years, male employees had posted magazine centerfold pictures over their work areas. Although many of the women employees has expressed unhappiness about this, no one wanted to make waves by filing a formal complaint. This situation changed when a young woman (Heather) became intensely distressed by the sexual overtures of another employee (Nat), who had repeatedly asked her to go out. As Heather declined Nat's invitations, he became angry and began making semiaudible negative comments about her to his male coworkers. When Nat posted a new centerfold and began making explicit comparisons between Heather and the centerfold, Heather went to Rachel for help.

Rachel was deeply troubled by the situation. She had worked many years with Nat and several of the other male employees and had grown accustomed to their "harmless" fun. She had never had problems setting limits with her male coworkers and sometimes enjoyed the light-hearted sexual banter. She recognized that Heather was a young woman many men found attractive, particularly because she tended to wear tight clothing, which emphasized her physical attributes. Even though Rachel viewed Nat's behavior as relatively innocuous, she feared that he may have crossed the fine line between fun and sexual harassment. With multiple misgivings, she went to Nat and pleaded with him to take the pictures down and "cool it" with Heather. Nat was highly offended by the request, but he agreed to comply as a personal favor to Rachel. Rachel was effusively grateful to Nat. She told Heather that she "shouldn't have to bother me with these complaints anymore." Heather was uneasy with Rachel's intervention, but because she did not want to be the cause of employee morale problems, she decided to let the matter drop.

An uneasy peace followed, but it was quickly disrupted by the annual controversy about selection of overtime workers. Each year, the mailroom was allotted several hundred hours of overtime work. Because most of the employees sought the hours, the matter had always created tension within the department. Rachel's predecessor (Harold) had doled out the coveted assignments to his "star performers," that is, those workers who had already generated the highest production numbers. Most of the women employees had felt that Harold's system was biased against them, because it fostered hostile competition, poor coordination between older and newer employees, and perpetuation of an old boy network. Additionally, they argued that two of the women employees had lower numbers because they had taken family leave; none of the men had taken any family leave.

Sensitive to this issue, Rachel suggested replacing the previous competition and reward policy with one emphasizing sharing and rotation of overtime opportunities. Rachel anticipated little resistance but was shocked by the rancor her suggestion received. The male employees, led by Nat, were outraged at Rachel, suggesting that she favored the women and had revealed herself to be unfit for her leadership position. They raised questions about the fairness of the process whereby she had been selected, feeling that the best male candidate had been subjected to reverse discrimination.

Just when it appeared that matters could not get any worse, Rachel received word that another employee from outside the mailroom had heard about Heather's encounters with Nat and was coaching her to file sexual harassment charges. The activist warned Heather that the only way to cope with "patriarchal male scum" was to rid the company of their vile and oppressive presence.

Gender Analysis

The mailroom of Diskettes International was facing an abundance of problems, many of them at least partly rooted in competing gender ideologies. We provide here a few highlights of the issues addressed and interventions attempted.

The most incendiary issue seemed to be Nat's interactions with Heather and her conflict about how to respond. Nat felt his behavior was harmless, and Rachel seemed to share his dismissal of Heather's distress. Although Rachel defensively met her legal obligations mandated by recent civil rights legislation prohibiting sexual harassment, she did so in a fashion that suggested Heather had been overly sensitive. Neither the men nor the women were comfortable with the resolution of the issue.

With the controversy about overtime pay, a number of intergender tensions were revealed. First, the conflict between individual competition strategy (favored by the male employees) and group cooperation strategy (favored by the female employees) created intense acrimony about fairness and justice. Rachel had tried to make allowances for culture-wide gender inequities hampering women, but when she presented her ideas, she encountered charges of reverse discrimination. Quickly, the superficial appearance of harmony was shattered as men's resentment of female leadership was uncovered.

Rachel's reluctance to take decisive authoritarian leadership inhibited the establishment of a firm antiharassment policy. Feeling uncomfortable with her lack of support, Heather was preparing to accept the services of a feminist activist. Polarization worsened as the male employees banded together defending Nat in a knee-jerk reaction (even though many of them privately were weary of his "adolescent macho" behavior).

Interventions

Interventions were made in several stages. First, the consultant met individually with Rachel to help her complete a gender inquiry. Rachel was encouraged to explore her background to identify experiences, attitudes, and beliefs that might have bearing on her actions. She was provided support for the delicateness of her dilemma and encouraged to speculate about the values and assumptions that guided her management policies.

Initially, Rachel was skeptical about the usefulness of gender inquiry, feeling that "my sex has no bearing on how I handle my supervisory responsibilities." From that point, Rachel went on to describe her strong feelings about needing to prove herself as a woman in a "man's world." She noted her pride at being able to succeed, both by working harder and learning how to work with men. She admitted to resentment about "women who want others to fight their battles for them" (Heather). She felt bitter that Heather "wanted it both ways," that is, "to be provocative, yet expect to be protected." Finally Rachel admitted that she had chronic problems taking firm, authoritarian positions. She admitted that she had learned to protect men's insecurities and found it painful to watch her male friends experience distress.

Having identified some of the gender-based values underlying Rachel's actions, the stage was set for consultation, discussion of alternative perspectives, and exploration of creative management strategies. The consultant then met separately with the male employees and the female employees, encouraging each group to present its perspectives.

The men were quick to voice their bitterness, resentment, and fear of women entering the workforce. They readily admitted their doubts about women's capacities to function as leaders. Over time, however, the consultant was able to probe beyond these issues and uncover some of the men's deeper anxieties. Ultimately, several men acknowledged their fears about how things were changing between women and men in the workplace. They admitted their discomfort with feeling "one-down" to a woman. Although they knew change was inevitable, they feared that they might become useless as women "took over." Finally, a few of the male employees confessed to shame over the abusive and sexist behavior of some of their colleagues.

The women were generally unhappy about the men's behavior but somewhat conflicted about how serious matters were. Two of them were supportive of Rachel's position and indirectly critical of Heather. Heather and a colleague were hurt by the other women's "betrayal" yet interested in their ideas about how to give men a chance. Eventually, the other women admitted to conflicts about Heather, in the form of both envy and feelings of moral superiority. They came to recognize that they were struggling with common obstacles and vowed to become less critical and more empathic toward each other. They agreed to form a solid opposition to sexism on the job but also agreed to meet with the men to explore reasonable accommodations.

After preparing each gender group, the consultant met with the entire workforce. Rachel sat with the consultant as a "listening ear." After hearing a brief description of the need for empathic knowing, the groups were guided through a process of intergender dialogue. Each was encouraged both to express their concerns and to listen attentively to the concerns of the other gender group.

Space permits only the briefest description of the outcome of these intergender dialogues. Although the dialogues did not provide conclusive answers to the many complex problems faced by the Diskettes International employees, they were highly successful in creating an atmosphere in which women and men could express their concerns about the difficulties inherent in close working relationships. They uncovered biases and misconceptions that interfered with team functioning. The men gained greater appreciation of the conflicts and double binds faced by women. The women gained greater appreciation of the insecurities faced by men in the new workplace environments. In the end, each group felt considerably more compassionate toward the other.

CONCLUSION

In this chapter, we have shown how greater empathy between women and men can improve parenting and workplace relationships. Similar principles would apply to relationships in many other settings, such as churches, schools, and recreational environments. The essence of these interventions is the development of methods to enable women and men to gain greater appreciation for the values and perspectives of another gender culture. Without this appreciation, relationships can be governed by accusation and mistrust. However, when differing values and communication styles are understood, intergender cooperation is facilitated. Often, a gender-informed consultation can make a big difference in improving relationships in nearly all mixed-gender settings.

Epilogue: The Therapist's Role in Social Revolution

We say it again: Our society is experiencing the drama of social revolution. At the close of the 20th century, particularly in the United States and other westernized cultures, women and men are struggling to redefine themselves in relationship to one another. Although the roles that men and women occupy as we enter the 21st century are in many ways different from those of 50 years ago, the messages of gender socialization have not kept pace. The people who have been caught in this transitional stage lack role models and rulebooks that can guide their interpersonal relationships. As a result, they are confused, angry, and struggling. We, as systemic therapists, are in an advantageous position to offer our clients a process that leads to empathic knowing and positive coevolution. This book has attempted to provide therapists with the ecosystemic knowledge base and the clinical methodology to accomplish this daunting task.

Thomas Kuhn (1962) identified distinct stages of scientific revolution that are relevant to this discussion. In his conceptualization, during the *essentialistic* period, a predominant theory exists, that is accepted unquestioned until anomalies occur that cannot be explained by that theory. The response to these inexplicable events in the traditional period is one of denial, negation, and suppression. Soon, a *revolutionary* period arises during which new theories emerge to explain the inexplicable. During this time, the new theory contradicts and competes with the old. Eventually, during the *ecological* period, a metatheory develops that connects and combines the old and the new, and what once seemed dichotomous becomes integrated.

The feminist movement was the articulate and powerful tool of the revolutionary period that defied suppression. It is our hope that we have now entered the ecological period. As we have documented throughout this book, both women and men suffer from the detrimental effects of a rigid gender socialization that stifles their potential and deprives them of a whole range of experiences and behaviors socially defined as belonging to the other gender. Rather than responding to feminism with a traditional cry to return to the old patriarchal values or distorting the feminist vision to mean the subjugation or devaluing of men, we suggest it is time for women and men to recognize that everyone suffers from traditional gender socialization.

In any social revolution, the pendulum swings from one extreme to the other in a reactionary manner. For centuries, women have been oppressed by a patriarchal society that seemed to value them only for their sexual and reproductive functions and, even in the most benevolent societies, treated them as children needing protection and guidance and not to be taken seriously. The most recent feminist movement has made major changes in that picture in the industrialized West, although most feminists would say that the improvements are minimal when contrasted to what is left to be accomplished. Nevertheless, changes have been made. Unfortunately, but understandably, those changes included a large dose of male bashing and a negation of the positive aspects of masculinity as well as a failure to recognize the contributions that men make to the society. The effect of this climate on couple relationships has been devastating in many cases. It is our conviction that the time is right for men and women to meet each other halfway. It is time for everyone to cooperate in the creation of a new social order that potentiates full, rich, and healthy lives.

Part of what makes this change possible is that many men have begun to question the meaning of masculinity and are finding that they too would like to redefine themselves. Because women and men both participate in the construction of gender and both are dissatisfied with the rules of old, the time is propitious for a cooperative effort to bring about constructive change. Therapists can help men and women explore their gender socialization, eliminate what is harmful, and retrieve and revitalize what is good. We can facilitate the sharing of their individual gender-role journeys, teaching them to listen empathically and respectfully. We can provide them with a therapeutic environment that leads to idiopathic solutions to creating a relationship in which parity, respect, and mutual appreciation are priorities.

We intend that the message of this book be evolutionary. We share a vision of what is possible between men and women in a society that respects the roles, values, and abilities of each. We began this project years ago with a dog and pony show—two men and two women with similar interests trying to find a way to alleviate the pain our clients experienced owing to sociological changes without losing the gains achieved for society by the feminist movement. Over the years, by sharing our views and our own gender stories, by listening empathically and growing to understand the pain of the other gender, we developed a communality—an ability to speak with one voice about the effect of gender socialization on all of us. Our vision of mutual respect and parity in male–female relationships may be optimistic, but it worked for us and it seems to work for many of our clients. This book is an attempt to share our vision of *what can be* and the important role that the therapist can play in *bridging separate gender worlds.*

Appendix:
Confidentiality

One element that encourages client confidence in the therapist is the assurance of confidentiality. Clients are more likely to share deeply when they are confident that their stories and feelings will not be reported to others. All states have laws regarding the confidentiality of professional records. For example, in Texas the General Rule of Privilege states the following:

> (1) Communication between a patient/client and a professional is confidential and shall not be disclosed.

> (2) Records of the identity, diagnosis, evaluation, or treatment of a patient/client which are created or maintained by a professional are confidential and shall not be disclosed.

> (3) Any person who receives information from confidential communications or records as defined herein, other than a representative of the patient acting on the patient's behalf, shall not disclose the information except to the extent that disclosure is consistent with the authorized purposes for which the information was first obtained. (Texas Civil Rule 510, Confidentiality of Mental Health Information)

In addition, the American Psychological Association (APA) Ethical Principles and Code of Conduct (APA, 1992) has specific directions for the protection of client confidentiality. The APA Code under Standard 5, Privacy and Confidentiality states the following:

> 5.02 Maintaining Confidentiality
> Psychologists have a primary obligation and take reasonable precautions to respect the confidentiality rights of those with whom they work or consult, recognizing that confidentiality may be established by law, institutional rules, or professional or scientific relationships.

Additional sections concern discussing the limits of confidentiality, minimizing intrusions on privacy, maintenance of records, disclosures, and consultations with others.

Concerning working families and couples, Standard 4.03, Couple and Family Relationships, of the code specifically states the following:

> (a) When a psychologist agrees to provide services to several persons who have a relationship (such as husband and wife or parents and children), the psychologist attempts to clarify at the outset
> (1) which of the individuals are patients or clients and
> (2) the relationship the psychologist will have with each person. This clarification includes the role of the psychologist and the probable uses of the services provided or the information obtained. (See also Standard 5.01, Discussing the Limits of Confidentiality.)
> (b) As soon as it becomes apparent that the psychologist may be called on to perform potentially conflicting roles (such as marital counselor to husband and wife and then witness for one party in a divorce proceeding), the psychologist attempts to clarify and adjust, or withdraw from, roles appropriately. (See also Standard 7.03, Clarification of Role, under Forensic Activities.)

Other professional groups such as the American Counseling Association, the American Association of Marriage and Family Therapists, and the national associations of social workers publish similar principles and codes. All discuss the ethical and legal needs to maintain confidentiality.

As can be seen in Standard 4.03 of the APA code, however, confidentiality issues are complicated in couples and family therapy. The confidentiality needs of different individuals may be in conflict. These conflicts focus most often in the areas of secrets and record keeping.

Different therapists have different rules regarding an individual's secrets. Some therapists see couples together only so that no individual secret material can emerge. Other therapists permit individual sessions with each partner. Individual sessions increase the likelihood that individual secrets will be shared. It is important to have a clearly articulated policy at the beginning of therapy about what will be done with such secrets. For some therapists, the ground rules are that no individual secrets will be kept. Any material shared in an individual session will be repeated in a couple session. Other therapists allow some material to be kept from couple sessions depending on their therapeutic judgment regarding importance, impact, and possible harm. There are various rationales for each therapeutic stance. Some therapists prefer the simplicity and openness of the no-secrets model, or the model may fit their theoretical stance that the relationship or system itself is the client. Other therapists value the material that they might gain only in an individual session and want to preserve that option and format. The APA Ethics Code (American Psychological Association, 1992) requires psychologists to discuss with clients "the relevant limitations on confidentiality, including where applicable in group, marital, and family therapy" (Standard 5.01[a][1]). Hence, regardless of the model chosen, the critical issue is that all clients be informed regarding how the therapist will treat confidentiality of all material presented.

In a similar manner, record keeping is impacted by issues of confidentiality. Most record-keeping guidelines and laws are written assuming that records contain material from individual sessions. Therapists who work with couples may choose to keep individual records for each partner and one record for the couple together. The rationale is that the relationship is also a client and the joint record is simpler and more useful.

Difficulty arises with the joint record, however, when disputes regarding confidentiality arise. For example, to release material from a joint record, written permission must be obtained from both partners. In the case of a dispute regarding divorce or child custody, both partners may not agree to give permission. Again, the critical issue is that the psychologist inform the couple at the beginning of therapy of policies regarding the type of record kept and the ramifications of that choice.

A final issue involves the limits of confidentiality. To create confidence in the therapeutic relationship, it is necessary to inform clients of these limits. Confidentiality laws vary across states: For example, Texas Rule 510, Confidentiality of Mental Health Information, lists the following exceptions:

> (1) when the proceedings are brought by the patient against a professional including but not limited to malpractice proceedings, and, in any license revocation proceedings in which the patient is a complaining witness and in which disclosure is relevant to the claim or defense of a professional;

> (2) when the patient waives his right in writing to the privilege of confidentiality of any information, or when a representative of the patient acting on the patient's behalf submits a written waiver to the confidentiality privilege;

> (3) when the purpose of the proceeding is to substantiate and collect on a claim for mental or emotional health services rendered to the patient; or

> (4) when the judge finds that the patient after having been previously informed that communications would not be privileged, had made communications to a professional in the course of a court-ordered examination relating to the patient's mental or emotional condition or disorder, providing that such communications shall not be privileged only with respect to issues involving the patient's mental or emotional health. On granting of the order, the court, in determining the extent to which any disclosure of all or part of any communication is necessary, shall impose appropriate safeguards against unauthorized disclosure;

(5) as to a communication or record relevant to an issue of the physical, mental or emotional condition of a patient in any proceeding in which he relies upon the condition as an element of his claim or defense, or, after the patient's death, in any proceeding in which any party relies upon the condition as an element of his claim or defense;

(6) when the disclosure is relevant in any suit affecting the parent-child relationship.

(7) in any proceeding regarding abuse or neglect, or cause of any abuse or neglect of the resident of an "institution" as defined in Tex. Rev. Civ. Stat. Ann. art. 5561h. . . .

Comment, This rule only governs disclosures of patient–professional communications in judicial or administrative proceedings.

In addition to exceptions listed in any confidentiality law, there are often exceptions defined in other state laws. For example, most states have laws requiring the mandatory reporting of child abuse to some appropriate authority such as a child protective services agency. In 1993, the Texas senate passed SB 210, which requires that "if a mental health services provider or the employer of a mental health services provider has reasonable cause to suspect that a patient has been the victim of sexual exploitation by a mental health services provider during the course of treatment, or if a patient alleges sexual exploitation by a mental health services provider during the course of treatment, the mental health services provider or the employer shall report the alleged conduct not later than the 30th day after the date the person became aware of the conduct or the allegations to: (1) the prosecuting attorney in the county in which the alleged sexual exploitation occurred; and (2) any state licensing board that has responsibility for the mental health services provider's licensing. Before making a report under this section, the reporter shall inform the alleged victim of the reporter's duty to report and shall determine if the alleged victim wants to remain anonymous. A report under this section need contain only the information needed to: (1) identify the reporter; (2) identify the alleged victim, unless the alleged victim has requested anonymity; and (3) express suspicion that sexual exploitation has occurred."

Most states allow confidentiality to be broken in the case of a suicidal client or patient when communicating with others is necessary to protect that person's life. Many states also have a Tarasoff-type duty-to-warn law that requires a mental health professional to report serious threats a patient makes against another person to either the intended victim or law enforcement officials. As stated earlier, the critical issues are that the therapist know the laws that govern therapeutic practice in the relevant state and that any limits of confidentiality be explained to all clients and patients.

References

Abramowitz, S. I., Abramowitz, C. V., Jackson, C., & Gomes, B. (1973). The politics of clinical judgment: What nonliberal examiners infer about women who do not stifle themselves. *Journal of Consulting and Clinical Psychology, 41,* 385–391.

Abusive Men Exploring New Directions. (1990). *AMEND's policy with regard to couples intervention and counseling.* Unpublished manuscript.

Ahlgren, A., & Johnson, W. (1979). Sex differences in cooperative and competitive attitudes from the second through the twelfth grades. *Developmental Psychology, 15,* 45–49.

Alexander, K., & Cook, M. (1982). Curricula and coursework: A surprise ending to a familiar story. *American Sociological Review, 47,* 626–640.

American Psychological Association. (1992). Ethical principles of psychologists and code of conduct. *American Psychologist, 47,* 1597–1611.

Anderson, C. M., & Holder, D. P. (1989). Women and serious mental disorders. In M. McGoldrick, C. M. Anderson, & F. Walsh (Eds.), *Women in families: A framework for family therapy.* New York: Norton.

Andronico, M. P. (Ed.). (1996). *Men in groups: Insights, interventions, and psychoeducational work.* Washington, DC: American Psychological Association.

Angier, N. (1993, April 11). Fashion's waif look makes strong women weep. *The New York Times,* p. E2.

Archer, J. (1987). Beyond sex differences: Comments on Borrill and Reid. *Bulletin of the British Psychological Society, 40,* 88–90.

Are men really that bad? (1994, February 15). *Time,* p. 1.

Arkin, W., & Dobrofsky, L. (1978). Military socialization and masculinity. *Journal of Social Issues, 34,* 151–168.

Arnold, F., & Kuo, E. C. (1984). The value of daughters and sons: A comparative study of the gender preferences of parents. *Journal of Comparative Family Studies, 15,* 299–318.

Atkinson, D., & Schein, S. (1986). Similarity in counseling. *The Counseling Psychologist, 14,* 319–354.

Avis, J. (1988). Deepening awareness: A private study guide to feminism and family therapy. In L. Braverman (Ed.), *A Guide to Feminist Family Therapy.* New York: Harrington Park Press.

Balswick, J. O. (1988). *The inexpressive male.* Lexington, MA: Lexington Books.

Bar-Tal, D., and Saxe, L. (1976). Physical attractiveness and its relationship to sex-role stereotyping. *Sex Roles, 2,* 123–133.

Barnett, O., Keyson, M., & Thelen, R. (1992, August 15). Women's violence as a response to male abuse. Paper presented at the 100th Annual Convention of the American Psychological Association, Washington, DC.

Barragan, M. (1976). The child-centered family. In P. Guerin (Ed.), *Family therapy: Theory and practice* (pp. 234–248). New York: Gardner Press.

Barry, R. J. (1980). Stereotyping of sex role in preschoolers in relation to age, family structure, and parental sexism. *Sex Roles, 6,* 795–806.

Basow, S. (1986). *Gender stereotypes: Traditions and alternatives.* Monterey, CA: Brooks/Cole.

Bates, C., & Brodsky, A. (1989). *Sex in the therapy hour: A case of professional incest.* New York: Guilford Press.

Bateson, G. (1935). Culture contact and schismogenesis. *Man, 35,* 178–183 (article 199). Reprinted in G. Bateson (1972), *Steps to an ecology of mind* (pp. 61–72). New York: Ballantine Books.

Belenky, M., Clinchy, B., Goldberger, N., & Tarule, J. (1986). *Women's ways of knowing: The development of self, voice, and mind.* New York: Basic Books.

Bell, R. R. (1981). Friendships of women and of men. *Psychology of Women Quarterly, 5,* 402–417.

Belote, B. (1981). Masochistic syndrome, hysterical personality, and the illusion of a healthy woman. In S. Cox (Ed.), *Female psychology: The emerging self* (2nd ed.). New York: St. Martin's Press.

Bem, S. L. (1974). The measurement of psychological androgyny. *Journal of Consulting and Clinical Psychology, 42,* 155–162.

Bem, S. L. (1981). Gender schema theory: A cognitive account of sex typing. *Psychological Review, 88,* 354–364.

Bem, S. L. (1982). Gender schema theory and self-schema theory compared: A comment on Markus, Crane, Bernstein, and Siladi's "self-schemas and gender." *Journal of Personality and Social Psychology, 43,* 1192–1194.

Bem, S. L. (1983). Gender schema theory and its implications for child development: Raising gender-aschematic children in a gender-schematic society. *Signs, 8,* 598–616.

Bem, S. L. (1984). Androgyny and gender schema theory: A conceptual and empirical integration. In T. B. Sonderegger (Ed.), *Nebraska Symposium on Motivation: Psychology of Gender.* Lincoln: University of Nebraska Press.

Bem, S. L. (1987). Gender schema theory and the romantic tradition. In P. Shaver & C. Hendrick (Eds.), *Sex and gender* (Vol. 7, pp. 251–271). Newbury Park, CA: Sage.

Bennett, N. (1986, February 14). They're falling in love again, say marriage counselors [Interview with L. Peterson]. *Stamford Advocate,* p. A1.

Bergin, A. E. (1980). Psychotherapy and religious values. *Journal of Consulting and Clinical Psychology, 48,* 95–105.

Bergin, A. E., & Garfield, S. L. (1994). *Handbook of psychotherapy and behavior change* (4th ed.). New York: Wiley.

Bergin, A. E., & Jensen, J. P. (1989). Religiosity of psychotherapists: A national survey. *Psychotherapy, 27,* 3–7.

Bergman, J. (1974). Are little girls being harmed by Sesame Street? In J. Stacey, S. Bereaud, & J. Daniels (Eds.), *And Jill came tumbling after: Sexism in American education.* New York: Dell.

Bernal, G., & Baker, J. (1979). Toward a metacommunication framework of couples' interaction. *Family Process, 18,* 292–302.

Bernal, G., & Baker, J. (1980). Multilevel couple therapy. Applying a metacommunication framework of couples' interaction. *Family Process, 19,* 367–376.

Bernard, J. (1981a). *The female world.* New York: Free Press.

Bernard, J. (1981b). The good-provider role: Its rise and fall. *American Psychologist, 36,* 1–12.

Betcher, R. W., & Pollack, W. S. (1993). *In a time of fallen heroes: The re-creation of masculinity.* New York: Atheneum.

Bettelheim, B. (1962). *Symbolic wounds.* New York: Collier Books.

Betz, N. E., & Fitzgerald, L. F. (1987). *The career psychology of women.* Orlando, FL: Harcourt Brace Jovanovich.

Beutler, L. E., & Bergan, J. (1991). Value change in counseling and psychotherapy: A search for scientific credibility. *Journal of Counseling Psychology, 38,* 16–24.

Beutler, L. E., Clarkin, J., Crago, M., & Bergan, J. (1991). Client–therapist matching. In C. R. Snyder & D. R. Forsyth (Eds.), *Handbook of social and clinical psychology: The health perspective* (pp. 699–716). Elmsford, NY: Pergamon Press.

Beutler, L. E., Crago, M., & Arizmendi, T. G. (1986). Therapist values in psychotherapy process and outcome. In S. L. Garfield & A. E. Bergin (Eds.), *Handbook of psychotherapy and behavior change* (3rd ed., pp. 257–310). New York: Wiley.

Biller, H. (1971). *Father, child, and sex role.* Lexington, MA; Lexington Books.

Block, J. H. (1973). Conceptions of sex-roles: Some cross-cultural and longitudinal perspectives. *American Psychologist, 28,* 512–526.

Bly, R. (1987). *The pillow and the key: Commentary on the fairy tale of Iron John, part one.* St. Paul, MN: Alley Press.

Bly, R. (with B. Moyers). (1990a). *A gathering of men* [Video]. (A Mystic Fire video. Public Affairs, Inc.)

Bly, R. (1990b). *Iron John: A book about men.* New York: Vintage Books.

Bograd, M. (1984). Family systems approaches to wife-battering: A feminist critique. *American Journal of Orthopsychiatry, 54,* 558–568.

Bograd, M. (Ed.). (1991). *Feminist approaches for men in family therapy.* New York: Harrington Park Press.

Bouhoutsos, J., Holroyd, J., Lerman, H., Forer, B., & Greenberg, M. (1983). Sexual intimacy between psychotherapists and patients. *Professional Psychology: Research and Practice, 4,* 85–196.

Bowen, M. (1978). *Family therapy in clinical practice.* New York: Jason Aronson.

Boyd-Franklin, N. (1989). *Black families in therapy: A multisystems approach.* New York: Guilford Press.

Bradbard, M. R., & Endsley, R. C. (1983). The effects of sex-typed labeling on preschool children's information-seeking and retention. *Sex Roles, 9,* 247–260.

Brehn, S. (Ed.). (1988). *Seeing female: Social roles and personal lives.* Westport, CT: Greenwood Press.

Briere, J., & Lanktree, C. (1983). Sex-role related effects of sex bias in language. *Sex Roles, 9,* 625–632.

Briscoe, J. (1989). Perceptions that discourage women attorneys from seeking public office. *Sex Roles, 21,* 557–567.

Brod, H. (1984). Work clothes and leisure suits: The class basis and bias of the men's movement. *Gentle Men for Gender Justice, 11,* 10–12.

Brod, H. (1988). (Ed.). *A mensch among men: Explorations in Jewish masculinity.* Freedom, CA: The Crossing Press.

Brodsky, A. M., & Hare-Mustin, R. T. (1980). *Women and psychotherapists: An assessment of research and practice.* New York: Guilford Press.

Bronstein, P., & Cowan, C. P. (Eds.). (1988). *Fatherhood today: Men's changing role in the family.* New York: Wiley Interscience.

Brooks, G. R. (1990). The inexpressive male and vulnerability to therapist–patient sexual exploitation. *Psychotherapy: Theory, Research, Training, 27,* 344–349.

Brooks, G. R. (1991a). The men's movement and the media. *Amplifier, 7,* 1, 6.

Brooks, G. R. (1991b). Traditional men in marital and family therapy. In M. Bograd (Ed.), *Feminist approaches for men in family therapy.* New York: Haworth Press.

Brooks, G. R. (1992). Gender-sensitive family therapy in a violent culture. *Topics in Family Psychology and Counseling, 1,* 24–36.

Brooks, G. R. (1995). *The centerfold syndrome: How men can overcome objectification and achieve intimacy with women.* San Francisco, CA: Jossey-Bass.

Brooks, G. R. (1996). Treatment for therapy-resistant men. In M. Andronico (Ed.), *Men in groups: Insights, interventions, and psychoeducational work* (pp. 7–19). Washington, DC: American Psychological Association.

Brooks, G. R., & Silverstein, L. B. (1995). Understanding the dark side of masculinity: An integrative systems model. In R. H. Levant & W. S. Pollack (Eds.), *A new psychology of men* (pp. 280–336). New York: Basic Books.

Broverman, I. K., Broverman, D. M., Clarkson, F. E., Rosenkrantz, P. A., & Vogel, S. R (1970). Sex-role stereotypes and clinical judgments of mental health. *Journal of Consulting and Clinical Psychology, 34,* 1–7.

Brown, E. (1991). *Patterns of infidelity and their treatment.* New York: Brunner/Mazel.

Browne, A. (1987). *When battered women kill.* New York: Free Press.

Brozan, N. A. (1985, February 18). Women and cocaine: A growing problem. *The New York Times,* p. C18.

Bullough, V. (1973). *The subordinate sex: A history of attitudes toward women.* Athens, GA: University of Georgia Press.

Burrell, I., & Brinkworth, L. (1994, November 27). Sugar n' spice but not at all nice. *The Sunday Times.*

Buss, D. (1995). Psychological sex differences: Origins through sexual selection. *American Psychologist, 50,* 164–168.

Cahill, S. (1986). Language practices and self-definition: The case of gender identity acquisition. *The Sociological Quarterly, 27,* 295–311.

Caldera, Y. M., Huston, A. C., & O'Brien, M. (1989). Social interactions and play patterns of parents and toddlers with feminine, masculine, and neutral toys. *Child Development, 60,* 70–76.

Cann, A., & Garnett, A. K. (1984). Sex stereotype impacts on competence ratings by children. *Sex Roles, 11,* 333–343.

Canter, R. J., & Meyerowitz, B. C. (1984). Sex-role stereotypes: Self-reports of behavior. *Sex Roles, 10,* 293–306.

Cantor, D. W., Bernay, T., & Stoess, J. (1992). *Women in power: The secrets of leadership.* Boston: Houghton Mifflin.

Cantor, M. G. (1987). Popular culture and the portrayal of women. In B. Hess & M. Ferree (Eds.), *Analyzing gender: A handbook of social science research.* Newbury Park, CA: Sage.

Carlson, N. (1987). Women therapist: Male client. In M. Scher, M. Stevens, G. Good, & G. Eichenfield (Eds.), *Handbook of counseling and psychotherapy with men* (pp. 39–50). Newbury Park, CA: Sage.

Carnes, P. (1983). *Out of the shadows: Understanding sexual addiction.* Minneapolis, MN: CompCare.

Carroll, S. J. (1984). Women candidates and support for feminist concerns: The closet feminist syndrome. *The Western Political Quarterly, 37,* 307–323.

Cartland, B. (1995). The legendary romanticist. *Greek News, 6,* p4.

Cash, T. F., & Brown, T. A. (1987). Body image in anorexia nervosa and bulimia nervosa: A review of the literature. *Behavior Modification, 11,* 487–521.

Cash, T. F., Gillen, B., & Burns, D. S. (1977). Sexism and "beautyism" in personnel consultant decision making. *Journal of Applied Psychology, 62,* 301–310.

Cash, T. F., & Trimer, C. A. (1984). Sexism and beautyism in women's evaluations of peer performance. *Sex Roles, 10,* 87–98.

Cazenave, N., & Leon, G. (1987). Men's work and family roles and characteristics: Race, gender, and class perceptions of college students. In M. Kimmel (Ed.), *Changing men: New directions in research on men and masculinity* (pp. 244–262). Newbury Park, CA: Sage.

Center for the American Woman and Politics. (1984). *Women holding elective office.* (Available from author, Eagleton Institute of Politics, Rutgers University, New Brunswick, NJ 08901)

Chafetz, J. S. (1978). *Masculine/feminine or human?* (2nd ed.). Itasca, IL: Peacock.

Change over a decade. (1985, March 10). *The New York Times,* p. E24.

Chernin, K. (1981). *The obsession: Reflections on the tyranny of slenderness.* New York: Harper & Row.

Chesler, P. (1972). *Women and madness.* Garden City, NY: Doubleday.

Chodorow, N. (1978). *The reproduction of mothering*. Berkeley, CA: University of California Press.

Choti, S., Marston, A., & Holston, S. (1987). Gender and personality variables in film-induced sadness and crying. *Journal of Social and Clinical Psychology, 5,* 535–544.

Clatterbaugh, K. (1990). *Contemporary perspectives on masculinity: Men, women, and politics in modern society*. Boulder, CO: Westview Press.

Clay, R. (1995, September). The spillover between work and family life. *APA Monitor*, pp. 44–45.

Cleary, P. D. (1987). Gender differences in stress-related disorders. In R. C. Barnett, L. Biener, & G. K. Baruch (Eds.), *Gender and stress* (pp. 39–72). New York: Free Press.

Cobb, N. J., Stevens-Long, J., & Goldstein, S. (1982). The influence of televised models on toy preference in children. *Sex Roles, 8,* 1075–1080.

Committee on Women in Psychology. (1989). If sex enters into the psychotherapy relationship. *Professional Psychology: Research and Practice, 20,* 112–115.

Condry, S. M., Condry, J. C., & Pogatshnik, L. W. (1983). Sex differences: A study of the ear of the beholder. *Sex Roles, 9,* 697–704.

Coombs, R. H., & Kenkel, W. F. (1966). Sex differences in dating aspirations and satisfaction with computer-selected partners. *Journal of Marriage and Family Therapy, 28,* 62–66.

Corrigan, C. D., Dell, D. M., Lewis, K. N., & Schmidt, L. D. (1980). Counseling as social influence process: A review. *Journal of Counseling Psychology, 27,* 395–441.

Costrich, N., Feinstein, J., Kidder, L., Maracek, J., & Pascale, L. (1975). When stereotypes hurt: Three studies of penalties for sex-role reversals. *Journal of Experimental Psychology, 11,* 520–530.

Courtney, A. E., & Whipple, T. W. (1983). *Sex stereotyping in advertising*. Lexington, MA: Heath.

Covey, H. C. (1988). Historical terminology used to represent older people. *Gerontologist, 28,* 291–297.

Cowan, G. (1984). The double standard in age-discrepant relationships. *Sex Roles, 11,* 17–23.

Cowan, P. (1988). Becoming a father: A time of change, an opportunity for development. In P. Bronstein & C. Cowan (Eds.), *Fatherhood today: Men's changing role in the family* (pp. 13–35). New York: Wiley.

Cowan, G., Warren, L. W., & Young, J. L. (1985). Medical perceptions of menopausal symptoms. *Psychology of Women Quarterly, 9,* 3–14.

Cox, C., & Glick, W. (1986). Resume evaluations and cosmetics use: When more is not better. *Sex Roles, 14,* 51–58.

Crits-Christoph, P., & Mintz, J. (1991). Implications of therapist effects for the design and analysis of comparative studies of psychotherapies. *Journal of Consulting and Clinical Psychology, 59,* 20–26.

Culp, R. E., Cook, A. S., & Housley, P. C. (1983). A comparison of observed and reported adult-infant interactions: Effects of perceived sex. *Sex Roles, 9,* 475–479.

Dahlberg, F. (Ed.). (1981). *Woman the gatherer.* New Haven, CT: Yale University Press.

Daly, M. (1974). *Beyond God the father.* Boston: Beacon Press.

David, D. S., & Brannon, R. (1976). *The forty-nine percent majority: The male sex role.* Reading, MA: Addison-Wesley.

Deaux, K., & Hanna, R. (1984). Courtship in the personals column: The influence of gender and sexual orientation. *Sex Roles, 11,* 363–375.

Decade of the Woman. (1992, December 31). *Providence Journal Bulletin,* p. A8.

De Cecco, J. (Ed.). (1985). *Bashers, baiters, and bigots: Homophobia in American society.* New York: Harrington Park Press.

DeLarossa, R. L. (1989). Fatherhood and social change. *Men's Studies Review, 6*(1), 3–9.

Del Boca, F. K., & Ashmore, R. D. (1980). Sex stereotypes through the life cycle. In L. Wheeler (Ed.), *Review of personal and social psychology* (Vol. 1, pp. 163–192). Beverly Hills, CA: Sage.

Diamond, J. (1987). Counseling male substance abusers. In M. Scher, M. Stevens, G. Good, & G. Eichenfield (Eds.), *Handbook of counseling and psychotherapy with men* (pp. 332–342). Newbury Park, CA: Sage.

Dicks, H. (1967). *Marital tensions.* New York: Basic Books.

Dinnerstein, D. (1976). *The mermaid and the minotaur: Sexual arrangements and the human malaise.* New York: Harper & Row.

Dobash, R. E., & Dobash, R. P. (1977–1978). Wives: The "appropriate" victims of marital violence. *Victimology, 2,* 426–442.

Dobash, R. E., & Dobash, R. P. (1979). *Violence against wives: A case against the patriarchy.* New York: Free Press.

Dominick, J. R. (1979). The portrayal of women in prime time, 1953–1977. *Sex Roles, 5,* 405–411.

Dowling, C. (1982). *The Cinderella complex.* New York: Pocket Books.

Downing, N. E., & Roush, K. L. (1985). From passive acceptance to active commitment: A model of feminist identity development for women. *The Counseling Psychologist, 13,* 695–709.

Downs, A. C. (1983). Letters to Santa Claus: Elementary school-age children's sex-typed toy preferences in a natural setting. *Sex Roles, 9,* 159–163.

Downs, A. C., & Gowan, C. (1980). Sex differences in reinforcement and punishment on prime-time television. *Sex Roles, 6,* 683–694.

Downs, A. C., & Harrison, S. K. (1985). Embarrassing age spots or just plain ugly? Physical attractiveness stereotyping as an instrument of sexism on American television commercials. *Sex Roles, 13,* 9–19.

Doyle, J. A. (1989). *The male experience.* (2nd ed.). Dubuque, IA: William C. Brown.

Doyle, J. A. (1994). *The male experience.* (3rd ed.). Dubuque, IA: William C. Brown.

Dullea, G. (1985, June 3). On corporate ladder, beauty can hurt. *The New York Times,* p. C13.

Dutton, M. (1988). Profiling of wife assaulters. Preliminary evidence for a trimodal analysis. *Violence and Victims, 3,* 5–30.

Dutton, M. (1994). Post-traumatic therapy with domestic violence survivors. In M. Williams & J. Sommer (Eds.), *Handbook of post-traumatic therapy.* Westport, CT: Greenwood Press.

Dworkin, A. (1974). *Woman hating.* New York: Dutton.

Dworkin, A. (1981). *Pornography: Men possessing women.* New York: Perigee/Putnam.

Eagly, A. (1995). The science and politics of comparing women and men. *American Psychologist, 50,* 145–158.

Edelson, J., Eisikovits, Z., & Guttman, E. (1985). Men who batter women: A critical review of the evidence. *Journal of Family Issues, 6,* 229–247.

Ehrenberg, M. (1989). *Women in prehistory.* London: British Museum Press.

Eisler, R. M., & Blulock, J. A. (1991). Masculine gender role stress: Implications for the assessment of men. *Clinical Psychology Review, 11,* 45–60.

Erikson, E. H. (1964). The inner and outer self: Reflections on womanhood. *Daedalus, 93,* 582–606.

Erikson, E. H. (1968). *Identity, youth and crisis.* New York: Norton.

Estriko-Griffin, A., & Griffin, P. (1981). Woman, the hunter: The Agta. In F. Dahlberg (Ed.), *Woman the gatherer.* New Haven, CT: Yale University Press.

Fabrikant, B. (1974). The psychotherapist and the female patient: Perceptions and change. In V. Franks & V. Burtle (Eds.), *Women in therapy.* New York: Brunner/Mazel.

Fabrikant, B., Landau, D., & Rollenhagen, J. (1973). Perceived female sex role attributes and psychotherapists' sex role expectations for female patients. *New Jersey Psychologist, 23,* 13–16.

Fagot, B. I. (1978). The influence of sex on parental reactions to toddler children. *Child Development, 49,* 459–465.

Fagot, B. I. (1981). Stereotypes versus behavioral judgements of sex differences in young children. *Sex Roles, 7,* 1093–1096.

Fagot, B. I. (1984). Teacher and peer reactions to boys' and girls' play styles. *Sex Roles, 11,* 691–702.

Fagot, B. I. (1985). A cautionary note: Parents' socialization of boys and girls. *Sex Roles, 12,* 471–476.

Faludi, S. (1991). *Backlash: The undeclared war against American women.* New York: Crown.

Farrell, W. T. (1987). *Why men are the way they are.* New York: McGraw-Hill.

Farrell, W. T. (1993). *The myth of male power.* New York: Simon & Schuster.

Fasteau, M. (1974). *The male machine.* New York: McGraw-Hill.

Fausto-Sterling, A. (1985). *Myths of gender: Biological theories about women and men.* New York: Basic Books.

Feldman, N. S., & Brown, E. (1984, April). *Male vs. female differences in control strategies: What children learn from Saturday morning television.* Paper presented at the meeting of the Eastern Psychological Association, Baltimore.

Fidell, L. (1980). Sex role stereotypes and the American physician. *Psychology of Women Quarterly, 4,* 313–330.

Fidell, L. (1981). Sex differences in psychotropic drug use. *Professional Psychology, 12,* 156–162.

Filene, P. (1987). The secrets of men's history. In H. Brod (Ed.), *The making of masculinities: The new men's studies* (pp. 103–119). Boston: Allen & Unwin.

Fiorenza, E. S. (1983). *In memory of her: A feminist theological reconstruction of Christian origins.* New York: Crossroad.

Fisk, W. R. (1985). Responses to "neutral" pronoun presentations and the development of sex-biased responding. *Developmental Psychology, 21,* 481–485.

Fitzgerald, L. F., & Cherpas, C. C. (1985). On the reciprocal relationship between gender and occupation: Rethinking assumptions concerning masculine career development. *Journal of Vocational Behavior, 27,* 109–122.

Fitzgerald, L. F., & Crites, J. O. (1980). Toward a career psychology of women: What do we know? What do we need to know? *Journal of Counseling Psychology, 27,* 44–62.

Fitzgerald, L. F., & Nutt, R. L. (1986). The Division 17 Principles Concerning the Counseling/Psychotherapy of Women: Rationale and implementation. *The Counseling Psychologist, 14,* 180–216.

Foreit, K. G., Agor, T., Byers, J., Larue, J., Lokey, H., Palazzini, M., Patterson, M., & Smith, L. (1980). Sex bias in the newspaper treatment of male-centered and female-centered news stories. *Sex Roles, 6,* 475–480.

Fox, G. L. (1978). "Nice girl": Social control of women through a value construct. *Signs, 2,* 805–817.

Frank, J. D., & Frank, J. B. (1991). *Persuasion and healing* (3rd ed.). Baltimore: Johns Hopkins University Press.

Franken, M. W. (1983). Sex role expectations in children's vocational aspirations and perceptions of occupations. *Psychology of Women Quarterly, 8,* 59–68.

Freedman, R. (1986). *Beauty bound.* Lexington, MA: Heath.

French, M. (1985). *Beyond power: On women, men and morals.* New York: Ballantine Books.

Freiberg, P. (1991). Self-esteem gap indexes in adolescence. *APA Monitor, 22*(4), 29.

Freudiger, P., & Almquist, E. (1978). Male and female roles in the lyrics of three genres of contemporary music. *Sex Roles, 4,* 51–65.

Friedan, B. (1963). *The feminine mystique.* New York: Norton.

Friedan, B. (1981). *The second stage.* New York: Summit.

Friedan, B. (1993). *The fountain of age.* New York: Simon & Schuster.

Friedl, E. (1978, April). Society and sex roles. *Human Nature, 1,* 68–75.

Frieze, I. H., Parsons, J. E., Johnson, P. B., Ruble, D. N., & Zellman, G. L. (1978). *Women and sex roles.* New York: Norton.

Frodi, A., Macauley, J., & Thorne, P. (1977). Are women always less aggressive than men? A review of the experimental literature. *Psychological Bulletin, 84,* 634–660.

Frisch, H. L. (1977). Sex stereotypes in adult–infant play. *Child Development, 48,* 1671–1675.

Gabbard, G. (Ed.). (1989). *Sexual exploitation in professional relationships.* Washington, DC: American Psychiatric Press.

Gallos, J. V. (1989). Exploring women's development: Implications for career theory, practice, and research. In M. B. Arthur, D. T. Hall, & B. S. Lawrence (Eds.), *Handbook of career theory.* Cambridge, England: Cambridge University Press.

Garcia, S., Stinson, L., Ickes, W., Bissonnette, V., & Briggs, S. (1991). Shyness and physical attractiveness in mixed-sex dyads. *Journal of Personality and Social Psychology, 61,* 35–49.

Geffner, R., Bartlett, M. J., & Rossman, B. B. R. (1995). Domestic violence and sexual abuse: Multiple systems perspective. In R. Mikesell, D.-D. Lusterman, & S. McDaniel (Eds.), *Integrating family therapy: A handbook of family psychology and systems therapy* (pp. 501–518). Washington, DC: American Psychological Association.

Geis, F. L. (1993). Self-fulfilling prophecies: A social psychological view of gender. In A. E. Beall & R. J. Sternberg (Eds.), *The psychology of gender* (pp. 9–54). New York: Guilford Press.

Gelles, R. J., & Straus, M. R. (1989). *Intimate violence: The causes and consequences of abuse in the American family.* New York: Simon & Schuster.

Gerson, K. (1993). *No man's land: Men's changing commitments to family and work.* New York: Basic Books.

Gerzon, M. (1982). *A choice of heroes.* Boston: Houghton Mifflin.

Gilbert, L. A. (1993). *Two careers/one family: The promise of gender equality.* Newbury Park, CA: Sage.

Gilbert, S. (1984, December 30). Feisty femme 40, seeks nurturant paragon. *The New York Times Book Review*, p. 11.

Gilligan, C. (1982). *In a different voice.* Cambridge, MA: Harvard University Press.

Gillis, J., & Avis, W. (1980). The male-taller norm in mate selection. *Personality and Social Psychology Bulletin, 6,* 396–401.

Gilmore, D. D. (1990). *Manhood in the making: Cultural concepts of masculinity.* New Haven, CT: Yale University Press.

Giordano, J. (1995, August). Ethnicity: The hidden dimension in family therapy. In *Gender and ethnicity in systems therapy.* Symposium conducted at the APA Mini-convention on Family Therapy, New York.

Glass, S., & Wright, T. (1985). Sex differences in type of extramarital involvement and marital dissatisfaction. *Sex Roles, 12,* 1101–1120.

Goldberg, H. (1976). *The hazards of being male.* New York: New American Library.

Goldberg, S., & Lewis, M. (1969). Play behavior in the year-old infant: Early sex differences. *Child Development, 40,* 21–31.

Goldner, V. (1985). Warning: Family therapy may be hazardous to your health. *Family Therapy Networker, 9,* 19–23.

Gondolf, E. (1988). Who are those guys? Towards a behavioral typology of men who batter. *Violence and Victims, 3,* 187–203.

Gondolf, E., & Foster, R. (1991). Preprogram attrition in batterer programs. *Journal of Family Violence, 6,* 337–349.

Good, G. E., Wallace, D. L., & Borst, T. S. (1994). Masculinity research: A review and critique. *Applied and Preventive Psychology, 3*, 3–14.

Goodman, M. J. (1982). A critique of menopause research. In A. M. Voda, M. Dinnerstein, & S. R. O'Donnell (Eds.), *Changing perspectives on menopause* (pp. 273–288). Austin: University of Texas Press.

Goodrich, T. J. (1991). *Women and power: Perspectives for family therapy.* New York: Norton.

Goodrich, T. J., Rampage, C., Ellman, B., & Halstead, L. (1988). *Feminist family therapy: A casebook.* New York: Norton.

Gorski, R. (1995, February 28). As quoted in G. Kolata, Man's world, woman's world? Brain studies point to differences. Science Times. *The New York Times,* p. 3.

Gottman, J. (1991). Predicting the longitudinal course of marriages. *Journal of Marital and Family Therapy, 17*, 3–7.

Gottman, J., Jacobson, N., Rushe, R., Shortt, J., Babcock, J., La Taillade, J., & Waltz, J. (1995). The relationship between heart rate reactivity, emotionally aggressive behavior, and general violence in batterers. *Journal of Family Psychology, 9*, 227–248.

Gottman, J., & Krokoff, L. (1989). Marital interaction and satisfaction: A longitudinal view. *Journal of Consulting and Clinical Psychology, 57*, 47–52.

Gottman, J., & Levenson, R. (1986). Assessing the role of emotion in marriage. *Behavioral Assessment, 8*, 31–48.

Gould, R. (1974). Measuring masculinity by the size of a paycheck. In J. Pleck & J. Sawyer (Eds.), *Men and masculinity* (pp. 96–100). Englewood Cliffs, NJ: Prentice-Hall.

Gove, W. R. (1972). The relationship between sex roles, mental illness and marital status. *Social Forces, 51*, 34–44.

Gove, W. R. (1979). Sex, marital status, and psychiatric treatment: A research note. *Social Forces, 58*, 89–93.

Gove, W. R. (1980). Mental illness and psychiatric treatment among women. *Psychology of Women Quarterly, 4*, 345–362.

Gove, W. R., & Tudor, J. R. (1973). Adult sex roles and mental illness. *American Journal of Sociology, 78*, 812–835.

Granleese, J., Trew, K., & Turner, I. (1988). Sex differences in perceived competence. *British Journal of Social Psychology, 27*, 181–184.

Grauerholz, E. (1987). Balancing the power in dating relationships. *Sex Roles, 17*, 563–571.

Gray, J. (1992). *Men are from Mars, women are from Venus: A practical guide for im-*

proving communication and getting what you want in your relationships. New York: HarperCollins.

Gray, J. (1995). *Mars and Venus in the bedroom.* New York: HarperCollins.

Greer, G. (1992). *The change: Women, ageing and the menopause.* New York: Knopf.

Griffin, S. (1981). *Pornography and silence: Culture's revenge against nature.* New York: Harper & Row.

Gross, A. (1978). The male role and heterosexual behavior. *Journal of Social Issues, 34,* 563–571.

Gross, L., & Jeffries-Fox, S. (1978). "What do you want to be when you grow up little girl?" In G. Tuchman, A. K. Daniels, & J. Benet (Eds.), *Hearth and home: Images of women in the mass media* (pp. 240–265). New York: Oxford University Press.

Gur, R. (1995). Sex differences in regional cerebral glucose metabolism during a resting state. *Science, 267,* 528–531.

Halas, C., & Matteson, R. (1978). *Paradoxes: Key to women's distress. I've done so well—why do I feel so bad?* New York: Ballantine Books.

Hammer, M. (1970). Preference for a male child: Cultural factors. *Journal of Individual Psychology, 26,* 54–56.

Hanley, R. (1983, November 22). Panel in Jersey finds bias against women in the State's courts. *The New York Times,* pp. B1, B2.

Hansen, M., & Goldenberg, I. (1993). Conjoint therapy with violent couples: Some valid considerations. In M. Hansen & M. Harway (Eds.), *Battering and family therapy: A feminist perspective* (pp. 82–92). Newbury Park, CA: Sage.

Hansen, M., & Harway, M. (Eds.). (1993). *Battering and family therapy: A feminist perspective.* Newbury Park, CA: Sage.

Hansen, M., Harway, M., & Cervantes, N. (1991). Therapists' perceptions of severity in cases of family violence. *Violence and Victims, 6,* 225–235.

Hare-Mustin, R. T. (1978). A feminist approach to family therapy. *Family Process, 17,* 181–194.

Hare-Mustin, R. T. (1983). An appraisal of the relationship between women and psychotherapy: 80 years after the case of Dora. *American Psychologist, 38,* 593–601.

Hare-Mustin, R. T. (1987). The problem of gender in family therapy theory. *Family Process, 26,* 15–33.

Hare-Mustin, R. (1990). On making a difference. In R. Hare-Mustin & J. Marecek, (Eds.), *Making a difference: Psychology and the construction of gender* (pp. 22–64). New Haven, CT: Yale University Press.

Harris, M. (1977). *Cannibals and kings*. New York: Random House.

Harris Poll. (1979, January). *The New York Times*.

Harrison, J. (1978). Warning: The male sex role may be hazardous to your health. *Journal of Social Issues, 34,* 65–86.

Harrison, J., Chin, J., & Ficcarrotto, T. (1989). Warning: Masculinity may be hazardous to your health. In M. S. Kimmel & M. A. Messner (Eds.), *Men's lives* (pp. 296–309). New York: Macmillan.

Hartley, R. E. (1959). Sex role pressures and the socialization of the male child. *Psychological Reports, 5,* 457–468.

Hartley, R. E. (1974). Sex role pressures and the socialization of the male child. In J. Pleck & J. Sawyer (Eds.), *Men and masculinity* (pp. 7–13). Englewood Cliffs, NJ: Prentice-Hall.

Hartrup, W. W. (1983). The peer system. In P. Mussen & E. Heatherington (Eds.), *Handbook of child psychology* (Vol. 4, 4th ed.). New York: Wiley.

Harway, M. (1980). Sex bias in educational-vocational counseling. *Psychology of Women Quarterly, 4,* 412–423.

Harway, M., & Astin, H. S. (1977). *Sex discrimination in career counseling and education*. New York: Praeger.

Harway, M., & Evans, K. (1996). Working in groups with men who batter. In M. Andronico (Ed.), *Men in groups: Insights, interventions, and psychoeducational work* (pp. 357–375). Washington, DC: American Psychological Association.

Harway, M., & Hansen, M. (1990). Therapists' recognition of wife battering: Some empirical evidence. *Family Violence Bulletin, 6*(3), 16–18.

Hatfield, E., & Sprecher, S. (1986). *Mirror, mirror . . . The importance of looks in everyday life*. Albany: State University of New York Press.

Hayman, A. S. (1976). Legal challenge to discrimination against men. In D. David & R. Brannon (Eds.), *The forty-nine percent majority* (pp. 297–321). Reading, MA: Addison-Wesley.

Healey, S. (1986). Growing to be an old woman: Aging and ageism. In J. Alexander, D. Berrow, L. Domitrovich, M. Donnelly, & C. McLean (Eds.), *Women and aging* (pp. 58–62), Corvallis, OR: Calyx.

Heilman, M. E., & Stopeck, M. H. (1985). Attractiveness and corporate success: Different causal attributions for males and females. *Journal of Applied Psychology, 70,* 379–388.

Heiman, J., & LoPiccolo, J. (1988). Becoming orgasmic: A sexual and personal growth program for women. New York: Prentice-Hall.

Helgesen, S. (1990). *The female advantage: Women's ways of leadership.* New York: Doubleday.

Hennig, M., & Jardim, A. (1977). *The managerial woman.* New York: Doubleday.

Heppner, P. P., & Claiborn, C. D. (1989). Social influence research in counseling: A review and critique. *Journal of Counseling Psychology, 36,* 365–387.

Heppner, P. P., & Dixon, D. N. (1981). A review of the interpersonal influence process in counseling. *Personnel and Guidance Journal, 59,* 542–550.

Heppner, P. P., & Gonzales, D. S. (1987). Men counseling men. In M. Scher, M. Stevens, G. Good, & G. Eichenfield (Eds.), *Handbook of counseling and psychotherapy with men* (pp. 30–50). Newbury Park, CA: Sage.

Herek, G. M. (1987). Of heterosexual masculinity: Some psychical consequences of the social construction of gender and sexuality. In M. S. Kimmel (Ed.), *Changing men: New directions in research on men and masculinity* (pp. 68–82). Newbury Park, CA: Sage.

Hetherington, E. M., & Parke, R. D. (1975). *Child psychology: A contemporary viewpoint.* New York: McGraw-Hill.

Heyn, D. (1989, July/August). Body hate. *Ms.,* pp. 35–36.

Hildebrandt, K. A., & Fitzgerald, H. E. (1979). Adults' perceptions of infant sex and cuteness. *Sex Roles, 5,* 471–481.

Hite, S. (1987). *Women and love: A cultural revolution in progress.* New York: Knopf.

Hochschild, A. (1989). *The second shift: Working parents and the revolution at home.* New York: Viking Penguin.

Hoff-Wilson, J. (1988). The unfinished revolution: Changing legal status of U.S. women. *Signs, 13,* 7–36.

Hoffman, L. (1989). Effects of maternal employment in the two parent family. *American Psychologist, 32,* 544–657.

Holahan, C. K., & Stephan, C. W. (1981). When beauty isn't talent: The influence of physical attractiveness, attitudes toward women, and competence on impression formation. *Sex Roles, 7,* 867–876.

Holroyd, J. C., & Brodsky, A. M. (1977). Psychologists' attitudes and practices regarding erotic and nonerotic physical contact with patients. *American Psychologist, 32,* 843–849.

Holtzworth-Munroe, A., Beatty, S., & Anglin, K. (1995). The assessment and treatment of marital violence: An introduction for the marital therapist. In N. Jacobson & A. Gurman (Eds.), *Clinical handbook of couple therapy.* New York: Guilford Press.

Holtzworth-Munroe, A., Waltz, J., Jacobson, N. S., Monaco, V., Fehrenback, P. A., & Gottman, J. M. (1992). Recruiting nonviolent men as control subjects for research on marital violence: How easily can it be done? *Violence and Victims,* 7(1), 79–88.

Honig, A. S., & Wittner, D. S. (1982). Teachers and low-income toddlers in metropolitan daycare. *Early Childhood Development and Care, 10,* 95–112.

Horner, M. (1968). *Sex differences in achievement motivation and performance competitive-noncompetitive situations.* Unpublished doctoral dissertation, University of Michigan, Ann Arbor.

Horner, M. (1970). Femininity and successful achievement: A basic inconsistency. In J. M. Bardwick, E. Douvan, M. S. Horner, & D. Gutman (Eds.), *Feminine personality and conflict.* Monterey, CA: Brooks/Cole.

Horner, M. (1972). Toward an understanding of achievement related conflicts in women. *Journal of Social Issues, 28,* 157–176.

Horney, K. (1973). *Feminine psychology.* New York: Norton.

Horvath, A. (1995, February 26). Death in the fast lane. *Sunday Newsday,* p. 1–2.

Horwitz, A. V. (1982). Sex-role expectations, power, and psychological distress. *Sex Roles, 8,* 607–623.

Hotaling, G., & Sugarman, D. (1986). An analysis of risk markers in husband to wife violence: The current state of knowledge. *Violence and Victims, 1,* 101–124.

Howard, J., Blumstein, P., & Schwartz, P. (1987). Social or evolutionary theories? Some observations on preferences in human mate selection. *Journal of Personality and Social Psychology, 53,* 194–200.

Huston, A. C. (1983). Sex-typing. In P. H. Mussen (Ed.), *Handbook of child psychology* (Vol. 4, 4th ed.). New York: Wiley.

Hyde, J. (1984a). Children's understanding of sexist language. *Developmental Psychology, 20,* 697–706.

Hyde, J. (1984b). How large are gender differences in aggression? A developmental analysis. *Developmental Psychology, 36,* 892–901.

Hyde, J. (1985). Black women and women as a minority group. In J. S. Hyde, *Half the human experience: The psychology of women* (3rd ed., pp. 379–400). Lexington, MA: Heath.

Hyde, J., & Linn, M. (1986). *The psychology of gender.* Baltimore: Johns Hopkins University Press.

Hyde, J., & Plant, E. A. (1995). Magnitude of psychological gender differences. *American Psychologist, 3,* 159–161.

Ipsaro, A. J. (1986). Male client–male therapist: Issues in a therapeutic alliance. *Psychotherapy, 23,* 257–266.

Jacklin, C. N., Dipietro, J. A., & Maccoby, E. E. (1984). Sex-typing behavior and sex-typing pressure in child-parent interaction. *Archives of Sexual Behavior, 13,* 413–415.

Jackson, L. A., Sullivan, L. A., & Rostker, R. (1988). Gender, gender role, and body image. *Sex Roles, 19,* 429–443.

Jacobson, N. S. (1993, October). *Domestic violence: What the couples look like.* Paper presented at the Annual Convention of the American Association for Marriage and Family Therapy, Anaheim, CA.

Jong, E. (1994). *Fear of fifty.* New York: HarperCollins.

Jordan, J. V., Kaplan, A. G., Miller, J. B., Stiver, I. P., & Surrey, J. L. (1991). *Women's growth in connection.* New York: Guilford Press.

Joyce, L. (1993, January 27). Commitment needed to tackle gender inequity, panel says. *Campus Report* (Stanford University), pp. 9–10.

Jump, T., & Haas, L. (1987). Fathers in transition: Dual-career fathers participating in child care. In M. Kimmel (Ed.), *Changing men: New directions in research on men and masculinity.* Newbury Park, CA: Sage.

Jurkovic, G. J., & Ulrici, D. K. (1980). *Developing conceptions of marital issues: A cognitive-developmental analysis.* Paper presented at the American Association of Psychiatric Services for Children, New Orleans, LA.

Kamerman, S. B. (1984). Women, children, and poverty: Public policies and female-headed families in industrialized countries. *Signs, 10,* 249–271.

Kaschak, E. (1992). *Engendered lives: A new psychology of women's experience.* New York: Basic Books.

Katz, P. (1979). The development of female identity. *Sex Roles, 5,* 115–178.

Kaufert, P. L., & Gilbert, P. (1986). Women, menopause, and medicalization. *Culture, Medicine and Psychiatry, 10,* 7–21.

Kaufman, M. (Ed.). (1987). *Beyond patriarchy: Essays by men on pleasure, power, and change.* Toronto, Ontario, Canada: Oxford University Press.

Keen, S. (1991). *Fire in the belly: On being a man.* New York: Bantam Books.

Kelly, M. (1981). Development and the sexual division of labor: An introduction. *Signs, 7,* 268–278.

Kelly, T. A. (1990). The role of values in psychotherapy: Review and methodological critique. *Clinical Psychology Review, 10,* 171–186.

Kimmel, M. (Ed.). (1987). *Changing men: New directions in research on men and masculinity.* Newbury Park, CA: Sage.

Kimmel, M. (1994). Masculinity as homophobia. In H. Brod & M. Kaufman (Eds.), *Theorizing masculinities* (pp. 119–141). Newbury Park, CA: Sage.

Kimmel, M., & Kaufman, M. (1994). Weekend Warriors: The New Men's Movement. In H. Brod & M. Kaufman, *Theorizing masculinities* (pp. 259–289). Beverly Hills, CA: Sage.

Kimmel, M., & Messner, M. A. (Eds.). (1992). *Men's lives.* New York: Macmillan.

Kinsey, A. C., Pomeroy, W. B., & Martin, C. E. (1948). *Sexual behavior in the human male.* Philadelphia: Saunders.

Kinsey, A. C., Pomeroy, W. B., Martin, C. E., & Gebhard, P. H. (1953). *Sexual behavior in the human female.* Philadelphia: Saunders.

Kiselica, M. S., Stroud, J., & Rotzien, A. (1992). Counseling the forgotten client: The teen father. *Journal of Mental Health Counseling, 14,* 338–350.

Kobrin, F. E., & Hendershot, G. E. (1977). Do family ties reduce mortality? Evidence for United States, 1966–1968. *Journal of Marriage, 39,* 737–745.

Kohlberg, L. (1969). Stage and sequence: The cognitive-development approach to socialization. In D. A. Goslin (Ed.), *Handbook of socialization and research* (pp. 347–480). Chicago: Rand McNally.

Kohn, A. (1986). *No contest: The case against competition.* Boston: Houghton Mifflin.

Kolata, G. (1995, February 28). Man's world, woman's world? Brain studies point to differences. Science Times. *The New York Times.*

Kolbenschlag, M. (1981). *Kiss Sleeping Beauty good-bye.* Toronto, Ontario, Canada: Bantam.

Kornheiser, T. (1995, July 23). Pa for the course. *The Washington Post,* pp. F1, F6.

Koss, M. (1990). The women's mental health research agenda: Violence against women. *American Psychologist, 45,* 374–380.

Krishnan, V. (1987). Preference for sex of children: A multivariate analysis. *Journal of Biosocial Science, 18,* 367–376.

Krupnick, C. G. (1985). Women and men in the classroom: Inequality in its remedies. *Teaching and Learning: The Journal of the Harvard University Derek Bok Center, 10,* 18–25.

Kubler-Ross, E. (1969). *On death and dying.* New York: Macmillan.

Kuhlenschmidt, S., & Conger, J. (1988). Behavioral components of social competence in females. *Sex Roles, 18,* 107–112.

Kuhn, T. (1962). *The structure of scientific revolutions.* Chicago: University of Chicago Press.

Kupers, T. A. (1993). *Revisioning men's lives: Gender, intimacy, power.* New York: Guilford Press.

Kurz, D. (1993). Physical assaults by husbands: A major social problem. In R. J. Gelles & D. R. Loseke (Eds.), *Current controversies on family violence.* Newbury Park, CA: Sage.

Kushner, H. I. (1985). Women and suicide in historical perspective. *Signs, 10,* 537–552.

Lakoff, R. T. (1975). *Language and women's place.* New York: Harper & Row.

Lakoff, R. T. (1990). *Talking power: The politics of language.* New York: Basic Books.

Lamb, M. (Ed.). (1986). *The father's role: Cross-cultural perspectives* (pp. 292–330). Hillsdale, NJ: Erlbaum.

Lamb, P. (1985, April). Heroine addicts. *Women's Review of Books,* pp. 16–17.

Lambert, M. J., & Bergin, A. E. (1983). Therapist characteristics and their contribution to psychotherapy outcome. In C. E. Walker (Ed.), *The handbook of clinical psychology* (Vol. 1, pp. 205–241). Homewood, IL: Dow Jones–Irwin.

Lambert, W., Yackley, A., & Hein, R. (1971). Child training values of English Canadian and French Canadian parents. *Canadian Journal of Behavioral Sciences, 3,* 217–236.

Lazur, R. F., & Majors, R. (1995). Men of color. In R. F. Levant & W. S. Pollack (Eds.), *A new psychology of men* (pp. 337–358). New York: Basic Books.

Lee, R., & DeVore, I. (Eds.). (1976). *Kalahari hunter-gatherers.* Cambridge, MA: Harvard University Press.

Leo, J. (1996, May 13). Things that go bump in the home. *U.S. News & World Report,* p. 25.

Lerner, H. E. (1981). The hysterical personality: A "woman's disease." In E. Howell & M. Bayes (Eds.), *Women and mental health.* New York: Basic Books.

Lerner, I. M. (1968). *Heredity, evolution, and society.* San Francisco: Freeman.

Levant, R. (1990). Psychological services designed for man: A psychoeductional approach. *Psychotherapy, 27,* 309–315.

Levant, R. F., & Kopecky, O. (1995/1996). *Masculinity reconstructed: Changing the rules of manhood—at work, in relationships, and in family life.* New York: Dutton/Plume.

Levant, R., & Kelley, J. (1989). *Between father and child.* New York: Viking Press.

Levant, R., & Pollack, W. S. (Eds.). (1995). *A new psychology of men.* New York: Basic Books.

Levinger, G., & Mole, O. (1976). In conclusion: Threads in the fabric. *Journal of Social Issues, 32,* 193–207.

Levinson, D., Darrow, C., Klein, E., Levinson, M., & McKee, B. (1978). *The seasons of a man's life.* New York: Knopf.

Lewis, H. B. (1983). Madness in women. In E. Howell & M. Bayes (Eds.), *Women and mental health.* New York: Basic Books.

Lewis, J. M., Beavers, W. R., Gossett, J. T., & Phillips, V. A. (1976). *No single thread: Psychological health in family systems.* New York: Brunner/Mazel.

Lewis, M. (1972). Parents and children: Sex role development. *The School Review, 80,* 229–240.

Liem, R., & Rayman, P. (1982). Health and social costs of unemployment: Research and policy considerations. *American Psychologist, 37,* 1116–1123.

Lipchik, E., & Geffner, R. (1994, February). A comment on Jacobson's findings. *Family Therapy News,* p. 21.

Lipman-Blumen, J., & Leavitt, H. (1976). Vicarious and direct achievement patterns in adulthood. *The Counseling Psychologist, 6,* 26–32.

Lipsyte, R. (1994, November 12–13). Male athletes and assault: A pattern of violence? *International Herald Tribune.*

Liss, M. B. (Ed.). (1983). *Social and cognitive skills: Sex roles and children's play.* New York: Academic Press.

Long, D. (1987). Working with men who batter. In M. Scher, M. Stevens, G. Good, & G. Eichenfield (Eds.), *Handbook of counseling and psychotherapy with men* (pp. 305–320). Newbury Park, CA: Sage.

Lopata, H. Z. (1973). Social relations of Black and White widowed women in a northern metropolis. *American Journal of Sociology, 78,* 1003–1010.

Lopata, H. Z. (1977). The meaning of friendship in widowhood. In L. E. Troll, J. Israel, & K. Israel (Eds.), *Looking ahead: A woman's guide to the problems and joys of growing older.* Englewood Cliffs, NJ: Prentice-Hall.

Lott, B. (1994). *Women's lives: Themes and variations in gender learning.* Pacific Grove, CA: Brooks/Cole.

Lott, B. (1996). Politics or science? The question of gender sameness/difference. *American Psychologist, 51,* 155–156.

Luborsky, L., Crits-Christoph, P., McLellan, A. T., Woody, G., Piper, W., Liberman, B., Imber, S., & Pilkonis, P. (1986). Do therapists vary much in their success? Findings from four outcome studies. *American Journal of Orthopsychiatry, 56,* 501–512.

Luepnitz, D. (1988). *The family interpreted.* New York: Basic Books.

Lusterman, D.-D. (1988). *Male role problems and infidelity.* Presented at the 96th Annual Convention of the American Psychological Association, Atlanta, GA.

Lusterman, D.-D. (1989). Empathic interviewing. In G. Brooks, D.-D. Lusterman, R. Nutt, & C. Philpot (Chairs), *Men and women relating: The carrot or the stick?* Symposium presented at the Annual Conference of the American Association of Marriage and Family Therapy, San Francisco.

Lusterman, D.-D. (1993). How to train for empathic interviewing. Unpublished manuscript.

Lynn, D. B. (1979). Daughters and parents: Past, present, and future. Monterey, CA: Brooks/Cole.

Maccoby, E. E., & Jacklin, C. M. (1974). The psychology of sex differences. Stanford, CA: Stanford University Press.

MacKinnon, C. A. (1979). *Sexual harassment of working women.* New Haven, CT: Yale University Press.

Majors, R. (1986). Cool pose: The proud signature of Black survival. *Changing Men, 17,* 5–6.

Majors, R. (1994). *The American Black male: His present status and future.* Chicago: Nelson-Hall.

Majors, R., & Billson, J. M. (1992). *Cool pose: The dilemmas of Black manhood in America.* Lexington, MA: Lexington Books.

Maracek, J., & Johnson, M. (1980). Gender and the process of therapy. In A. Brodsky & R. T. Hare-Mustin (Eds.), *Women and psychotherapy: An assessment of research and practice.* New York: Guilford Press.

Martin-Knudson, C. (1994). The female voice: Applications to Bowen family systems theory. *Journal of Marital and Family Therapy, 20,* 35–46.

Matteo, S. (1984, August). *The effect of sex role stereotyping on sport participation.* Paper presented at the meeting of the American Psychological Association, Toronto, Ontario, Canada.

Matteo, S. (1988). The risk of multiple addictions: Guidelines for assessing a woman's alcohol and drug use. *Western Journal of Medicine, 149,* 741–745.

McArthur, L. Z., & Eisen, S. V. (1976). Achievements of male and female storybook characters as determinants of achieving behavior by boys and girls. *Journal of Personality and Social Psychology, 33,* 467–473.

McGhee, P. E., & Frueh, T. (1980). Television viewing and the learning of sex-role stereotypes. *Sex Roles, 6,* 179–188.

McGoldrick, M., Anderson, C. M., & Walsh, F. (Eds.). (1989). *Women and families: A framework for family therapy.* New York: Norton.

McGoldrick, M., Pearce, J., & Giordano, J. (Eds.). (1982). *Ethnicity and family therapy.* New York: Guilford Press.

McGrath, E. (1992). *When feeling bad is good.* New York: Henry Holt & Co.

McGrath, E., Keita, G., Strickland, B. R., & Russo, N. F. (1990). *Women and depression: Risk factors and treatment issues.* Final report of the American Psychological Association's National Task Force on Women and Depression. Washington, DC: American Psychological Association.

Mellen, J. (1973). *Women and their sexuality in the new film.* New York: Dell.

Mellen, J. (1978a). *Big bad wolves: Masculinity in the American film.* New York: Dell.

Mellen, J. (1978b, April 23). Hollywood rediscovers the American woman. *The New York Times,* Section 2, p. 1ff.

Merritt, S. (1982). Sex roles and political ambition. *Sex Roles, 8,* 1025–1036.

Messner, M. (1992). *Power at play: Sports and the problem of masculinity.* Boston: Beacon Press.

Meth, R. L., & Pasick, R. S. (1990). *Men in therapy: The challenge of change.* New York: Guilford Press.

Miedzian, M. (1991). *Boys will be boys. Breaking the link between masculinity and violence.* New York: Doubleday.

Miller, A. (1949) *Death of a salesman.* New York: *Viking.*

Miller, J. B. (1984). The effects of inequality on psychology. In P. P. Rieker & E. H. Carmen (Eds.), *The gender gap in psychotherapy: Social realities and psychological processes.* New York: Plenum Press.

Miller, J. B. (1986). *Toward a new psychology of women* (2nd ed.). Boston: Beacon Press.

Mintz, L. B., & O'Neil, J. M. (1990). Gender roles, sex, and the process of psychotherapy: Many questions and few answers. *Journal of Counseling and Development, 68,* 381–387.

Morgan, L. (1991). *After marriage ends: Economic consequences for midlife women.* Newbury Park, CA: Sage.

Mowbray, C., Lanir, S., & Hulce, M. (Eds.). (1984). *Women and mental health: New directions for change.* New York: Haworth Press.

Nardi, P. M. (Ed.). (1992). *Men's friendships.* Newbury Park, CA: Sage.

Nathanson, C. A. (1977). Sex roles as variables in preventive health behavior. *Journal of Community Health, 3,* 142–155.

National Center for Education Statistics. (1983). Faculty salaries, tenure, and benefits survey. Washington, DC: Author.

Neugarten, B. L. (Ed.). (1964). *Personality in middle and later life.* New York: Atherton Press.

Neugarten, B. L. (1968). *Middle age and aging.* Chicago: University of Chicago Press.

Nevid, J. S. (1984). Sex differences in factors of romantic attraction. *Sex Roles, 11,* 401–411.

Nielsen Media Research. (1985). *'85 Nielsen Report on Television.* Northbrook, IL: Author.

Noble, B. (1993, February 7). The family leave bargain. *The New York Times,* p. F25.

Nolen-Hoeksema, S. (1990). *Sex differences in depression.* Stanford, CA: Stanford University Press.

Norcross, J. C., & Goldfried, M. R. (Eds.). (1992). *Handbook of psychotherapy integration.* New York: Basic Books.

Nutt, R. (1991). Ethical principles for gender-fair family therapy. *The Family Psychologist, 7*(3), 32–33.

Nutt, R. (1995). Unpublished class survey. Denton, Texas Women's University.

Nutt, R., & Gottlieb, M. (1993). Gender diversity in clinical psychology: Research, practice, and training. *The Clinical Psychologist, 46,* 64–73.

O'Brien, M., & Huston, A. C. (1985a). Activity level and sex stereotyped toy choice in toddler boys and girls. *Journal of Genetic Psychology, 146,* 527–534.

O'Brien, M., & Huston, A. C. (1985b). Development of sex-typed play in toddlers. *Developmental Psychology, 21,* 866–871.

Ogilvie, B. C., & Tutko, T. (1971, October). Sport: If you want to build character, try something else. *Psychology Today,* p. 61ff.

Okun, L. (1986). *Women and abuse: Facts replacing myths.* Albany: State University of New York Press.

O'Leary, V. E., & Donahue, J. M. (1978). Latitudes of masculinity: Reactions to sex-role deviance in men. *Journal of Social Issues, 34,* 17–28.

O'Neil, J. M. (1982). Gender-role conflict and strain in men's lives. In K. Solomon & N. Levy (Eds.), *Men in transition: Theory and therapy.* New York: Plenum Press.

O'Neil, J. M., & Egan, J. (1992a). Abuses of power against women: Sexism, gender role conflict, and psychological violence. In E. P. Cook (Ed.), *Women, relationships, and power: Implications for counseling.* Alexandria, VA: ACA Press.

O'Neil, J. M., & Egan, J. (1992b). Men's and women's gender role journeys: A metaphor for healing, transition, and transformation. In B. R. Wainrib (Ed.), *Gender issues across the life cycle* (pp. 107–123). New York: Springer.

O'Neil, J. M., Helms, B., Gable, R., David, T., & Wrightsman, L. (1986). Gender role conflict scale: College men's fear of femininity. *Sex Roles, 14,* 335–350.

O'Neil, J. M., & Roberts-Carroll, M. (1988). A gender role journey. *Journal of Counseling and Development, 67,* 193–197.

Orlinsky, D. E., & Howard, K. I. (1980). Gender and psychotherapeutic outcome. In A. M. Brodsky & R. T. Hare-Mustin (Eds.), *Women and psychotherapy: An assessment of research and practice.* New York: Guilford Press.

Ornduff, S., Kelsey, R., & O'Leary, D. (1995). What do we know about typologies of batterers? Comment on Gottman et al. (1995). *Journal of Family Psychology, 9,* 249–252.

Osherson, S. (1986). *Finding our fathers: The unfinished business of manhood.* New York: Free Press.

Osherson, S., & Krugman, S. (1990). Men, shame, and psychotherapy. *Psychotherapy, 27,* 327–339.

Parsons, J. E., & Bryan, J. (1978). Adolescence: Gateway to androgyny. *Michigan Occasional Paper,* No. VIII.

Parsons, R. D., & Wicks, R. J. (1994). *Counseling strategies and intervention techniques for the human services* (4th ed.). Boston: Allyn & Bacon.

Pasick, R. (1994). *What every man needs to know.* San Francisco: HarperCollins.

Patterson, C. H. (1984). Empathy, warmth, and genuineness in psychotherapy: A review of reviews. *Psychotherapy, 21,* 431–438.

Payne, B., & Whittington, F. (1976). Older women: An examination of popular stereotypes and research evidence. *Social Problems, 23,* 488–504.

Pearson, J. C. (1985). *Gender and communication.* Dubuque, IA: William C. Brown.

Pence, E., & Paymar, M. (1990). *Power and control, tactics of men who batter: An educational curriculum.* Duluth, MN: Minnesota Program Development.

Perry, D. G., White, A. J., & Perry, L. C. (1984). Does early sex-typing result from children's attempts to match their behavior to sex role stereotypes? *Child Development, 55,* 2114–2121.

Peterson, L. (1986, February 14). They're falling in love again, say marriage counselors. *Stamford Advocate,* p. A1.

Philpot, C. (1991). Gender-sensitive couples' therapy: A systemic definition. *Journal of Family Psychotherapy, 2*(3), 19–40.

Philpot, C., & Brooks, G. (1988). *Guidelines for gender-sensitive psychotherapy.* Unpublished manuscript.

Philpot, C., & Brooks, G. (1995). Intergender communication and gender-sensitive family therapy. In R. Mikesell, D.-D. Lusterman, & S. McDaniel (Eds.), *Integrating family therapy: Handbook of family psychology and systems theory* (pp. 303–325). Washington, DC: American Psychological Association.

Philpot, C., & Howze, S. (1994). Marital expectations of graduate and undergraduate psychology students. Unpublished survey.

Pittman, F. (1985). Gender myths: When does gender become pathology? *Family Therapy Networker, 9,* 24–33.

Pittman, F. (1989). *Private lies: Infidelity and the betrayal of intimacy.* New York: Norton.

Pittman, F. (1990). The masculine mystique. *The Family Therapy Networker, 14,* 40–53.

Pittman, F. (1991). The secret passions of men. *Journal of Marital and Family Therapy, 17,* 17–23.

Pleck, E., & Pleck, J. H. (Eds.). (1980). *The American man.* Englewood Cliffs, NJ: Prentice-Hall.

Pleck, J. H. (1976). My male sex role and ours. In D. David & R. Brannon (Eds.), *The forty-nine percent majority* (pp. 253–264). Reading, MA: Addison-Wesley.

Pleck, J. H. (1981). *The myth of masculinity.* Cambridge, MA: MIT Press.

Pleck, J. H. (1987). American fathering in historical perspective. In M. S. Kimmel (Ed.), *Changing men: New directions in research on men and masculinity* (pp. 83–97). Beverly Hills, CA: Sage.

Pleck, J. H. (1993). Are "family-supportive" employer policies relevant to men? In J. C. Hood (Ed.), *Work, family, and masculinities.* Beverly Hills, CA: Sage.

Pleck, J. H., & Sawyer, J. (1980). *Men and masculinity.* Englewood Cliffs, NJ: Prentice-Hall.

Pope, K. S. (1987). Sex with patients: New data, standards, and liabilities. *The Independent Practitioner, 7*(2), 15–20.

Pope, K. S. (1990). Therapist–patient sex as sex abuse: Six scientific, professional, and practical dilemmas in addressing victimization and rehabilitation. *Professional Psychology: Research and Practice, 21,* 277–289.

Pope, K. S., & Vetter, V. A. (1991). Prior therapist–patient sexual involvement among patients seen by psychologists. *Psychotherapy, 28,* 429–438.

Public eye: Does father know best? (1995, March 20). *Time,* pp. 40–45.

Purcell, P., & Stewart, L. (1990). Dick and Jane in 1989. *Sex Roles, 22,* 177–185.

Radway, J. (1984). *Reading the romance: Women, patriarchy, and popular literature.* Chapel Hill: University of North Carolina Press.

Ramirez, A. (1988). Racism toward Hispanics: The culturally monolithic society. In P. Katz & D. Taylor (Eds.), *Eliminating racism: Profiles in controversy* (pp. 137–157). New York: Plenum Press.

Randolph, R., Schneider, D., & Diaz, M. (Eds.). (1988). *Dialectics and gender: Anthropological approaches.* Boulder, CO: Westview Press.

Rebecca, M., Hefner, R., & Oleshansky, B. (1976). A model of sex-role transcendence. *Journal of Social Issues, 32,* 197–206.

Reinartz, K. F. (1975). The paper doll: Images of American women in popular songs. In J. Freeman (Ed.), *Women: A feminist perspective* (pp. 293–308). Palo Alto, CA: Mayfield.

Rheingold, H. L., & Cook, K. V. (1975). The contents of boys' and girls' rooms as an index of parents' behavior. *Child Development, 46,* 459–463.

Ridenour, R. I. (1984). The military, service families, and the therapist. In F. W. Kaslow & R. I. Ridenour (Eds.), *The military family.* New York: Guilford Press.

Rieker, P. P., & Carmen, E. H. (Eds.). (1984). *The gender gap in psychotherapy: Social realities and psychological processes.* New York: Plenum Press.

Roberts, J. M. (1991). Sugar and spice, toads and mice: Gender issues in family therapy training. *Journal of Marital and Family Therapy, 17*(2), 121–132.

Robertson, J., & Fitzgerald, L. F. (1990). The (mis)treatment of men: Effects of client gender role and life-style on diagnosis and attribution of pathology. *Journal of Counseling Psychology, 37,* 3–9.

Robins, L. N., Helzer, J. E., Weissman, M. M., Orvaschel, H., Gruenberg, E., Burker, J. D., & Regier, D. A. (1984). Lifetime prevalence of specific psychiatric disorders in three sites. *Archives of General Psychiatry, 41,* 949–958.

Robinson, C. C., & Morris, J. T. (1986). The gender-stereotyped nature of Christmas toys received by 36-, 48-, and 60-month-old children: A comparison between nonrequested and requested toys. *Sex Roles, 15,* 21–32.

Rogers, C. R. (1951). *Client-centered therapy.* Boston: Houghton Mifflin.

Rogers, C. R. (1954). *Psychotherapy and personality change.* Chicago: University of Chicago Press.

Rogers, C. R. (1957). The necessary and sufficient conditions of therapeutic personality change. *Journal of Consulting Psychology, 21,* 95–103.

Rogers, C. R. (1959). A theory of therapy, personality, and interpersonal relationships, as developed in the client-centered framework. In S. Koch (Ed.), *Psychology: A study of science; Vol. III. Formulations of the personal and the social context* (pp. 184–256). New York: McGraw-Hill.

Rohrbaugh, J. B. (1979, August). Femininity on the line. *Psychology Today,* p. 30.

Roopnarine, J. L. (1986). Mothers' and fathers' behaviors toward the toy play of their infant sons and daughters. *Sex Roles, 14,* 59–68.

Root, M. P. P. (1990). Disordered eating in women of color. *Sex Roles, 22,* 525–536.

Rosenberg, K. (1984, April 14). Peaceniks and soldier girls. *The Nation,* pp. 453–457.

Ross, L., & Mirowsky, J. (1984). Men who cry. *Social Psychology Quarterly, 47,* 138–146.

Rotundo, E. A. (1993). *American manhood: Transformations in masculinity from the Revolution to the modern era.* New York: Basic Books.

Ruben, H. (1981). *Competing.* New York: Pinnacle Books.

Rubin, J. Z., Provenzano, F. J., & Luria, Z. (1974). The eye of the beholder: Parents' views on sex of newborns. *American Journal of Orthopsychiatry, 44,* 512–519.

Ruether, R. R. (1983). *Sexism and God-talk: Toward a feminist theology.* Boston: Beacon Press.

Ruitenbeek, H. (1967). *The male myth.* New York: Dell.

Russianoff, P. (1981). *Why do I think I am nothing without a man?* Toronto, Ontario, Canada: Bantam Books.

Russo, N. F. (1976). The motherhood mandate. *Journal of Social Issues, 32*(3), 143–153.

Russo, N. F. (Ed.). (1985). *A women's mental health agenda.* Washington, DC: American Psychological Association.

Russo, N. F., & Sobel, S. B. (1981). Sex differences in the utilization of mental health facilities. *Professional Psychology, 12,* 7–19.

Sadd, S., Lenauer, M., Shaver, P., & Dunivant, N. (1978). Objective measurement of fear of success and fear of failure: A factor analytic approach. *Journal of Consulting and Clinical Psychology, 46,* 405–416.

Sadker, M. P., & Sadker, D. M. (1985, March). Sexism in the schoolroom of the 80's. *Psychology Today,* pp. 54–57.

Sager, C. (1976). *Marriage contracts and couple therapy: Hidden forces in intimate relationships.* New York: Brunner/Mazel.

Scarf, M. (1989). *Intimate partners.* New York: Random House.

Scharff, D., & Scharff, J. (1987). *Object relations family therapy.* Northvale, NJ: Jason Aronson.

Scher, M. (1990). Effect of gender-role incongruities on men's experience as clients in psychotherapy. *Psychotherapy, 27,* 322–326.

Schmidt, P. (1985, March 24). For the women, still a long way to go. *The New York Times,* Section 12, pp. 14–15.

Schnarch, D. M. (1991). *Constructing the sexual crucible: An integration of sexual and marital therapy.* New York: Norton.

Schnarch, D. M. (1995). A family systems approach to sex therapy and intimacy. In R. Mikesell, D.-D. Lusterman, & S. McDaniel (Eds.), *Integrating family therapy: Handbook of family psychology and systems theory.* Washington, DC: American Psychological Association.

Schwartz, F. N. (1989, January-February). Management women and new facts of life. *Harvard Business Review,* pp. 65–76.

Schwartz, L. A., & Markham, W. T. (1985). Sex stereotyping in children's toy advertisements. *Sex Roles, 12,* 157–170.

Schwartz, P. (1994, September 7). How men act as parents can improve marriages. *St. Paul Pioneer Press,* AE.

Scrivner, R., & Eldridge, N. (1995). Lesbian and gay family psychology. In R. Mikesell, D.-D. Lusterman, & S. McDaniel (Eds.), *Integrating family therapy: A handbook for family psychology and systems therapy.* Washington, DC: American Psychological Association.

Secunda, V. (1992). *Women and their fathers.* New York: Delta.

Sekaran, U. (1986). *Dual-career families.* San Francisco: Jossey-Bass.

Shakin, M., Shakin, D., & Sternglanz, S. H. (1985). Infant clothing: Sex labeling for strangers. *Sex Roles, 12,* 955–964.

Shaver, P., & Hendrick, C. (1987). *Sex and gender.* Newbury Park, CA: Sage.

Shaywitz, S., & Shaywitz, B. (1995). Sex differences in the functional organization of the brain for language. *Nature, 373,* 607–609.

Sheehy, G. (1992). *The silent passage.* New York: Random House.

Shiffman, M. (1987). The men's movement: An empirical investigation. In M. S. Kimmel (Ed.), *Changing men: New directions in research on men and masculinity* (pp. 295–314). Beverly Hills, CA: Sage.

Shinar, E. H. (1978). Person perception as a function of occupation and sex. *Sex Roles, 4,* 679–693.

Silverberg, R. (1986). *Psychotherapy for men: Transcending the masculine mystique.* Springfield, IL: Charles C Thomas.

Silverstein, L. (1991). Transforming the debate about child care and maternal employment. *American Psychologist, 46,* 1025–1032.

Simon, F., Stierlin, H., & Wynne, L. (1985). *The language of family therapy.* New York: Family Process Press.

Skord, K. G., & Schumacher, B. (1982). Masculinity as a handicapping condition. *Rehabilitation Literature, 43*(9–10), 284–289.

Slobogin, K. (1977, November 20). Stress. *The New York Times Magazine,* pp. 48–55.

Smith, K. (1971). Homophobia: A tentative personality profile. *Psychological Reports, 29,* 1091–1094.

Smith, T. (1993). *American sexual behavior: Trends, sociodemographic differences, and risk behavior* (Version 1.2). Chicago: National Opinion Research Center, University of Chicago.

Sobel, S. B., & Russo, N. F. (1981). Sex roles, equality and mental health. *Professional Psychology, 12,* 1–5.

Sontag, S. (1972, September 23). The double standard of aging. *Saturday Review,* pp. 29–38.

Spacks, P. (1975). *The female imagination.* New York: Knopf.

Spence, J. T., & Swain, L. L. (1985). Images of masculinity and femininity: A reconceptualization. In V. O'Leary, R. Unger, & B. Wallston (Eds.), *Women, gender and social psychology* (pp. 35–66). Hillsdale, NJ: Erlbaum.

Stake, J., & Lauer, M. L. (1987). The consequences of being overweight: A controlled study of gender differences. *Sex Roles, 17,* 31–47.

Steinmetz, S. (1978). The battered husband syndrome. *Victimology, 2*(3–4), 499–509.

Steinmetz, S., & Lucca, J. (1988). Husband battering. In V. B. Van Hasselt (Ed.), *Handbook of family violence* (pp. 233–245). New York: Plenum Press.

Sternglanz, S. H., & Serbin, L. A. (1974). Sex role stereotyping in children's TV programs. *Developmental Psychology, 10,* 710–715.

Stiles, D., Gibbons, J. L., Hardardottir, S., & Schnellman, J. (1987). The ideal man or woman as described by young adolescents in Iceland and the United States. *Sex Roles, 17,* 313–320.

Stoltenberg, J. (1989). *Refusing to be a man: Essays on sex and justice.* New York: Meridian.

Stone, J. (1993, May/June). He's just big, she's fat. *Health,* pp. 67–70.

Straus, M. A. (1993). Husband abuse and the woman offender are important issues. In R. J. Gelles & D. Loseke (Eds.), *Current controversies in family violence* (pp. 67–87). Newbury Park, CA: Sage.

Straus, M. A., & Gelles, R. J. (1986). Societal change and change in family violence from 1975 to 1985 as revealed by two national surveys. *Journal of Marriage and the Family, 48,* 465–479.

Straus, M. A., & Gelles, R. J. (1988). How violent are American families? Estimates from the National Family Violence Resurvey and other studies. In G. T. Hotaling, D. Finkelhor, J. T. Kirkpatrick, & M. A. Straus (Eds.), *Family abuse and its consequences: New directions in research* (pp. 14–36). Newbury Park, CA: Sage.

Stuart, R. (1980). *Helping couples change.* New York: Guilford Press.

Sue, D. W., & Sue, D. (1990). *Counseling the culturally different: Theory and practice.* New York: Wiley.

Tamashiro, R. T. (1978, July). Developmental stages in the conceptualization of marriage. *The Family Coordinator,* pp. 237–244.

Tannen, D. (1990). *You just don't understand: Women and men in conversation.* New York: Ballantine Books.

Tanner, N. (1981). *On becoming human.* New York: Cambridge University Press.

Task Force on Sex Bias and Sex-Role Stereotyping in Psychotherapeutic Practice. (1978). Guidelines for therapy with women. *American Psychologist, 33,* 122–123.

Tavris, C. (1992). *The mismeasure of woman.* New York: Simon & Schuster.

Thomas, A. H., & Stewart, N. R. (1971). Counselor ratings of female clients with deviate and conforming career goals. *Journal of Counseling Psychology, 18,* 352–357.

Thompson, E. H., & Pleck, J. H. (1986). The structure of male role norms. *American Behavioral Scientist, 29,* 531–543.

Tiger, L. (1969). *Men in groups.* New York: Random House.

Tjelvelt, A. C. (1986). The ethics of value conversion in psychotherapy: Appropriate and inappropriate therapist influence on client values. *Clinical Psychology Review, 6,* 515–537.

Tomm, K. (1988). Interventive interviewing: Part III. Intending to ask lineal, circular, strategic, or reflexive questions? *Family Process, 27,* 1–15.

Ungar, S. B. (1982). The sex-typing of adult and child behavior in toy sales. *Sex Roles, 8,* 251–260.

Unger, R., & Crawford, M. (1992). *Women and gender.* New York: McGraw-Hill.

U.S. Commission on Civil Rights. (1977). *Window dressing on the set: Women and minorities on television.* Washington, DC: U.S. Government Printing Office.

U.S. Commission on Civil Rights. (1979). *Window dressing on the set: An update.* Washington, DC: U.S. Government Printing Office.

U.S. Department of Health, Education, and Welfare, Bureau of Occupational and Adult Education. (1979). *Summary data vocational education, project year 1978.* Washington, DC: U.S. Government Printing Office.

U.S. Department of Labor, Bureau of Labor Statistics. (1985). *Employment and earnings, April 1985*. Washington, DC: U.S. Government Printing Office.

U.S. support for equality is growing, study reveals. (1983, August 31). *The Easton Express*, p. A10.

Ussher, J. (1989). *The psychology of the female body*. London: Routledge & Kegan Paul.

Verbrugge, L. M. (1985). Gender and health: An update on hypothesis and evidence. *Journal of Health and Social Behavior, 26*, 156–182.

Vessey, J. T., & Howard, K. I. (1993). Who seeks psychotherapy? *Psychotherapy, 30*, 546–553.

Wagenvoord, J., & Bailey, J. (1978). *Men: A book for women*. New York: Avon Books.

Waldron, I. (1976). Why do women live longer than men? *Journal of Human Stress, 2*, 1–13.

Walker, B. Z., Reis, S. M., & Leonard, J. S. (1992). A developmental investigation of the lives of gifted women. *Gifted Child Quarterly, 36*, 201–206.

Walker, L. (1984). *The battered woman syndrome*. New York: Springer.

Walker, L. (1989). *Terrifying love: Why battered women kill and how society responds*. New York: HarperCollins.

Wallston, B., & O'Leary, V. (1981). Sex makes a difference: Differential perceptions of women and men. In L. Wheeler (Ed.), *Review of personality and social psychology* (Vol. 2, pp. 9–41). Beverly Hills, CA: Sage.

Walsh, J. (1984). Total doctorates edge up in science, engineering. *Science, 226*, 815.

Walters, M., Carter, B., Papp, P., & Silverstein, O. (1988). *The invisible web: Gender patterns in family relationships*. New York: Guilford Press.

Washburn, S., & Moore, R. (1974). *Ape into man: A study of human evolution*. Boston: Little, Brown.

Watzlawick, P., Beavin, J. H., & Jackson, D. D. (1967). *Pragmatics of human communication*. New York: Norton.

Watzlawick, P., Weakland, J., & Fisch, R. (1974). *Change: Principles of problem formation and problem resolution*. New York: Norton.

Weisheit, R. (1984). Women and crime: Issues and perspectives. *Sex Roles, 11*, 567–581.

Weitz, S. (1977). *Sex roles: Biological, psychological and social foundations*. New York: Oxford University Press.

Weitzman, L. (1985). *The divorce revolution: The unexpected social and economic consequences for women and children in America.* New York: Free Press.

Weitzman, L., Eifler, E., & Ross, C. (1972). Sex-role socialization in picture books for preschool children. *American Journal of Sociology, 77,* 1125–1150.

White, J. (1988). Influence tactics as a function of gender, insult, and goal. *Sex Roles, 18,* 433–448.

Widom, C. S. (Ed.). (1984). *Sex roles and psychopathology.* New York: Plenum Press.

Williams, D. (1982). Weeping by adults: Personality correlates and sex differences. *Journal of Psychology, 100,* 217–226.

Williams, J. (1977). *The psychology of women: Behavior in a biosocial context.* New York: Norton.

Williams, J. (1987). *The psychology of women* (3rd ed.). New York: Norton.

Williams, J. B. W., & Spitzer, R. L. (1983). The issue of sex bias in *DSM-III. American Psychologist, 38,* 793–798.

Wilson, J. (1977, May 29). Hollywood flirts with the New Woman. *The New York Times,* Section 2, pp. 1ff.

Witelson, S. (1989). Hand and sex differences in the isthmus and genu of the human corpus callosum: A post-mortem morphological study. *Brain, 112,* 799–835.

Wolf, N. (1991). *The beauty myth.* New York: Morrow.

Wolf, N. (1993). *Fire with fire: The new female power and how it will change the 21st century.* New York: Random House.

Wolfe, T. (1988). *Bonfire of the vanities* (p. 8). New York: Bantam Books.

Wolowitz, H. M. (1972). Hysterical character and feminine identity. In J. M. Bardwick (Ed.), *Readings on the psychology of women.* New York: Harper & Row.

Women on Words and Images. (1972). *Dick and Jane as victims.* Princeton, NJ: Author.

Women on Words and Images. (1975a). *Channeling children.* Princeton, NJ: Author.

Women on Words and Images. (1975b). *Dick and Jane as victims: An update.* Princeton, NJ: Author.

Women on Words and Images. (1975c). *Doctor, lawyer, Indian chief. . . ? Sex stereotyping in career education materials.* Princeton, NJ: Author.

Zelen, S. L. (1985). Sexualization of therapeutic relationships: The dual vulnerability of patient and therapist. *Psychotherapy, 22,* 178–185.

Zilbergeld, B. (1992). *The new male sexuality: The truth about men, sex, and pleasure.* New York: Bantam Books.

Zuckerman, D. M., Singer, D. S., & Singer, J. L. (1980). Children's television viewing, racial and sex-role attitudes. *Journal of Applied Social Psychology, 10,* 281–294.

Suggested Readings on
Women's Issues

*Dowling, C. (1982). *The Cinderella complex*. New York: Pocket Books.

Erikson, E. H. (1968). *Identity, youth and crisis*. New York: Norton.

*Faludi, S. (1991). *Backlash: The undeclared war against American women*. New York: Crown.

*Friedan, B. (1993). *The fountain of age*. New York: Simon & Schuster.

*Gilligan, C. (1982). *In a different voice*. Cambridge, MA: Harvard University Press.

*Gray, J. (1992). *Men are from Mars, women are from Venus*. New York: HarperCollins.

*Greer, G. (1992). *The change: Women, ageing and the menopause*. New York: Knopf.

*Hochschild, A. (1989). *The second shift: Working parents and the revolution at home*. New York: Viking Penguin.

Horney, K. (1973). *Feminine psychology*. New York: Norton.

*Jong, E. (1994). *Fear of fifty*. New York: HarperCollins.

Kaschak, E. (1992). *Engendered lives*. New York: Basic Books.

Lips, H. M. (1991). *Women, men, and power*. Mountain View, CA: Mayfield.

Miller, J. B. (1986). *Toward a new psychology of women*. Boston, MA: Beacon Press.

Polster, M. F. (1992). *Eve's daughters*. San Francisco: Jossey-Bass.

*Russianoff, P. (1981). *Why do I feel like I'm nothing without a man*. Toronto, Ontario, Canada: Bantam Books.

*Sheehy, G. (1992). *The silent passage*. New York: Random House.

*Tannen, D. (1990). *You just don't understand: Women and men in conversation*. New York: Ballantine Books.

*Tavris, C. (1992). *The mismeasure of woman*. New York: Simon & Schuster.

Unger, R., & Crawford, M. (1992). *Women and gender*. New York: McGraw-Hill.

*Wolf, N. (1991). *The beauty myth*. New York: Morrow.

*Suitable for client reading.

Suggested Readings on Men's Issues

*Balswick, J. O. (1988). *The inexpressive male.* Lexington, MA: Lexington Books.

Barnett, R. C., & Baruch, G. K. (1987). Social roles, gender, and psychological distress. In R. C. Barnett, L. Biener, & G. K. Baruch (Eds.), *Gender and stress* (pp. 122–143). New York: Free Press.

Blumstein, P., & Schwartz, P. (1983). *American couples: Money, work, sex.* New York: Morrow.

*Bly, R. (1990). *Iron John: A book about men.* New York: Vintage Books.

Brooks, G. R. (1990). The inexpressive male and vulnerability to therapist–patient sexual exploitation. *Psychotherapy: Theory, Research, Training, 27,* 344–349.

*Brooks, G. R. (1995). *The centerfold syndrome.* San Francisco: Jossey-Bass.

Carnes, P. (1983). *Out of the shadows: Understanding sexual addiction.* Minneapolis, MN: CompCare.

Clatterbaugh, K. (1990). *Contemporary perspectives on masculinity: Men, women, and politics in modern society.* Boulder, CO: Westview Press.

David, D. S., & Brannon, R. (1976). *The forty-nine percent majority: The male sex role.* Reading, MA: Addison-Wesley.

Doyle, J. A. (1994). *The male experience* (3rd ed.). Dubuque, IA: William C. Brown.

*Farrell, W. T. (1974). *The liberated man.* New York: Bantam Books.

*Farrell, W. T. (1987). *Why men are the way they are.* New York: McGraw-Hill.

*Farrell, W. T. (1993). *The myth of male power.* New York: Simon & Schuster.

*Fasteau, M. F. (1975). *The male machine.* New York: Dell.

*Gerson, K. (1993). *No man's land: Men's changing commitments to family and work.* New York: Basic Books.

Gilbert, L. A. (1993). *Two careers/one family: The promise of gender equality.* Newbury Park, CA: Sage.

*Suitable for client reading.

Gilmore, D. D. (1990). *Manhood in the making: Cultural concepts of masculinity.* New Haven, CT: Yale University Press.

*Goldberg, H. (1976). *The hazards of being male.* New York: New American Library.

*Hochschild, A. (1989). *The second shift.* New York: Viking Press.

*Keen, S. (1991). *Fire in the belly: On being a man.* New York: Bantam Books.

Kimmel, M. S. (Ed.). (1987). *Changing men: New directions in research on men and masculinity.* Beverly Hills, CA: Sage.

*Levant, R. (1989). *Between father and child.* New York: Viking Press.

*Levant, R., and Kopecky, G. (1995/1996). *Masculinity reconstructed: Changing the rules of manhood—at work, in relationships, and in family life.* New York: Dutton.

Levinson, D., Darrow, C., Klein, E., Levinson, M., & McKee, B. (1978). *The seasons of a man's life.* New York: Knopf.

Messner, M. (1992). *Power at play: Sports and the problem of masculinity.* Boston: Beacon Press.

Meth, R. L., & Pasick, R. S. (1990). *Men in therapy: The challenge of change.* New York: Guilford Press.

*Miedzian, M. (1991). *Boys will be boys: Breaking the link between masculinity and violence.* New York: Doubleday.

Myers, M. (1989). *Men and divorce.* New York: Guilford Press.

Nardi, P. M. (Ed.). (1992). *Men's friendships.* Newbury Park, CA: Sage.

*Pasick, R. (1992). *Awakening from the deep sleep: A practical guide for men in transition.* San Francisco: HarperCollins.

*Pasick, R. (1994). *What every man needs to know.* San Francisco: HarperCollins.

Pleck, J., & Sawyer, J. (Eds.). (1980). *Men and masculinity.* Harmonsworth, Middlesex, England: Penguin Books.

*Tannen, D. (1990). *You just don't understand: Women and men in conversation.* New York: Morrow.

*Zilbergeld, B. (1992). *The new male sexuality: The truth about men, sex, and pleasure.* New York: Bantam Books.

Index

About the Authors

Carol Philpot, PsyD, is associate dean, associate director of clinical training, and professor of psychology at the School of Psychology, Florida Institute of Technology, where she also directs the marriage and family track and teaches psychology of gender. Dr. Philpot also serves as director of community psychological services of Florida Tech, a training clinic for upper-level doctoral students. She is a fellow of the American Psychological Association (APA), a past president of APA's Division of Family Psychology, a member of the American Family Therapy Academy, and an American Association for Marriage and Family Therapy approved supervisor. She is on the editorial board of the *Journal of Family Psychology* and has authored numerous articles and book chapters in the area of gender-sensitive psychotherapy.

Gary R. Brooks, PhD, is an associate professor in psychiatry and behavioral science with the Texas A & M University Health Sciences Center, adjunct faculty member at Baylor University, and instructor of men's studies with Texas Women's University. He is also the chief of psychology service at the O. E. Teague Veterans Center in Temple, Texas. Dr. Brooks is past president of APA's Division of Family Psychology and president elect of the Division for the Study of Men and Masculinity. He is the author of numerous publications dealing with men's issues, including *The Centerfold Syndrome.*

Don-David Lusterman, PhD, is in private practice in Baldwin, New York. He founded the program in family counseling at Hofstra University. He was the founding executive director of the American Board of Family Psychology, which is now a part of the American Board of Professional Psychology (ABPP). He is an ABPP diplomate in family psychology, a fellow of the APA and of the American Association for Marriage and Family Therapy, and a member of the American Family Therapy Academy, and was named APA Family Psychologist of the Year in 1987. He is coeditor of *Integrating Family Therapy: Handbook of Family Psychology and Systems Theory*, serves as consulting editor for the *Journal of Family Psychology*, and is on the editorial board of *American Journal of Family Therapy*.

Roberta L. Nutt, PhD, is professor of psychology and director of the counseling psychology doctoral and master's programs at Texas Women's University. She is the chair of the Texas State Board of Examiners of Psychologists. She received the Distinguished Psychologist Award from the Dallas Psychological Association in 1992. Dr. Nutt is a fellow of the APA and president elect of the Division of Family Psychology. She has presented widely and has written numerous articles and book chapters in the area of gender-sensitive psychotherapy.